Teach Yourself VISUALLY™

Zoom™

by Paul McFedries

Published by John Wiley & Sons, Inc., Hoboken, New Jersey.

Published simultaneously in Canada.

978-1-119-83584-4

978-1-119-83591-2 (ebk.)

978-1-119-83592-9 (ebk.)

For general information on our other products and services or for technical support, please contact our Customer Care Department within the United States at (800) 762-2974, outside the United States at (317) 572-3993 or fax (317) 572-4002.

For technical support please visit https://hub.wiley.com/community/support.

Wiley also publishes its books in a variety of electronic formats. Some content that appears in print may not be available in electronic formats. For more information about Wiley products, visit our web site at www.wiley.com.

Library of Congress Control Number: 2021942366

Cover Images: © Cobalt/Adobe Stock; Screenshot courtesy of Paul McFedries

Cover design: Wiley

SKY10028957_082421

About the Author

Paul McFedries is a full-time technical writer. Paul has been authoring computer books since 1991, and he has more than 100 books to his credit. Paul's books have sold more than four million copies worldwide. These books include the Wiley titles *Teach Yourself VISUALLY Windows 11*, *Teach Yourself VISUALLY Excel 2016*, *Amazon Fire TV For Dummies*, *Alexa For Dummies*, and *Cord Cutting For Dummies*. Paul invites you to drop by his personal website at www.paulmcfedries.com or follow him on Twitter @paulmcf.

Author's Acknowledgments

It goes without saying that writers focus on text, and I certainly enjoyed focusing on the text that you'll read in this book. However, this book is more than just the usual collection of words and phrases. A quick thumb-through the pages will show you that this book is also chock full of images, from sharp screenshots to fun and informative illustrations. Those colorful images sure make for a beautiful book, and that beauty comes from a lot of hard work by Wiley's immensely talented group of designers and layout artists. I thank them for creating another gem. Of course, what you read in this book must also be accurate, logically presented, and free of errors. Ensuring all of this was an excellent group of editors that included project editor Lynn Northrup, technical editor Doug Holland, copy editor Kim Wimpsett, and production editor Barath Kumar Rajasekaran. Thanks to all of you for your exceptional competence and hard work. Thanks, as well, to acquisitions editor Devon Lewis for asking me to write this book.

How to Use This Book

Who This Book Is For

This book is for the reader who has never used this particular technology or software application. It is also for readers who want to expand their knowledge.

The Conventions in This Book

1 Steps

This book uses a step-by-step format to guide you easily through each task. **Numbered steps** are actions you must do; **bulleted steps** clarify a point, step, or optional feature; and **indented steps** give you the result.

2 Notes

Notes give additional information — special conditions that may occur during an operation, a situation that you want to avoid, or a cross-reference to a related area of the book.

3 Icons and Buttons

Icons and buttons show you exactly what you need to click to perform a step.

4 Tips

Tips offer additional information, including warnings and shortcuts.

5 Bold

Bold type shows command names, options, and text or numbers you must type.

6 Italics

Italic type introduces and defines a new term.

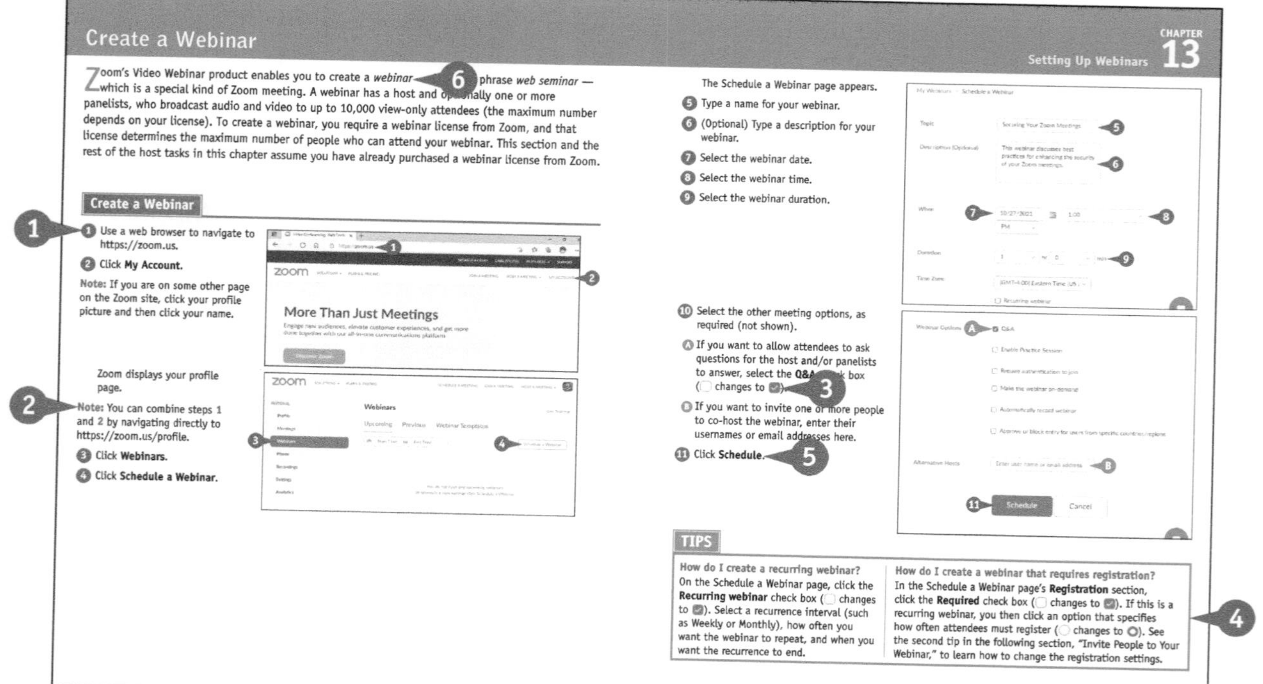

Create a Webinar

CHAPTER 13 Setting Up Webinars

Zoom's Video Webinar product enables you to create a *webinar* — a phrase *web seminar* — which is a special kind of Zoom meeting. A webinar has a host and optionally one or more panelists, who broadcast audio and video to up to 10,000 view-only attendees (the maximum number depends on your license). To create a webinar, you require a webinar license from Zoom, and that license determines the maximum number of people who can attend your webinar. This section and the rest of the host tasks in this chapter assume you have already purchased a webinar license from Zoom.

Create a Webinar

1. Use a web browser to navigate to https://zoom.us.
2. Click **My Account**.

Note: If you are on some other page on the Zoom site, click your profile picture and then click your name.

Zoom displays your profile page.

Note: You can combine steps 1 and 2 by navigating directly to https://zoom.us/profile.

3. Click **Webinars**.
4. Click **Schedule a Webinar**.

The Schedule a Webinar page appears.

5. Type a name for your webinar.
6. (Optional) Type a description for your webinar.
7. Select the webinar date.
8. Select the webinar time.
9. Select the webinar duration.
10. Select the other meeting options, as required (not shown).
   - A If you want to allow attendees to ask questions for the host and/or panelists to answer, select the **Q&A** check box (changes to ☑).
   - B If you want to invite one or more people to co-host the webinar, enter their usernames or email addresses here.
11. Click **Schedule**.

TIPS

How do I create a recurring webinar?
On the Schedule a Webinar page, click the **Recurring webinar** check box (changes to ☑). Select a recurrence interval (such as Weekly or Monthly), how often you want the webinar to repeat, and when you want the recurrence to end.

How do I create a webinar that requires registration?
In the Schedule a Webinar page's **Registration** section, click the **Required** check box (changes to ☑). If this is a recurring webinar, you then click an option that specifies how often attendees must register (changes to ◉). See the second tip in the following section, "Invite People to Your Webinar," to learn how to change the registration settings.

Table of Contents

Chapter 1 Getting Started

SIGN UP FREE

Always free, no credit card required

Chapter 2 Hosting a Meeting

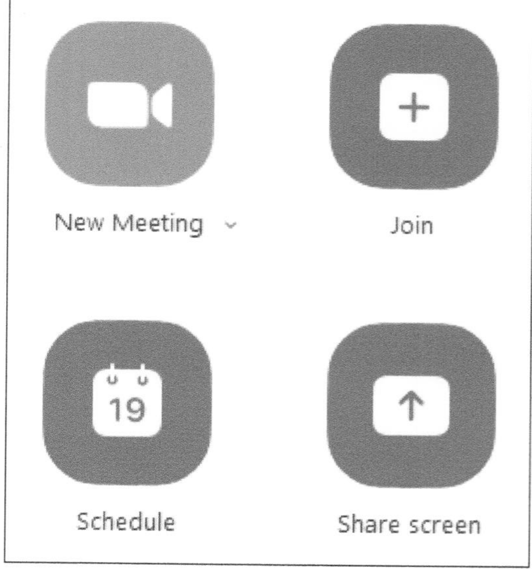

Chapter 3 Joining a Meeting

Table of Contents

Chapter 4 Working with Meeting Audio

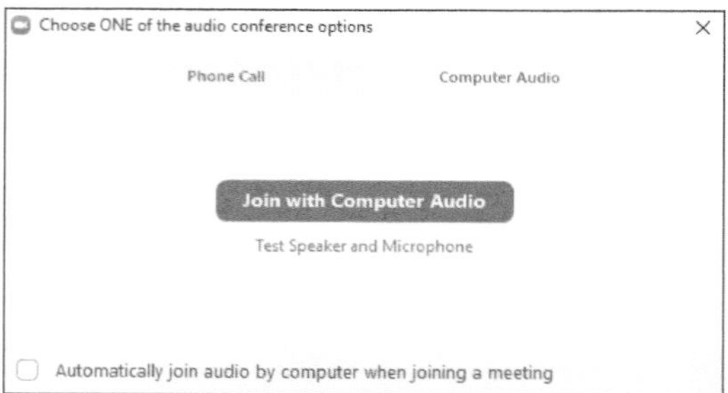

Chapter 5 Working with Meeting Video

Chapter 6 Sharing Your Screen

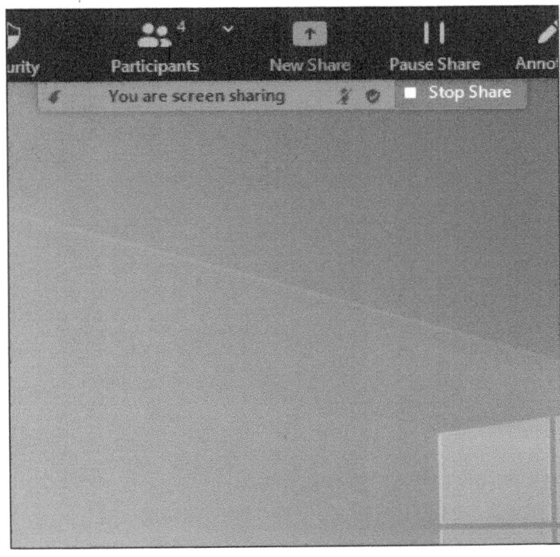

Chapter 7 Recording a Meeting

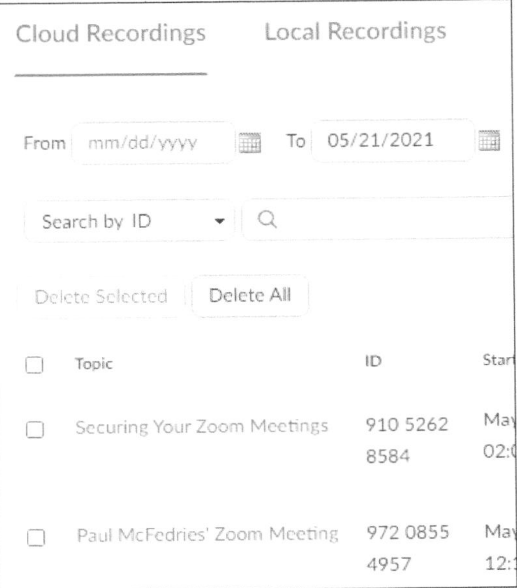

Table of Contents

Chapter 8 Configuring Settings

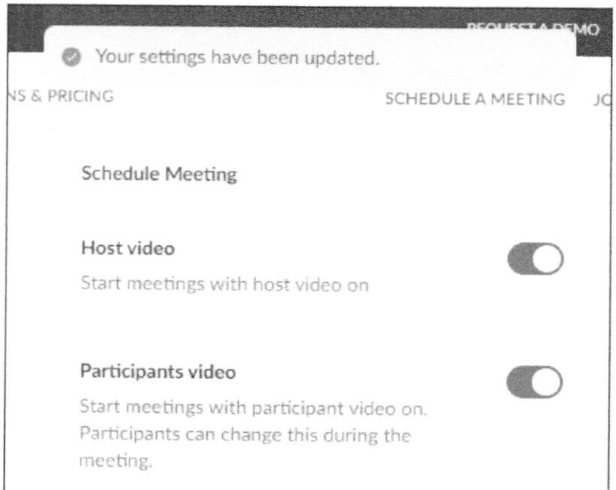

Chapter 9 Configuring Security

Sign-In Password
Old Password
New Password
Password must:

- Have at least 8 characters
- Have at least 1 letter (a, b, c...)
- Have at least 1 number (1, 2, 3...)
- Include both uppercase and lowercase characters

Chapter 10 Managing Users and Contacts

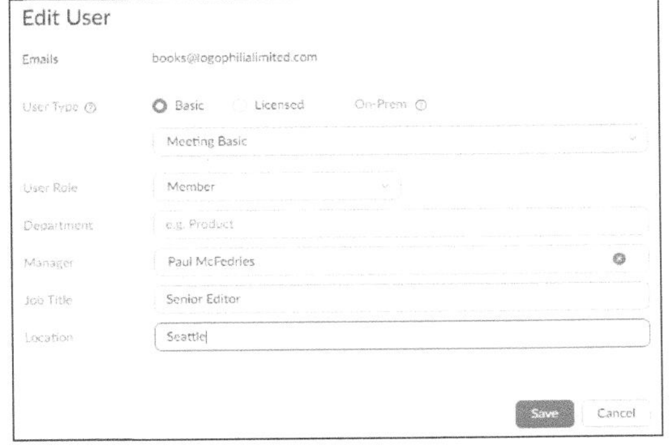

Table of Contents

Chapter 11 Chatting with Zoom

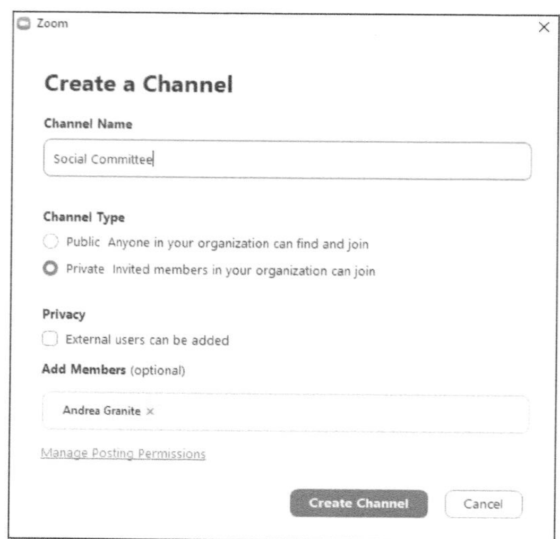

Chapter 12 Making Calls with Zoom Phone

zoom

Paul Walker, you have been assigned a direct number

(647) 555-5925

You can use your **Zoom Applications** to make or receive calls.

Chapter 13 Setting Up Webinars

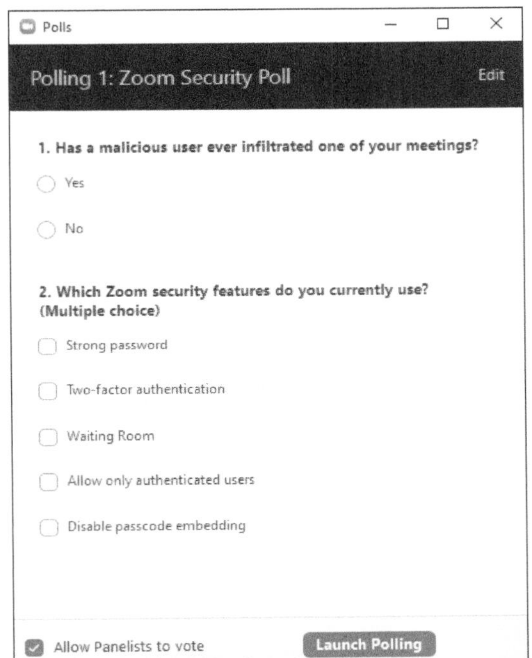

Chapter 14 Integrating with Other Apps

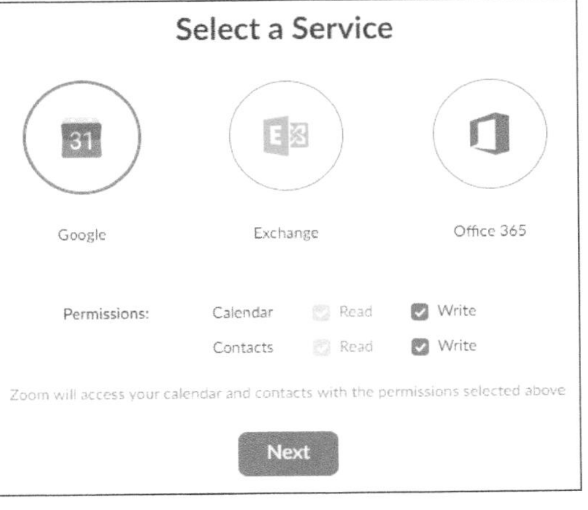

CHAPTER 1

Getting Started

To get the most out of Zoom, you need to understand Zoom meetings and other Zoom products and then create and sign in to your Zoom account. From there, you can download the Zoom client, join a test meeting, and examine the Zoom desktop and mobile windows.

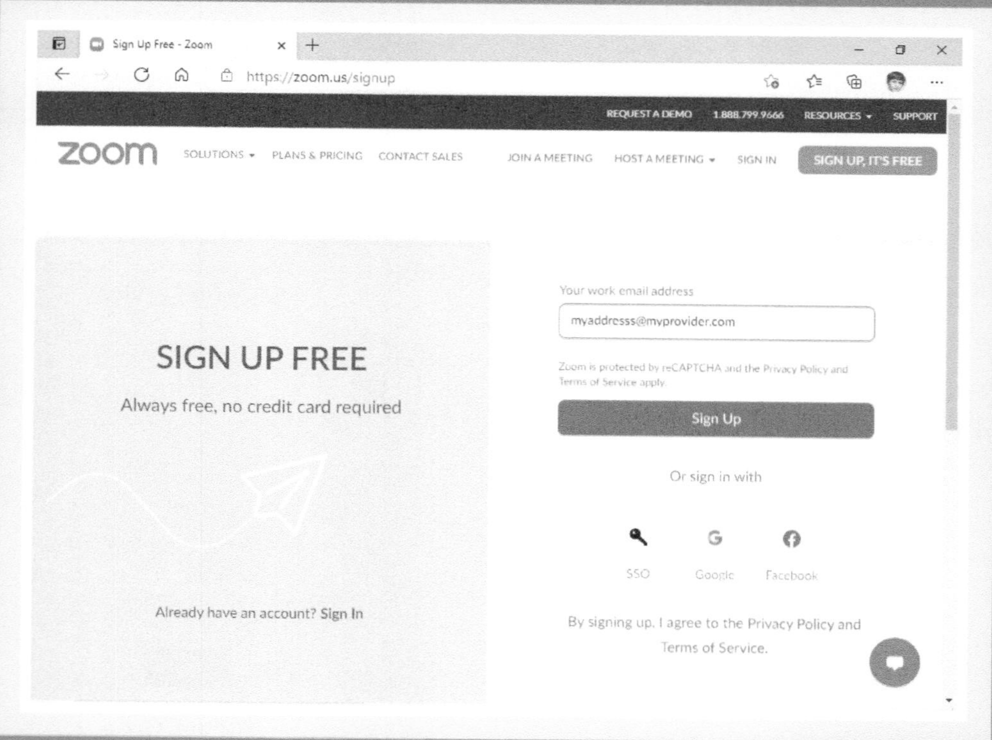

Understanding Zoom Meetings

A Zoom *meeting* is an online connection point where multiple people in multiple locations can gather to socialize or to exchange ideas and information. In most Zoom meetings, each attendee interacts using both audio and video, which enables the meeting participants to hear and see each other.

Each Zoom meeting is created and moderated by the meeting host, who is also responsible for inviting the other attendees to the meeting. Besides conversing and discussing ideas, meeting participants can also share their computer screen with others, and the meeting host can record the meeting for later playback.

Hosting a Meeting

Every Zoom meeting must be created by a person called the *host*. The host sets the parameters of the meeting (for example, whether attendees can share their screens), sends out invitations to the meeting participants, and controls access to the meeting. Hosts can create instant meetings that start right away or can schedule meetings that start at a specified time. Hosts are also responsible for moderating the meetings, which can include muting or removing participants, as well as ending the meeting.

Joining a Meeting

To participate in a Zoom meeting, you must *join* the meeting. For almost all Zoom meetings, you can join only if you receive an invitation from the meeting host and if the host allows you access to the meeting when you request it. Once you are in the meeting, you normally share your device's camera feed so that other attendees can see you. Your microphone is normally muted, but you can quickly unmute the microphone to participate in the conversation.

Sharing a Screen

If allowed by the meeting host, during the meeting you can request to share your device screen. *Sharing* usually refers to allowing other attendees to see some or all of your screen, usually so that you can demonstrate a procedure or display something. You can also share by writing on a digital whiteboard, playing a video file, or playing an audio file. You can also share a presentation by showing the slides as a virtual background.

Recording a Meeting

The meeting host can elect to *record* the meeting, which saves the meeting video and audio to a file. The recording can be used to document the meeting or to allow people who were unable to attend the meeting to view the meeting. The host can store the meeting recording using either the host's computer or the cloud storage provided with the host's Zoom account.

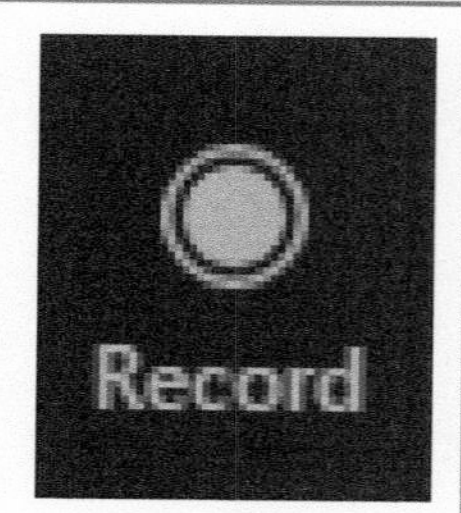

CHAPTER 1

Understanding Other Zoom Products

Most people use Zoom only for hosting and joining meetings. However, Zoom offers several other products. For example, Zoom Chat enables you to exchange messages with other Zoom users, Zoom Phone enables you to make and receive phone calls with other Zoom users, and Zoom Video Webinar enables you to broadcast a meeting to hundreds or even thousands of people.

It's important to understand that although Zoom offers the option of setting up a free account for Zoom Meetings and that a free account includes Zoom Chat, there are no free versions of either Zoom Phone or Zoom Video Webinar.

Zoom Chat

Zoom Chat is available to all Zoom users and enables each user to send instant messages to other Zoom users and to external users. Besides exchanging text messages, Zoom Chat also enables you to exchange data such as screenshots, files, and audio messages. You can set up *channels*, which are private or public groups where you can quickly send messages to the channel members.

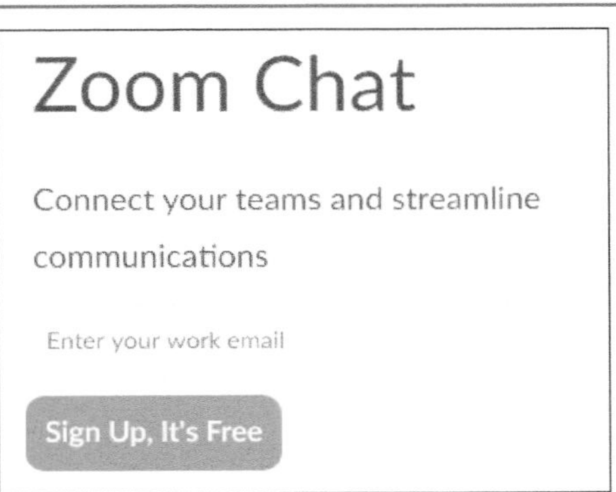

Zoom Phone

Crystal-clear audio, even if the lingo isn't.

Zoom Phone. Powering modern business communications.

With Zoom Phone, you can use the Internet to place calls to and receive calls from other Zoom users and external contacts. During a call you can add other callers, transfer a call, and start an instant meeting with people on the call. Zoom Phone also provides a voicemail service and a history of the calls you make and receive. Zoom Phone is an extra feature that requires a subscription.

Zoom Video Webinar

Zoom Webinar enables you to broadcast a meeting to as many as 10,000 attendees. Each person joins the meeting as a view-only attendee, so only the webinar host or one of the designated webinar panelists can participate. That participation includes not only the audio and video feed, but also screen sharing. Webinar attendees have access to the meeting's chat facilities and can answer questions posed by the host or a panelist. Zoom Webinar is an extra feature that requires a subscription. The number of people who can attend depends on the license you purchase.

My Webinars › Schedule a Webinar

Schedule a Webinar

Topic: My Webinar

Description (Optional): Enter your webinar description

Create a Basic Zoom Account

To get the most out of your Zoom experience, you should create a Zoom account. You can join Zoom meetings without an account, but having an account enables you to host meetings, customize your Zoom profile, configure settings for meetings and other Zoom products, and access extra meeting features. A Basic Zoom account has some restrictions — most notably the meetings you host are limited to 40 minutes if you have three or more participants — but the account is free and takes only a few steps to set up.

Create a Basic Zoom Account

1. Using a web browser, navigate to https://zoom.us/signup.

   The Zoom sign-up page appears and asks you to enter your date of birth.

2. Select the month of your date of birth.
3. Select the day of your date of birth.
4. Select the year of your date of birth.
5. Click **Continue**.
6. Type your email address.
7. Click **Sign Up**.

   Zoom sends an email to the address you provided in step 6.

8. In the Zoom email, click the confirmation link (not shown).

   The Welcome to Zoom screen appears.

9. Type your name, type a password (twice), and then click **Continue** (not shown).

   Zoom activates your new account.

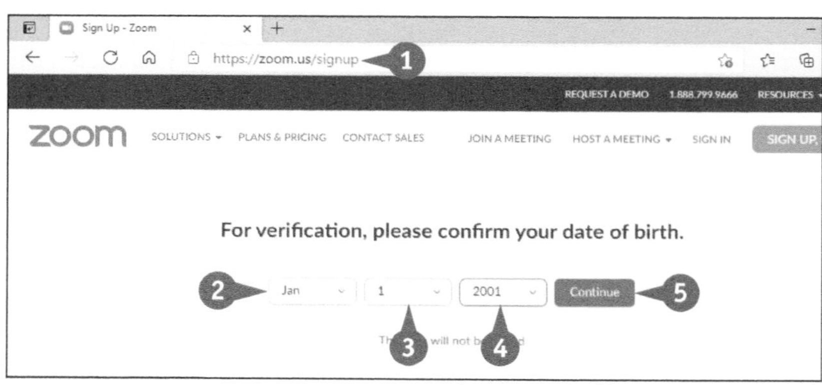

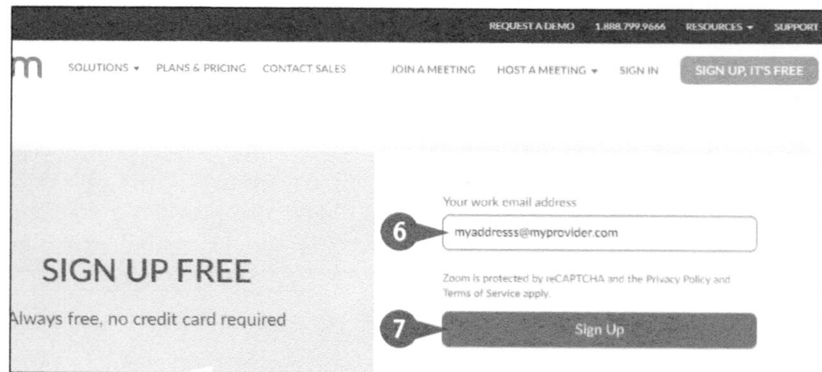

CHAPTER 1

Sign In to Your Zoom Account

Once your Zoom account has been created, you can sign in to your account to modify your settings, join a meeting, or host a meeting. When you first activate a new Zoom account, Zoom signs you in automatically. In subsequent visits to the Zoom website, you will often need to sign in manually.

Once you have completed your work on the Zoom site, it is a good idea to sign out of your account. This ensures that nobody who has access to your computer can make changes to your Zoom account.

Sign In to Your Zoom Account

1. Using a web browser, navigate to https://zoom.us/signin.

   The Zoom Sign In page appears.

2. Type the email address you used to sign up with Zoom.
3. Type your Zoom account password.
4. Click **Sign In**.

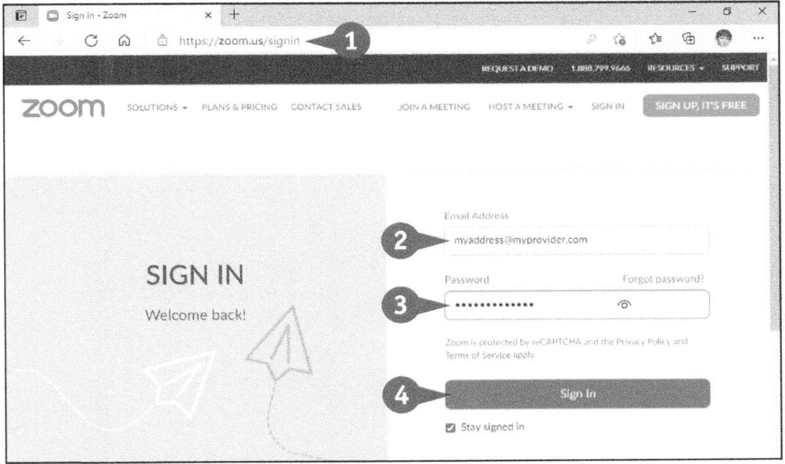

Zoom signs you in to your account and displays your profile page.

A. To sign out of your Zoom account, click your profile picture and then click **Sign Out**.

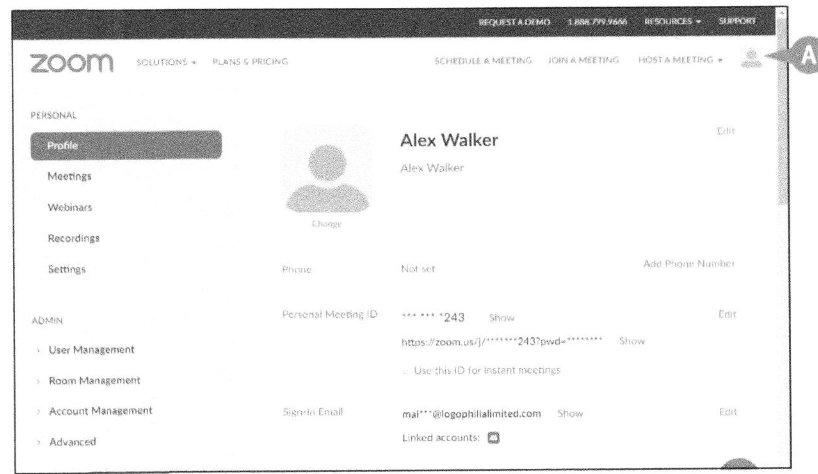

Upgrade Your Zoom Account

If you are currently using a free Basic account, you can get more features by upgrading to one of Zoom's paid account types. With the Basic license, you can join meetings and host meetings, but your hosted sessions are limited to 100 people and cannot be longer than 40 minutes if three or fewer people participate.

Besides hosting meetings with no time limit, upgrading your account also enables you to record meetings to cloud storage, work with expanded controls for users, and work with advanced administration controls.

Upgrade Your Zoom Account

1. Using a web browser, navigate to https://zoom.us/billing.
2. Sign in to your account.

   Zoom displays a summary of your current plan.
3. Click **Upgrade Account**.

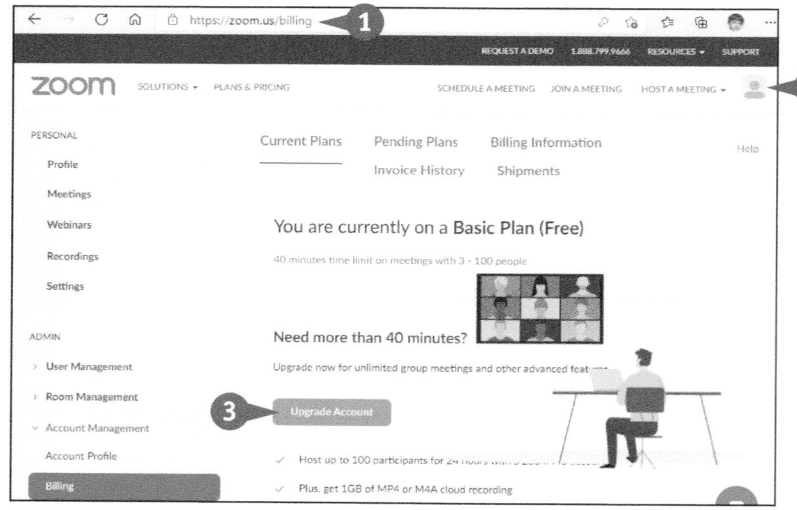

4. Click the type of plan you want.
5. Click **Save & Continue.**

   If you see a window asking if you want Zoom United (which combines Zoom Meetings, Chat, and Phone), click **No, thanks.**

   If you see a window asking if you are interested in other Zoom products, click **Skip This Step**.

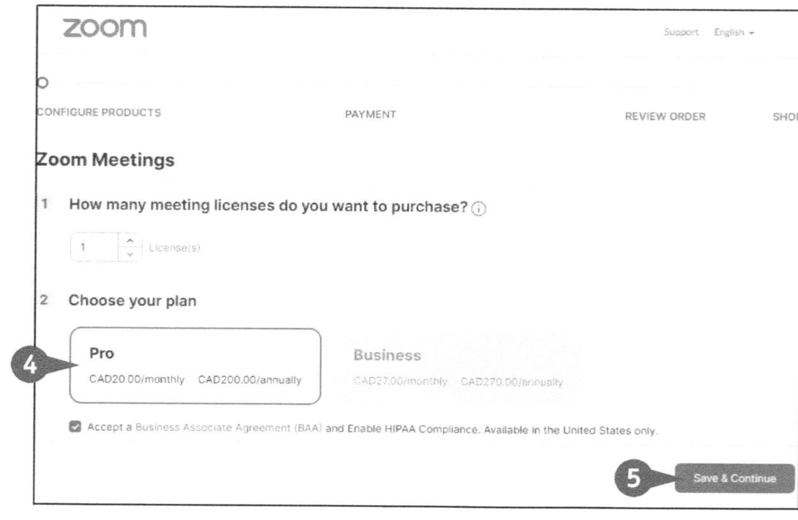

6. Complete your contact information.
7. Click **Save & Continue**.

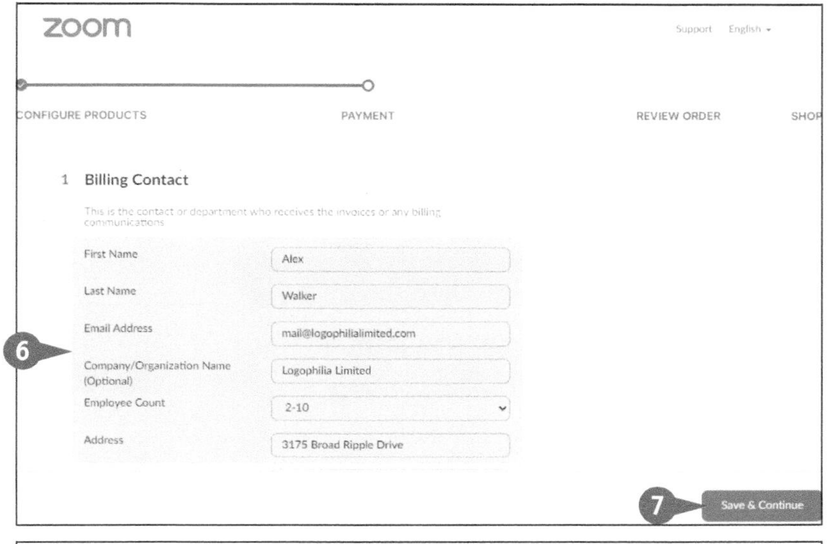

8. Complete your payment information.
9. Click **Save & Continue**.

   Zoom displays the Review Order window with a summary of your order.
10. Click **Place Order** (not shown).

   Zoom upgrades your account.

TIPS

What is the difference between a Pro account and a Business account?

The Pro plan is designed for small teams, so it limits meeting sizes to 100 participants. The Business plan is geared toward small and medium-sized businesses, so it allows meeting sizes up to 300 attendees. With a Business license you can also use your own domain name and add your company's branding to your meetings.

How do I cancel a plan?

Navigate your web browser to https://zoom.us/billing and sign in to your account. Under the Admin heading, click **Billing** and then click the **Current Plans** tab. Click the **Cancel Plan** link that appears beside the plan you want to cancel.

Download and Install the Zoom App

Although you can use the Zoom website to perform tasks related to meetings, most Zoom users prefer to host and join meetings using the Zoom app (sometimes called the Zoom *client*). The Zoom app is a software program that runs on your computer or mobile device. There are versions of the Zoom app available for Windows and Mac computers, as well as iOS and Android smartphones and tablets. Once you have installed the Zoom app, you need to run the app and then sign in to your Zoom account.

Download and Install the Zoom App

Install the Zoom App on Windows or Mac

1. Using a web browser, navigate to https://zoom.us/download.
2. Click **Download**.
3. Open the downloaded file and follow the instructions that appear on-screen.

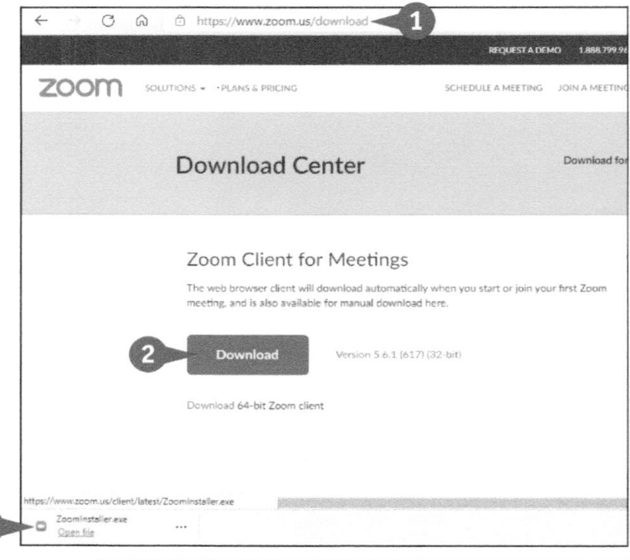

Install the Zoom App on iOS

1. On the Home screen, tap **App Store** (not shown).
2. Locate the Zoom Cloud Meetings app.
3. Tap **Get** and follow the instructions that appear on-screen.

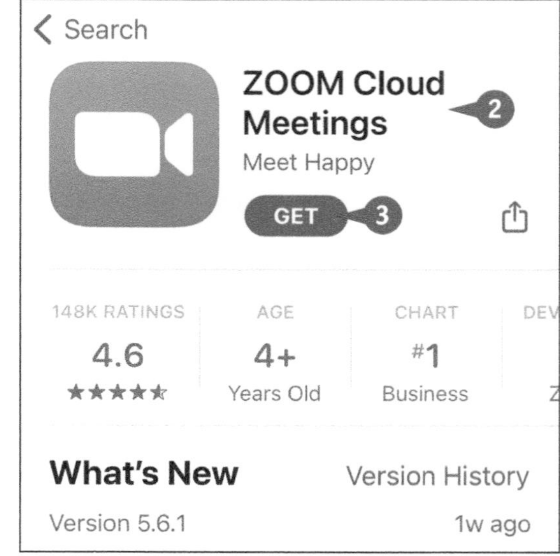

Install the Zoom App on Android

1. On the Home screen, tap **Play Store** (not shown).
2. Locate the Zoom Cloud Meetings app.
3. Tap **Install** and follow the instructions that appear on-screen.

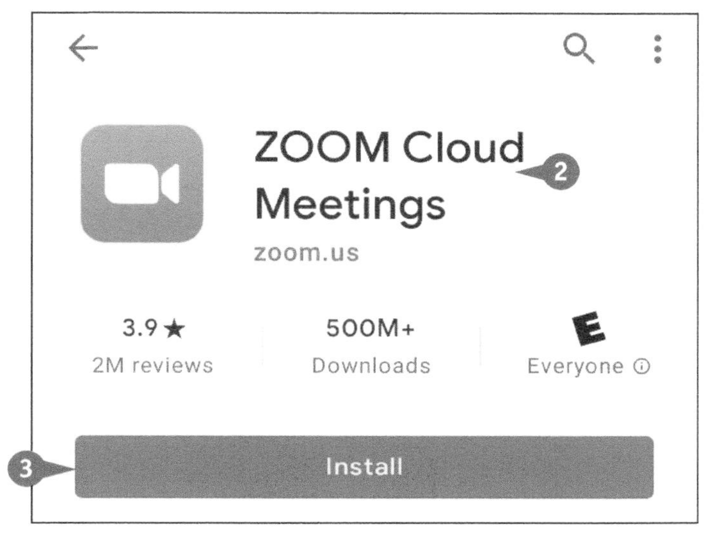

Sign In to the Zoom App

1. Open the Zoom app.
2. Select **Sign In**.
3. Type your Zoom account email address.
4. Type your Zoom account password.
5. Select **Sign In**.

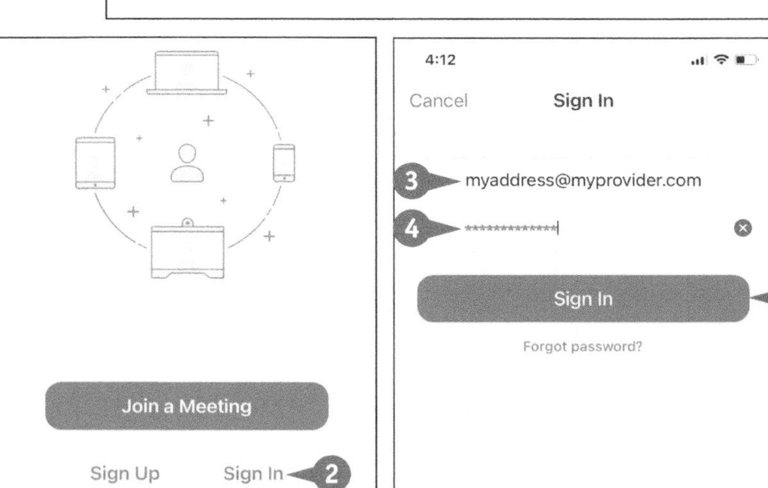

TIP

Is it possible to launch the Zoom app automatically each time I start Windows?

Yes, by following these steps:

1. Run the Windows Zoom app and sign in to your Zoom account.
2. Click your profile icon in the upper-right corner of the Zoom window.
3. Click **Settings**.
4. Click the **General** tab.
5. Click **Start Zoom when I start Windows** (☐ changes to ☑).

Join a Test Meeting

Before you host your own meetings and join other people's meetings, it is worthwhile to take a few minutes to get to know the Zoom environment. The easiest way to become familiar with Zoom is to join a test meeting. You can do this on your own at any time, and the resulting meeting is just like a regular Zoom meeting. This enables you to look around and try some meeting features.

This section shows you how to join a test meeting. The next two sections take you through the major features of the desktop and mobile meeting windows.

Join a Test Meeting

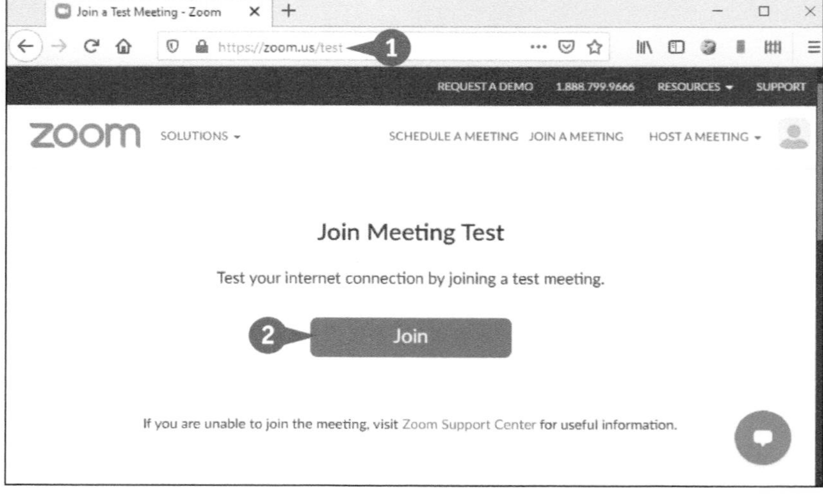

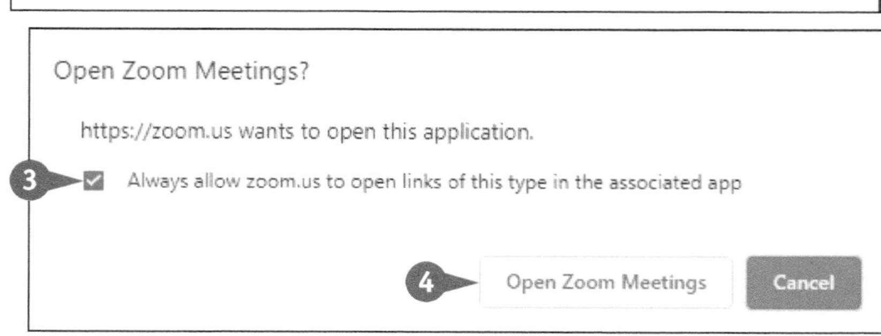

1. Using a web browser, navigate to https://zoom.us/test.
2. Select **Join**.

Note: If you do not have the Zoom app installed, your web browser will either download the app or prompt you to download it from your device's app store.

   Your browser asks for permission to launch the Zoom app. The steps vary depending on your browser and operating system.

3. Select the check box that tells the operating system to always allow your web browser to launch the Zoom app (☐ changes to ☑).
4. Select the button that launches the Zoom app (such as the **Open Zoom Meetings** button shown here).

Note: On a Mac, click **Allow**; on iOS, tap **Launch Meeting** and then tap **Open**; on Android, tap **Zoom** in the Open With window.

5 If you see the Video Preview window, click **Join with Video**.

6 If you're prompted to enter your name (not shown), type your name and then tap **OK** (Android) or **Continue** (iOS).

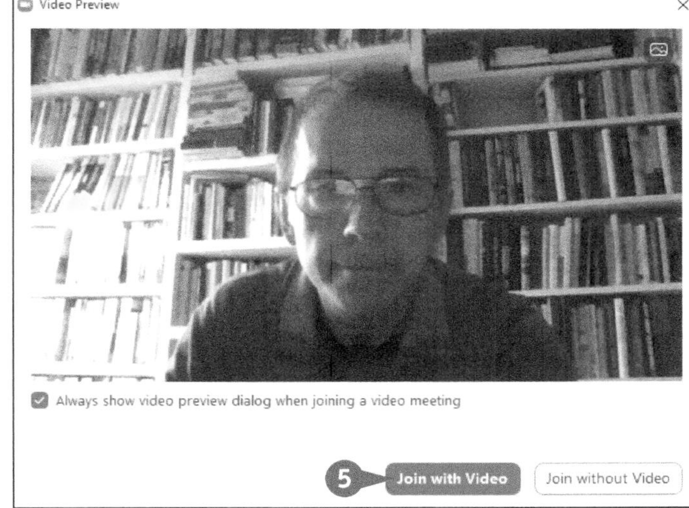

The Join Audio window appears.

7 Select **Join with Computer Audio**.

Note: On some devices, you need to select **Call using Internet Audio** instead.

8 If you joined the meeting with video, click **Yes** when Zoom asks if you can see yourself.

9 The Zoom app now tests your audio (not shown); to learn more about audio testing, see Chapter 4.

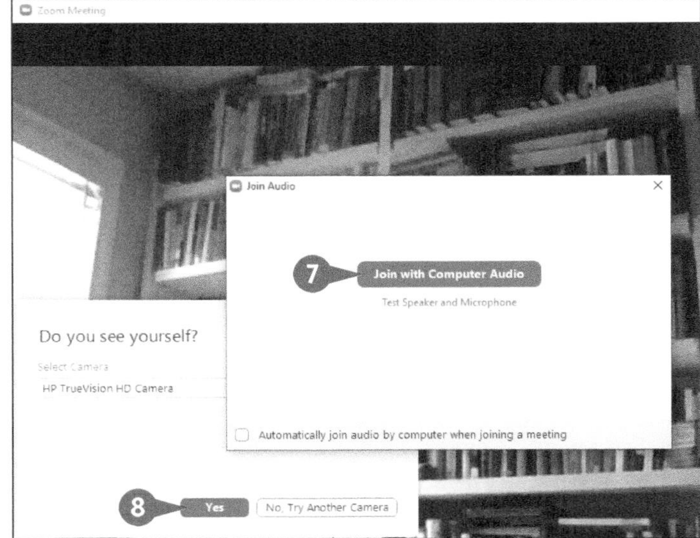

TIPS

Why am I seeing a message that the meeting was ended by the host?
The test meeting is not designed for extended interaction. Instead, the purpose of a test meeting is to take a quick look around and make sure your video and audio are working. Zoom configures every test meeting to automatically end after several minutes.

I started the test meeting without video. How do I turn on my video during the meeting?
Move your mouse within the Zoom window to display the attendee controls and then select the **Start Video** button. To learn more about the attendee controls in a Zoom meeting window, see the next two sections.

Explore the Zoom Desktop Window

If you use the Zoom app on a Windows computer or on a Mac, you can get more out of your Zoom meetings by becoming familiar with the major features of the Zoom desktop window. These features include where the video feeds appear, the meeting controls, and the icons for obtaining meeting data and for entering full-screen mode.

The image used in this section to demonstrate the Zoom desktop window is from a Windows computer, but the macOS version of the window is identical.

A Video Feed

The main section of the Zoom desktop window displays the participant video feeds. In a test meeting or when you first start an instant meeting, you see just your own video feed.

B Controls

The bottom strip of the Zoom window displays a set of controls that you can use to configure the meeting and access meeting features. If you do not see the controls, move the mouse within the Zoom window to display them. The controls you see depend on whether you are the meeting host (see Chapter 2) or a meeting attendee (see Chapter 3).

C Enter Full Screen

Clicking **Enter Full Screen** () expands the Zoom window so that it takes up the entire desktop. You can also enter full-screen mode by pressing Alt+F (Windows) or Shift+⌘+F (Mac). To exit full-screen mode, either press Esc or double-click the mouse.

D Meeting Information

Clicking the **Meeting Information** icon () displays a dialog box that shows the meeting ID and passcode, the name of meeting host, and a link that can be used to invite people to the meeting. You can also click **Settings** () to open the Zoom app's Settings dialog box.

Explore the Zoom Mobile Window

CHAPTER 1

If you use the Zoom app on an Android or iOS smartphone or tablet, you can get more out of your Zoom meetings by becoming familiar with the major features of the Zoom mobile window. These features include where the video feeds appear, the meeting controls, and how you obtain meeting data.

The image used in this section to demonstrate the Zoom mobile window is from an iPad, but the iPhone and Android mobile windows are similar.

Ⓐ Video Feed

The main section of the Zoom mobile window displays the participant video feeds. In a test meeting or when you first start an instant meeting, you see just your own video feed.

Ⓑ Controls

This strip (which might appear at the bottom of the window, depending on your device) displays a set of controls that you can use to configure the meeting and access meeting features. If you do not see the controls, tap the screen to display them. The controls you see depend on whether you are the meeting host (see Chapter 2) or a meeting attendee (see Chapter 3).

Ⓒ Meeting Information

Click **Zoom** to display a dialog that shows the meeting ID and passcode, the name of meeting host, and a link that can be used to invite people to the meeting.

Understanding Presence Status

The Zoom desktop and mobile apps use presence status icons to indicate the current status of users you interact with on Zoom. A user's *presence status* is an indication of the person's current engagement with the Zoom app. The presence status is useful because it lets you know whether a user is available for a meeting, chat, or phone call. For example, if you want to invite a user to an instant meeting, you would delay that meeting if the user's presence status indicates that person is not currently available.

The following table describes the main presence status icons.

Icon	Presence Status	The User Is . . .
	Available (desktop)	Signed in to the Zoom desktop app
	Available (mobile)	Signed in to the Zoom mobile app
	Offline	Not signed in to the Zoom desktop or mobile app
	Away	Signed in to the Zoom desktop or mobile app, but their device is in sleep mode or the user has manually set their status to Away
	Do not disturb	Signed in to the Zoom desktop or mobile app, but has chosen not to receive any Zoom notifications for a period of time
	In a Zoom meeting	Hosting or has joined a Zoom meeting
	On a call	Currently on a Zoom Phone call
	In a calendar event	Taking part in an event that was scheduled using a synced calendar

Set Your Presence Status

CHAPTER **1**

When you are hosting or attending a Zoom meeting or on a Zoom Phone call, the Zoom app automatically sets your presence status accordingly so that other users know that you are currently busy. However, there will be times when you prefer to set your presence status manually. For example, if you are signed in to the Zoom desktop app, you might require some uninterrupted time. In that case, you can manually set your presence status to Do Not Disturb.

The Zoom desktop app supports three presence statuses: Available, Away, and Do Not Disturb.

Set Your Presence Status

1. Sign in to the Zoom desktop app.

   A. Your user icon displays your current presence status.

2. Click your user icon.

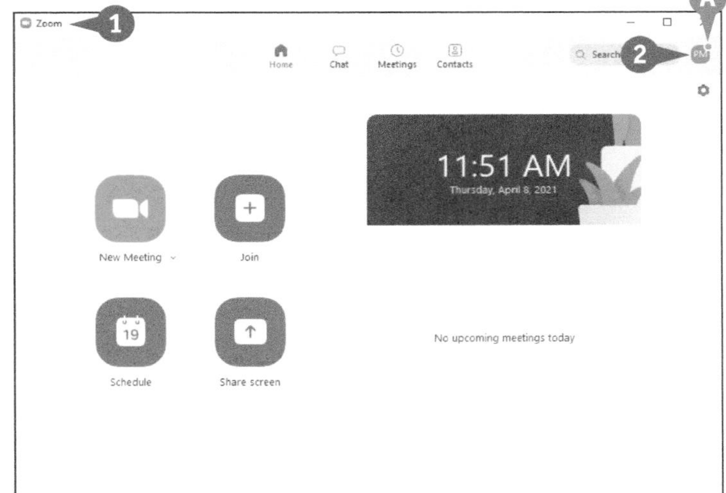

3. Click the presence status you want to set.
4. If you click **Do not disturb**, click the amount of time you want to be undisturbed.

   B. Zoom updates your presence status icon.

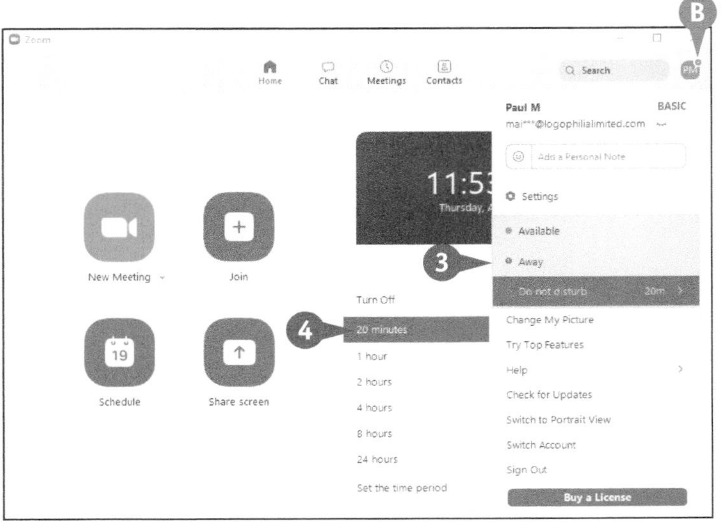

CHAPTER 2

Hosting a Meeting

You can host your own Zoom meetings and invite other people to attend. You can create instant meetings that start right away, or you can schedule a future meeting. As host, you can also allow participants into the meeting, rename attendees, enable participants to share a screen or record the meeting, remove participants, and more.

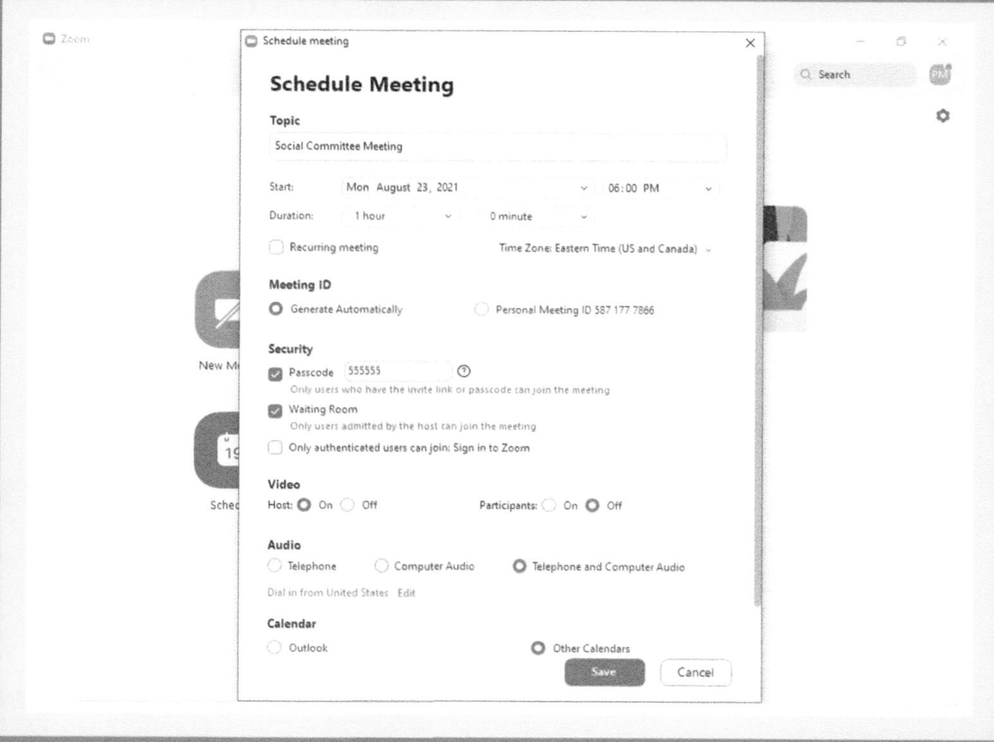

Start an Instant Meeting

If you have a Zoom account, you can host a meeting immediately by starting an instant meeting. An *instant meeting* is a meeting that begins right away and to which you invite users after the meeting has begun, as described in the section "Invite People to a Meeting" later in this chapter. You can start an instant meeting either using the Zoom desktop app or using the Zoom mobile app.

You can also start an instant meeting from a Zoom chat conversation. For the details, see Chapter 11.

Start an Instant Meeting

Using the Zoom Desktop App

1. Click **Home**.
2. Click **New Meeting**.

(A) If you prefer to start the instant meeting with your video turned off, click the **New Meeting** ⌄ and then click **Start with video** (☑ changes to ☐).

Zoom starts the instant meeting.

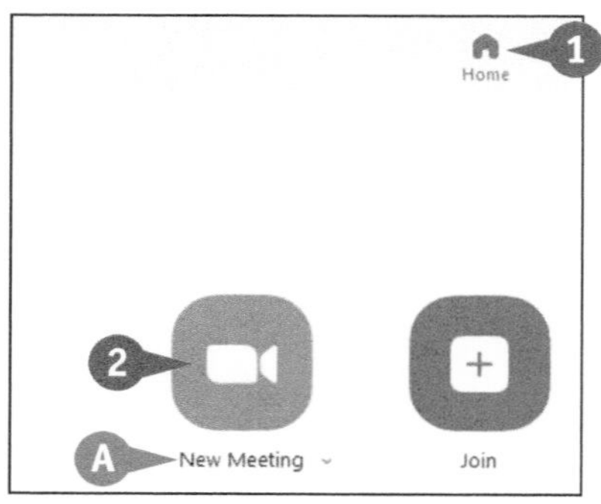

Using the Zoom Mobile App

1. Tap **Meet & Chat**.
2. Tap **New Meeting**.

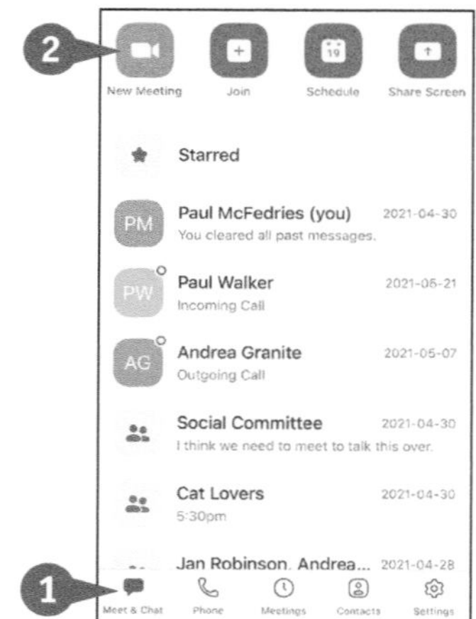

Zoom displays the Start a Meeting screen.

(B) If you prefer to start the instant meeting with your video turned off, tap **Video On** (toggle on changes to toggle off).

3. Tap **Start a Meeting.**

Zoom starts the instant meeting.

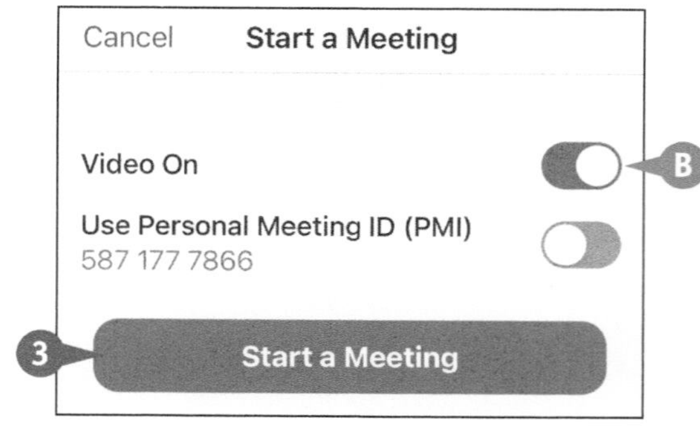

Start an Instant Meeting in Your Personal Meeting Room

CHAPTER **2**

If you have a paid Zoom account, you can create an instant meeting that takes place in your personal meeting room. When you sign up for a paid Zoom account, you are automatically assigned a *personal meeting room*, which is a virtual room that's permanently reserved just for your own use. Your personal meeting room is identified by your Personal Meeting ID (PMI), which is a ten-digit number unique to your account. When you start an instant meeting in your personal meeting room, Zoom uses your PMI as part of the meeting web address.

Start an Instant Meeting in Your Personal Meeting Room

Using the Zoom Desktop App

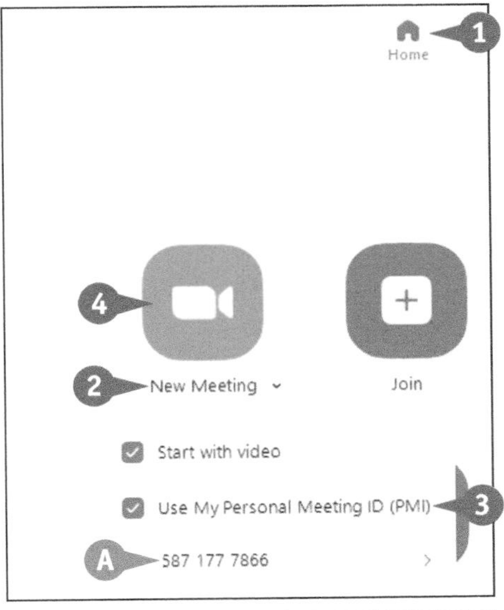

1 Click **Home**.

2 Click the **New Meeting** ⌄.

3 Click **Use My Personal Meeting ID (PMI)** (☐ changes to ☑).

A Your PMI appears here.

4 Click **New Meeting**.

Zoom starts the instant meeting in your personal meeting room.

Using the Zoom Mobile App

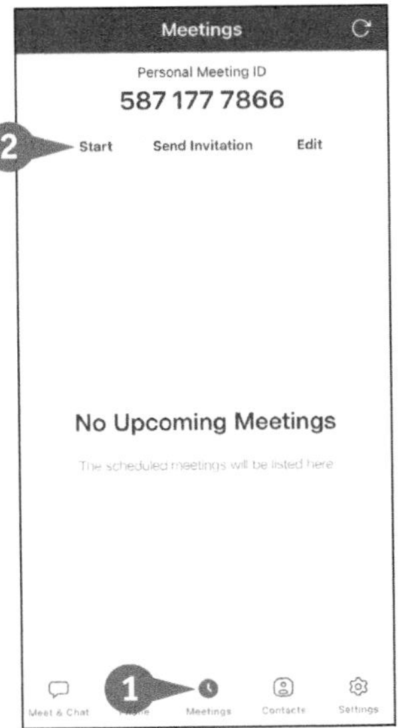

1 Tap **Meetings**.

2 Tap **Start**.

Zoom starts the instant meeting in your personal meeting room.

Invite People to a Meeting

After you start an instant meeting, as described in the previous two sections, you can invite one or more users to attend. By default, an instant meeting starts with just you as the meeting host. Your next step is to invite people to participate in your meeting. Zoom gives you three ways to invite users: by email, by contact name (see Chapter 10), or by copying the meeting link or the meeting invitation and pasting the information into an email or text message. In the Zoom mobile app, you can also invite people via text message.

Invite People to a Meeting

Start the Invitation

1. In the Zoom desktop app, click the **Participants**.
2. Click **Invite**.

Note: You can also select the Invite command by pressing Alt + I.

Zoom displays the Invite People to Join Meeting dialog.

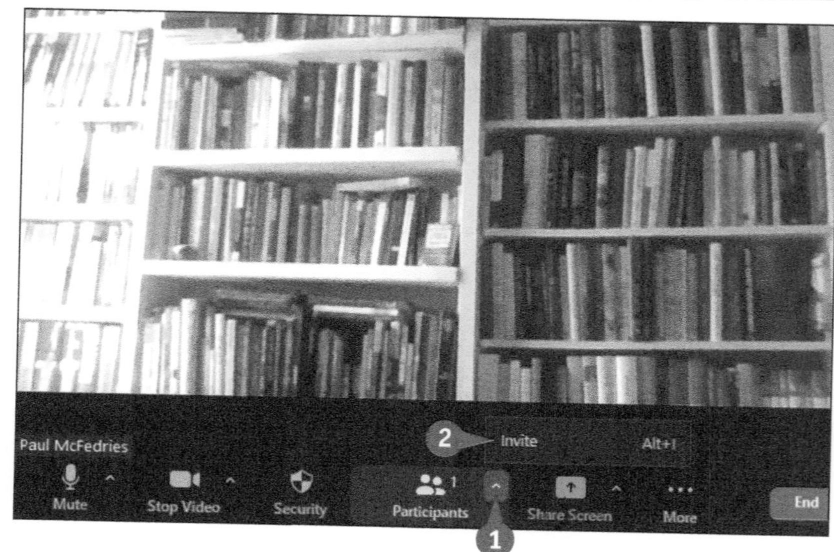

Invite Via Email

1. Click **Email**.
2. Click the email service you want to use.
3. Address and send the email message (not shown).

Zoom sends the invitation to the email recipients.

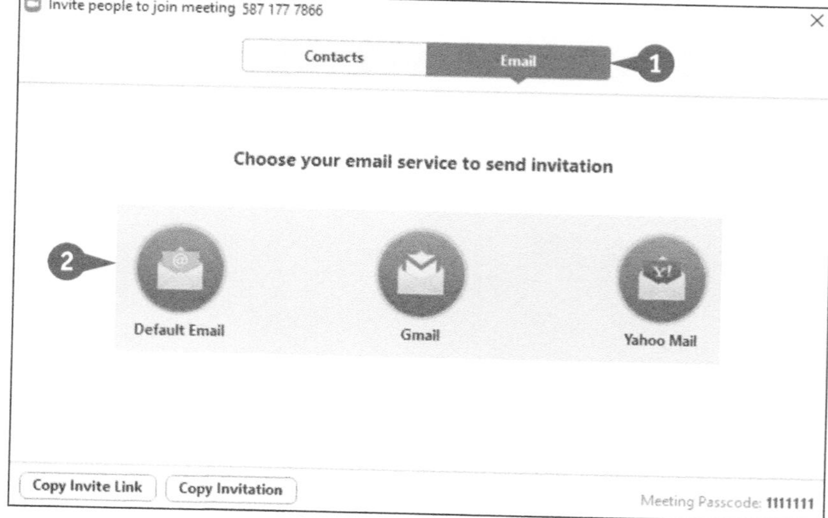

Invite Contacts

1. Click **Contacts**.
2. Click each contact you want to invite.
3. Click **Invite**.

   Zoom sends the invitation to the selected contacts.

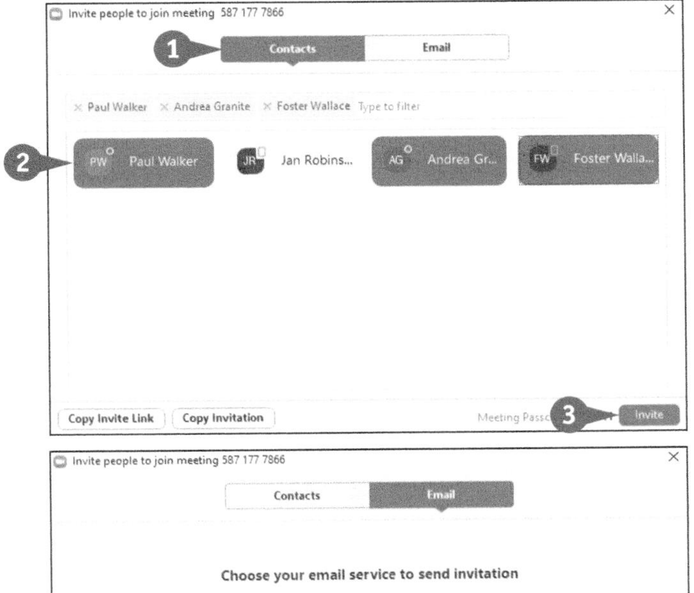

Copy the Invitation

1. Click **Copy Invitation**.

   A. If you prefer to copy just the meeting link instead of the full invitation, click **Copy Invite Link** instead.

2. Paste the invitation where you want to share it, such as an email message, text message, or web page.

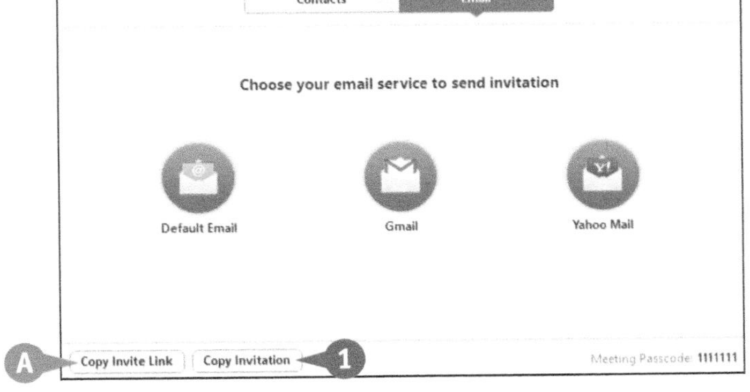

TIP

How do I invite people if I am using the Zoom mobile app?

Here are the steps to follow:

1. Tap **Participants**.
2. Tap **Invite**.
3. Tap the method you want to use:

   A. **Send Email**. Sends the invitation via email message

   B. **Send Message**. Sends the invitation via text message

   C. **Invite Contacts**. Sends the invitation to one or more of your Zoom contacts

   D. **Copy Invite Link**. Copies the invitation so that you can paste it elsewhere

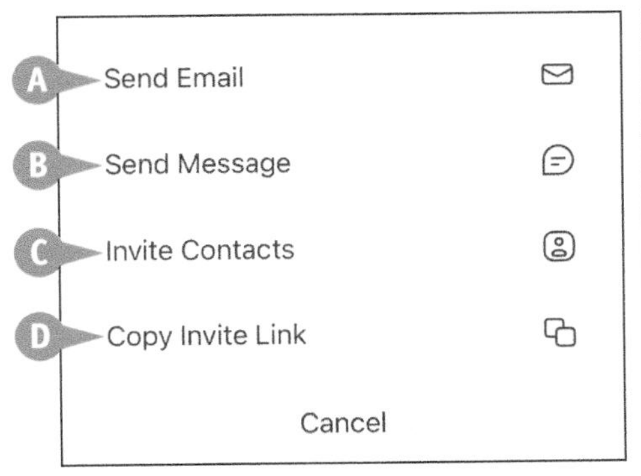

Schedule a Meeting

If you have a Zoom account, you can schedule a meeting to occur at a future date and time. Instant meetings are often useful, but to ensure that meeting invitees can attend, it is usually better to schedule a meeting for a date and time that is convenient for everyone you want to attend your meeting. With a scheduled meeting, you can also set the duration of the meeting, security options such as the passcode and waiting room (see Chapter 9), and whether the participants have video on or off at the start of the meeting.

Schedule a Meeting

1 In the desktop Zoom app, click **Home**.

2 Click **Schedule**.

The Schedule Meeting dialog appears.

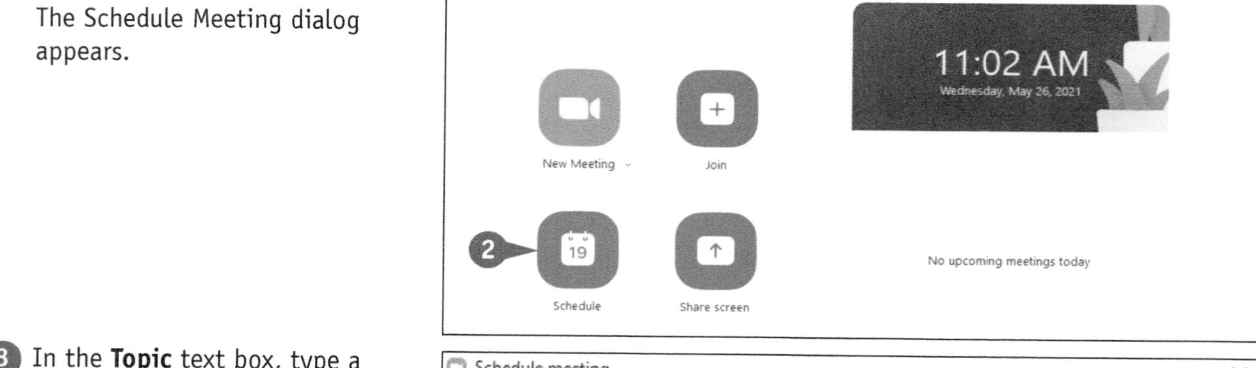

3 In the **Topic** text box, type a meeting name.

4 Click the first **Start** ⌄ and then click the date of your meeting.

5 Click the second **Start** ⌄ and then click the start time of your meeting.

6 Click the first **Duration** ⌄ and then click the length of your meeting in hours.

7 Click the second **Duration** ⌄ and then click the length of your meeting in minutes.

Note: If you have a free Zoom account, your maximum meeting duration is 40 minutes.

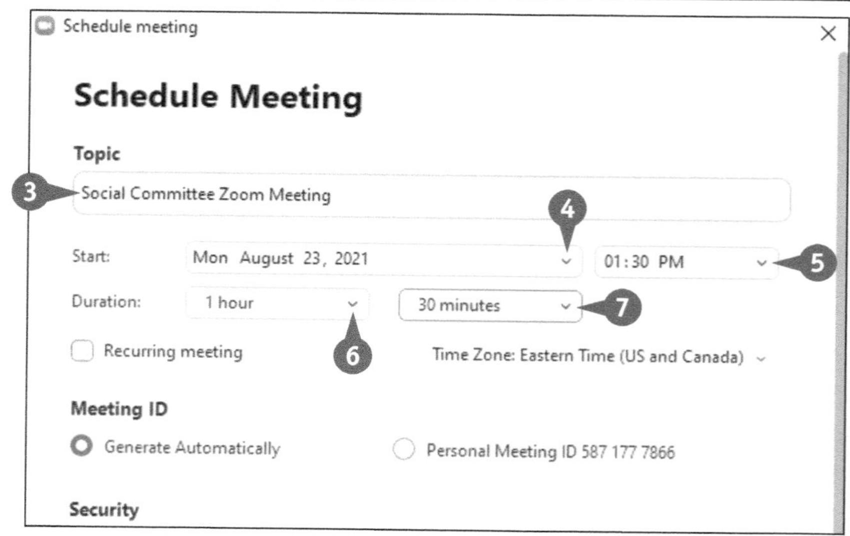

8 (Optional) If you want to use your personal meeting room for the meeting, click **Personal Meeting ID** (◯ changes to ◉).

9 Click **Passcode** (☐ changes to ☑).

10 Enter the passcode.

11 Click **Waiting Room** (☐ changes to ☑).

Note: You must select one or both of **Passcode** and **Waiting Room**; you cannot deselect both.

12 If you want your video on when you start your meeting, click **Host: On** (◯ changes to ◉).

13 If you want your attendees' video on when they join your meeting, click **Participants: On** (◯ changes to ◉).

14 Click **Save**.

Zoom schedules your meeting.

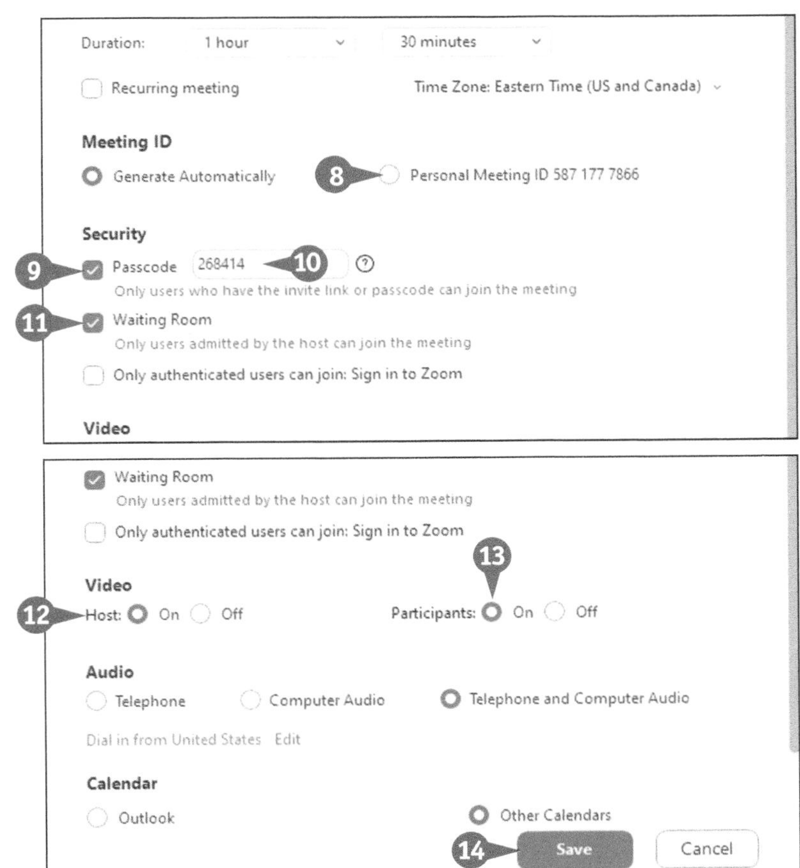

TIPS

Are there other methods I can use to schedule a meeting?

Yes, Zoom gives you two other ways to schedule a meeting:

- **Zoom mobile app**. Tap **Meet & Chat** and then tap **Schedule**.
- **Zoom web portal**. Navigate to https://zoom.us, sign in to your account, and then click **Schedule a Meeting**.

How do I invite people to my scheduled meeting?

After you save your meeting, Zoom displays the Your Meeting Has Been Scheduled dialog, which shows the meeting invitation. Click **Copy to Clipboard** (A) to copy the invitation. You can then paste the invitation into an email, text message, or social media post.

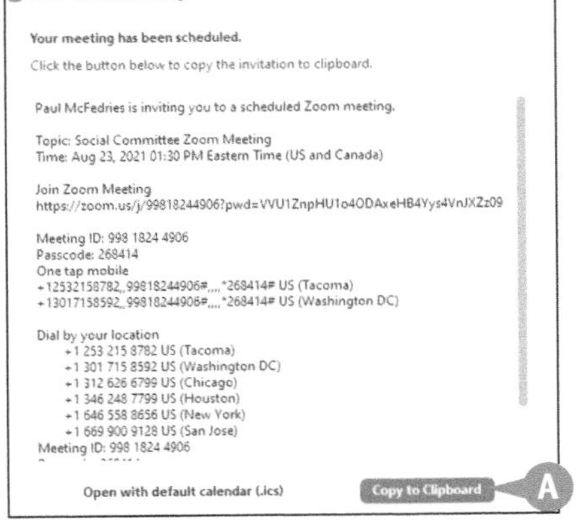

Schedule a Recurring Meeting

If a group or topic requires regular meetings, you can schedule a recurring meeting. A *recurring* meeting is one that repeats regularly, such as daily, weekly, or monthly. You can set a custom frequency — for example, every two days or every three weeks — and you can set the recurrence to end on a specific date or after a specified number of occurrences.

If you use the desktop app to create a recurring meeting, you must specify the recurrence interval using your calendar application. Therefore, it is easier to schedule a recurring meeting in the Zoom web portal.

Schedule a Recurring Meeting

1. Use a web browser to navigate to https://zoom.us/meeting.

A Zoom displays the **Upcoming** tab, which shows a list of your upcoming meetings.

2. Click **Schedule a Meeting**.

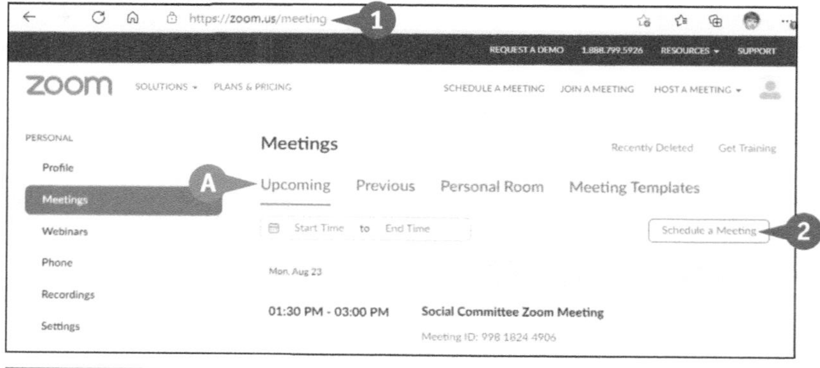

The Schedule a Meeting page appears.

3. In the **Topic** text box, type a name for your meeting.
4. Click the first **When** box and then click the date of your meeting.
5. Click the second **When** ⌄ and then click the start time of your meeting.
6. Click the first **Duration** ⌄ and then click the length of your meeting in hours.
7. Click the second **Duration** ⌄ and then click the length of your meeting in minutes.

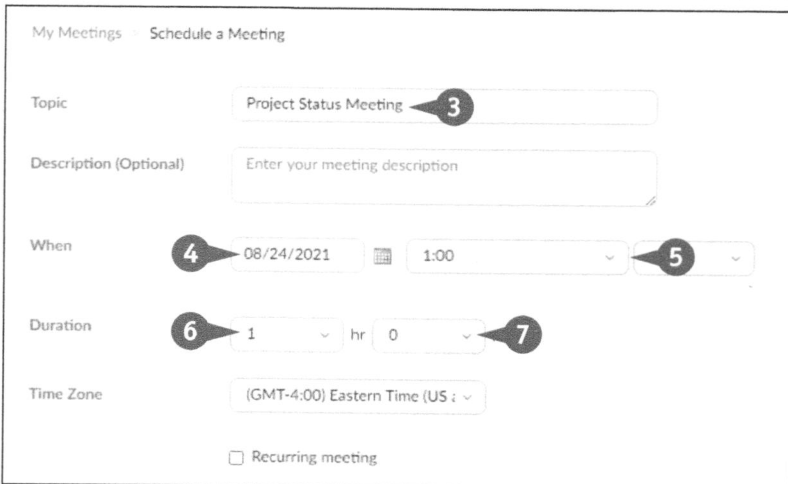

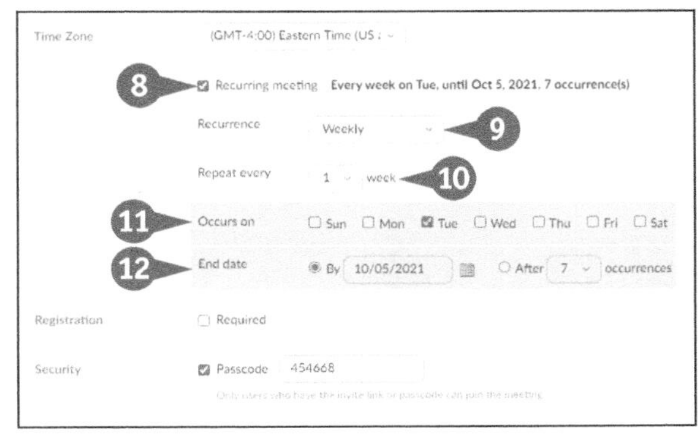

8 Click **Recurring meeting** (☐ changes to ☑).

Zoom displays the recurrence options.

9 Click the **Recurrence** ⌄ and then click the interval you want to use.

10 Click the **Repeat every** ⌄ and then click a repeat frequency.

11 Fill in the other recurrence options, which vary depending on the interval.

12 Click the **End date** option you want to use (○ changes to ◉) and then specify either the last date or the number of occurrences.

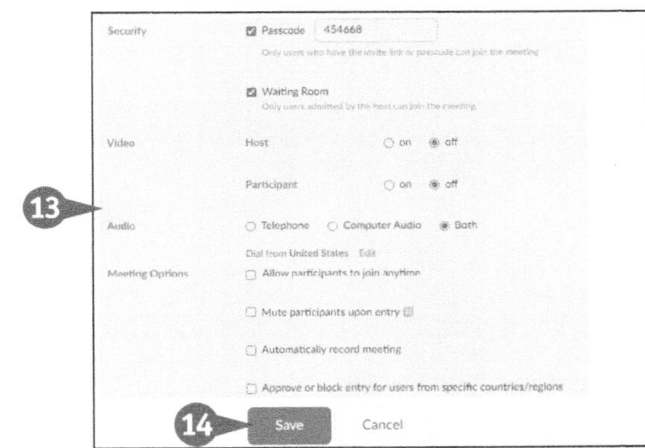

13 Select the other options you want to apply to your meeting.

Note: See the previous section, "Schedule a Meeting," for the details on the options you can apply.

14 Click **Save**.

Zoom schedules your recurring meeting.

TIP

Can I schedule a recurring meeting in the Zoom mobile app?
Yes, by following these steps:

1 Tap **Meet & Chat**.

2 Tap **Schedule**.

3 Specify a topic, starting date and time, and duration.

4 Tap **Repeat**.

5 Tap the recurrence interval you want to use.

6 Tap **Done**.

7 Tap **End Repeat**.

8 Specify the date of the last occurrence (or tap **Repeat Forever**).

9 Tap **Done**.

10 Fill in the rest of the meeting details.

11 Tap **Save**.

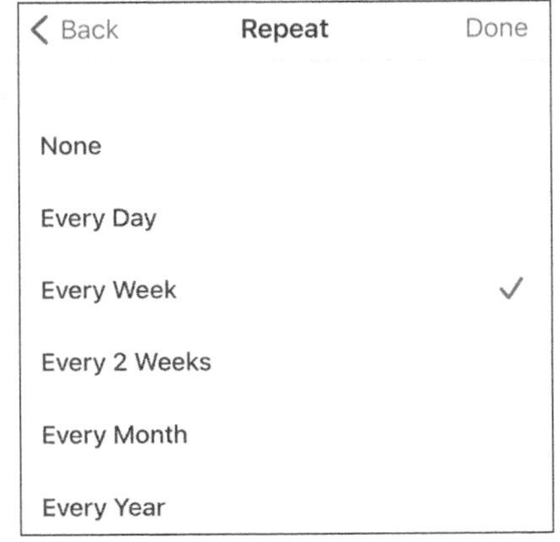

Start a Scheduled Meeting

When the date and time arrives for a scheduled meeting, your first task as meeting host is to start the meeting. You can start a scheduled meeting using the Zoom desktop app, the Zoom web portal, or the Zoom mobile app.

Start a Scheduled Meeting

Using the Zoom Desktop App

1. Click **Meetings**.
2. Click the meeting you want to start.
3. Click **Start**.

   Zoom starts the meeting.

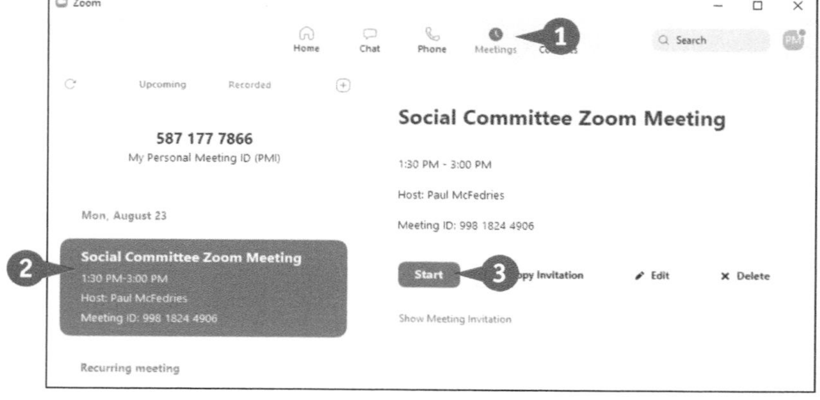

Using the Zoom Web Portal

1. Use a web browser to navigate to https://zoom.us/meeting.

   A. Zoom displays the **Upcoming** tab, which shows a list of your upcoming meetings.

2. Click the **Start** button that appears next to the meeting you want to start.

   Zoom starts the meeting.

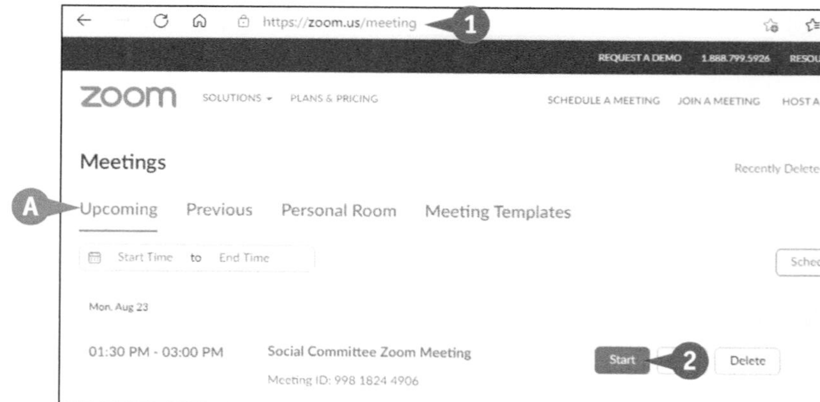

Using the Zoom Mobile App

1. Tap **Meetings**.
2. Tap the meeting you want to start.

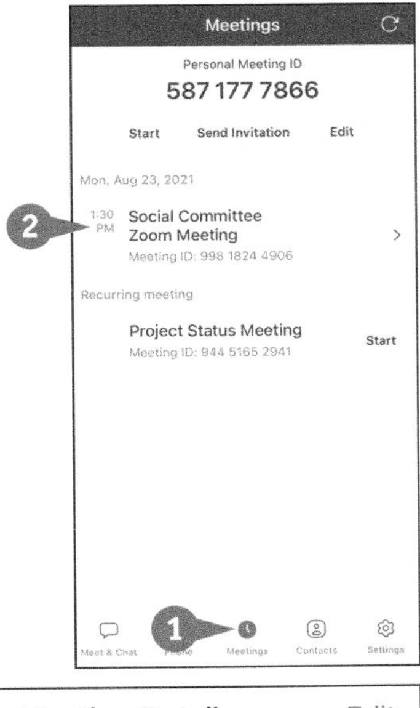

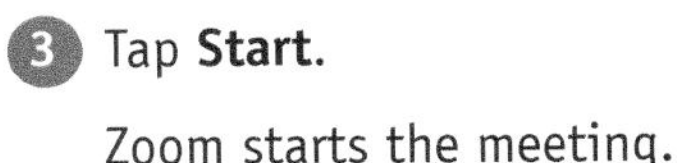

3. Tap **Start**.

   Zoom starts the meeting.

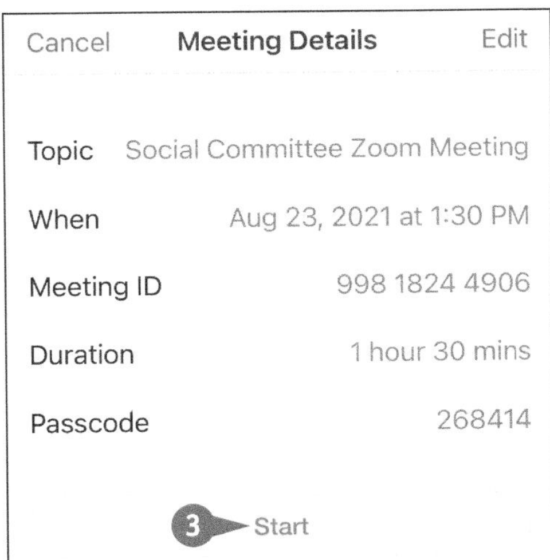

TIP

What happens if an attendee attempts to join my meeting before I have started it?

If you have not started your meeting yet, someone attempting to join the meeting sees a dialog that says *Please wait for the host to start this meeting*. Note that you can configure your Zoom account to allow users to join a meeting before you do. See Chapter 8.

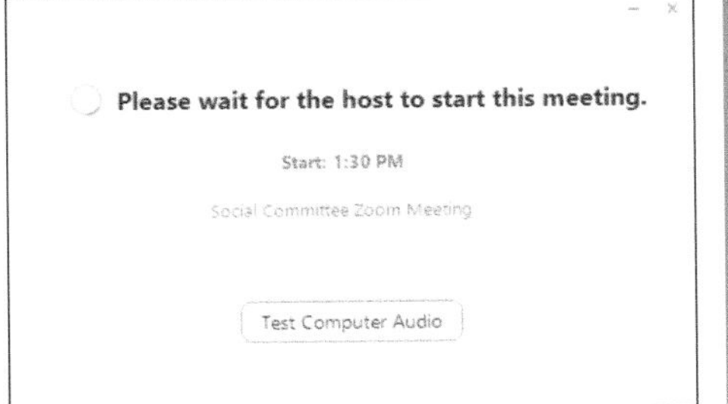

Explore Host Controls

As the meeting host, you have access to a number of features that enable you to control various aspects of the meeting and its participants. When you start a meeting using the desktop app, Zoom opens the meeting in a new window. At the bottom of that window, you see a toolbar that offers a number of icons. If you host a meeting using the Zoom mobile app, you see a similar set of icons.

Zoom hides the toolbar after a few seconds of inactivity, so if you do not see the toolbar, move your mouse or tap the screen.

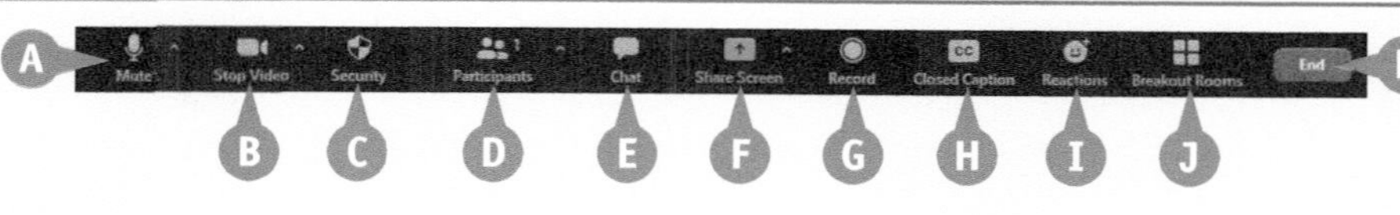

A Mute/Unmute

Turns off your audio. Select **Unmute** to turn your audio back on.

B Stop Video/Start Video

Turns off your video. Select **Start Video** to turn your video back on.

C Security

Displays a menu of security settings for the meeting. See Chapter 9.

D Participants

Displays the Participants pane, which contains a list of the meeting attendees.

E Chat

Displays the Chat pane, which enables you to exchange messages with other meeting attendees. See Chapter 11.

F Share Screen

Displays a window of options for sharing content with the participants. See Chapter 6.

G Record

Records the meeting locally or to the cloud. See Chapter 7.

H Closed Caption

Assigns an attendee to type closed captions. See the section "Assign an Attendee to Type Closed Captions" later in this chapter.

I Reactions

Adds a reaction icon to your video feed. See Chapter 3.

J Breakout Rooms

Creates one or more breakout rooms. See the section "Enable Breakout Rooms for Participants" later in this chapter.

K End

Stops the meeting. See the section "End a Meeting" later in this chapter.

Allow a Person into Your Meeting

CHAPTER 2

If you have enabled the Waiting Room feature for your meeting, you need to allow authorized users into the meeting when they ask to join. The Waiting Room security feature (see Chapter 9) prevents unauthorized users from joining your meeting. This is highly recommended for all meetings, but it does give you as the meeting host an extra task: you must watch for users in the waiting room, determine whether they are authorized, and then allow access to legitimate meeting participants.

Allow a Person into Your Meeting

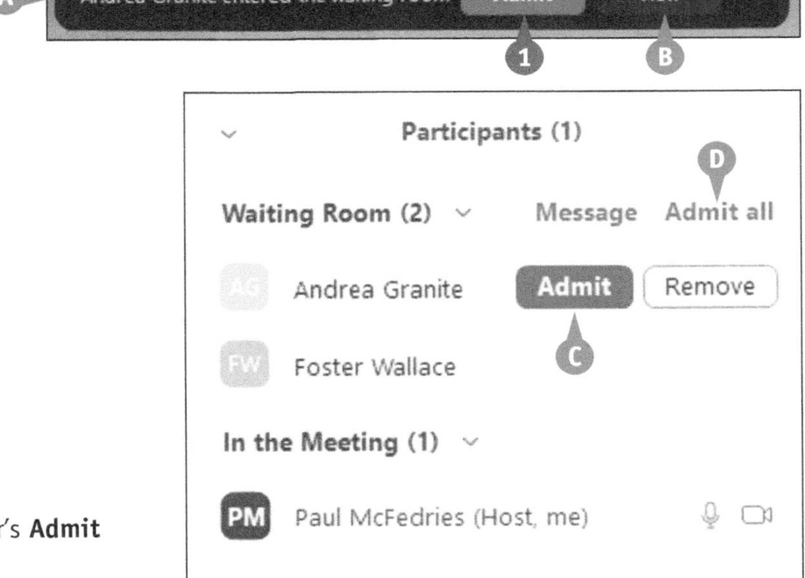

A Zoom displays a bar similar to the one shown here if one or more users are in the waiting room.

1 To allow a single authorized user into the meeting, click **Admit**.

Zoom allows the user to join the meeting.

B If multiple users are in the waiting room, click **View** instead; then continue with step 2.

Zoom opens the Participants pane.

2 Admit the authorized users:

C To admit a single user, click that user's **Admit** button.

D To admit everyone in the waiting room, click **Admit all**.

Zoom allows the users to join the meeting.

Note: To remove a person from your meeting, first click the attendee's **Menu** icon (...). To remove the user temporarily, click **Put in Waiting Room**; to remove the user permanently, click **Remove**.

Enable the Co-Host Option

If you want to make one of your meeting participants a co-host of your meeting, you need to enable that option in your Zoom profile. You can share hosting duties by assigning a participant to be a meeting co-host. The capability of making an attendee a co-host is disabled by default. You can enable the co-host feature by modifying your meeting settings.

Once you have enabled the co-host setting, in subsequent meetings you will be able to assign co-host duties to an attendee, as described in the next section, "Make an Attendee a Meeting Co-Host."

Enable the Co-Host Option

1. Use a web browser to navigate and sign in to https://zoom.us/profile/setting.
2. Click **Meeting**.

   Zoom displays the meeting settings.
3. Click **Co-host** (◯ changes to ◯).

   You can now assign a co-host in a meeting.

Note: If you change the co-host setting during a meeting, the option to assign a co-host will not be available in that meeting.

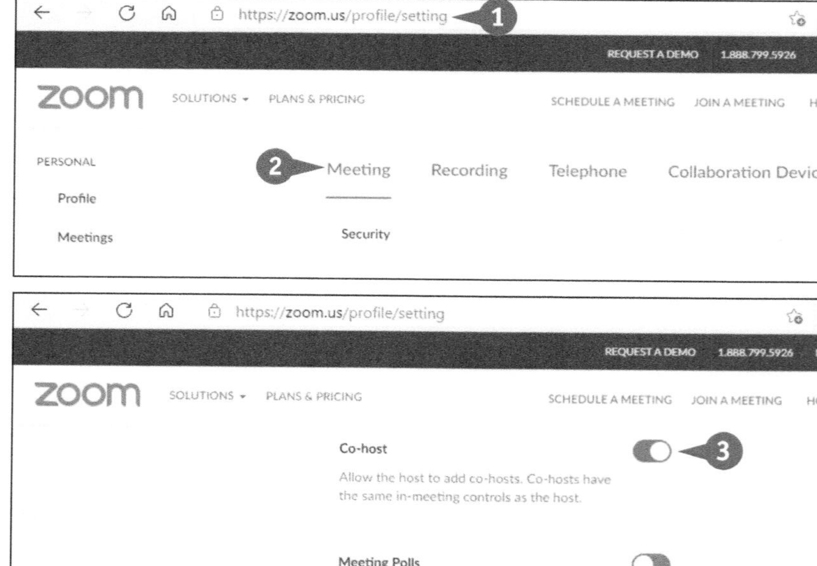

Make an Attendee a Meeting Co-Host

Hosting a meeting comes with a number of responsibilities, including admitting authorized users, controlling attendee audio and video when needed, setting security options, removing users, and more. If you are hosting a meeting with many participants, you might find all these tasks burdensome. If so, you can share that burden and make hosting a large meeting easier by making one or more attendees a co-host.

To make someone a co-host, you need to enable this feature in your profile settings. See the previous section, "Enable the Co-Host Option."

Make an Attendee a Meeting Co-Host

1. In the host controls, click **Participants**.

Note: You can also display the Participants pane by pressing Alt + U.

Zoom opens the Participants pane.

2. Click the attendee's **More** button.
3. Click **Make Co-host**.

Alternatively, click the attendee's **Menu** icon (...) and then click **Make Co-host**.

Note: You can repeat steps 2 and 3 to add more co-hosts, as needed. There is no limit on the number of co-hosts you can add.

Zoom lets the attendee know that they are now a co-host of the meeting.

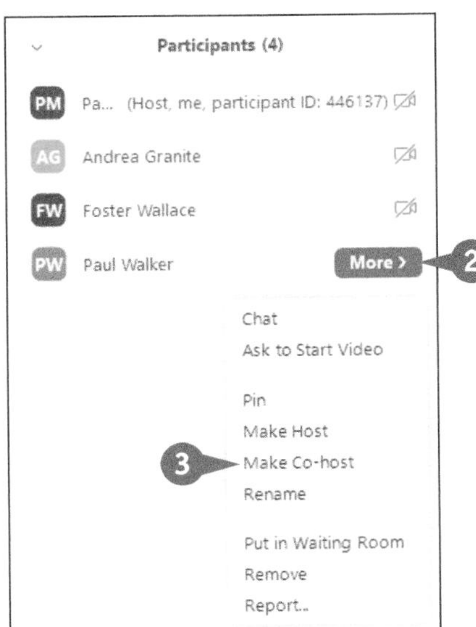

Assign an Attendee to Type Closed Captions

If your meeting includes participants who are hearing impaired, you can assign another participant to type closed captions. Zoom offers a feature that enables you to assign a third-party service to create closed captions. However, if you do not have access to such a service and your meeting either has one or more hearing-impaired participants or is required to provide such accessibility, you as the meeting host can assign another attendee to provide the closed captioning. Ideally, it is best to contact that user before the meeting to ensure the person is willing and able to type closed captions.

Assign an Attendee to Type Closed Captions

1. In the host controls, click **Closed Caption**.
2. Click **Assign a participant to type**.

   A. Alternatively, you can click **I will type** to assign this task to yourself.

   B. If you have access to a third-party closed captioning service, click **Copy the API token** and then paste the token into the service's closed captioning tool.

   Zoom opens the Participants pane.
3. Click the attendee's **More** button.
4. Click **Assign to Type Closed Caption**.

   Alternatively, click the attendee's **Menu** icon (…) and then click **Assign to Type Closed Caption**.

Note: If you do not see the Assign to Type Closed Caption command, it means the user is attending the meeting using a mobile device.

Zoom lets the attendee know that they have been assigned to type closed captions.

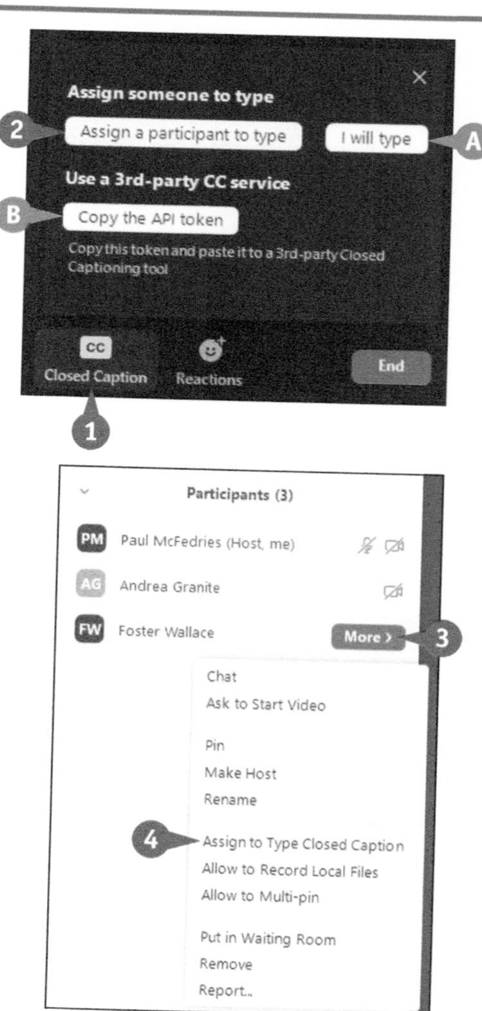

Enable Screen Sharing for Participants

You can make your meetings more valuable and productive by enabling participants to use screen sharing. *Screen sharing* is a feature that enables you to show your screen, an open window, a running application, or other types of content to the participants in your meeting. By default, only the meeting host can share content in this way. However, it is often useful to allow participants to share content. To allow this, you must enable participant screen sharing in your Zoom profile settings. For the full details on using screen sharing, see Chapter 6.

Enable Screen Sharing for Participants

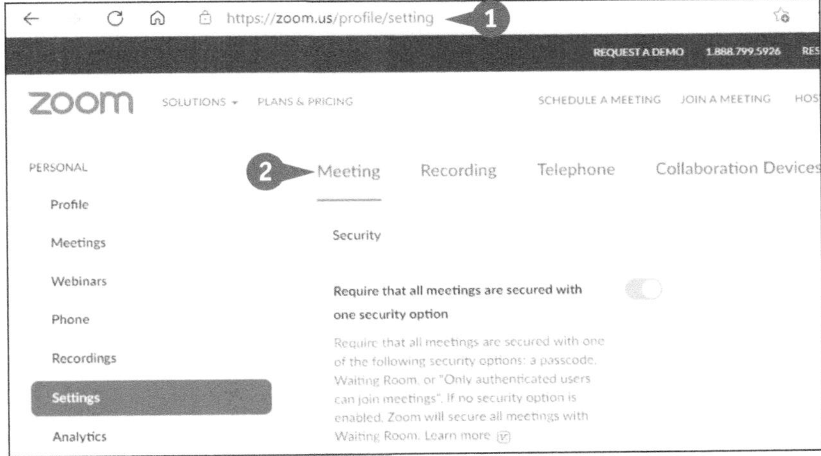

1. Use a web browser to navigate and sign in to https://zoom.us/profile/setting.
2. Click **Meeting**.

Zoom displays the meeting settings.

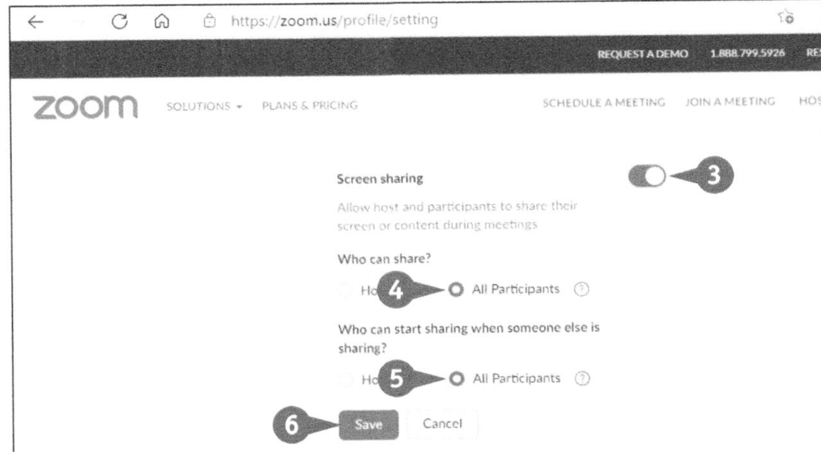

3. Click **Screen sharing** (changes to).
4. Under Who Can Share?, click **All Participants** (changes to).
5. Under Who Can Start Sharing When Someone Else Is Sharing?, click **All Participants** (changes to).
6. Click **Save**.

Meeting participants can now use screen sharing.

Note: Changes to screen sharing settings do not apply to existing meetings.

Enable Breakout Rooms for Participants

You can make your large meetings more efficient and productive by enabling participants to be split into multiple breakout rooms. A *breakout room* is a separate session that includes a subset of the participants from the main meeting. By splitting a large meeting into several breakout rooms, you make it easier for participants to talk and share information. Breakout rooms are disabled by default, so to use them you must enable a setting in your Zoom profile. To learn how to create breakout rooms, see the next section, "Create Breakout Rooms."

Enable Breakout Rooms for Participants

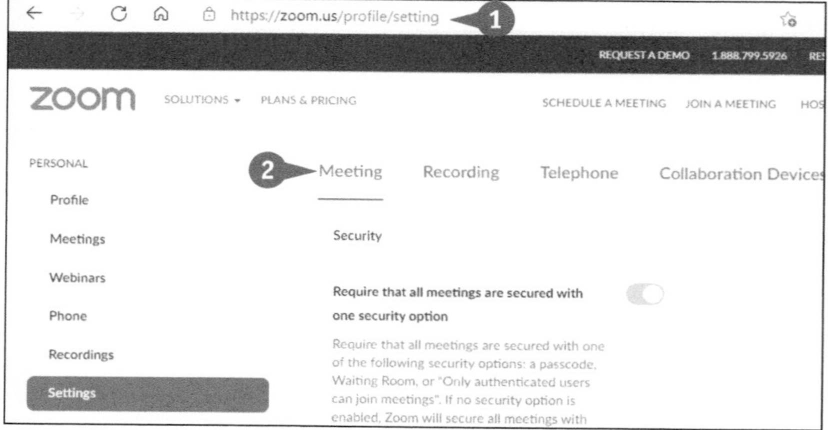

1. Use a web browser to navigate and sign in to https://zoom.us/profile/setting.
2. Click **Meeting**.

   Zoom displays the meeting settings.

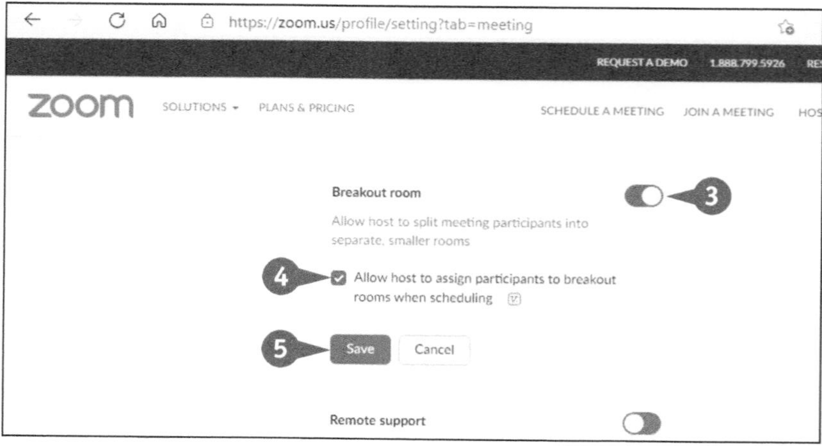

3. Click **Breakout room** (toggle changes to toggle).
4. Click **Allow host to assign participants to breakout rooms when scheduling** (☐ changes to ☑).

Note: To pre-assign breakout rooms, use the Zoom web portal to schedule a meeting and click **Breakout Room pre-assign** (☐ changes to ☑).

5. Click **Save**.

   You can now create breakout rooms in meetings.

Note: Changes to breakout room settings do not apply to existing meetings.

Create Breakout Rooms

In a large meeting, you can enhance communication and sharing by creating breakout rooms. Each breakout room contains a subset of the participants from the main meeting. Breakout room participants get the same audio, video, and screen sharing features as they do in the main meeting, but the smaller number of participants in the breakout room makes for easier communication. You can create up to 50 breakout rooms. You can have Zoom automatically assign participants to each room, assign the participants yourself, or allow participants to choose rooms themselves. See the previous section, "Enable Breakout Rooms for Participants," to activate this feature.

Create Breakout Rooms

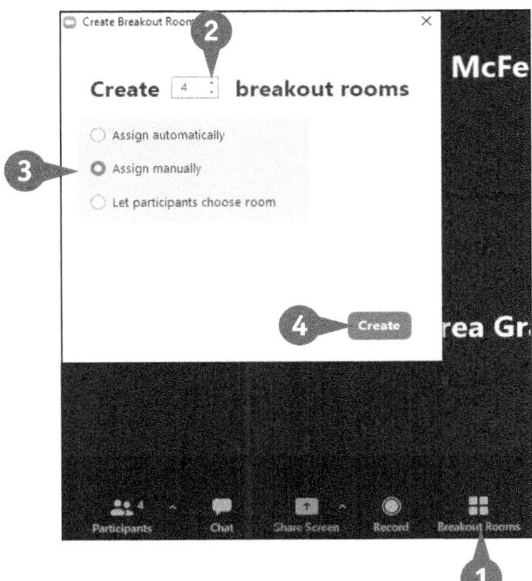

1. In the host controls, click **Breakout Rooms**.

   Zoom displays the Create Breakout Rooms dialog.

2. Click the **Create *X* breakout rooms** ⁝ to set the number of rooms.

3. Click how you want the rooms assigned to the participants (○ changes to ◉):

   - **Assign automatically.** Let Zoom assign the participants.
   - **Assign manually.** Assign the participants yourself.
   - **Let participants choose room.** Let each participant choose the room they want.

4. Click **Create**.

   The Breakout Rooms dialog appears.

   A. You can click **Rename** to give a room a different name.

5. If you opted to assign the rooms yourself, click **Assign** and then click each user (☐ changes to ☑).

6. Click **Open All Rooms**.

   Zoom opens the breakout rooms.

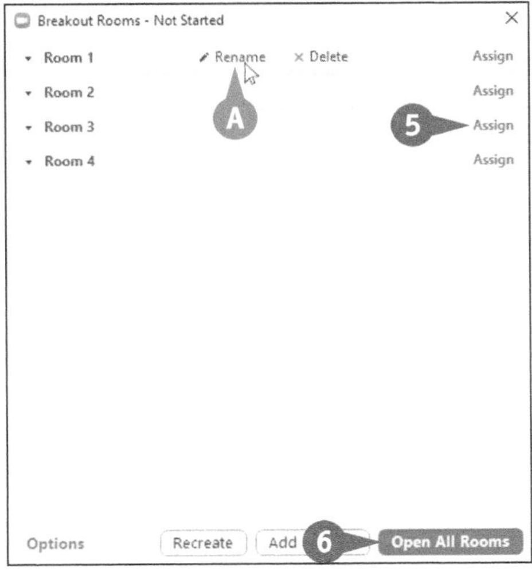

Enable Recording for Participants

You can make a meeting more valuable to the participants by enabling them to record the meeting. *Recording* is a feature that saves the meeting audio and video to a file for later playback. See Chapter 7 to learn more. By default, the meeting host can record the meeting, and that recording can be saved either locally to the host's computer or online in the cloud. If you enable participants to record the meeting, they can record locally only. However, before you can give a participant permission to record the meeting, you must activate that setting in your Zoom profile.

Enable Recording for Participants

1. Use a web browser to navigate and sign in to https://zoom.us/profile/setting.
2. Click **Recording**.

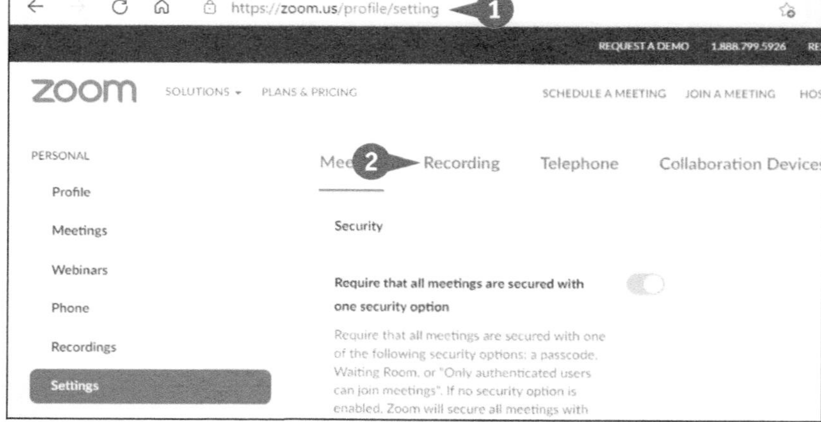

Zoom displays the recording settings.

3. Click **Local recording** (toggle changes to toggle).
4. Click **Hosts can give meeting participants permission to record locally** (☐ changes to ☑).

You can now allow meeting participants to record meetings locally.

Note: Changes to recording settings do not apply to existing meetings.

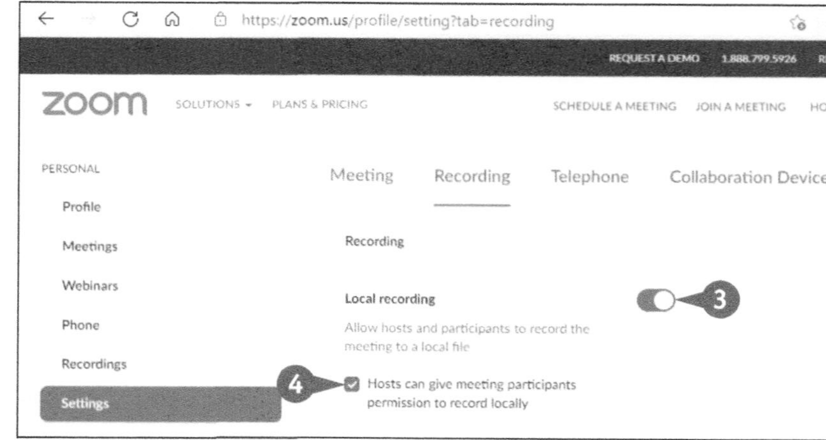

End a Meeting

When your meeting time is done, your final duty as the meeting host is to end the meeting. Even though you specify a meeting duration when you schedule a meeting, that duration is a courtesy so that the meeting participants know how much time to set aside in their calendar. When the duration you specified is reached, Zoom does not end the meeting automatically. Instead, when the meeting is complete, whether the meeting is exactly as long as the duration you set or the meeting is a little longer or shorter, you as the meeting host must end the meeting.

End a Meeting

1. In the host controls, click **End**.

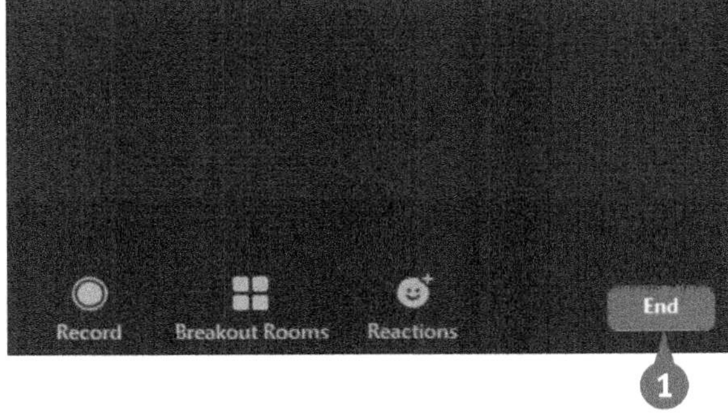

2. Click **End Meeting for All**.

   Zoom ends your meeting.

Note: If your meeting is idle — that is, no talking and no activity — for 40 minutes, Zoom ends the meeting automatically. Zoom also ends the meeting automatically after 40 minutes if you created the meeting using a Basic (free) Zoom account.

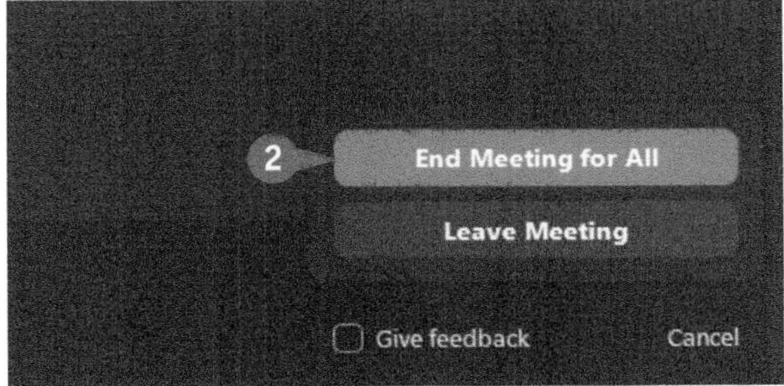

CHAPTER 3

Joining a Meeting

To participate in a Zoom meeting hosted by someone else, you must first join that meeting. You can join a meeting in several ways, including via the Zoom desktop and mobile apps, from an email invitation, from the Web, and by phone. Once you are in the meeting, you have several controls at your disposal for participating in the meeting.

Join a Meeting via the Desktop App

You can use the Zoom desktop app to join a meeting. Before you can join the meeting, though, you need to know the meeting ID, which is a 10- or 11-digit number that uniquely identifies the meeting. Most meetings also require you to enter a six-digit passcode. These steps assume you have not received an invitation link; if you do have such a link, it is easier to use the method described in the section "Join a Meeting via an Invitation Link" later in this chapter.

You can join a Zoom meeting using the desktop app either before or after signing in to the app.

Join a Meeting via the Desktop App

Join Before Signing In

1. Launch the Zoom desktop app.
2. Click **Join a Meeting**.

   Zoom displays the Join Meeting dialog. Continue with the steps in the later "Join the Meeting" section.

Join After Signing In

1. Launch the Zoom desktop app and sign in to your account.
2. Click **Home**.
3. Click **Join**.

   Zoom displays the Join Meeting dialog. Continue with the steps in the later "Join the Meeting" section.

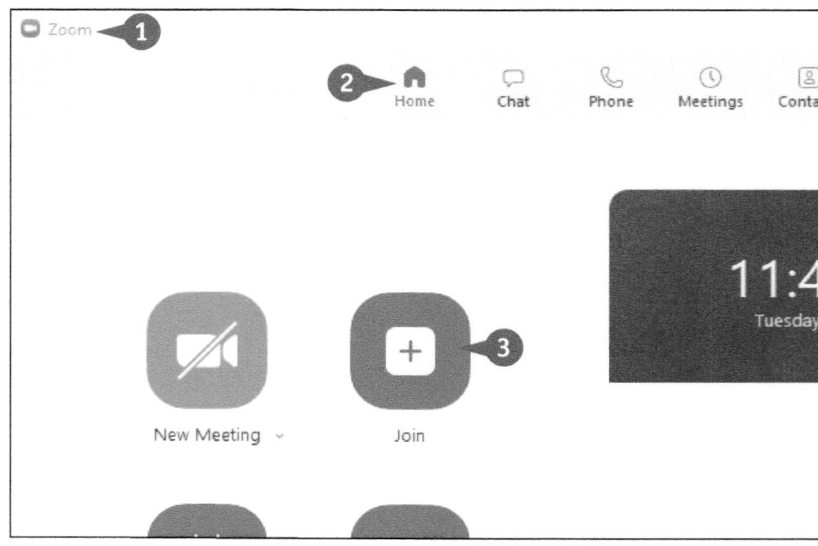

Join the Meeting

1. Type the meeting ID.
2. Type your display name.

A. If you are joining before signing in, you can click **Remember my name for future meetings** to save the name (☐ changes to ☑).

3. If you want to start with audio turned off, click **Do not connect to audio** (☐ changes to ☑).
4. If you want to start with video turned off, click **Turn off my video** (☐ changes to ☑).
5. Click **Join**.

   If the meeting is protected by a passcode, the Enter Meeting Passcode dialog appears.

6. Type the passcode.

B. For security purposes, the passcode digits appear as asterisks.

7. Click **Join Meeting**.

   Zoom lets you in to the meeting.

Note: If the meeting uses a waiting room (see Chapter 9), then instead of letting you into the meeting directly, Zoom will display the message *Please wait, the meeting host will let you in soon.*

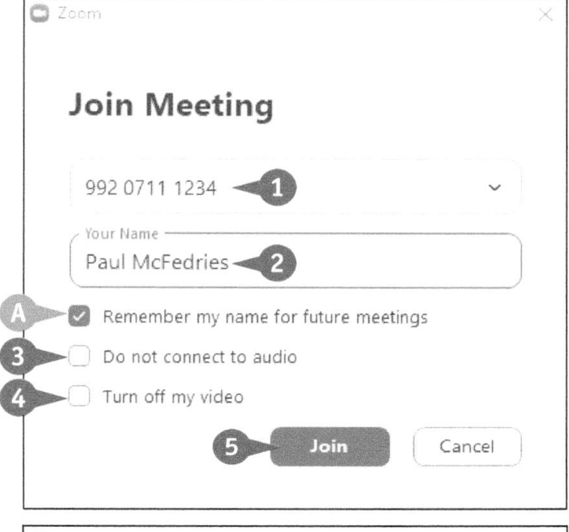

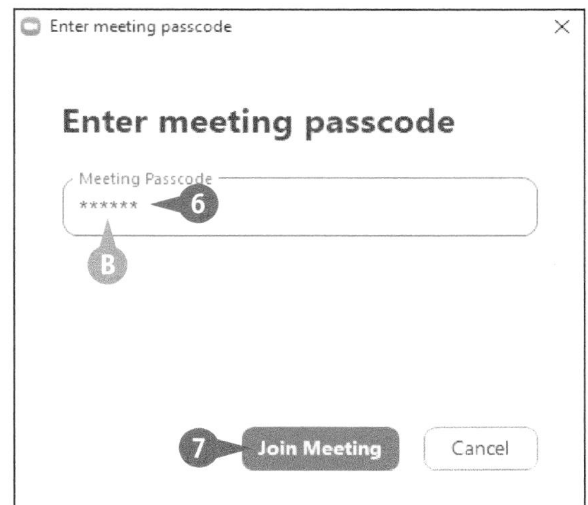

TIP

Why does Zoom tell me the meeting is for authorized attendees only?

For security purposes, the meeting host can configure the meeting so that only authenticated users — that is, people who have Zoom accounts and are signed in to those accounts — can join the meeting. (See Chapter 9 to learn more about this security feature.) If you see this dialog, you need to click **Sign in to Join** (A), enter your Zoom credentials, and then click **Sign In**.

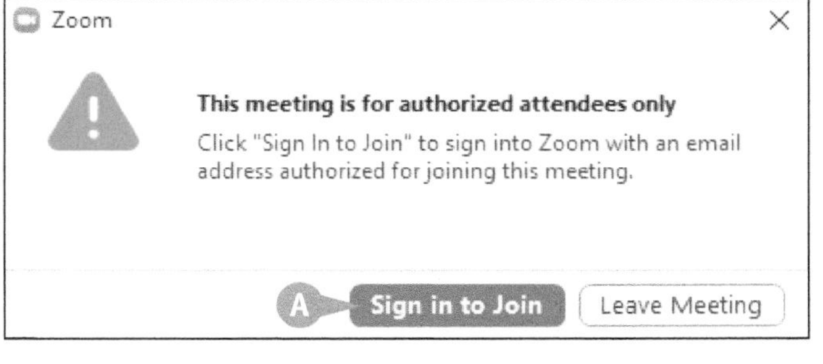

Join a Meeting via the Mobile App

You can use the Zoom mobile app on a smartphone or tablet to join a meeting. To join a meeting using the mobile app, you usually need two pieces of information. First, you need the meeting ID, a 10- or 11-digit number that is unique to the meeting. Second, for most meetings you also need the passcode, which is usually a six-digit number.

With the Zoom mobile app, you can join a meeting either before or after signing in to the app.

Join a Meeting via the Mobile App

Join Before Signing In

1. Launch the Zoom mobile app.
2. Tap **Join a Meeting**.

   Zoom displays the Join a Meeting screen. Continue with the steps in the later "Join the Meeting" section.

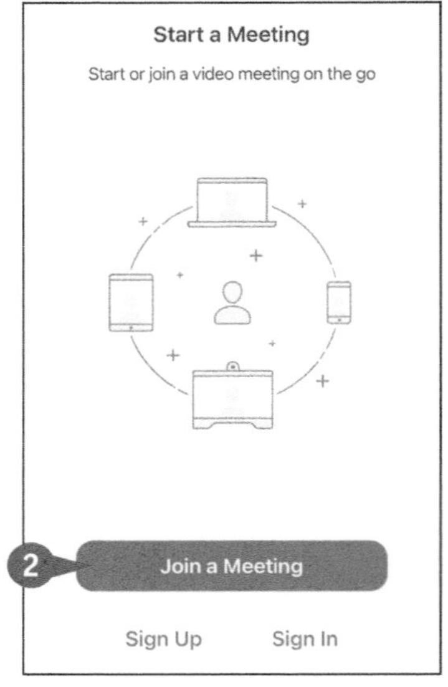

Join After Signing In

1. Launch the Zoom mobile app and sign in to your account.
2. Tap **Meet & Chat**.
3. Tap **Join**.

   Zoom displays the Join a Meeting screen. Continue with the steps in the later "Join the Meeting" section.

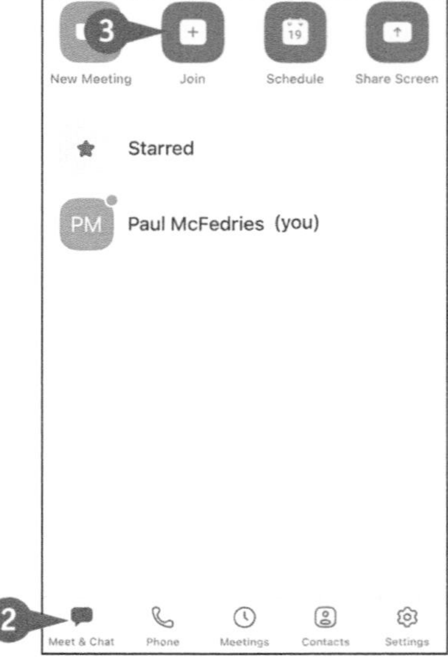

Join the Meeting

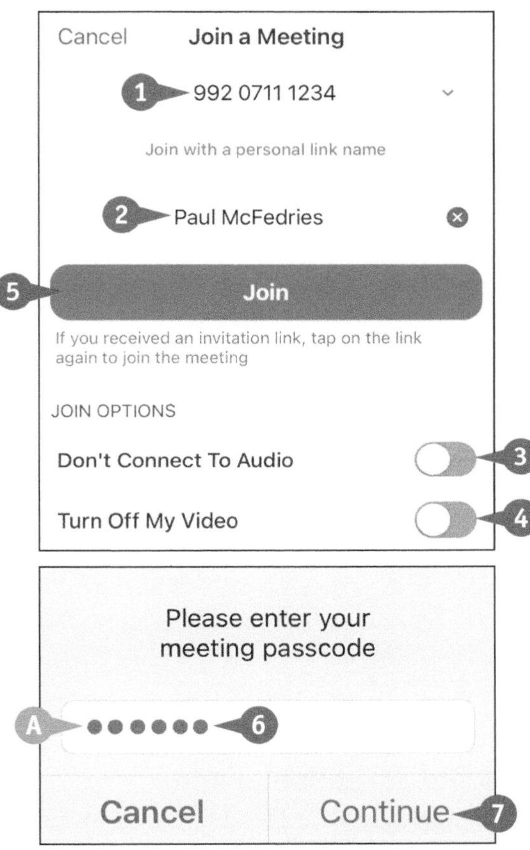

1. Type the meeting ID.
2. Type your display name.
3. If you want to start with audio turned off, tap **Don't Connect To Audio** (◯ changes to ◯).
4. If you want to start with video turned off, tap **Turn Off My Video** (◯ changes to ◯).
5. Tap **Join**.

   If the meeting is protected by a passcode, Zoom prompts you to enter the passcode.

6. Type the passcode.

   A For security purposes, the passcode digits appear as dots.

7. Tap **Continue**.

   Zoom lets you in to the meeting.

Note: If the meeting uses a waiting room (see Chapter 9), then instead of letting you into the meeting directly, Zoom will display the message *Please wait, the meeting host will let you in soon.*

TIP

Why does Zoom tell me the meeting requires authentication?

As a security precaution, the person who created the meeting configured it to allow only authenticated users. An authenticated user is someone who has a Zoom account and is signed in to that account. (To learn more about this security setting, see Chapter 9.) If you see the Sign In to Join dialog, tap **Sign In** (A), enter your Zoom account credentials, and then tap **Sign In**.

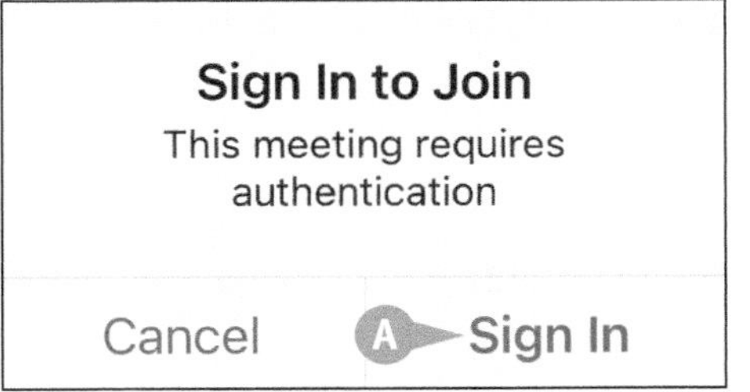

Accept a Direct Meeting Invitation

If you are in the contacts list of the meeting host (see Chapter 10), the host can send you a direct invitation to join a meeting that is already in progress. You can use either the Zoom desktop app or the Zoom mobile app to accept the invitation.

If the host has configured the meeting with a waiting room (see Chapter 9 to learn how to do this), then you will not be allowed in to the meeting directly. Instead, you will see the message *Please wait, the meeting host will let you in soon.*

Accept a Direct Meeting Invitation

With the Zoom Desktop App

1 Click **Join**.

A If you cannot join the meeting at this time, click **Decline** instead.

Zoom lets you in to the meeting.

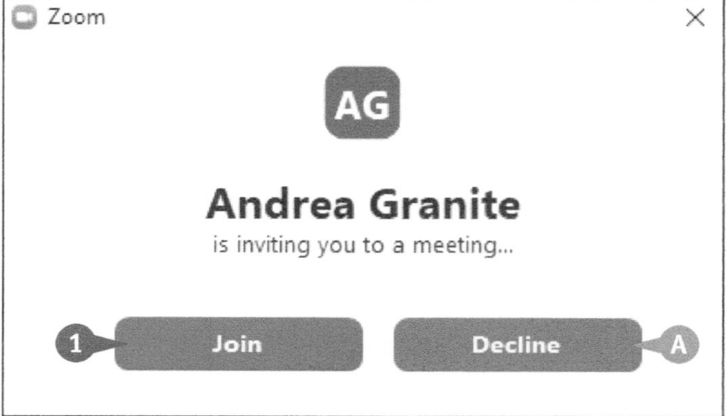

With the Zoom Mobile App

1 Tap **Accept**.

B If you cannot join the meeting, tap **Decline** instead.

Zoom lets you in to the meeting.

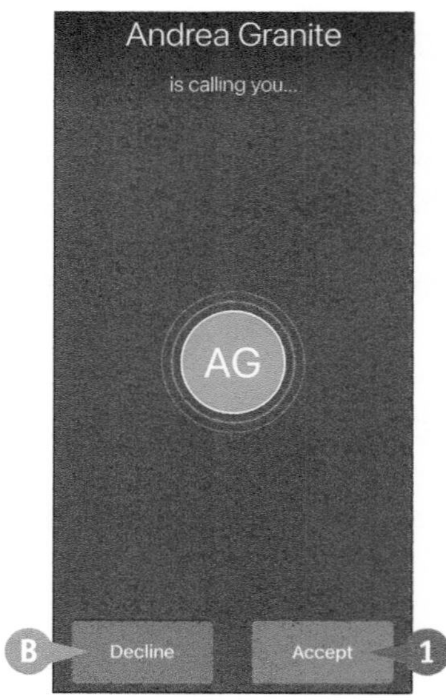

Join a Meeting via an Invitation Link

If you receive a meeting invitation link via email, text, or social media post, you can use that link to join the meeting. In most cases, clicking or tapping the link takes you directly to the meeting because the meeting passcode is included in the link. However, for extra security the host might have configured the meeting link to not include the passcode. (See Chapter 9 to learn more about this setting.) In that case, you need to know the passcode to join the meeting.

Join a Meeting via an Invitation Link

1. Open the email, text, or post that contains the meeting invitation.
2. Click the invitation link.

   If the meeting is protected by a passcode and the passcode was not embedded in the invitation link, the Enter Meeting Passcode dialog appears.

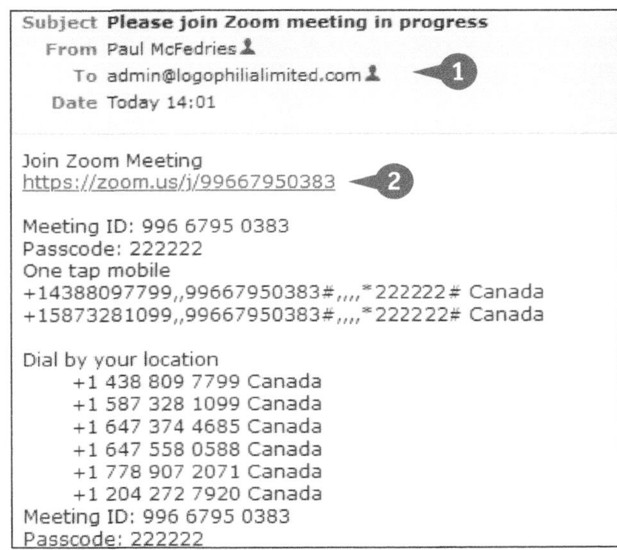

3. Type the passcode.

   A For security purposes, the passcode digits appear as asterisks.

4. Click **Join Meeting**.

   Zoom lets you in to the meeting.

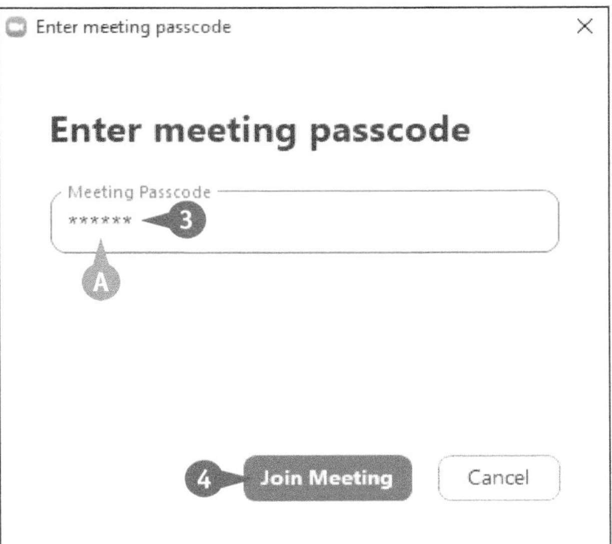

Note: If the host has configured the meeting with a waiting room (see Chapter 9), then you will not be allowed in to the meeting directly. Instead, you will see the message *Please wait, the meeting host will let you in soon.*

Join a Meeting via the Web

You can use a web browser to join a meeting using the Zoom web portal. To join a meeting via the Web, you need to know the meeting ID, which is a 10- or 11-digit number that uniquely identifies the meeting. In most cases, to join the meeting you also need to know the meeting's six-digit passcode.

Although this section shows you how to begin the process of joining a meeting via the Web, note that to actually join the meeting, you require the Zoom app. If you cannot use or install the app, see the tip at the end of this section.

Join a Meeting via the Web

1. Use a web browser to navigate to https://zoom.us/.
2. Click **Join a Meeting**.

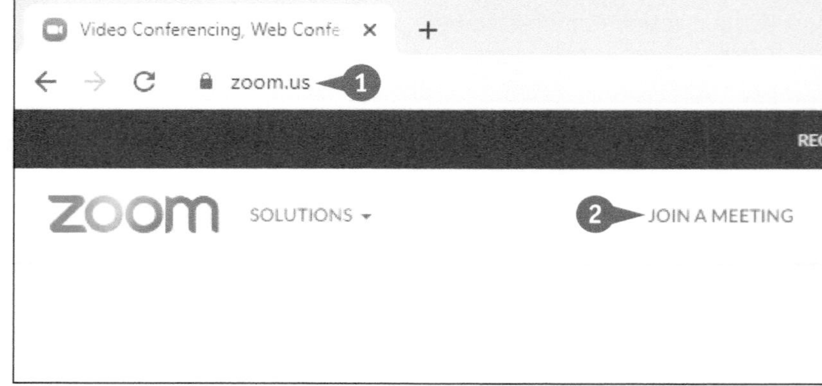

The Join Meeting page appears.

Note: You can browse directly to the Join Meeting page by using the address https://zoom.us/join.

3. Type the meeting ID.
4. Click **Join**.

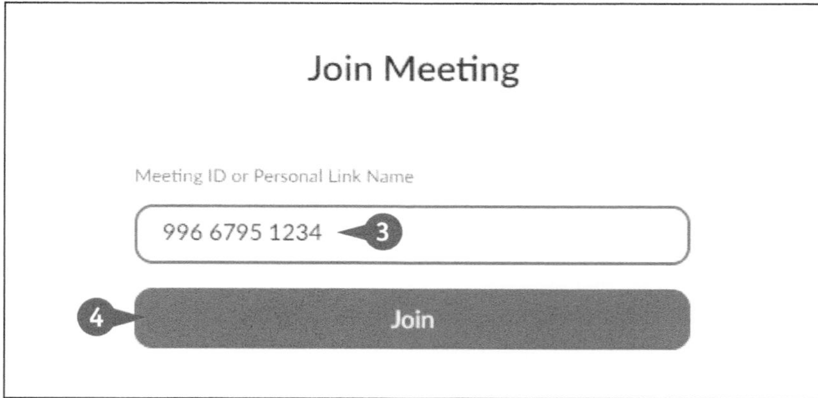

Your web browser asks for your permission to open the Zoom app.

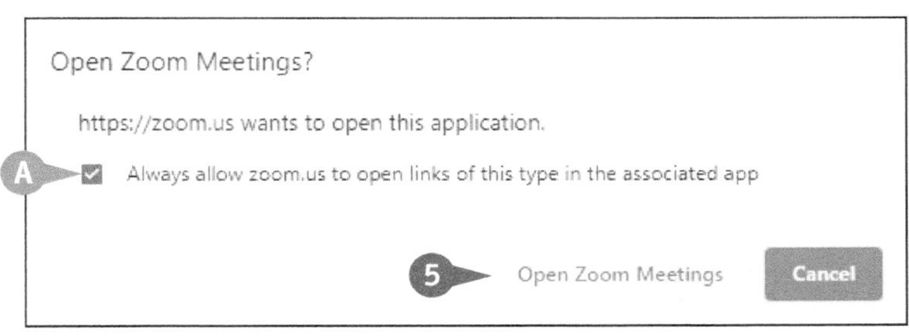

Note: The steps you follow to give permission vary depending on the browser. The following steps are for Google Chrome.

A To avoid this step in the future, click **Always allow zoom.us to open links of this type in the associated app** (☐ changes to ☑).

5 Click **Open Zoom Meetings**.

Your web browser launches the Zoom app.

If the meeting is protected by a passcode, the Enter Meeting Passcode dialog appears.

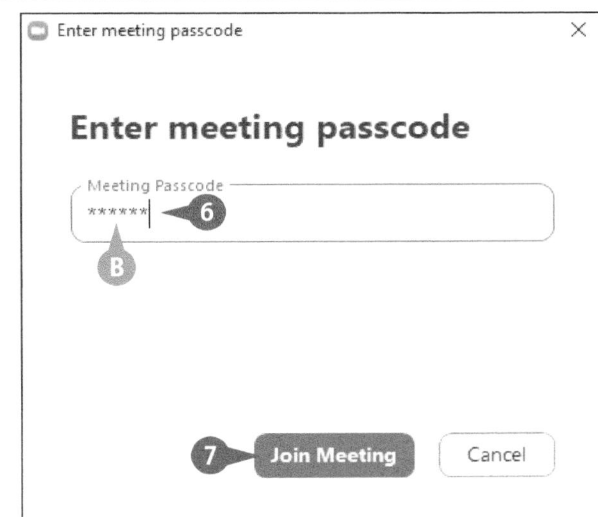

6 Type the passcode.

B For security purposes, the passcode digits appear as asterisks.

7 Click **Join Meeting**.

Zoom lets you in to the meeting.

Note: If the host has configured the meeting with a waiting room (see Chapter 9), then you will not be allowed in to the meeting directly. Instead, you will see the message *Please wait, the meeting host will let you in soon.*

TIP

I cannot install or run the Zoom app. Can I still join a meeting?

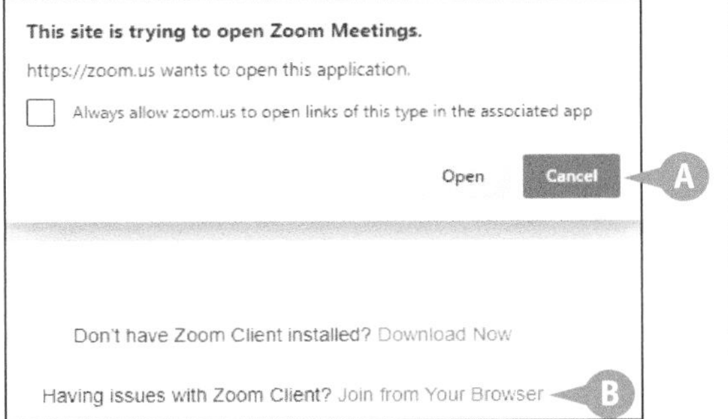

Yes, it is possible to join and participate in a meeting using your web browser. However, this option is turned off by default for meetings, so before the meeting you must ask the meeting host to enable the Show a "Join from Your Browser" Link setting, as described in Chapter 8.

To join from your web browser, follow steps **1** to **4** and then click **Cancel** (A) when your browser requests permission to open the Zoom app. Click the **Join from Your Browser** link (B). Follow the prompts on-screen, which might include giving your web browser permission to use your camera and microphone.

Configure Meeting Settings

When you join a meeting, you can configure a number of settings to make your meeting experience easier and more efficient. For example, as described in the tip at the end of this section, you can configure Zoom to take advantage of your computer's dual-monitor setup.

Many of the tasks in the rest of this chapter show you how to configure some useful settings. See also Chapter 8 for more information on settings you can apply as a host and a participant.

Configure Meeting Settings

Using the Zoom Desktop App

1. Move the mouse to display the meeting controls.
2. Click **Meeting Information** (🛡).
3. Click **Settings** (⚙).

Zoom opens the Settings dialog.

A By default, Zoom displays the Statistics tab, which shows various metrics for the current meeting.

B When you have completed your work with the settings, click **Close** (✕).

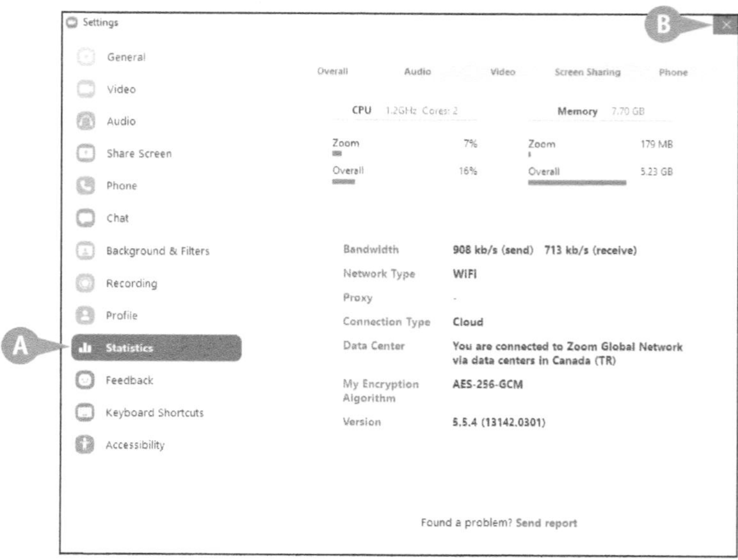

Using the Zoom Mobile App

1. Tap the screen to display the meeting controls.
2. Tap **More**.
3. Tap **Meeting Settings**.

   Zoom displays the Meeting Settings screen.

Note: When you have finished working with the settings, tap **Done** to return to the meeting.

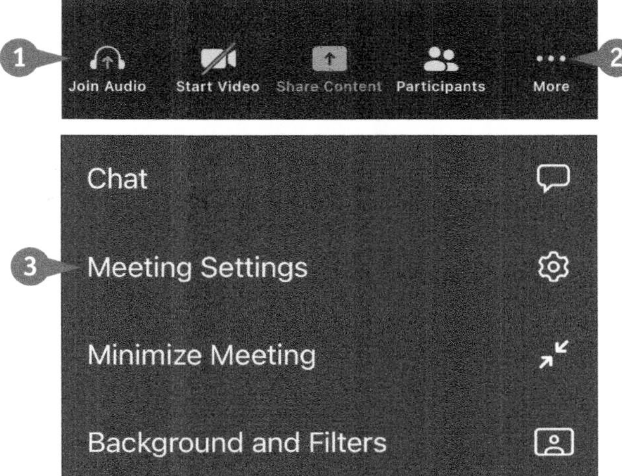

TIP

Is it possible to use Zoom with two monitors?

Yes. If you have a dual-monitor setup configured on your computer, you can use both monitors while in a Zoom meeting. This is most useful when you share content (see Chapter 6) because it enables you to view your meeting controls and participant videos on one monitor and the information you are sharing on the other monitor.

To enable Zoom to use your computer's dual-monitor setup, display the meeting settings using the Zoom desktop client, click the **General** tab, and then click **Use dual monitors** (☐ changes to ☑).

Explore Attendee Controls

As a meeting attendee, you have access to a number of features that enable you to control various aspects of your meeting profile and participation. When you join a meeting using the desktop app, Zoom opens the meeting in a new window. At the bottom of that window, you see a toolbar that offers a number of icons. If you join a meeting using the Zoom mobile app, you see a similar set of icons.

Zoom hides the toolbar after a few seconds of inactivity, so if you do not see the toolbar, move your mouse or tap the screen.

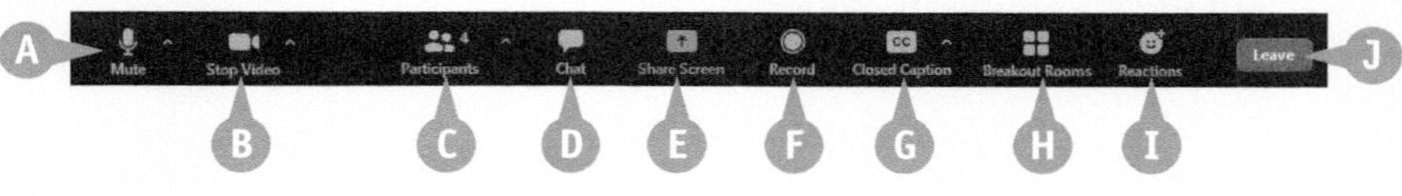

A Mute/Unmute

Turns off your audio. Select **Unmute** to turn your audio back on.

B Stop Video/Start Video

Turns off your video. Select **Start Video** to turn your video back on.

C Participants

Displays the Participants pane, which contains a list of the meeting attendees.

D Chat

Displays the Chat pane, which enables you to exchange messages with other meeting attendees. See Chapter 11.

E Share Screen

Displays a window of options for sharing content with the participants. See Chapter 6.

F Record

Records the meeting locally if the host has enabled this feature. See Chapter 7.

G Closed Caption

Appears when the meeting host has assigned you to type closed captions. See Chapter 2.

H Breakout Rooms

Enables you to join a breakout room, as described in the section "Join a Breakout Room" later in this chapter. You see this icon only if the meeting host has activated this option. See Chapter 2.

I Reactions

Enables you to raise your hand (see the section "Raise Your Hand" later in this chapter) or send a reaction (see the section "Send a Reaction" later in this chapter).

J Leave

Leaves the meeting. See the section "Leave a Meeting" later in this chapter.

Keep Meeting Controls On-Screen

You can configure your meeting settings to keep the attendee controls on-screen all the time. By default, Zoom automatically hides the attendee controls after a few seconds. Hiding the attendee controls is usually what you want because it enables you to focus on the meeting. However, if you find you use the attendee controls frequently for muting your audio or chatting with other participants, having to frequently redisplay the controls can become bothersome. Instead, you can configure the meeting to always show the attendee controls.

Keep Meeting Controls On-Screen

Using the Zoom Desktop App

1. Open the meeting settings.

Note: See the section "Configure Meeting Settings" earlier in this chapter.

2. Click **General**.
3. Click **Always show meeting controls** (☐ changes to ☑).
4. Click **Close** (☒).

Zoom now leaves the attendee controls on-screen all the time.

Using the Zoom Mobile App

1. Open the meeting settings.

Note: See the section "Configure Meeting Settings" earlier in this chapter.

2. Tap **Always Show Meeting Controls** (toggle off changes to toggle on).
3. Tap **Done**.

Zoom now leaves the attendee controls on-screen all the time.

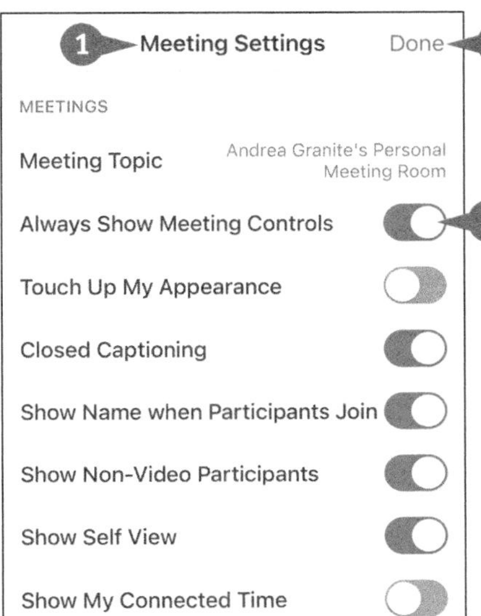

Change Your Display Name

You can change the name that appears along with your video feed. In your Zoom profile, you can specify a display name, which is the name that appears in the lower-left corner of your video window while you are in a meeting. Zoom also shows your display name if you have turned off your video feed and you do not have a profile picture. You can change your display name during the meeting. For example, if you are attending the meeting along with another person, you might want to change the display name to show both your names.

Change Your Display Name

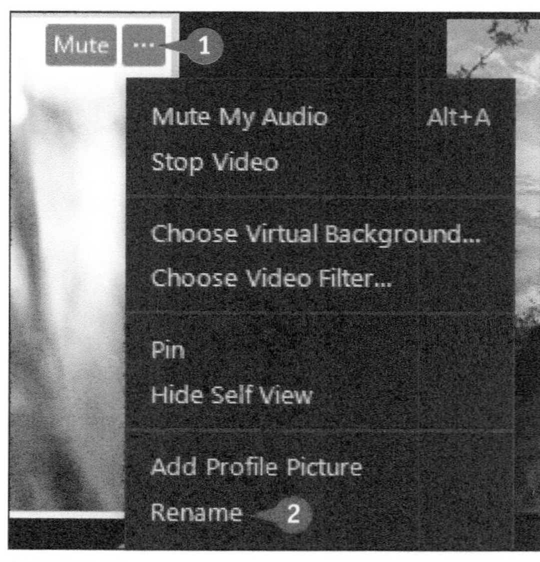

1. In the Zoom desktop app, click **More** (...) in the upper-right corner of your video window.
2. Click **Rename**.

Note: If you do not see the Rename command, it means your meeting host has disabled this feature.

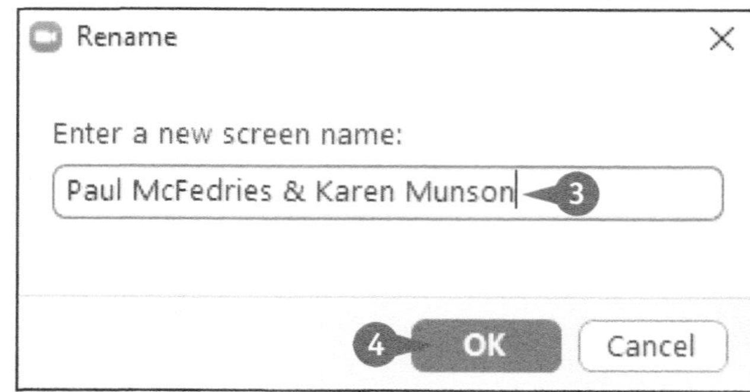

The Rename dialog appears.

3. Type the name you want to display.
4. Click **OK**.

Zoom displays the new name in your video window.

Note: To change your display name in the Zoom mobile app, tap **Participants**, tap your name, tap **Rename**, enter the new name, and then tap **Done**.

Raise Your Hand

You can ask to speak next in a meeting by raising your hand. In a large or active meeting, it can be difficult to break into the conversation. One way to ask for the floor is to raise your hand. In the context of a Zoom meeting, *raising your hand* means that you add an icon of a raised hand to your video window. The idea is that when the meeting host sees your raised-hand icon, the host asks you to speak next.

Raise Your Hand

Using the Zoom Desktop App

1. Display the meeting controls.
2. Click **Reactions**.
3. Click **Raise Hand.**

   Zoom displays the Raised Hand icon () in the upper-left corner of your video window.

Using the Zoom Mobile App

1. Display the meeting controls.
2. Tap **More**.
3. Tap **Raise Hand**.

   Zoom displays the Raised Hand icon () in the upper-left corner of your video window.

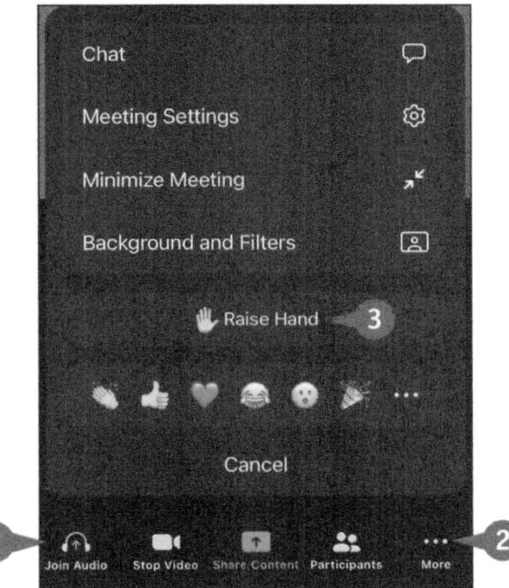

Send a Reaction

You can respond nonverbally to what is happening in a meeting by sending a reaction. In a large or busy meeting, you might not want to unmute or break into the conversation with a short verbal response, such as a laugh. Instead, you can send a nonverbal *reaction*, an icon that appears in the upper-left corner of your video window for a few seconds. The icon could be clapping hands, a thumbs-up, a heart, or one of hundreds of smileys and emojis.

Send a Reaction

Using the Zoom Desktop App

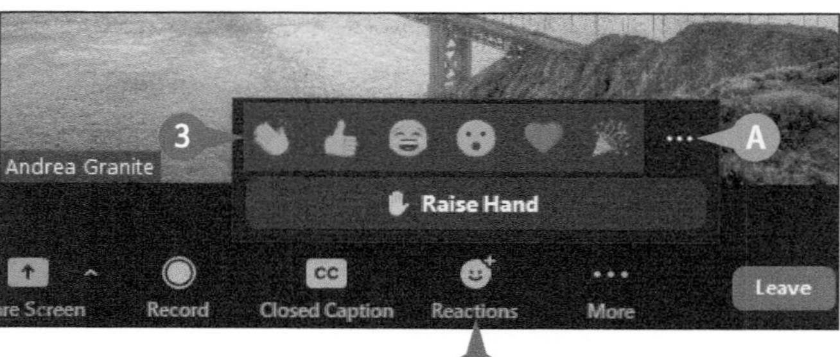

1 Display the meeting controls.

2 Click **Reactions**.

3 Click the reaction you want to send.

A You can click **More** (▪▪▪) to access the full list of reactions.

Zoom displays the reaction icon in the upper-left corner of your video window.

Note: In the Zoom desktop app, you can change the skin tone of your reactions. Open the meeting settings and click **General**. In the **Reaction Skin Tone** section, click the icon for the skin tone you want to use.

Using the Zoom Mobile App

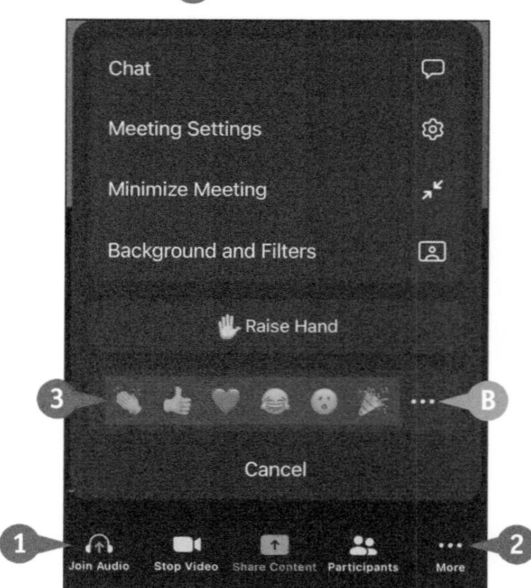

1 Display the meeting controls.

2 Tap **More**.

3 Click the reaction you want to send.

B You can click **More** (▪▪▪) to access the full list of reactions.

Zoom displays the reaction icon in the upper-left corner of your video window.

Send Nonverbal Feedback

You can communicate with meeting participants by sending nonverbal feedback. During a meeting, you might want to respond to something by saying "yes" or "no," or you might want to ask the current speaker to slow down or speed up. These short feedback responses are not usually a problem in a small meeting, but they can be difficult to get across in a large meeting. Instead, you can send your feedback nonverbally, which means an icon appears in the top-left corner of your video window. Unlike a reaction, your nonverbal feedback stays in your feed until you remove it.

Send Nonverbal Feedback

Using the Zoom Desktop App

1. Display the meeting controls.
2. Click **Reactions**.
3. Click the nonverbal feedback you want to send.

   Zoom displays the feedback icon in the upper-left corner of your video window. To remove the icon, repeat steps 1 to 3.

Note: If you do not see the feedback icons, it means the host did not enable them for this meeting.

Using the Zoom Mobile App

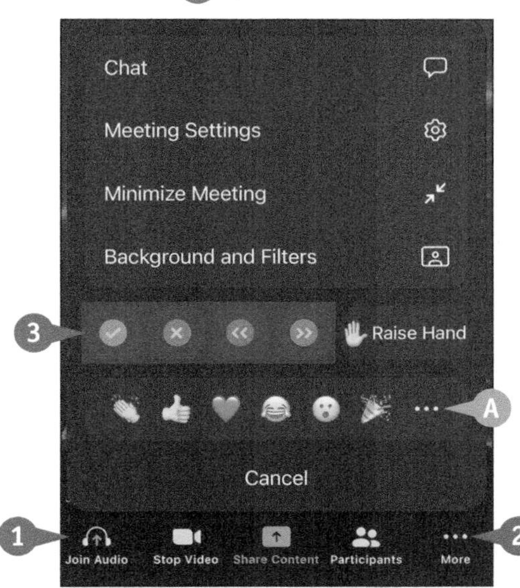

1. Display the meeting controls.
2. Tap **More**.
3. Click the reaction you want to send.

   A. You can click **More** (•••) to access the full list of reactions.

   Zoom displays the feedback icon in the upper-left corner of your video window. To remove the icon, repeat steps 1 to 3.

Note: If you do not see the feedback icons, it means the host did not enable them for this meeting.

Join a Breakout Room

If your meeting offers breakout rooms and your meeting host has allowed participants to choose their own rooms, then you can join the room you want. As detailed in Chapter 2, a breakout room is a separate session that includes a subset of the participants from the main meeting. The idea of a breakout room is to make it easier for participants to talk and share information. Some hosts create breakout rooms that are dedicated to specific topics from the main meeting. If one of those topics is of particular interest to you, then you can join that breakout room to meet with like-minded people.

Join a Breakout Room

Using the Zoom Desktop App

1. Display the meeting controls.
2. Click **Breakout Rooms**.

   The Breakout Rooms dialog appears.

   A. Zoom shows the names of other participants who have joined each room.

3. Click the **Join** link next to the breakout room you want to enter.

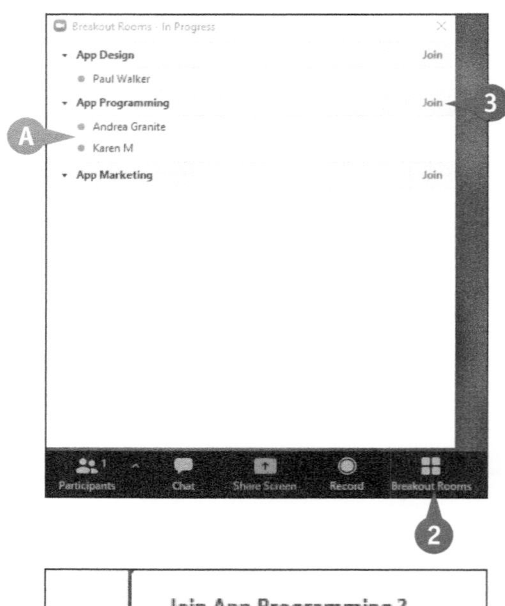

   Zoom asks you to confirm.

4. Click **Yes**.

   Zoom moves your video window from the main meeting to the breakout room.

Join App Programming ?

Yes No

Using the Zoom Mobile App

1. Display the meeting controls.
2. Tap **Join Breakout Room**.

The Join Breakout Room screen appears.

3. Tap the breakout room you want to join.
4. Tap **Join**.

Zoom moves your video window from the main meeting to the breakout room.

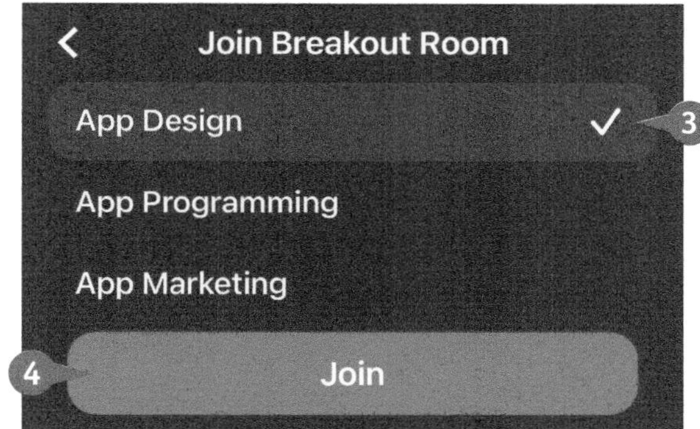

TIPS

Can I switch to a different breakout room?
Yes. If you accidentally joined the wrong breakout room or you want to try a different room, you can switch at any time. In the desktop app, click **Breakout Rooms**, click **Choose Breakout Room**, click **Join** beside the room you want, and then click **Yes**. In the mobile app, repeat the steps in the earlier "Using the Zoom Mobile App" section.

How do I return to the main meeting?
In the desktop app, display the meeting controls, click **Leave Room**, and then click **Leave Breakout Room**. In the mobile app, display the meeting controls, tap **Leave**, and then tap **Leave Breakout Room**.

Change the View

While in a meeting, you can change the video layout by switching between Zoom's two views: Speaker view and Gallery view. Speaker view (sometimes called Active Speaker view) is the default layout, and it shows the participant who is currently speaking in a large video window and some or all of the other participants in thumbnail windows. Gallery view shows all the participants in thumbnail windows. In the desktop app, you can see up to 49 video thumbnails at a time per screen, although less powerful computers might show fewer thumbnails.

Change the View

Using the Zoom Desktop App

1. Display the meeting controls.
2. Click **View**.
3. Click the layout you want to use.

   Zoom switches to the layout you selected.

Note: In Gallery view, you can click and drag a video thumbnail to a new location within the Gallery grid.

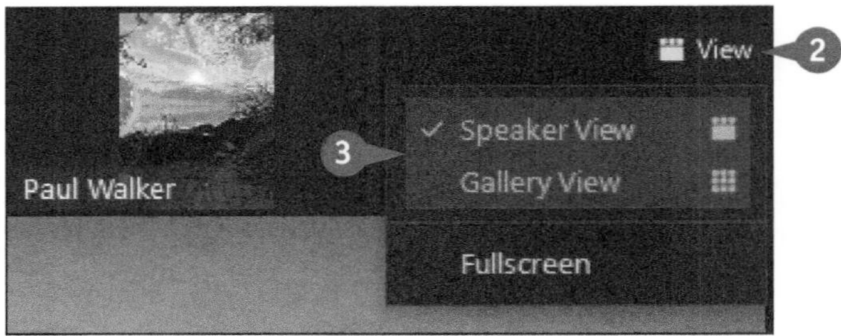

Using the Zoom Mobile App on a Tablet

1. Display the meeting controls.
2. Tap **Switch to *View***, where *View* is either *Gallery View* or *Active Speaker*.

   Zoom switches to the layout you selected.

Note: To change the view using the Zoom mobile app on a smartphone, swipe left for Gallery view or swipe right for Speaker view.

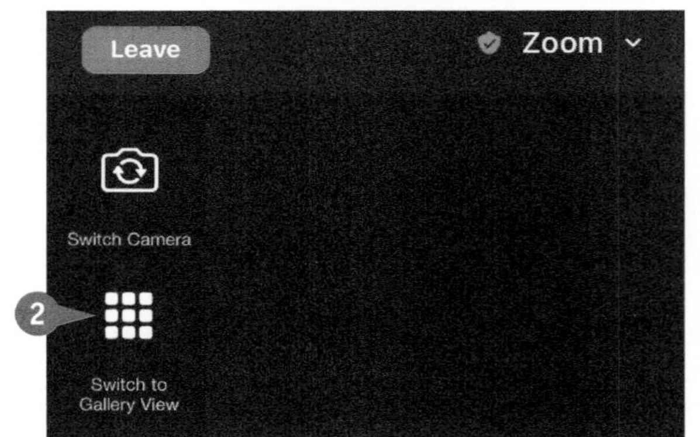

Show Your Connected Time

You can configure your meeting settings to show your connected time, which is how long you have been in the meeting. When you join a meeting, you might not be able to stay for the entire session because of another obligation. Rather than checking a clock constantly, display your connected time so you know exactly when to leave the meeting. Displaying your connected time is also useful if you bill for your time. In the desktop app, your connected time appears in your video window; in the mobile app, your connected time appears at the top of the Zoom screen.

Show Your Connected Time

Using the Zoom Desktop App

1. Open the meeting settings.

Note: See the section "Configure Meeting Settings" earlier in this chapter.

2. Click **General**.
3. Click **Show my connected time** (☐ changes to ☑).
4. Click **Close** (☒).

   Zoom displays the hours, minutes, and seconds you have been in the meeting in the upper-right corner of your video window.

Using the Zoom Mobile App

1. Open the meeting settings.

Note: See the section "Configure Meeting Settings" earlier in this chapter.

2. Tap **Show My Connected Time** (toggle off changes to toggle on).
3. Tap **Done**.

   Zoom displays the hours, minutes, and seconds you have been in the meeting at the top of the screen.

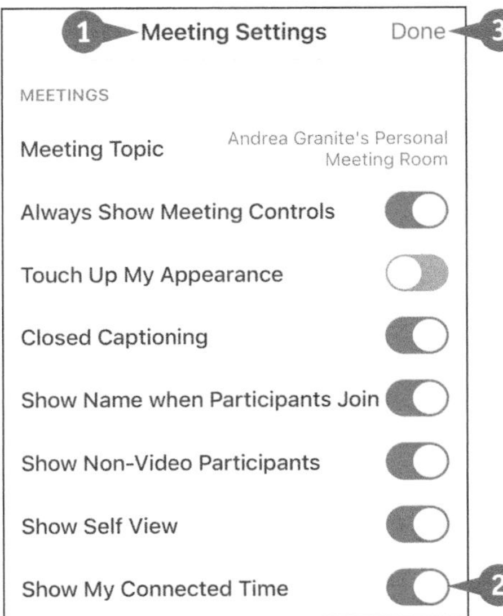

Leave a Meeting

When you no longer want or need to participate in a meeting, you leave the meeting to remove your video window. Some meetings end automatically. For example, if the host uses a free Zoom account, most meetings are restricted to 40 minutes and will end automatically at that time. Other meetings stop when the host ends the meeting for everyone. However, you might want to stop your participation before the meeting itself ends. In that case, you need to leave the meeting. As a courtesy, you should use the meeting chat feature to mention that you are leaving. Note that the meeting host receives a notification when you leave.

Leave a Meeting

Using the Zoom Desktop App

1. Display the meeting controls.
2. Click **Leave**.

Zoom asks you to confirm.

3. Click **Leave Meeting**.

Zoom removes you from the meeting.

Using the Zoom Mobile App

1. Display the meeting controls.
2. Tap **Leave**.

   Zoom asks you to confirm.

3. Tap **Leave Meeting**.

   Zoom removes you from the meeting.

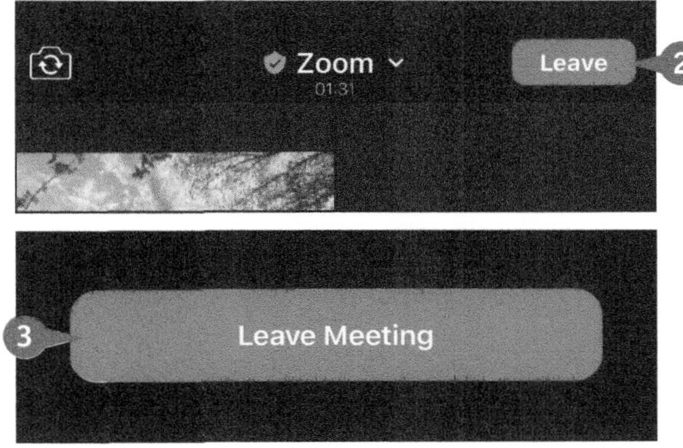

TIP

Can I prevent Zoom from displaying the confirmation that I want to leave the meeting?

Yes, if you use the Zoom desktop app, you can configure your meeting settings to not display the confirmation. Here are the steps to follow:

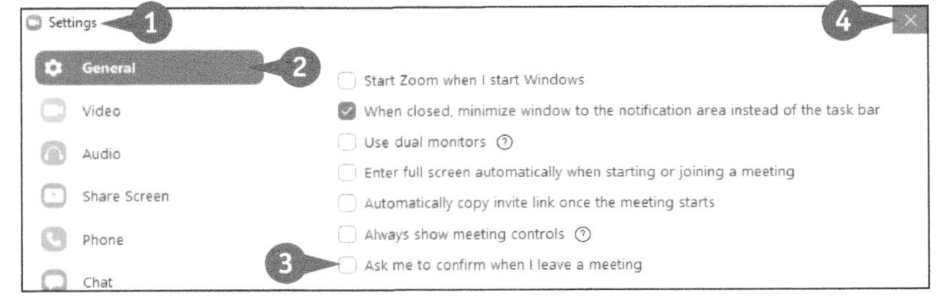

1. Open the meeting settings. (See the section "Configure Meeting Settings" earlier in this chapter.)
2. Click **General**.
3. Click **Ask me to confirm when I leave a meeting** (☑ changes to ☐).
4. Click **Close** (☒).

   Now, when you click **Leave**, Zoom immediately removes you from the meeting.

CHAPTER 4

Working with Meeting Audio

Zoom offers a number of features and tools for working with the audio portion of a meeting. For example, you can test the microphone and speakers you want to use in a meeting. You can also choose a different microphone or speakers, mute and unmute your audio, use push-to-talk, and suppress background noises.

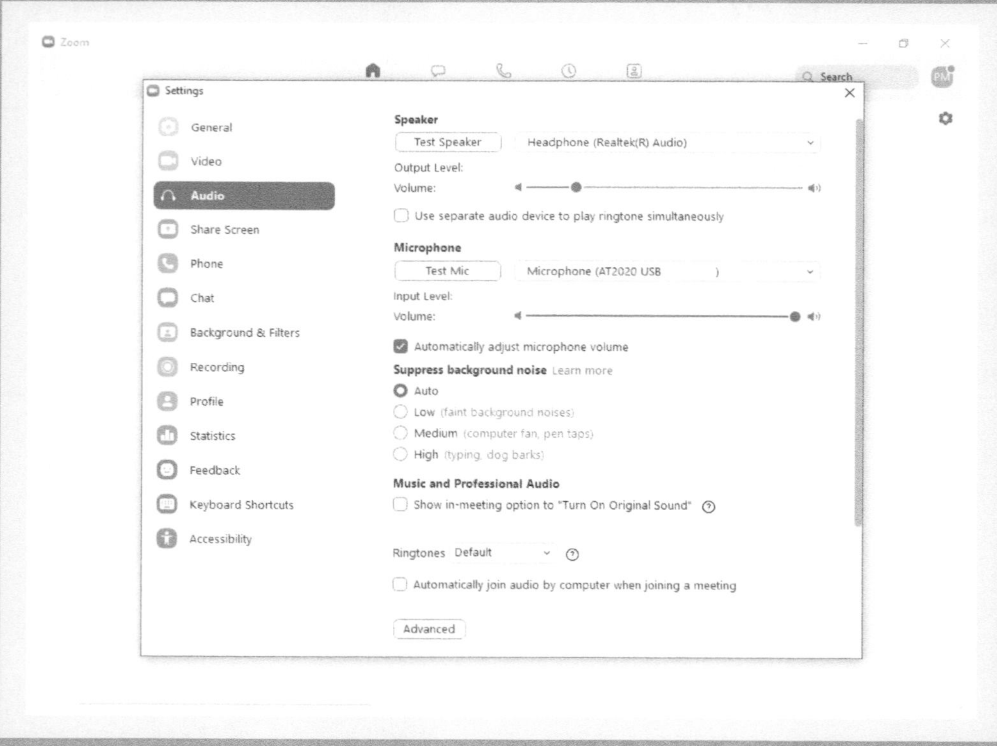

Test Your Audio Devices

To get the most out of a Zoom meeting, you should test your audio devices to make sure they are working optimally. By far the most common cause of Zoom problems is a faulty audio setup. This could be a speaker not connected or a microphone on mute. You can prevent such problems by testing your audio devices to make sure they are working.

You can test your audio devices at any time using the Settings dialog of the Zoom desktop app. You can also test your audio devices just before joining a meeting.

Test Your Audio Devices

Test Audio in the Desktop App

1. Click your profile picture.
2. Click **Settings**.

The Settings dialog appears.

3. Click **Audio**.
4. Click the **Speaker** ⌄ and then select the speaker you want to use in your Zoom meetings.
5. Click **Test Speaker**.
6. Click and drag the **Volume** slider (●) to adjust the output volume.
7. Click the **Microphone** ⌄ and then select the microphone you want to use in your Zoom meetings.
8. Click **Test Mic**.
9. Click and drag the **Volume** slider (●) to adjust the input volume.

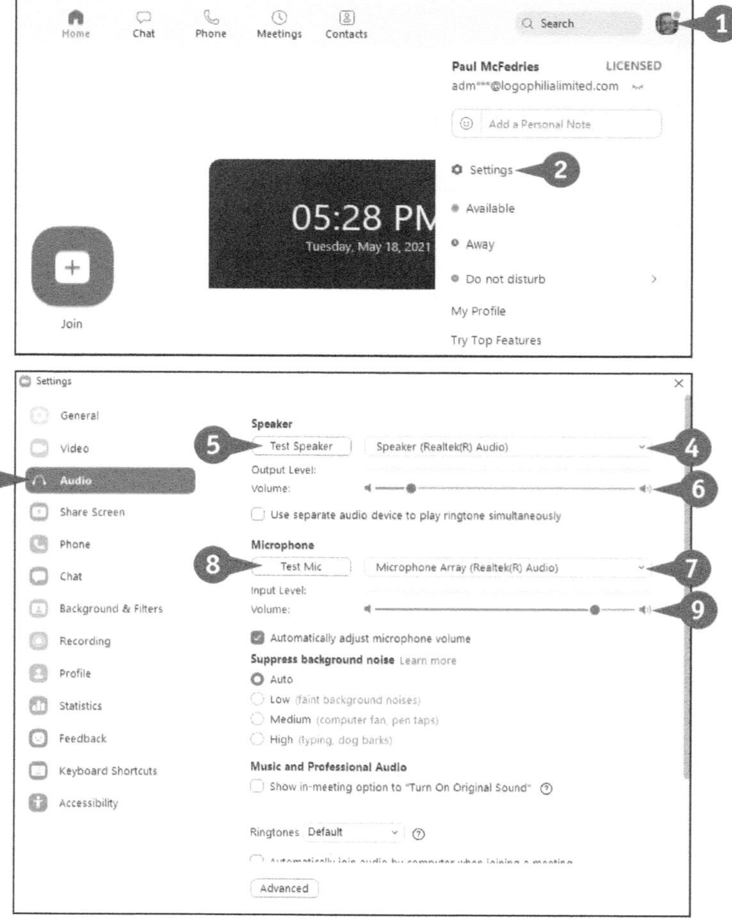

Test Audio Before a Meeting

1. Start or join the meeting.
2. Click **Test Speaker and Microphone**.

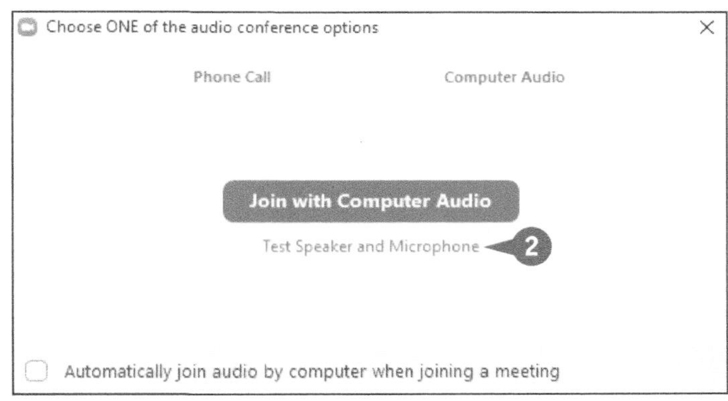

The Do You Hear a Ringtone? dialog appears.

3. If you hear the ringtone being played through your speakers, click **Yes**.

A. If you do not hear the ringtone, click the **Select Speaker** ⌄ and try a different speaker.

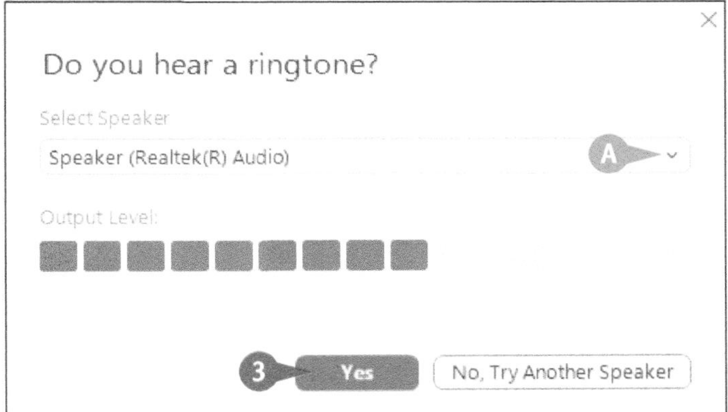

The Speak and Pause, Do You Hear a Replay? dialog appears.

4. Speak a short phrase into your microphone.
5. If you hear your phrase replayed, click **Yes**.

B. If you do not hear the phrase, click the **Select Microphone** ⌄ and try a different microphone.

6. Click **End Test** (not shown).

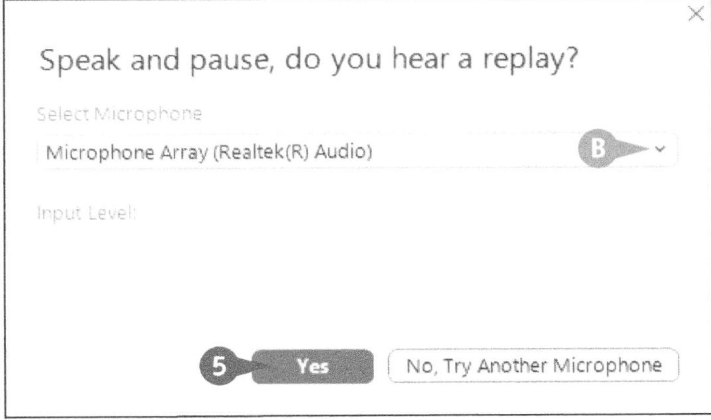

TIP

Is there a way to test my audio devices during a meeting?

Yes, you can also access the audio settings after you have joined a meeting. Click **Meeting Information** (🛡), click **Settings** (⚙), and then follow steps 3 to 9 in the "Test Audio in the Desktop App" subsection.

Select a Different Audio Output Device

During a Zoom meeting, you can switch to a different audio output device. When you join a Zoom meeting, you might find you cannot hear the other meeting participants. The most common cause of this glitch is that the currently selected speaker is not working or not attached to your computer. You can often fix this problem by selecting a different audio output device. The output device could be an external speaker, a headset, earbuds, or the speakers that are built in to the device you are using.

Select a Different Audio Output Device

1. Click **Meeting Information** (🛡).
2. Click **Settings** (⚙).

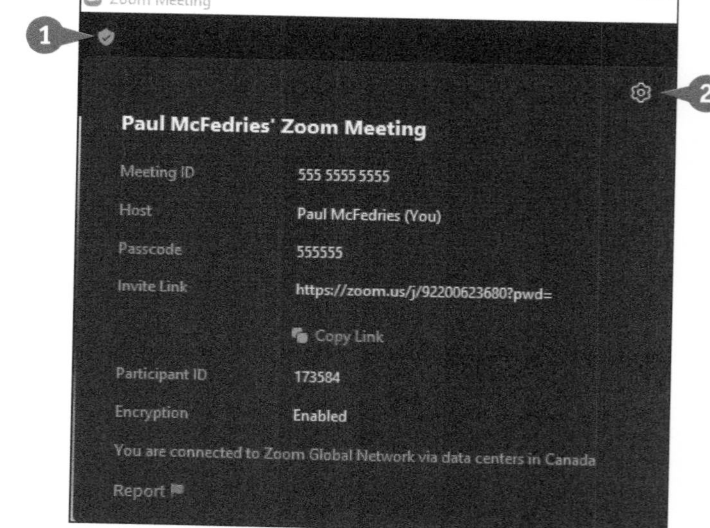

3. Click **Audio**.
4. Click the **Speaker** ⌄ and then select the speaker you now want to use in the meeting.

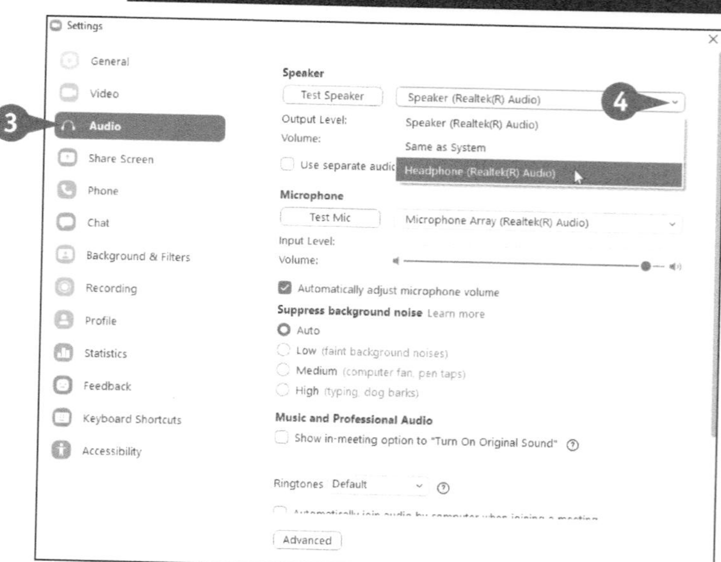

5. Click and drag the **Volume** slider (●) to adjust the output volume.

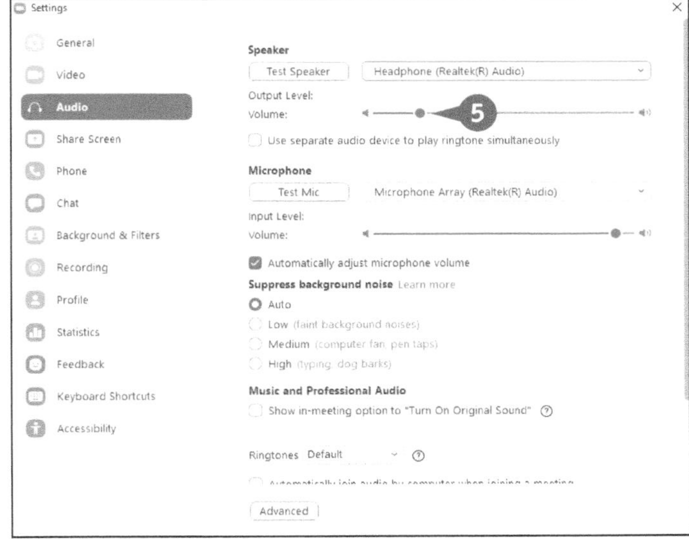

6. Click **Close** (✕).

Zoom returns you to the meeting and uses the device you selected for the audio output.

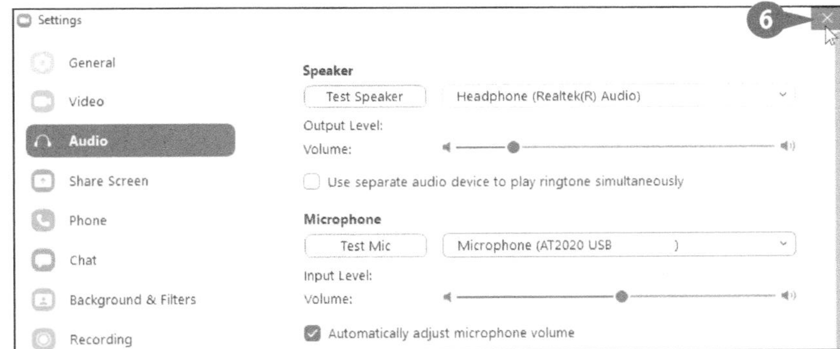

TIP

Is there a quicker way to switch between audio output devices?
Yes, although this faster method does not give you a direct way to adjust the volume of the selected device. Display the meeting controls and click the **Audio** (A). In the menu that appears, you can change the output device by selecting a device in the **Select a Speaker** section of the menu (B).

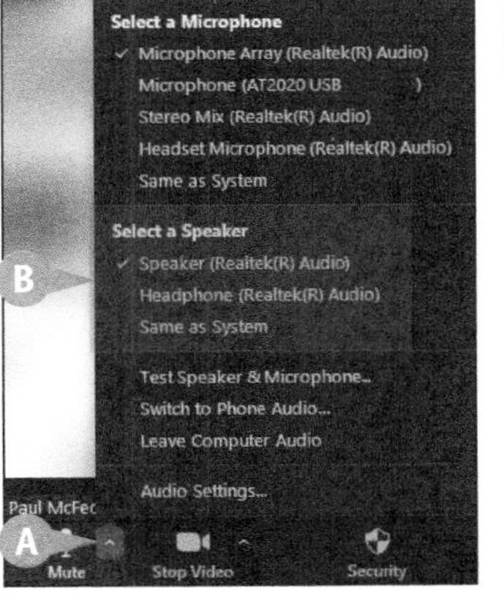

Select a Different Audio Input Device

During a Zoom meeting, you can switch to a different audio input device. One of the most common Zoom meeting difficulties is when the other meeting participants cannot hear you. The most common cause of this kind of problem is that the default microphone is not working or not connected. You can often fix this problem by selecting a different audio input device. The input device could be an external microphone, a headset, or the microphone that is built in to the device you are using.

Select a Different Audio Input Device

1. Click **Meeting Information** (🛡).
2. Click **Settings** (⚙).

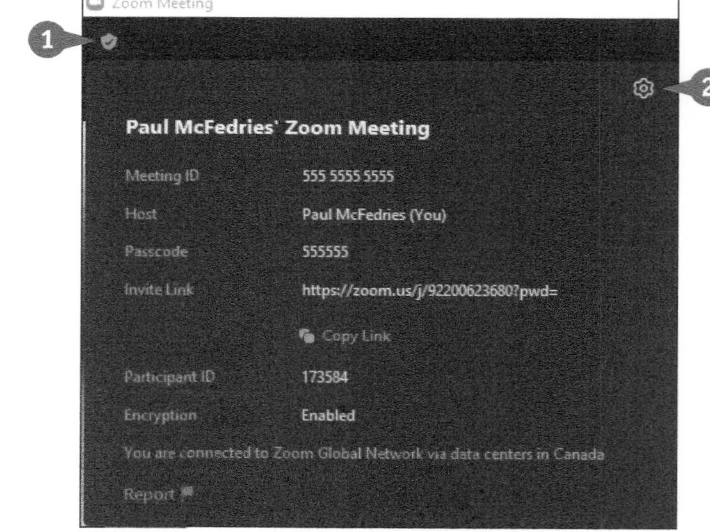

3. Click **Audio**.
4. Click the **Microphone** ⌄ and then select the microphone you now want to use in the meeting.

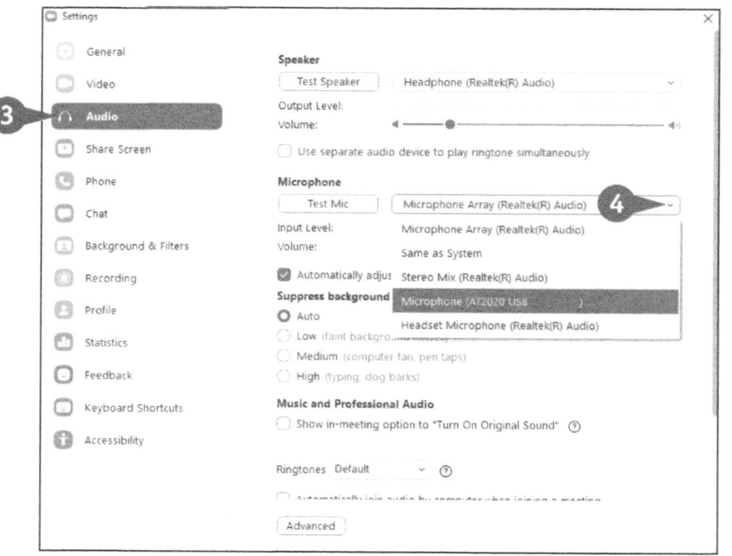

5 Click and drag the **Volume** slider (●) to adjust the input volume.

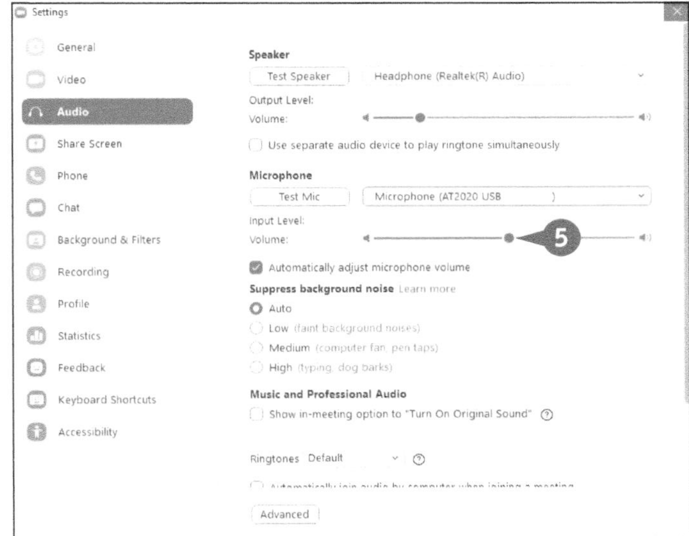

6 Click **Close** (×).

Zoom returns you to the meeting and uses the device you selected for the audio input.

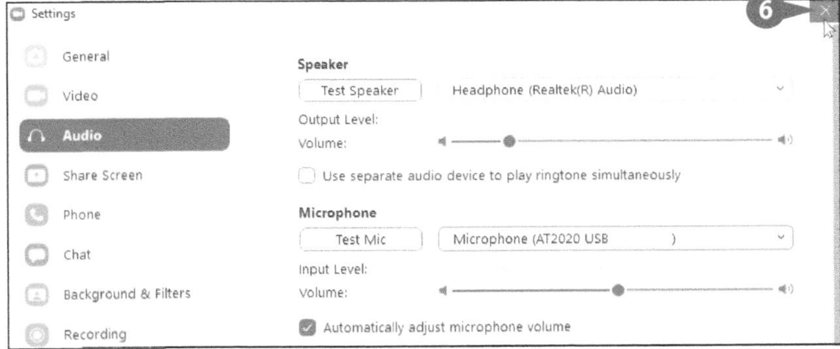

TIP

Is there a quicker way to switch between audio input devices?
Yes, although this faster method does not give you a direct way to adjust the volume of the selected device. Display the meeting controls and click the **Audio** (A). In the menu that appears, you can change the input device by selecting a device in the **Select a Microphone** section of the menu (B).

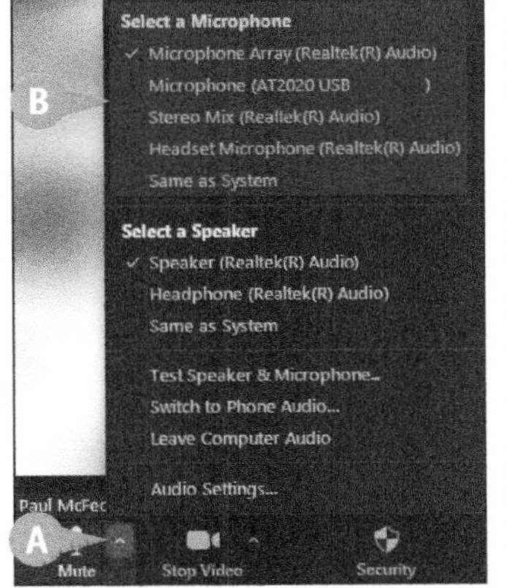

Mute and Unmute Participants

If you are the meeting host or co-host, you can mute some or all of the meeting participants. Muting participants is often useful if a particular attendee's audio feed is creating excessive background noise or is distracting the meeting in some other way. The host can mute either individual users or all the meeting's participants.

Note, however, that for privacy reasons, the meeting host cannot directly unmute any participant. Instead, the host can ask a muted participant to unmute, and that user has the option of unmuting or staying muted.

Mute and Unmute Participants

Mute a Participant

1. In the host controls, click **Participants**.

Note: In the desktop app, you can also view the participants by pressing Alt + U.

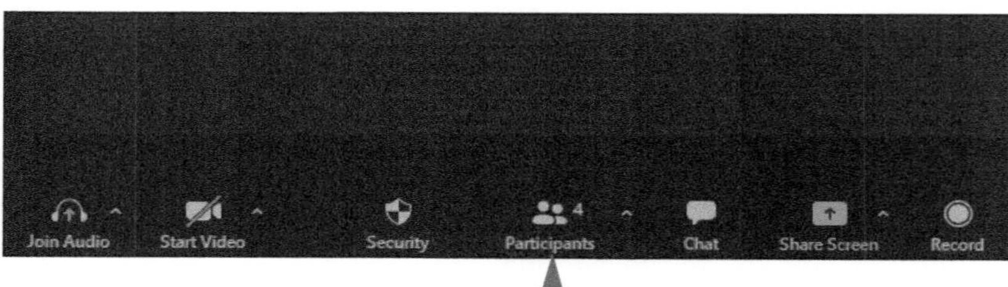

Zoom displays the Participants pane.

2. Click **Mute** for the participant you want to mute.

A. Alternatively, you can mute every participant at once by clicking **Mute All** and then clicking **Yes** (not shown) when Zoom asks you to confirm.

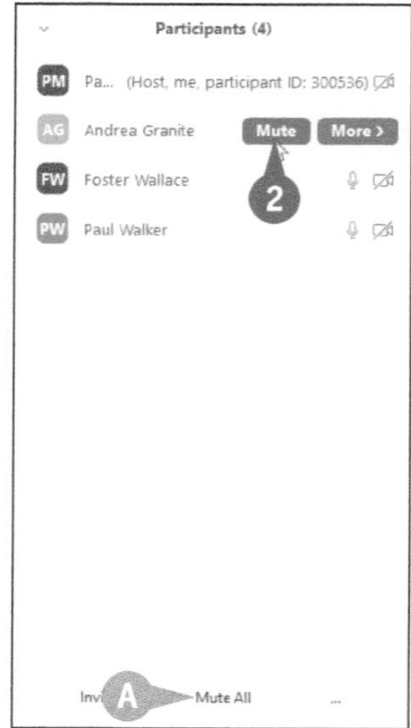

Ask a Participant to Unmute

1. In the host controls, click **Participants**.

Note: In the desktop app, you can also view the participants by pressing Alt + U.

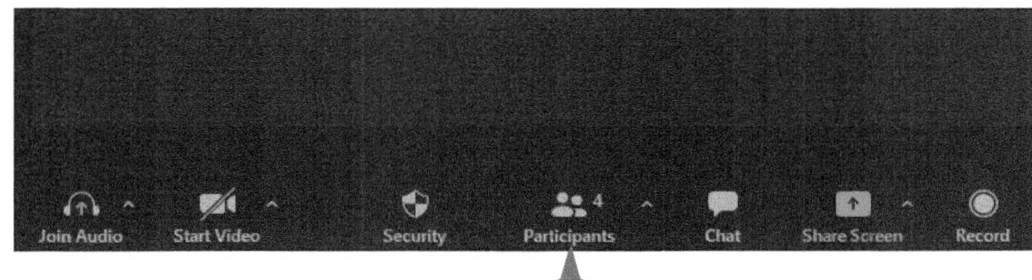

Zoom displays the Participants pane.

2. Click **Ask to Unmute** for the participant you want to unmute.

B Alternatively, you can ask every participant to unmute by clicking **More** (···) and then clicking **Ask All to Unmute**.

Zoom asks the participant to unmute, and that person can select either **Unmute** or **Stay Muted**.

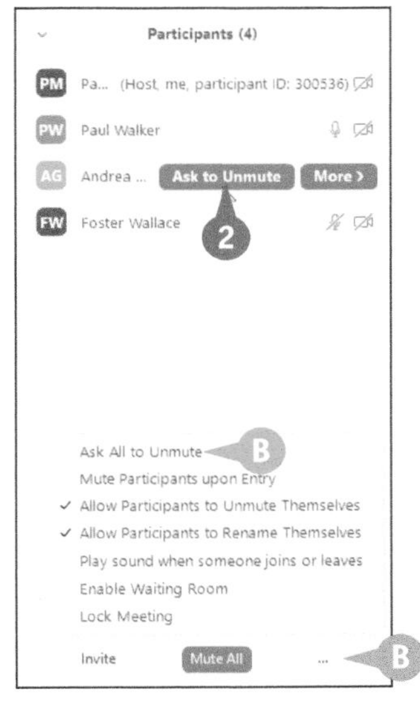

TIPS

Is there a way to prevent muted participants from unmuting themselves?
Yes, you can prevent users from unmuting themselves until you are ready to ask them to unmute. Click **Participants**, click **More** (···) at the bottom of the Participants pane, and then click to deselect the **Allow Participants to Unmute Themselves** command.

Can I automatically mute attendees when they join the meeting?
Yes. Click **Participants**, click **More** (···) at the bottom of the Participants pane, and then click to select the **Mute Participants upon Entry** command.

Mute and Unmute Your Microphone

You can mute and unmute your microphone as needed during a meeting. A primary etiquette rule for meetings is to not distract other attendees or disrupt the meeting with unnecessary or excessive noise. This is particularly true if there's any possibility of noises happening that are outside of your control, such as the phone or doorbell ringing, another person nearby making noise, or a construction crew close to your location. You can ensure that noises don't disrupt the meeting by muting your microphone when you're not talking. When it's time for you to talk, you can unmute your microphone.

Mute and Unmute Your Microphone

Mute Your Microphone

1. In the meeting controls, select **Mute**.

Note: In the desktop app, you can also mute your microphone by pressing Alt+A.

Zoom mutes your microphone.

Unmute Your Microphone

1. In the meeting controls, select **Unmute**.

Note: In the desktop app, you can also unmute your microphone by pressing Alt+A.

Zoom unmutes your microphone.

Mute Your Microphone Automatically

CHAPTER 4

You can configure your Zoom account to automatically mute your microphone when you join a meeting. When they join a meeting, most people mute their microphones so as not to disrupt either the meeting itself if it has already started or a pre-meeting conversation that might be taking place. If you find that you always mute your microphone after you join a meeting, you can avoid this step in the future by configuring your Zoom account to automatically mute your microphone whenever you join a meeting.

Mute Your Microphone Automatically

1. In the Zoom desktop app, click your profile picture.
2. Click **Settings**.

The Settings dialog appears.

3. Click **Audio**.
4. Click **Mute my microphone when joining a meeting** (☐ changes to ☑).

Note: In the Zoom mobile app, tap **Settings**, tap **Meetings**, and then tap either the **Always Mute My Microphone** (Android) or the **Mute My Microphone** (iOS) switch to **On** (toggle changes to toggle).

Zoom now automatically mutes your microphone each time you join a meeting.

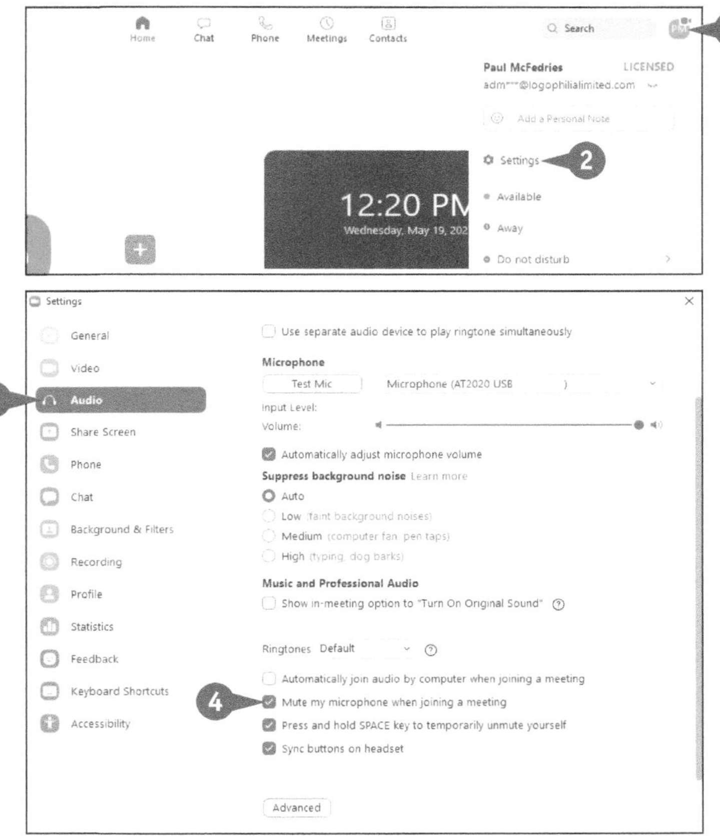

Enable Push-to-Talk

If you use the Zoom desktop app, you can enable the push-to-talk feature. Unmuting your microphone during a meeting is not a difficult task, but it can often take a few seconds to either click the Unmute button or press Alt+A. Then, when you're done talking, you have to remember to mute your microphone again. If you find yourself unmuting and muting frequently during your meetings, try push-to-talk, which enables you to temporarily unmute your microphone by holding down Spacebar. When you're done, release Spacebar to mute your microphone again.

Enable Push-to-Talk

1. In the Zoom desktop app, click your profile picture.
2. Click **Settings**.

   The Settings dialog appears.
3. Click **Audio**.
4. Click **Press and hold SPACE key to temporarily unmute yourself** (☐ changes to ☑).

   Zoom now temporarily unmutes your microphone while you hold down Spacebar.

Note: If you are using Zoom muted on a smartphone, swipe right until you see the Safe Driving Mode screen, tap the **Tap to Speak** button, state what you have to say, and then tap **Done Speaking**.

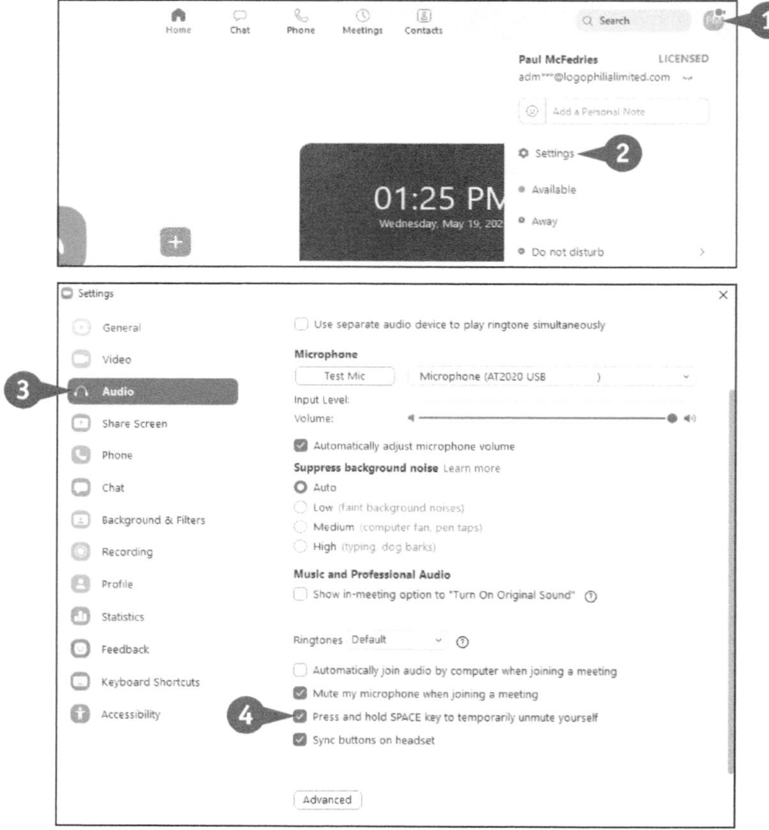

Suppress Background Noise

You can improve the meeting experience for other participants by configuring how Zoom filters out background noises. Background noises in your environment, such as paper crunching or a dog barking, can be annoying and distracting for other meeting participants. By default, Zoom applies a moderate level of background noise suppression. However, if you are in a noisy environment, you might want to increase the level of background noise suppression. Similarly, if you are in a quiet environment, you might want to reduce the level of background noise suppression to ensure that your own words are not suppressed.

Suppress Background Noise

1. In the Zoom desktop app, click your profile picture.
2. Click **Settings**.

   The Settings dialog appears.

3. Click **Audio**.
4. Click a **Suppress background noise** option (◯ changes to ◉):
   - **Auto**. Zoom adjusts the level of background noise suppression based on the background sounds it detects.
   - **Low**. Zoom applies minimal suppression of background noises.
   - **Medium**. Zoom suppresses moderate background noises such as pen tapping and fans.
   - **High**. Zoom aggressively suppresses noises such as typing, barking, and wrapper crunching.

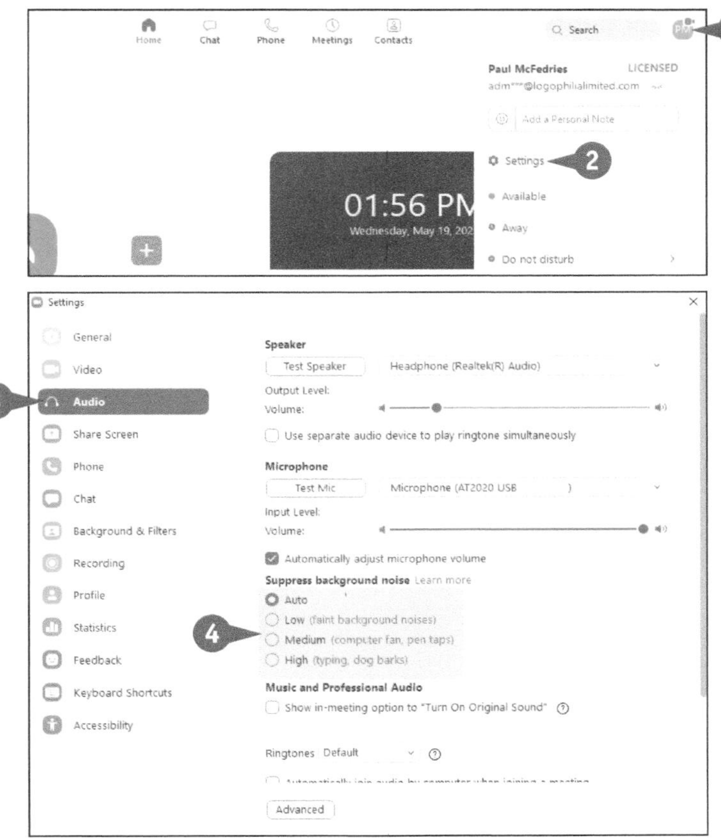

Join a Meeting with Audio Automatically

You can save a step when joining a meeting by configuring your Zoom account to automatically join each meeting with audio connected. When you start or join a meeting, Zoom displays a dialog asking how you want to connect your audio. If you find that you always click the Join with Computer Audio button, you can eliminate this extra step by configuring Zoom to always join with computer audio. For mobile devices, you can also configure Zoom to connect using a specified network, such as cellular or Wi-Fi.

Join a Meeting with Audio Automatically

Using the Zoom Desktop App

1. Click your profile picture.
2. Click **Settings**.

The Settings dialog appears.

3. Click **Audio**.
4. Click **Automatically join audio by computer when joining a meeting** (☐ changes to ☑).

When you join a meeting from now on, Zoom automatically connects your audio devices.

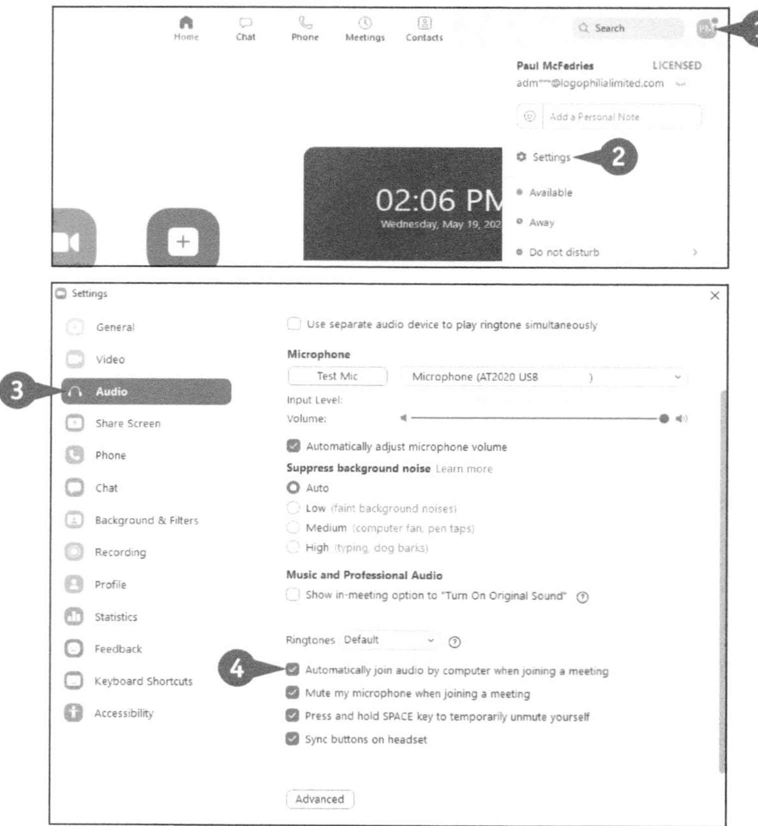

Using the Zoom Mobile App

1. Tap **Settings.**
2. Tap **Meetings.**

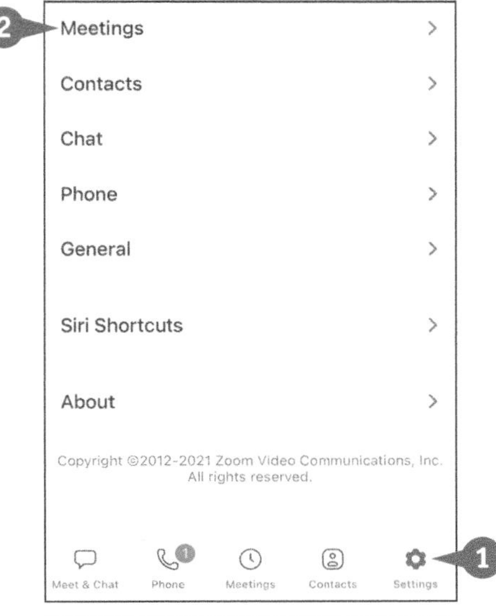

The Meeting Settings screen appears.

3. Tap **Auto-Connect to Audio** (Android) or **Auto Connect Audio** (iOS).
4. Select how you want to connect.
5. Tab **Done** (iOS only).

Zoom now connects audio automatically when you join a meeting.

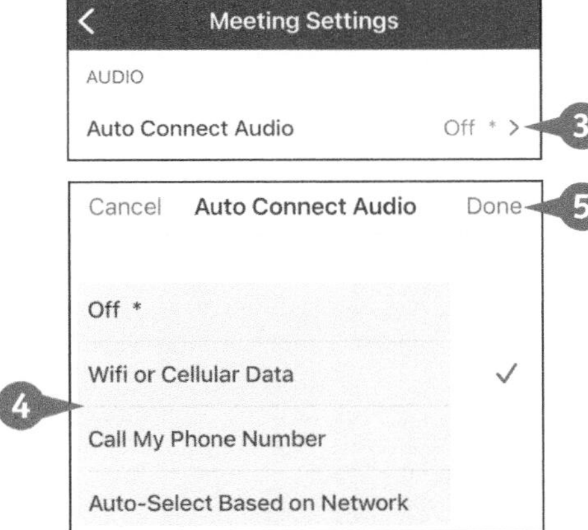

TIP

What do the various connection types mean?

Here is a summary of the options you see:

- **Off**. Zoom does not connect your audio automatically when you join a meeting.
- **Wifi or Cellular Data**. Zoom connects your audio using your Wi-Fi network or your phone's cellular network.
- **Call My Phone Number**. Zoom connects your audio by calling a phone number that you provide.
- **Auto-Select Based on Network**. Zoom automatically selects the audio connection based on your device's current network connection.

CHAPTER 5

Working with Meeting Video

Zoom offers a number of features and tools for working with a meeting's video feed. For example, you can choose a different camera, stop and start your video, apply a video filter and background, and view a meeting using two monitors.

Select a Different Camera

During a Zoom meeting, you can switch to a different camera for a better image or if your original camera stops working. Most Zoom users have just one camera, which is the one built in to the device they are using to join the meeting. However, if you have a second camera connected to your device, you might find that camera has better light or a better image quality. If so, or if your original camera is not working, then you can switch to the other camera during the meeting.

Select a Different Camera

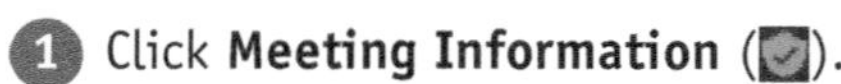

1 Click **Meeting Information** (![icon]).

2 Click **Settings** (![icon]).

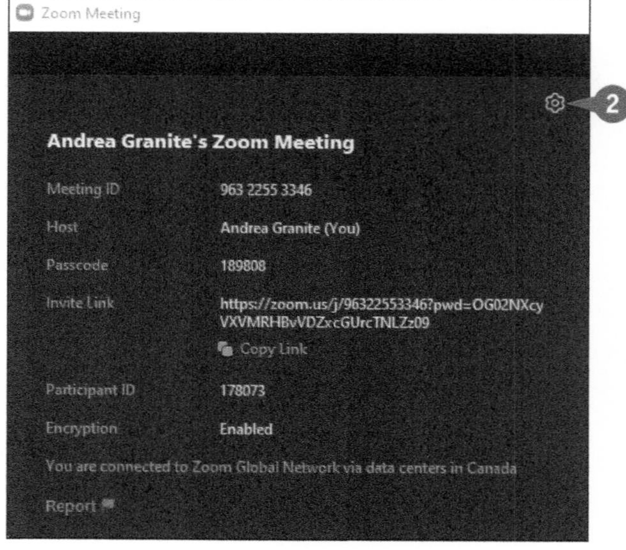

3. Click **Video**.
4. Click the **Camera** ⌄ and then select the camera you want to use in the meeting.

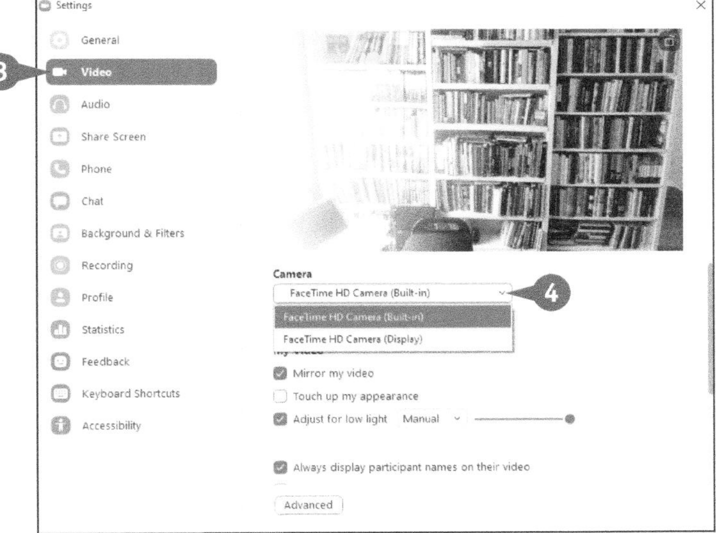

6. Click **Close** (✕).

   Zoom returns you to the meeting and uses the camera you selected.

TIP

Is there a quicker way to switch between cameras?

Yes, there are two faster methods you can use:

- Press Alt + N to switch between your cameras.
- Display the meeting controls and click the **Video** (A). In the menu that appears, you can change the camera by selecting a device in the **Select a Camera** section of the menu (B).

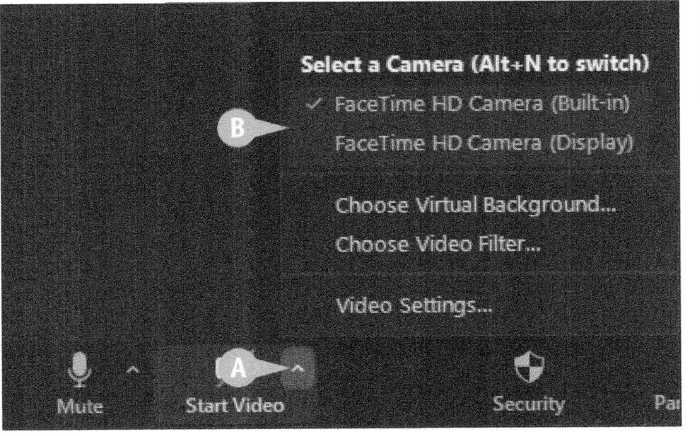

Stop and Start a Participant's Video

If you are the meeting host or co-host, you can stop the video of a meeting participant. Stopping video is a useful feature if a user's video feed is inappropriate, distracting, or problematic in some way. The host or co-host can stop the video of individual users only, not all the meeting's participants at once.

Note, however, that for privacy reasons, the meeting host cannot directly start the video of any participant. Instead, the host can ask a participant with stopped video to start the feed, and that user has the option of starting the video or leaving it stopped.

Stop and Start a Participant's Video

Stop a Participant's Video

1. In the host controls, click **Participants**.

Note: In the desktop app, you can also view the participants by pressing Alt + U.

Zoom displays the Participants pane.

2. Click **More** for the participant you want to work with.
3. Click **Stop Video**.

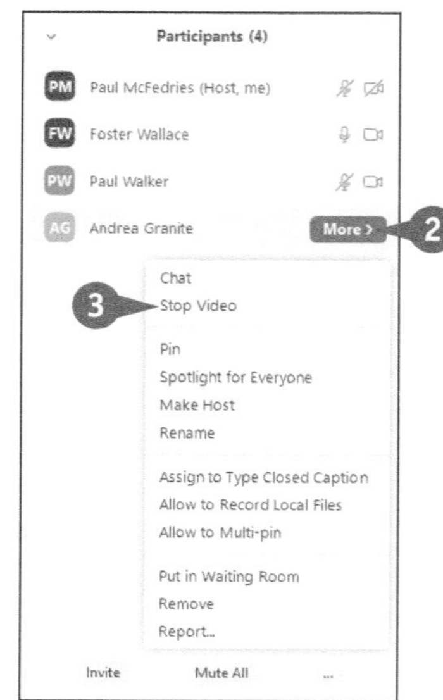

Ask a Participant to Start Video

1. In the host controls, click **Participants**.

Note: In the desktop app, you can also view the participants by pressing Alt + U.

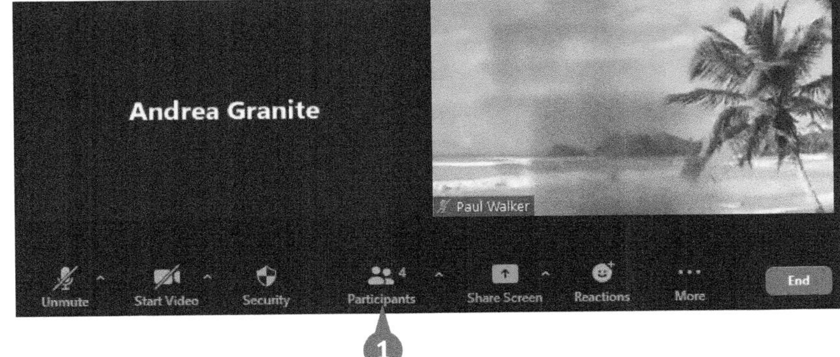

Zoom displays the Participants pane.

2. Click **More** for the participant you want to work with.
3. Click **Ask to Start Video**.

Zoom asks the participant to unmute, and that person can select either **Start Video** or **Later**.

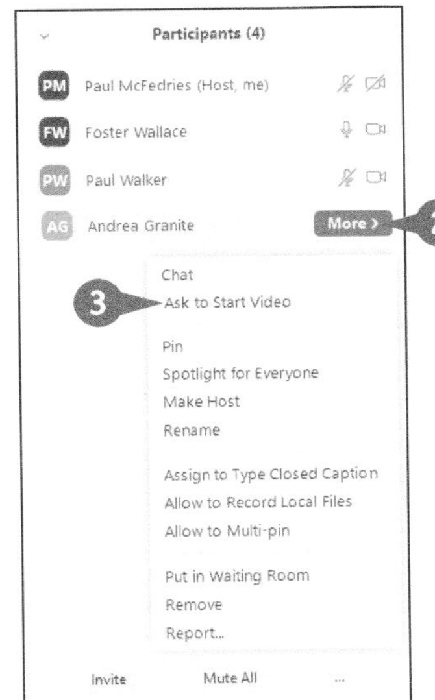

TIP

Is there a way to not show users who have stopped video?

Yes, you can temporarily hide a nonvideo user from the meeting. When the video feed resumes, the user is automatically unhidden. Use either of the following techniques to hide participants with stopped video:

- In the Zoom desktop app, click **Settings** (⚙), click **Video**, and then click **Hide non-video participants** (☐ changes to ☑).
- In the Zoom mobile app, tap **Settings**, tap **Meetings**, and then tap the **Show Non-Video Participants** switch to **Off** (toggle on changes to toggle off).

Stop and Start Your Video

You can start and stop your video feed as needed during a meeting. Although not universally followed, one of the unofficial rules of Zoom etiquette is if everyone else in a meeting is showing video, then you should, too. Similarly, if everyone else in the meeting is not showing video, then you should not show yours, either. This rule means that you might need to stop or start your video when you join a meeting to match what the host wants or what other people are doing.

Stop and Start Your Video

Stop Your Video

1 In the meeting controls, select **Stop Video**.

Note: In the Zoom desktop app, you can also stop your video by pressing Alt + V.

Zoom stops your video. Meeting participants now see just your profile picture. If you have not added a profile picture, Zoom shows your account display name.

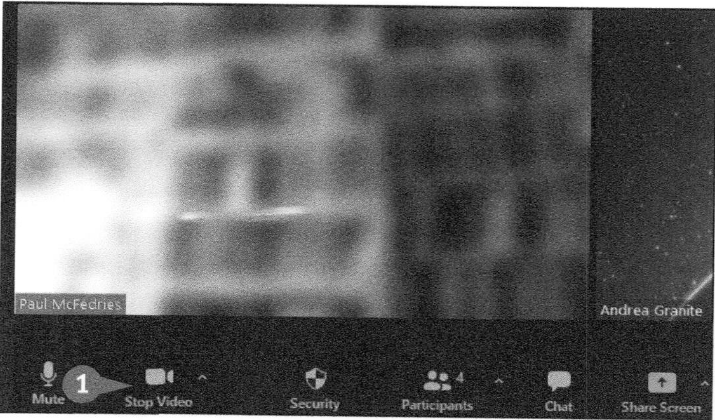

Start Your Video

1 In the meeting controls, select **Start Video**.

Note: In the Zoom desktop app, you can also start your video by pressing Alt + V.

Zoom starts your video.

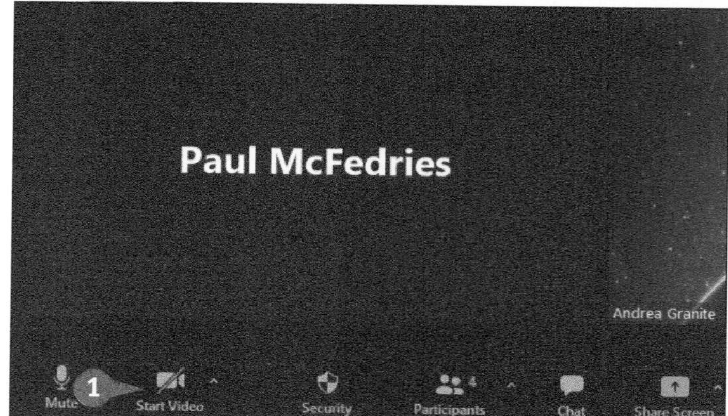

Turn Off Video Automatically

You can configure your Zoom account to automatically turn off your video when you join a meeting. When they join a meeting, many people turn off their video until they see whether others in the meeting are using video or until they get settled. If you find that you always turn off your video feed when you join a meeting, you can avoid this step in the future by configuring your Zoom account to automatically start with your video turned off whenever you join a meeting.

Turn Off Video Automatically

1. In the Zoom desktop app, click **Settings** (⚙).

The Settings dialog appears.

2. Click **Video**.
3. Click **Turn off my video when joining meeting** (☐ changes to ☑).

Note: In the Zoom mobile app, tap **Settings**, tap **Meetings**, and then tap either the **Always Turn Off My Video** (Android) or the **Turn Off My Video** (iOS) switch to **On** (◯ changes to ◯).

Zoom now automatically turns off your video each time you join a meeting.

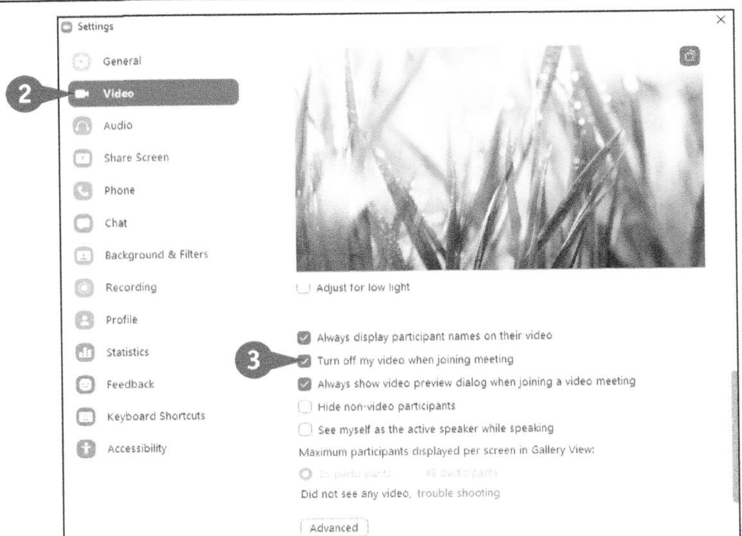

Bypass the Video Preview

You can configure Zoom to not show the video preview when you join a meeting. When you join a meeting, Zoom displays a preview of your device video. This is usually a good idea because it enables you to ensure that your video is working and that your lighting and background are acceptable. However, if you do not need to perform these checks — particularly if you always start meetings with your video turned off, as described in the previous section, "Turn Off Video Automatically" — then you can save a step and configure Zoom to bypass the video preview.

Bypass the Video Preview

1 In the Zoom desktop app, click **Settings** (⚙).

The Settings dialog appears.

2 Click **Video**.

3 Click **Always show video preview dialog when joining a video meeting** (☑ changes to ☐).

Note: In the Zoom mobile app, tap **Settings**, tap **Meetings**, and then tap either the **Always Show Video Preview** (Android) or the **Show Video Preview** (iOS) switch to **On** (◯ changes to ⬤).

Zoom no longer displays the video preview each time you join a meeting.

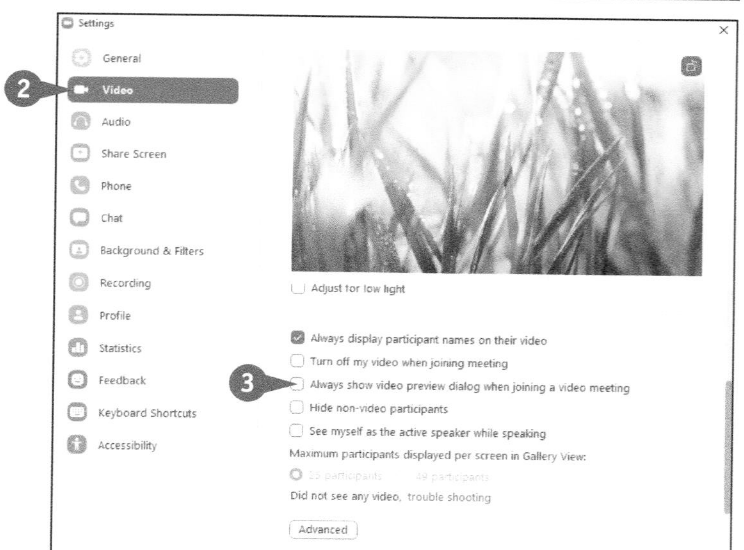

Adjust Video for Low Light

You can adjust the lighting level of your video to compensate for low light conditions in your environment. When choosing a location for a meeting, it's best to find a well-lit spot so that the meeting participants can see you clearly. However, there might be times when good lighting is not available. For example, your computer might be in a dark office, or it might be a cloudy day. If you cannot increase the ambient lighting to compensate, the desktop app has a feature that enables you to adjust the light level of your video feed.

Adjust Video for Low Light

1. In the Zoom desktop app, click the **Video** menu (▲).
2. Click **Video Settings**.

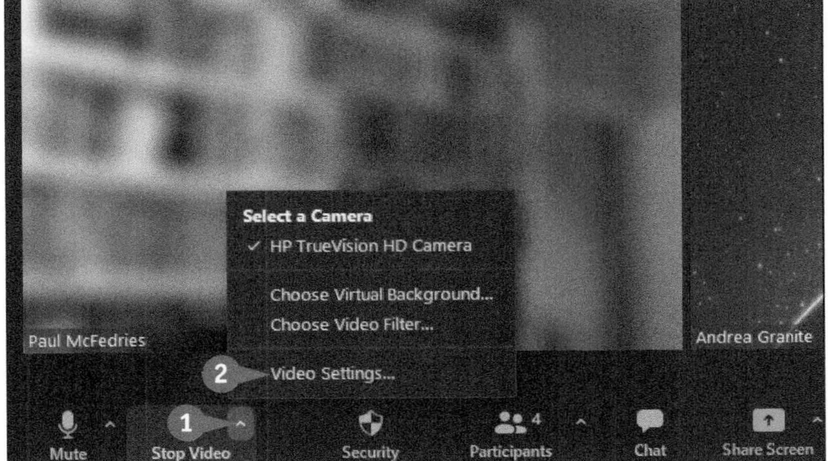

Zoom opens the Settings dialog with the Video page displayed.

3. Click **Adjust for low light** (☐ changes to ☑).
4. Click the **Adjust for low light** ⌄ and then select how you want the low-light adjustment made:
   - **Auto**. Zoom adjusts the light automatically.
   - **Manual**. Drag the slider (●) to set the light level you prefer (A).
5. Click **Close** (☒).

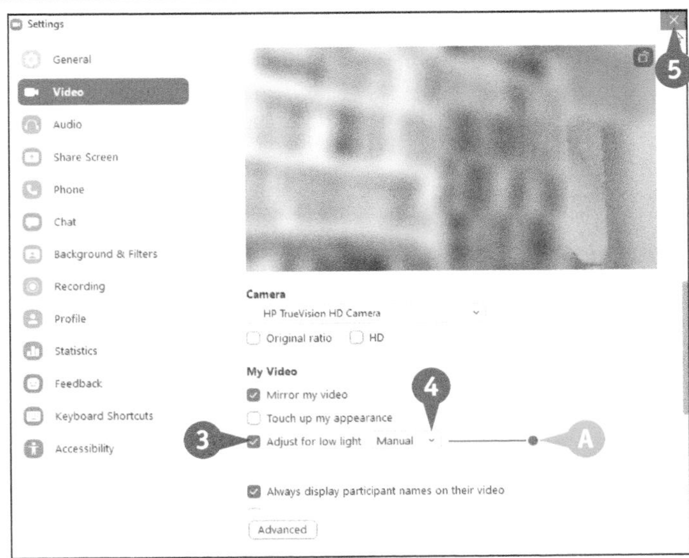

Zoom applies the low-light adjustment to your video.

Choose a Video Filter

You can add visual interest to your video feed by applying a filter. A *video filter* is a special effect that Zoom applies to your video. There are three types of video filters: a *tint filter* applies an overall color to your video, an *overlay filter* superimposes a static image on your video feed, and a *personal overlay filter* superimposes a static image on your head (for example, a crown or party hat) or face (for example, a mustache or sunglasses).

Video filters add an element of whimsy to your video, but they are often not appropriate for business meetings.

Choose a Video Filter

Using the Zoom Desktop App

1. Click the **Video** menu (▲).
2. Click **Choose Video Filter**.

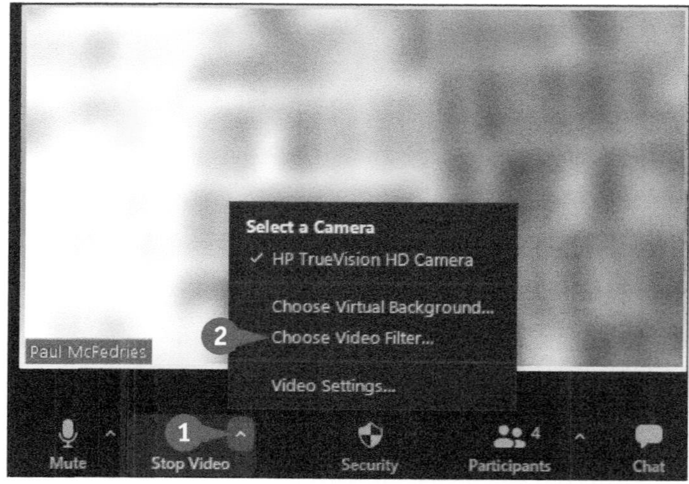

Zoom opens the Settings dialog with the Background & Filters page displayed and the Video Filters tab selected.

3. Click the video filter you want to apply.

A Zoom shows you a preview of the filter.

4. Click **Close** (✕).

Zoom applies the filter to your video.

B To remove the filter, follow steps 1 and 2 in this subsection and then click **None**.

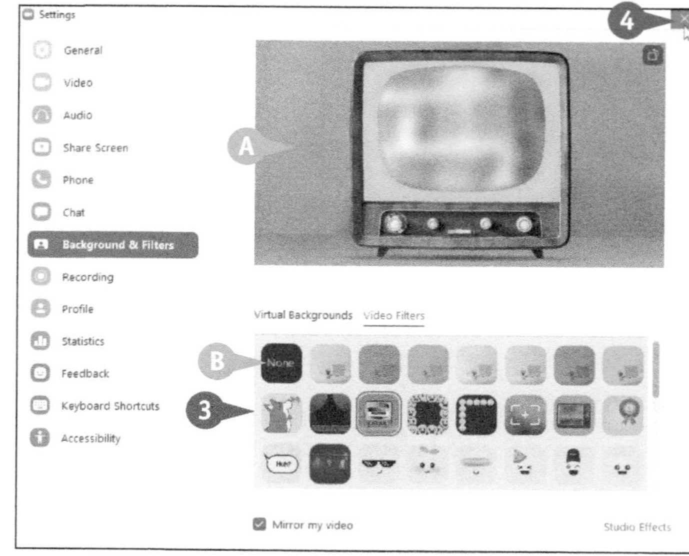

Using the Zoom Mobile App

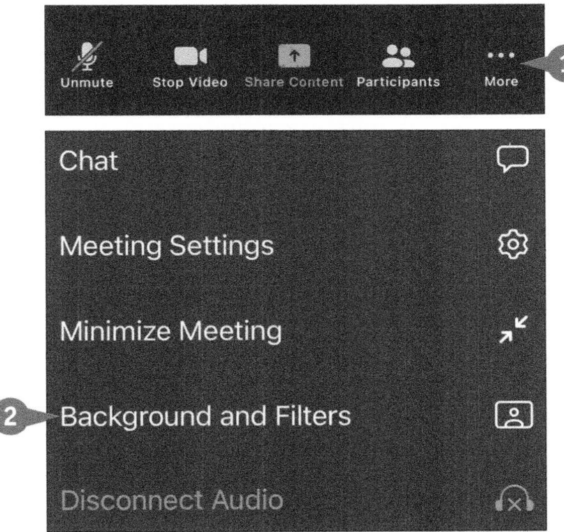

1. Tap **More**.
2. Tap **Background and Filters**.

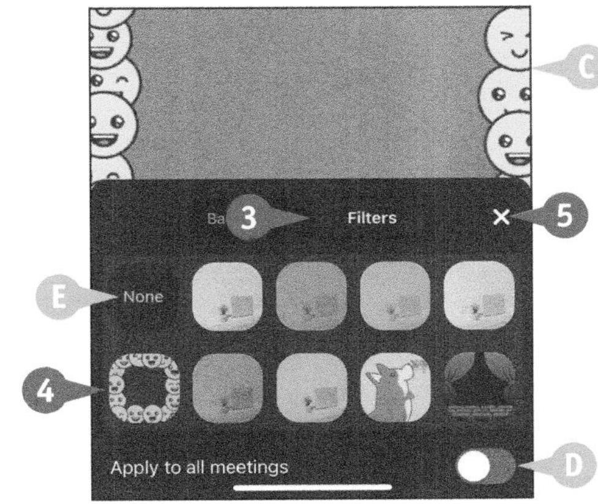

3. Tap **Filters**.
4. Tap the video filter you want to apply.
   - C Zoom shows you a preview of the filter.
   - D You can tap the **Apply to all meetings** switch to **On** (◯ changes to ◯) to use this filter in all your meetings.
5. Click **Close** (☒).

   Zoom applies the filter to your video.

   - E To remove the filter, follow steps 1 to 3 in this subsection and then tap **None**.

TIP

What are studio effects?

Studio effects enable you to alter your appearance by applying eyebrows, facial hair, and a lip color. To apply studio effects, use the Zoom desktop app to display the Video Filters tab and then click **Studio Effects**. Use the Studio Effects pane to apply the effects you want and then click **Close**.

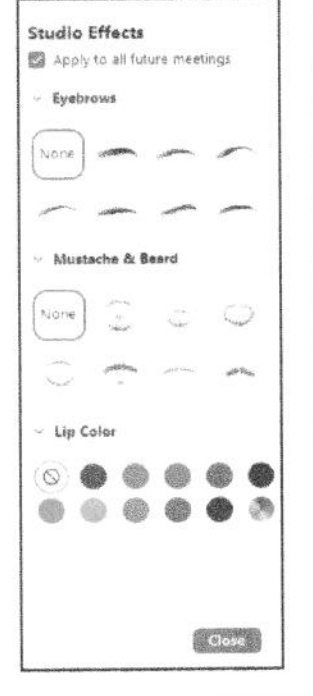

Choose a Virtual Background

You can enhance the look of your video feed by applying a virtual background. A *virtual background* is a special effect that Zoom applies to your video where it replaces the actual background of the video feed with a static image. This works best if you have a solid color or a green screen behind you. If you are using the Zoom desktop app, you can improve Zoom's ability to differentiate between you and the virtual background by downloading the Smart Virtual Background package.

Virtual backgrounds are fun, but they are not suitable for all types of meetings.

Choose a Virtual Background

Using the Zoom Desktop App

1. Click the **Video** menu (▲).
2. Click **Choose Virtual Background.**

   Zoom opens the Settings dialog with the Background & Filters page displayed and the Virtual Background tab selected.

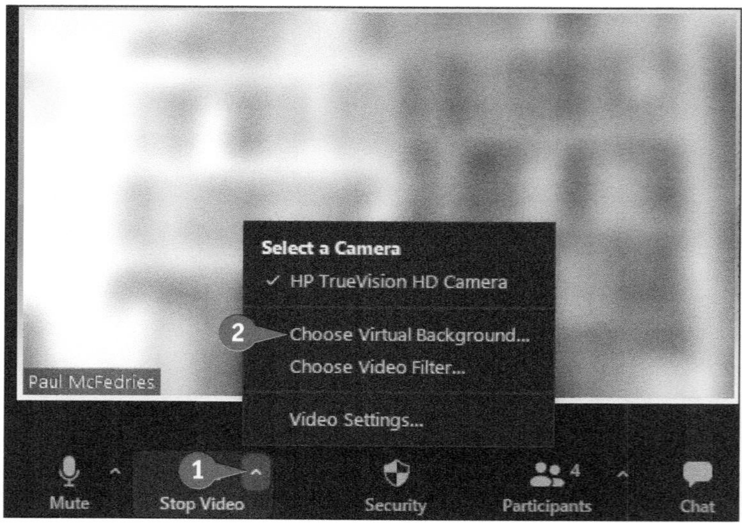

3. Click the virtual background you want to apply.

   The first time you select a background, Zoom prompts you to download the Smart Virtual Background package.
4. Click **Download.**

A. Zoom shows you a preview of the filter.

5. Click **Close** (×).

   Zoom applies the virtual background to your video.

B. To remove the background, follow steps 1 and 2 in this subsection and then click **None.**

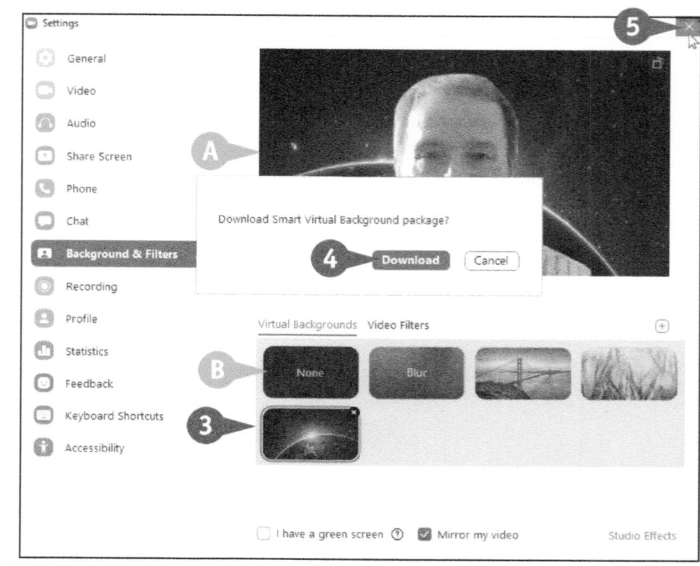

Using the Zoom Mobile App

1. Tap **More**.

2. Tap **Background and Filters**.

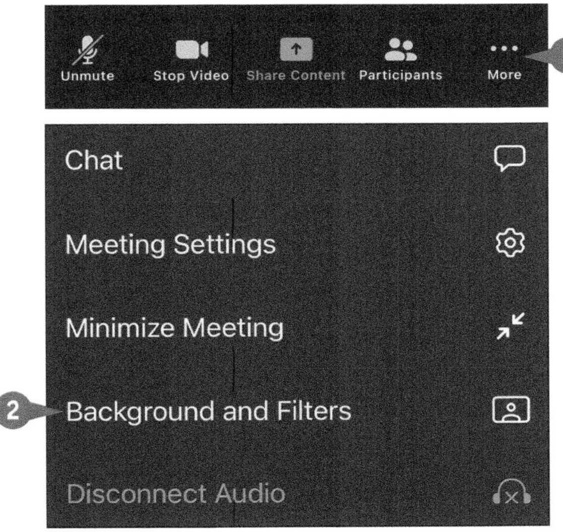

3. Tap **Background**.
4. Tap the virtual background you want to apply.

C Zoom shows you a preview of the filter.

5. Click **Close** (☒).

Zoom applies the virtual background to your video.

D To remove the background, follow steps 1 to 3 in this subsection and then tap **None**.

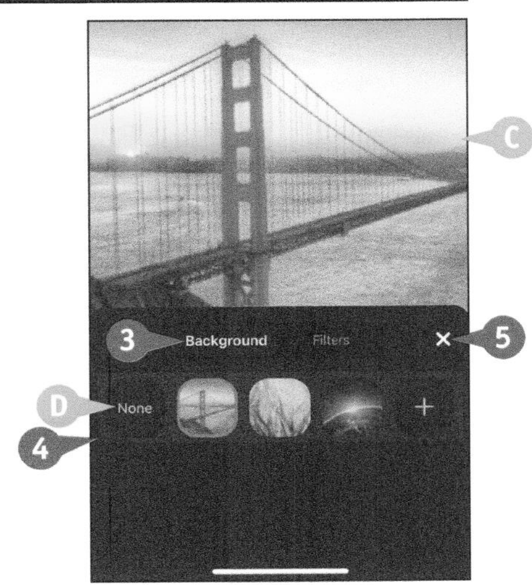

TIPS

How can I get better results with virtual backgrounds?
Here are a few tips:

- Use a real background that's a solid color.
- Use a green screen as your real background.
- Do not wear clothing that matches the color of your real background.
- Try to make your environment's lighting as uniform as possible.

Can I use a mobile device photo as a virtual background?
Yes. Follow steps 1 to 3 in the "Using the Zoom Mobile App" subsection and then tap **Add** (+). When your mobile device asks if Zoom can access your photos, tap **Allow** or **OK**. Tap the photo you want to use as your virtual background, tap **Done**, and then tap **Close** (☒).

Pin a Participant's Video

You can pin a participant to view only that person's video in Zoom's Speaker view. By default, when you use Zoom's Speaker view (see Chapter 3), the only video feed you see is the user who is currently talking. However, some meetings have a main speaker, and Zoom might sometimes display other users who are unmuted and make a noise. To prevent this, you can *pin* the main speaker's video, which means you see only that user in Speaker view. If you are the meeting host or co-host, you can pin up to nine participants.

Pin a Participant's Video

Pin a Video in the Desktop App

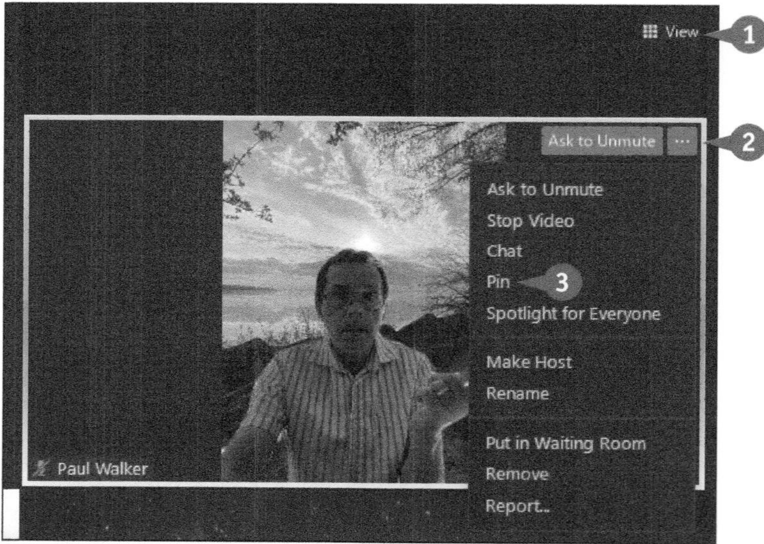

1. Switch to Gallery view (▦) (not shown).
2. Click **More** (···) in the upper-right corner of the participant's video.
3. Click **Pin**.

   Zoom switches to Speaker view and displays an enlarged version of the participant's video.

Note: If you are the meeting host or co-host, you can repeat steps **1** to **3** as needed to pin up to nine participants.

Pin a Video in the Mobile App

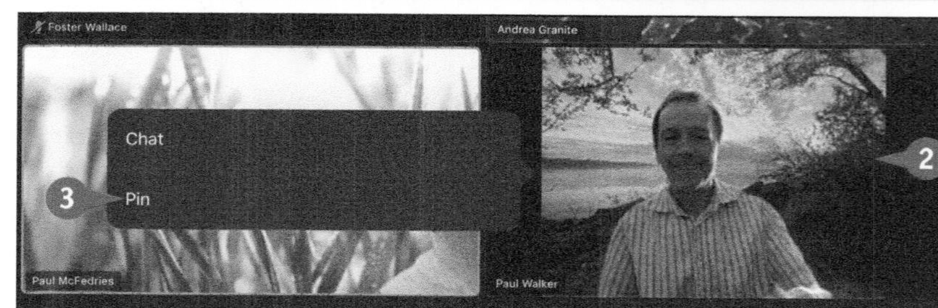

1. Switch to Gallery view (▦) (not shown).
2. Double-tap the participant.
3. In a tablet, tap **Pin**.

   Zoom switches to Speaker view and displays the participant's video.

Remove a Pin in the Desktop App

1. Switch to Speaker view (▦).
2. Click **Remove Pin**.

   Zoom removes the pin and returns to the regular Speaker view.

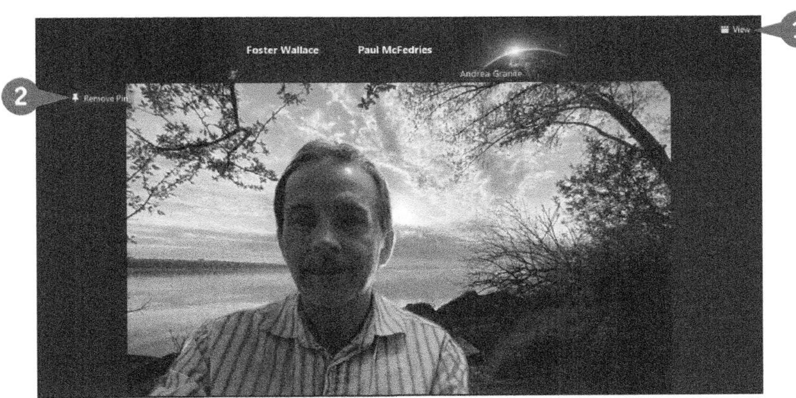

Remove a Pin in the Mobile App

1. Switch to Speaker view (▦) (not shown).
2. Double-tap the pinned participant.
3. In a tablet, tap **Remove Pin**.

   Zoom removes the pin and returns to the regular Speaker view.

TIPS

I am not the meeting host, but I would like to pin a second video. Is there a way I can do this?

Yes, as long as your device is set up to use a second monitor (see Chapter 3). In that case, you can use the techniques in this section to pin the first video. Follow the same steps for the second video, but this time select the **Pin video on second screen** command.

As the meeting host, can I allow meeting participants to pin multiple videos?

Yes, as long as the participant is using a device that supports multi-pinning: a desktop computer or a tablet. To enable multi-pinning for an attendee, click **Participants** (or press Alt + U), click the user's **More** button, and then click **Allow to Multi-pin**.

Spotlight Participant Videos

As a host, you can designate one or more participants to be the only videos seen by the other attendees. Some Zoom meetings have a participant who is meant to be the only speaker for all or part of the meeting. The participant might be making a speech or presenting findings. As the host, you want to ensure that the other attendees see only the featured speaker. Rather than asking each attendee to pin the speaker, you can *spotlight* the speaker, which means others only see that user in Speaker view. You can spotlight up to nine participants.

Spotlight Participant Videos

Spotlight a Participant

1. Switch to Gallery view (▦) (not shown).
2. Click **More** (···) in the upper-right corner of the participant's video.
3. Click **Spotlight for Everyone**.

   Zoom switches to Speaker view and displays an enlarged version of the participant's video.

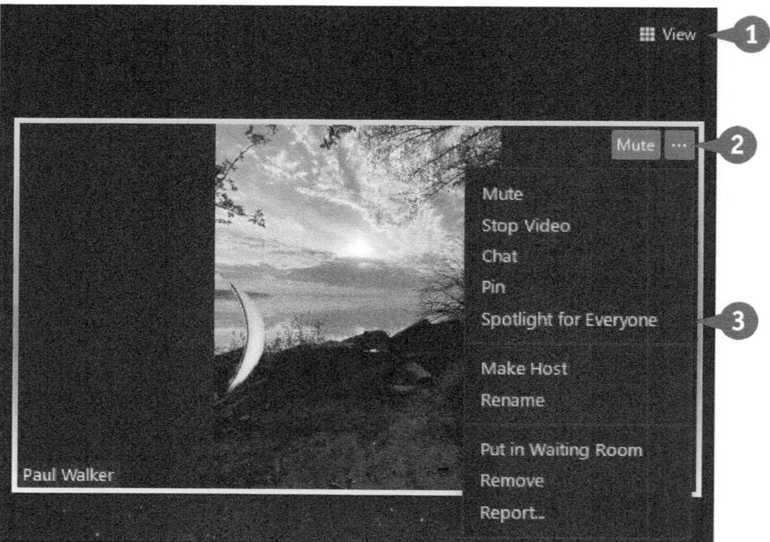

Replace a Spotlight

1. Switch to Gallery view (▦) (not shown).
2. Click **More** (···) in the upper-right corner of the participant's video.
3. Click **Replace Spotlight**.

   Zoom replaces the current spotlight participant.

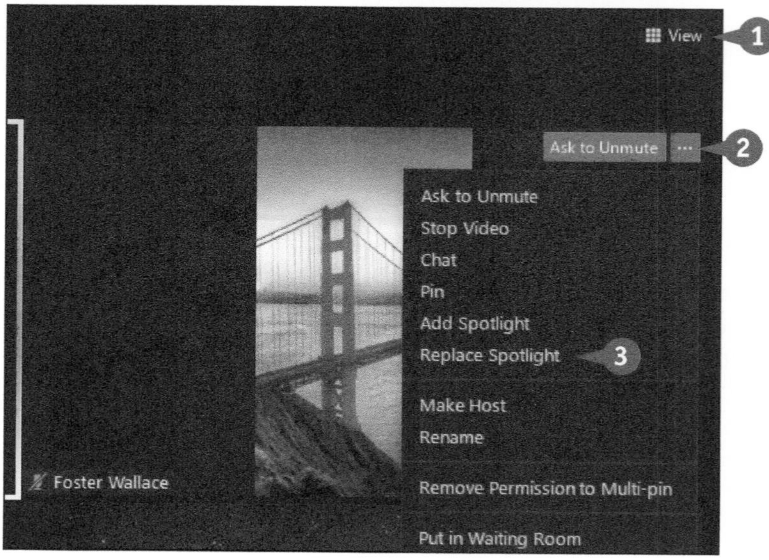

Add a Spotlight

1. Switch to Gallery view (▦) (not shown).
2. Click **More** (···) in the upper-right corner of the participant's video.
3. Click **Add Spotlight**.

Zoom adds the user to the spotlighted participants.

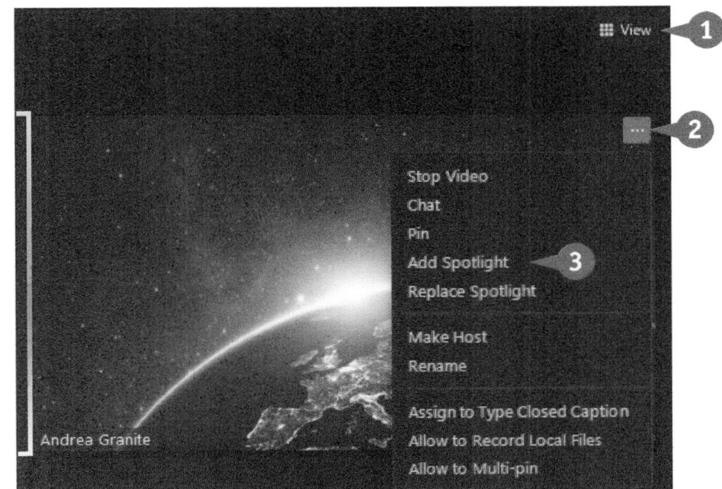

Remove a Spotlight

1. Switch to Gallery view (▦) (not shown).
2. Click **More** (···) in the upper-right corner of a spotlighted participant.
3. Click **Remove Spotlight**.

Zoom removes the participant from the spotlight.

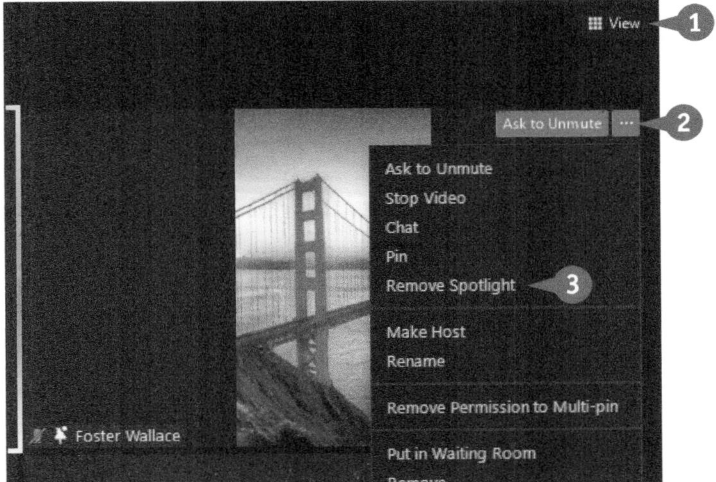

TIP

Can I spotlight a participant's video using the Zoom mobile app?

Yes, by following these steps:

1. Tap **Participants** (not shown).
2. Tap the participant you want to spotlight.
3. Tap **Spotlight For Everyone**.

Zoom spotlights the participant for the other attendees.

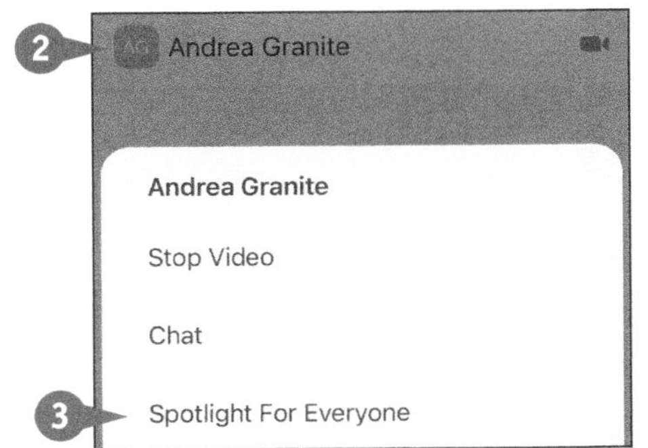

CHAPTER 6

Sharing Your Screen

You can make your Zoom meetings more productive and more useful by sharing information with the other participants. You can share some or all of your screen, video and audio clips, and files. You can also write on a whiteboard, share presentation slides, and control another person's screen share.

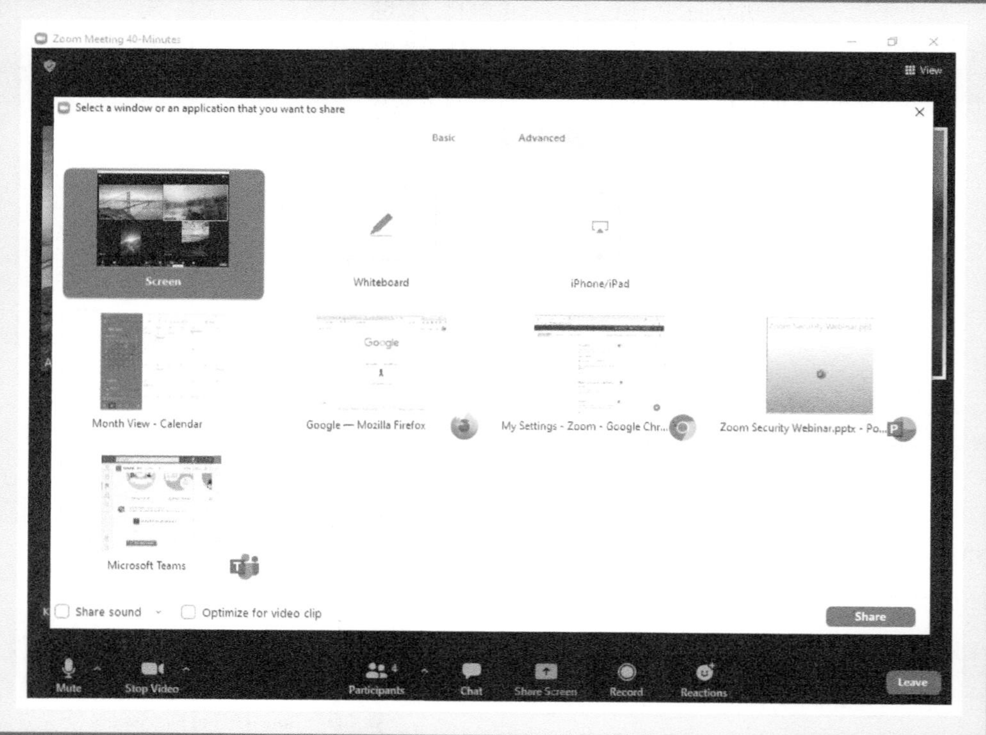

Share Your Screen

You can share with the meeting participants content that appears on your screen. You can share your entire screen or, in the desktop app, the window of a running application. Sharing your screen is useful if you have a running application that contains content you think the meeting attendees would find interesting or educational. Sharing your screen is also useful for demonstrating how to perform a task.

Participant screen sharing is disabled by default, so you can share your screen only if your meeting host has enabled this. See the Tip at the end of this section for more information.

Share Your Screen

Using the Zoom Desktop App

1. Display the meeting controls (not shown).
2. Click **Share Screen**.

Note: You can also select the Share Screen command by pressing Alt + S.

Zoom displays the sharing options.

3. Select what you want to share:

   A. To share your entire screen, click **Screen**.

   B. To share the window of a running application, click the window thumbnail.

4. Click **Share**.

Zoom shares your screen with the meeting participants.

Note: To stop sharing your screen, click the **Stop Share** button that appears at the top of your screen.

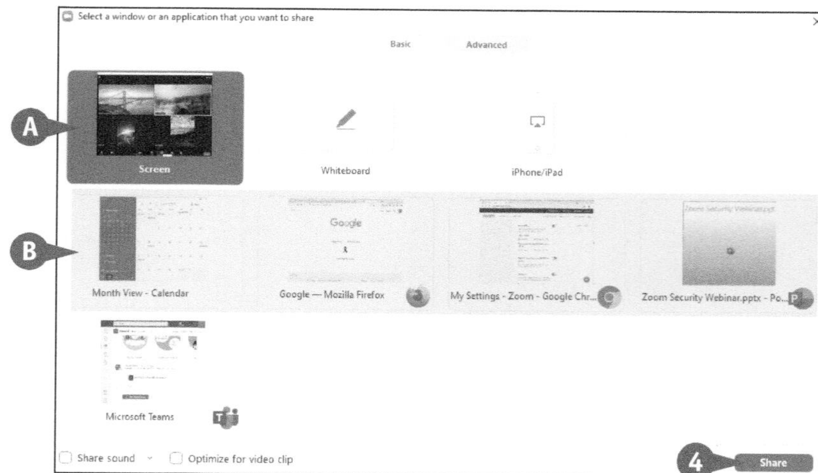

Using the Zoom Mobile App

1. Display the meeting controls.
2. Tap **Share** (Android) or **Share Content** (iOS).
3. Tap **Screen**.

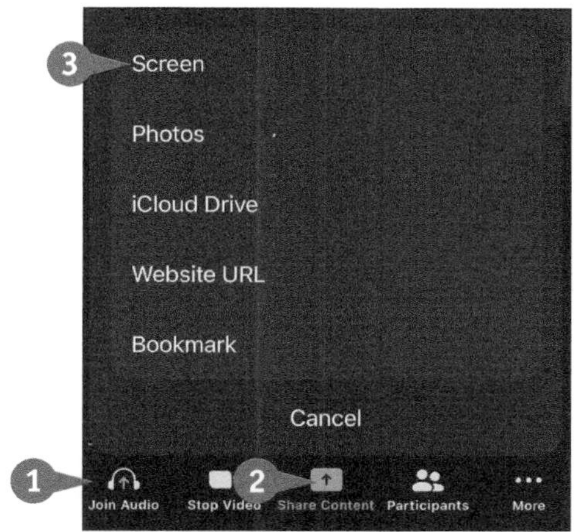

4. Tap **Start now** (Android) or **Start Broadcast** (iOS).

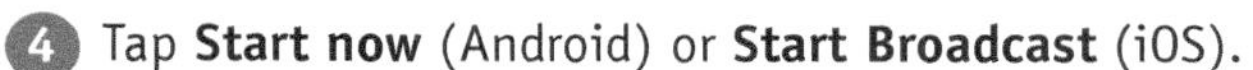

Note: If your Android device asks for "Appear on top" permission, click **Allow permission** (toggle changes to toggle).

Zoom shares your screen with the meeting participants.

Note: To stop sharing your screen, tap **Stop Share** in the sharing controls.

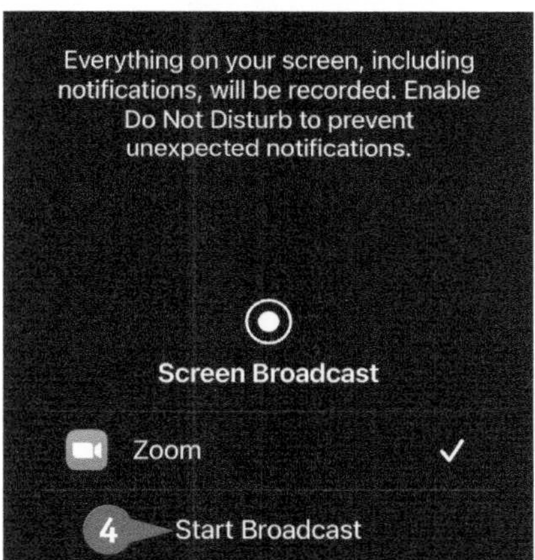

TIP

When I start screen sharing, why do I see a message telling me that participant screen sharing is disabled?

When configuring meeting options, the host can disable screen sharing entirely or can enable screen sharing but allow only the host to share (see Chapter 2).

If you are the meeting host, you can enable participant screen sharing during the meeting by selecting the **Screen Sharing** menu (icon), then **Advanced Sharing Options**, and finally **All Participants** (○ changes to ◉) (A).

Explore Sharing Controls

When you share content with the meeting participants, Zoom hides its default toolbar of attendee controls. In its place, Zoom displays a revised set of controls in a toolbar that appears at the top of the screen. This toolbar includes all the controls from the default toolbar, but adds several controls related to sharing content. This toolbar remains visible even as you switch from one application to another. Only you see this toolbar; the meeting participants see just what you are sharing. The layout of the sharing toolbar changes depending on the type of content you share.

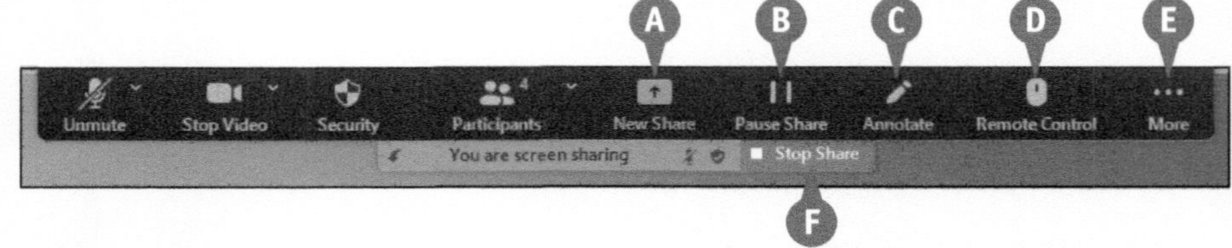

A New Share

Replaces the current shared content with new shared content.

B Pause Share/ Resume Share

Temporarily stops sharing your content. Select **Resume Share** to turn sharing back on.

C Annotate

Displays the Annotation toolbar so that you can add text, drawings, and other markup to the screen. See the sections "Share a Whiteboard" and "Annotate a Shared Screen" later in this chapter.

D Remote Control

Enables you to give a participant mouse and keyboard control of your share. See also the section "Request Control of a Screen Share" later in this chapter.

E More

Displays a menu with extra meeting and sharing commands.

F Stop Share

Ends your sharing of the content.

CHAPTER 6

Share a Portion of the Screen

Rather than sharing your entire desktop or an entire application window, Zoom enables you to share only a portion of your screen. If your screen or application contains personal or private information, you can prevent that data from being shared with the meeting participants. You do this by sharing just the portion of the screen that does not include the content. When you share a portion of the screen, Zoom displays a rectangle that defines that portion. You can move the rectangle to the area you want to share, and you can change the rectangle size as needed.

Share a Portion of the Screen

1. In the Zoom desktop app, display the meeting controls (not shown).
2. Click **Share Screen**.

Note: You can also select the Share Screen command by pressing Alt + S.

Zoom displays the sharing options.

3. Click **Advanced**.
4. Click **Portion of Screen**.
5. Click **Share**.

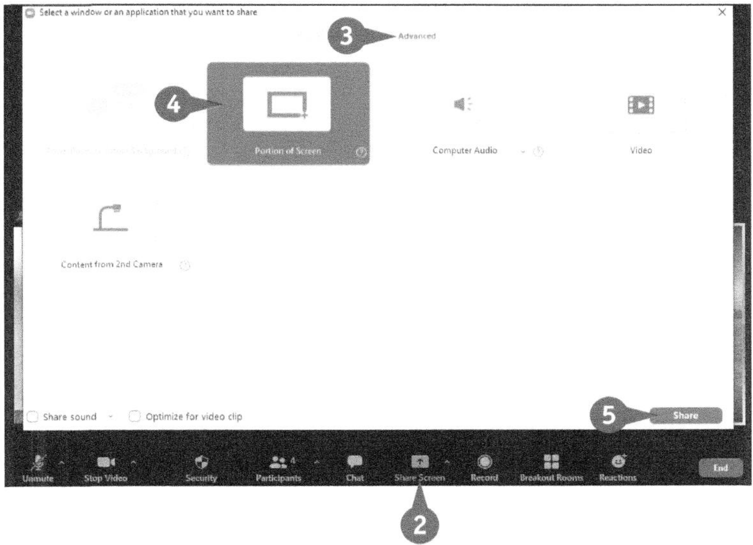

A. Zoom displays a rectangle. Any screen content within that rectangle is shared with the meeting participants.

B. Click and drag the top of the rectangle to move it.

C. Click and drag any edge or corner of the rectangle to change its size.

Note: To stop sharing the portion of the screen, tap **Stop Share** in the sharing controls.

Share Your iPhone or iPad Device Screen

From the Zoom desktop app, you can share with meeting participants content on the screen of your iPhone or iPad. If you are attending a meeting using the Zoom desktop app, you might want to share some content that appears on your iPhone or iPad. You can accomplish this using Zoom's Screen Sharing feature and the Screen Mirroring feature on your iPhone or iPad. Screen Mirroring enables you to send the iPhone or iPad screen to your Zoom desktop app, which then shares the screen with the meeting.

Share Your iPhone or iPad Device Screen

1. Display the meeting controls (not shown).
2. Click **Share Screen**.

Note: You can also select the Share Screen command by pressing Alt + S.

Zoom displays the sharing options.

3. Click **iPhone/iPad**.
4. Click **Share**.

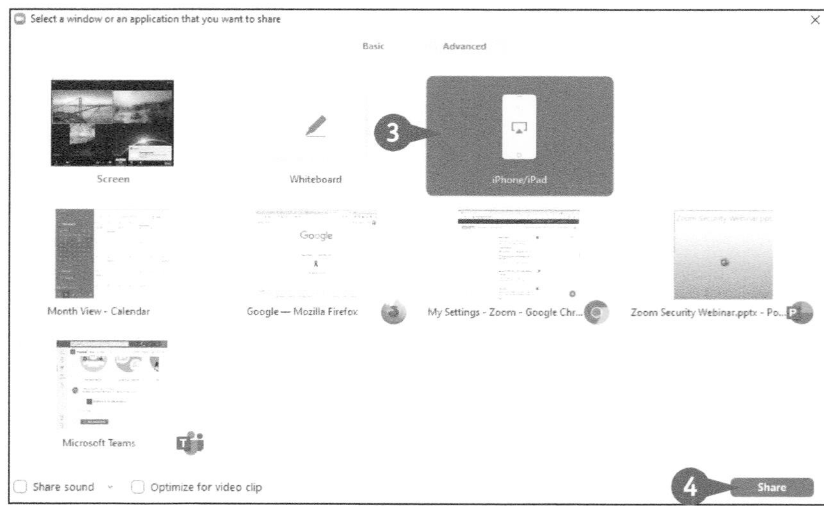

The first time you attempt to share your iPhone or iPad screen, Zoom tells you that a plug-in is required.

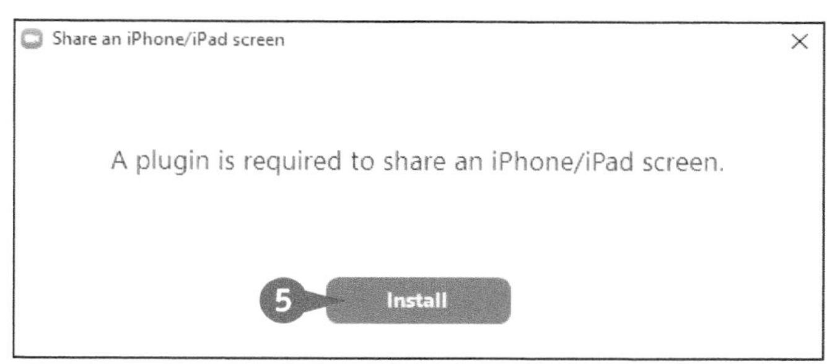

5 Click **Install**.

If you see a Windows Security Alert dialog, click **Allow Access** and then enter your administrator account credentials.

6 On your iPhone or iPad, display the Control Center.

7 Tap **Screen Mirroring**.

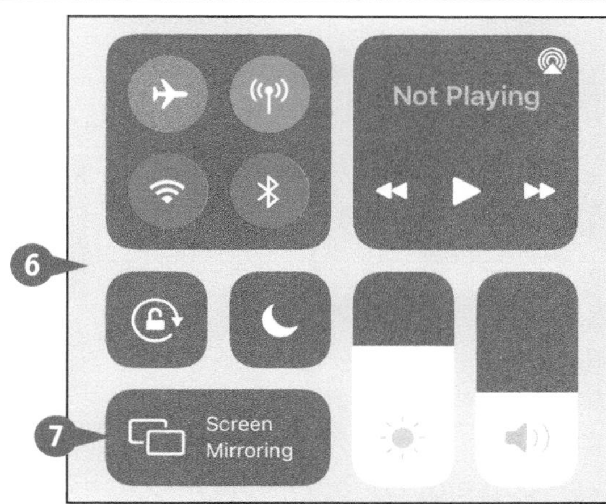

The Screen Mirroring dialog appears.

8 Tap the Zoom device, which has a name that begins with **Zoom-**.

Zoom connects to your iPhone or iPad and shares the device screen with the meeting participants.

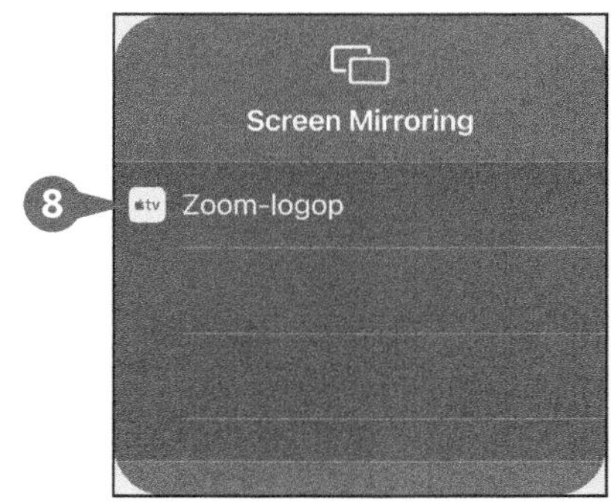

TIPS

How do I display the Control Center on my iPhone or iPad?
For the iPhone: If your iPhone has a notch at the top, swipe down from the top-right corner of the screen; for all other iPhones, swipe up from the bottom of the screen.

For the iPad: If you are running iPadOS 12 or later, swipe down from the top-right corner of the screen; for all other iPads, swipe up from the bottom of the screen.

How do I stop sharing my iPhone or iPad screen?
First, on your iPhone or iPad, open Control Center, tap **Screen Mirroring**, and then tap **Stop Mirroring**. Second, in your Zoom desktop app, click **Stop Sharing** at the top of the screen.

Share a Whiteboard

You can share annotations with other meeting attendees by sharing Zoom's whiteboard feature. A *whiteboard* is a blank white canvas on which you can create annotations. You can annotate Zoom's whiteboard feature with text, freehand drawings, arrows, and stamps, which are icons such as a heart or check mark. You can share a whiteboard using the desktop app or the mobile app, although this feature is not available on the iPhone.

Zoom also enables multiple attendees to annotate the shared whiteboard, which enables attendees to share ideas and contribute to brainstorming sessions.

Share a Whiteboard

Using the Zoom Desktop App

1. Display the meeting controls (not shown).
2. Click **Share Screen**.

Note: You can also select the Share Screen command by pressing Alt+S.

Zoom displays the sharing options.

3. Click **Whiteboard**.
4. Click **Share**.

Zoom displays the whiteboard and shares it with the meeting participants.

Note: To stop sharing the portion of the screen, tap **Stop Share** in the sharing controls.

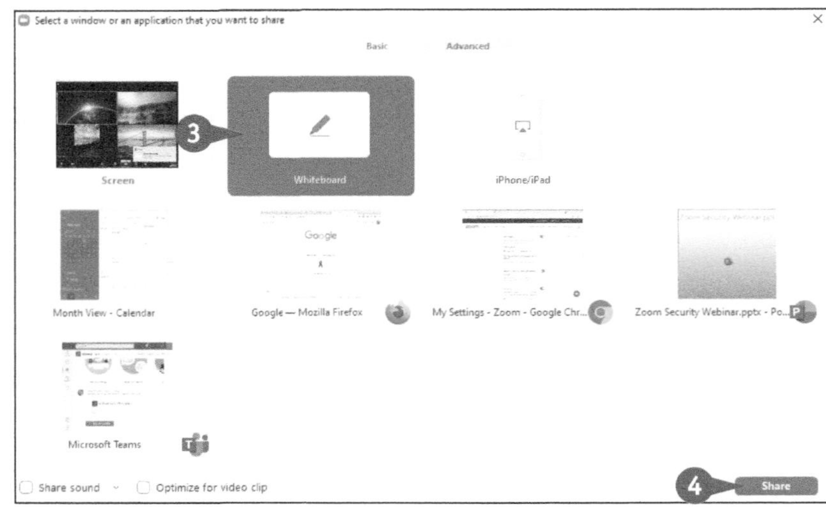

Using the Zoom Mobile App (Android or iPad Only)

1. Display the meeting controls (not shown).
2. Tap **Share** (Android) or **Share Content** (iPad).
3. Tap **Share Whiteboard** (Android) or **Whiteboard** (iPad).

   Zoom displays the whiteboard and shares it with the meeting participants.

Note: To stop sharing your whiteboard, tap the **Stop Share** button.

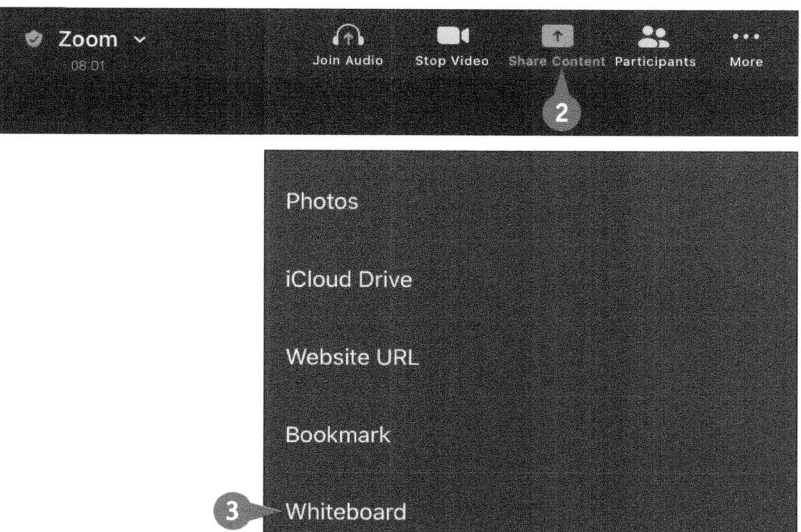

TIP

How do I use the whiteboard?

The desktop app version of the whiteboard offers the following controls:

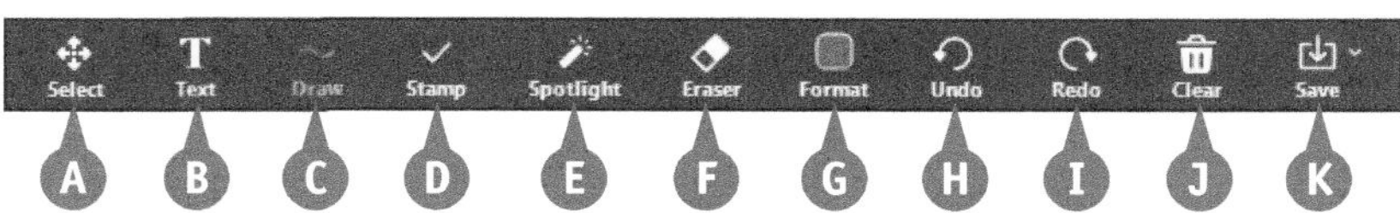

- A **Select**. Select and move whiteboard objects.
- B **Text**. Enter text.
- C **Draw**. Draw objects, including lines, arrows, curves, rectangles, and ovals.
- D **Stamp**. Add an icon object.
- E **Spotlight**. Add a spotlight to the mouse cursor for pointing out objects.
- F **Eraser**. Erase objects.
- G **Format**. Add formatting to the current object.
- H **Undo**. Reverse the most recent action.
- I **Redo**. Redo an action reversed by Undo.
- J **Clear**. Remove some or all of the objects.
- K **Save**. Save your annotations as a PNG image.

Share a Video

If you have video content you want to show to the meeting, you can share a video clip. One way to share video content would be to share your screen or a window and play the video there. However, it is better to share a video directly. When you share the video directly, Zoom displays it in its own window. You also get playback controls that enable you to pause and play the video, skip to any part of the video, adjust the volume, and more. Note that only you see the playback controls; meeting participants just see the video.

Share a Video

1. In the Zoom desktop app, display the meeting controls (not shown).
2. Click **Share Screen**.

Note: You can also select the Share Screen command by pressing Alt + S.

Zoom displays the sharing options.

3. Click **Advanced**.
4. Click **Video**.
5. Click **Share**.

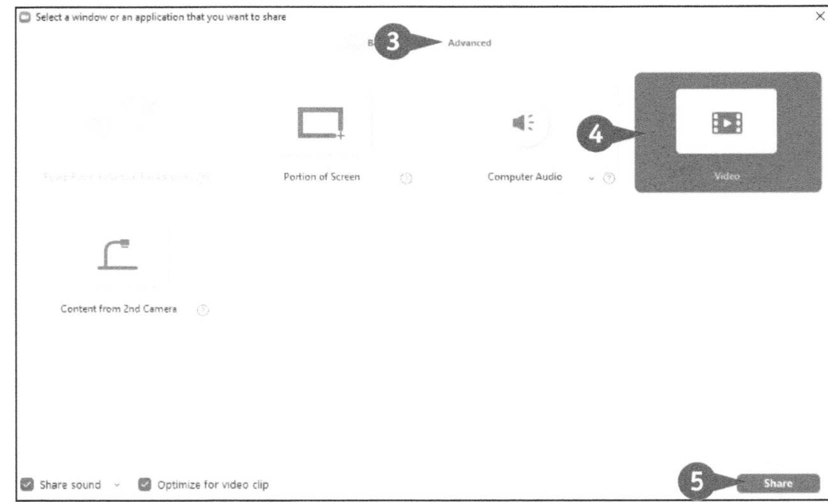

Zoom displays the Open dialog.

6. Select the video file you want to share.
7. Click **Open**.

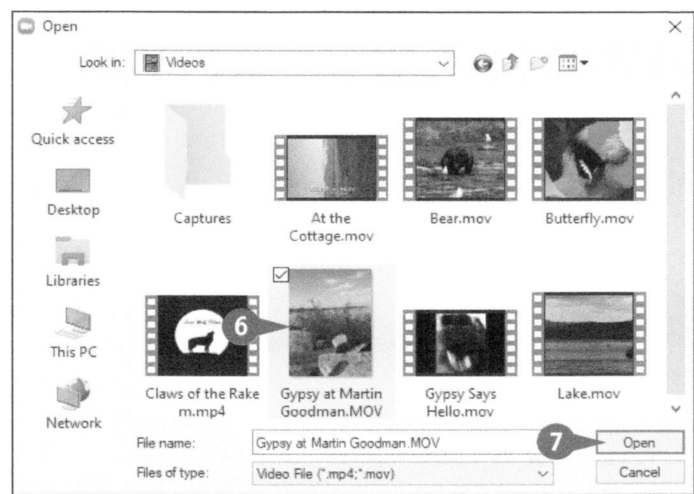

Zoom starts sharing the video.

8. Click **Play** (▶) to begin the video.

Zoom plays the video for the meeting participants.

A. To stop sharing your video, click **Stop Share**.

TIPS

What video file formats does Zoom support?

Zoom supports two file formats: the QuickTime video file format developed by Apple, which uses the .mov file extension; and the MPEG-4 video file format, which uses the .mp4 file extension. In both cases, only the H.264 AVC codec is supported.

Can I share a video using the Zoom mobile app?

No, video sharing is not supported by the mobile app. However, you can use the mobile app to share photos with the meeting participants. Tap **Share** (Android) or **Share Content** (iOS), tap **Photo** (Android) or **Photos** (iOS), select the photos you want to share, and then tap **Select** (Android) or **Done** (iOS). Swipe left and right to navigate the shared photos.

Share Audio

If you have audio content you want meeting participants to hear, you can share either content audio or computer audio. When you share your desktop or an application window, Zoom does not directly include any associated audio output, although some audio might play through your microphone. If the audio portion of the content is important, you can tell Zoom to include audio when you share your screen. Similarly, you can share any audio from your computer to the meeting. Either way, sharing audio directly in this way provides better-quality sound.

Share Audio

Share Content Audio

1. In the Zoom desktop app, display the meeting controls (not shown).
2. Click **Share Screen**.

Note: You can also select the Share Screen command by pressing Alt + S.

Zoom displays the sharing options.

3. Select what you want to share.
4. Click **Share sound** (☐ changes to ☑).
5. Click the **Share sound** ⌄ and then click either **Mono** or **Stereo**.
6. Click **Share**.

Zoom shares your screen and its audio with the meeting participants.

Note: To stop sharing the portion of the screen, tap **Stop Share** in the sharing controls.

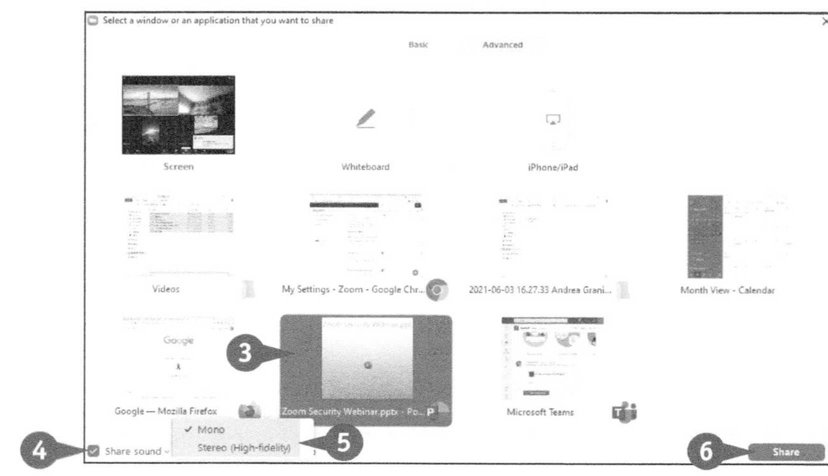

Share Computer Audio

1. In the Zoom desktop app, display the meeting controls (not shown).
2. Click **Share Screen.**

Note: You can also select the Share Screen command by pressing Alt + S.

Zoom displays the sharing options.

3. Click **Advanced.**
4. Click **Computer Audio.**
5. Click the **Computer Audio** ⌄ and then click either **Mono** or **Stereo.**
6. Click **Share.**

Zoom shares all audio output from your computer with the meeting participants.

To stop sharing your computer, click **Stop Share.**

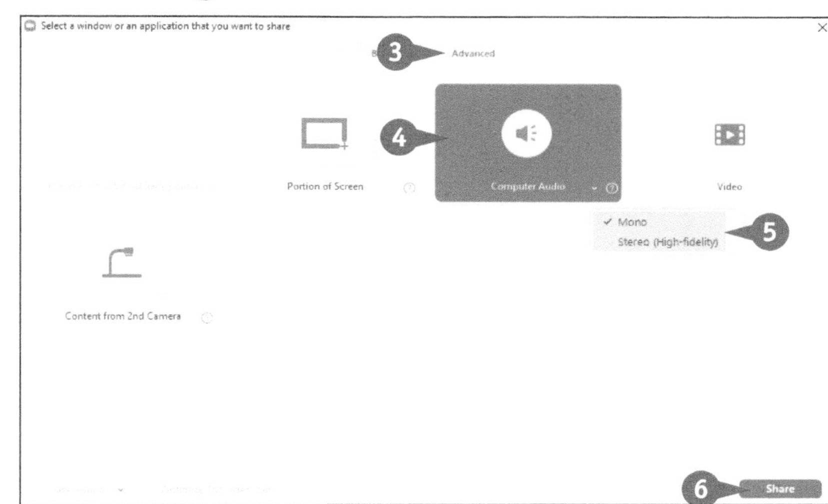

TIP

I have already shared my desktop or an app window without sound. Is there a way to add the audio to the share?

Yes, by following these steps:

1. In the Zoom meeting controls, click **More.**
2. Click **Share sound.**

Zoom adds audio to your share and closes the More menu.

3. Click **More.**
4. Click either **Mono** or **Stereo.**

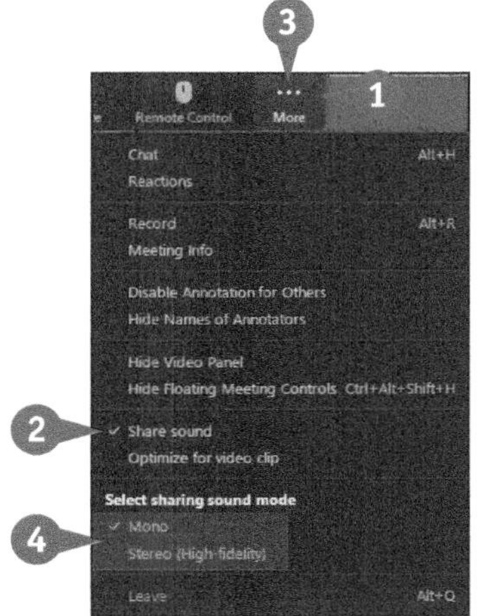

Share Video from a Second Camera

You can share with the meeting participants the feed from a second camera connected to your computer. If your computer has two cameras — for example, an internal camera built into a second monitor or an external camera connected via USB — the Zoom desktop app enables you to share the video feed from that second camera. This is useful if you want to show the meeting participants a nearby object or scene without interfering with your normal Zoom video display. Once you have shared the second camera video, you can switch between the two cameras as needed.

Share Video from a Second Camera

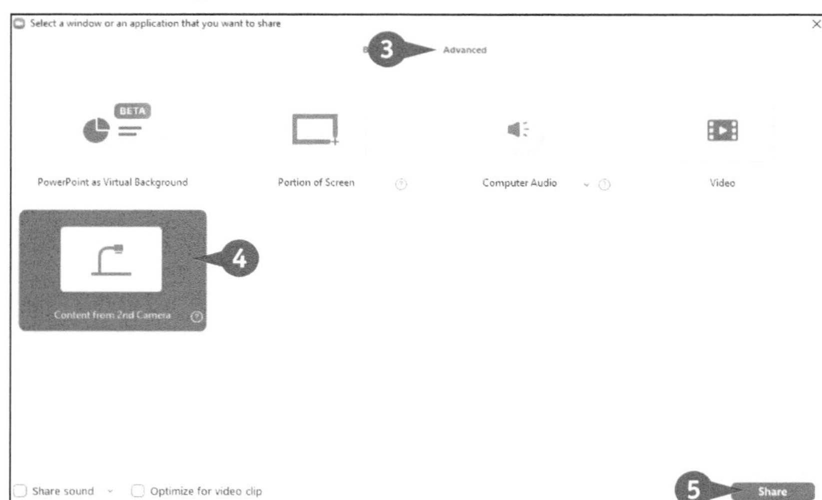

1. In the Zoom desktop app, display the meeting controls (not shown).
2. Click **Share Screen**.

Note: You can also select the Share Screen command by pressing Alt + S.

Zoom displays the sharing options.

3. Click **Advanced**.
4. Click **Content from 2nd Camera**.
5. Click **Share**.

Zoom shares the feed from your second camera with the meeting participants.

Note: You can switch between your two cameras by clicking the **Switch Camera** button in the upper-left corner of the screen.

Note: To stop sharing the portion of the screen, tap **Stop Share** in the sharing controls.

CHAPTER
6
Annotate a Shared Screen

After you share a screen, you and the other meeting participants can add annotations to the screen. Annotations are useful for pointing out screen objects, adding quick notes, and sharing ideas. You can annotate your shared screen with text, freehand drawings, shapes, arrows, and stamps, which are icons such as a heart or check mark. Zoom also enables other attendees to annotate someone else's shared screen, and those annotations are visible to everyone else in the meeting.

You can annotate a shared screen using the desktop app or the mobile app, although this feature is not available on the iPhone.

Annotate a Shared Screen

Annotate Your Shared Screen

1. Share your screen.

Note: See the section "Share Your Screen" earlier in this chapter.

2. In the sharing controls, click **Annotate**.

Ⓐ Zoom displays the annotation tools.

3. Use the annotation tools to mark up the screen.

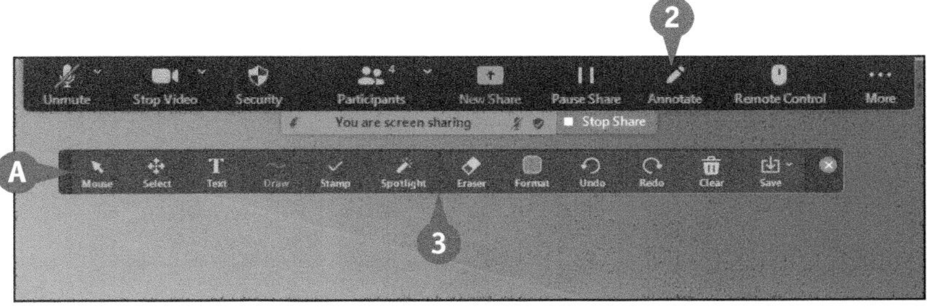

Annotate Another User's Shared Screen

1. Click **View Options**.

2. Click **Annotate**.

Ⓑ Zoom displays the annotation tools.

3. Use the annotation tools to mark up the screen.

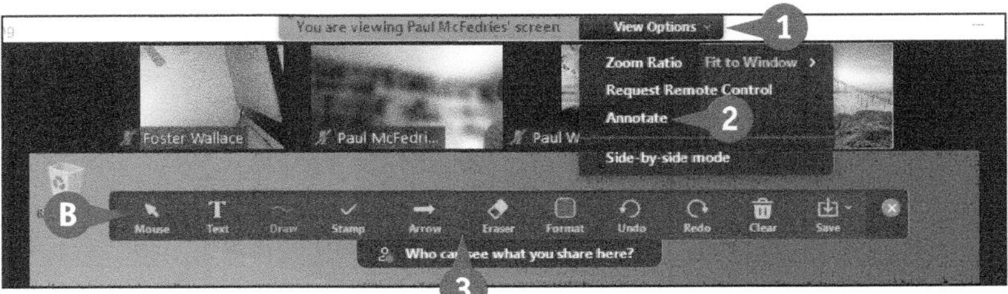

Note: You can annotate a user's shared screen with an Android device or iPad by tapping the **Annotate** icon (⊘).

Share Slides as a Virtual Background

You can share PowerPoint or Keynote presentation slides as a virtual background for your video. It is possible to share a presentation by sharing the PowerPoint or Keynote application window. However, sharing a presentation as a virtual background means that your regular Zoom video background is replaced by each slide in the presentation. This creates a more immersive experience and also enables you to control the presentation from within Zoom. To use this feature, you need PowerPoint installed on your Windows PC, or PowerPoint or Keynote installed on your Mac.

Share Slides as a Virtual Background

1. In the Zoom desktop app, display the meeting controls (not shown).
2. Click **Share Screen**.

Note: You can also select the Share Screen command by pressing Alt + S.

Zoom displays the sharing options.

3. Click **Advanced.**
4. Click **PowerPoint as Virtual Background.**

Note: If you use Keynote, you would click **Keynote as Virtual Background** instead.

5. Click **Share.**

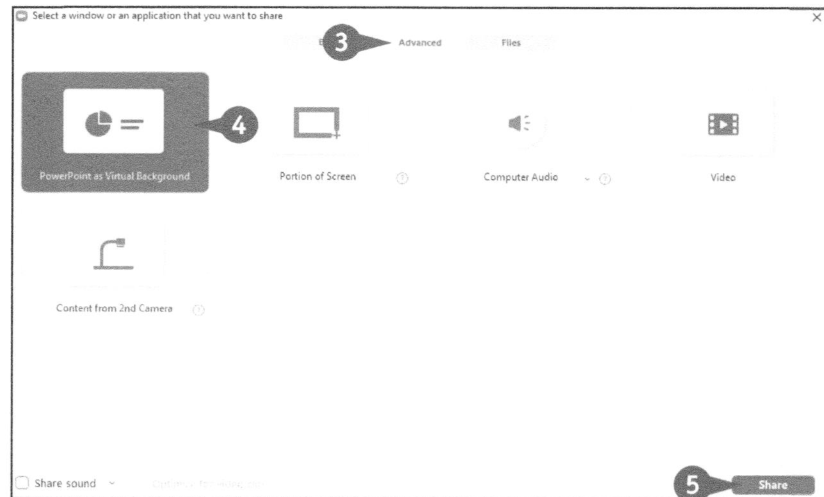

Zoom displays the Open dialog.

6 Select the presentation file you want to share.

7 Click **Open**.

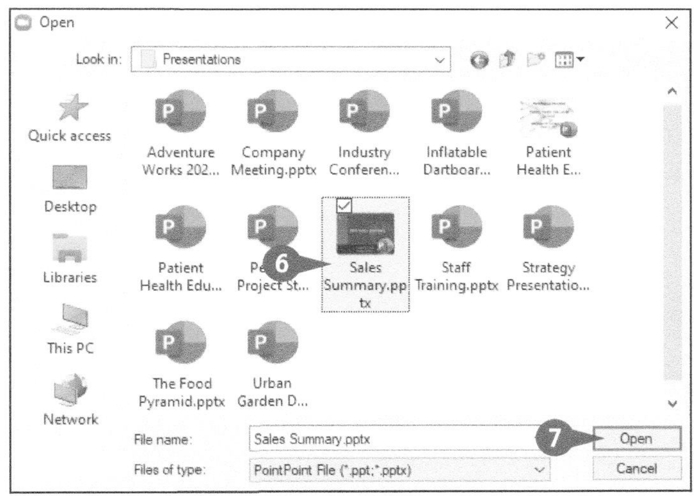

A Zoom starts sharing the presentation by displaying the first slide as your virtual background.

B To stop sharing your video, click **Stop Share**.

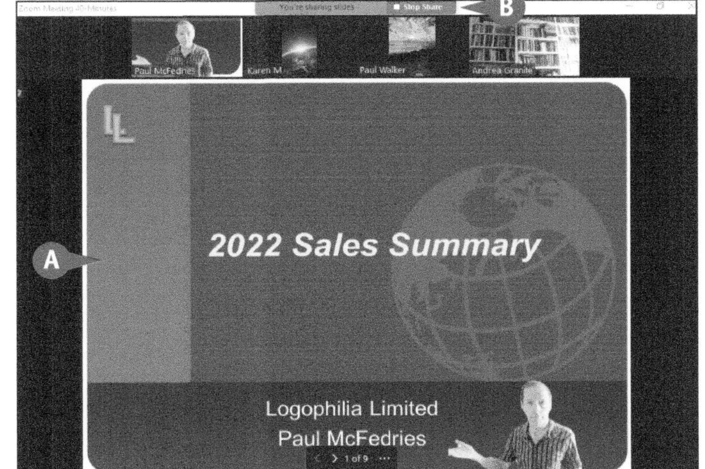

TIPS

How do I navigate the slides?

With your mouse, you can click the **Next** (>)(A) and **Previous** (<)(B) buttons at the bottom of the slides. You can also press → to go to the next slide and ← to go to the previous slide.

Can I temporarily remove my video from the presentation?

Yes. If you find your video is blocking important information on a particular slide, you can temporarily remove your video by clicking **More** (···) and then clicking **Split Video from PowerPoint**. To return your video to the slide, click **More** (···) and then click **Merge Video and PowerPoint**.

Host a Screen Share–Only Meeting

You can host and launch a meeting that uses only the screen sharing feature. You might decide to host an instant meeting with some colleagues to share a spreadsheet, video, or presentation. If sharing that content is all you want to do, you can simplify the meeting hosting by creating a screen share–only meeting. When you launch the meeting, Zoom immediately displays the sharing options that are discussed in this chapter. When you stop sharing the content, Zoom automatically ends the meeting.

Host a Screen Share–Only Meeting

1. Use a web browser to sign in to https://zoom.us/.
2. Click **Host a Meeting**.
3. Click **Screen Share Only**.

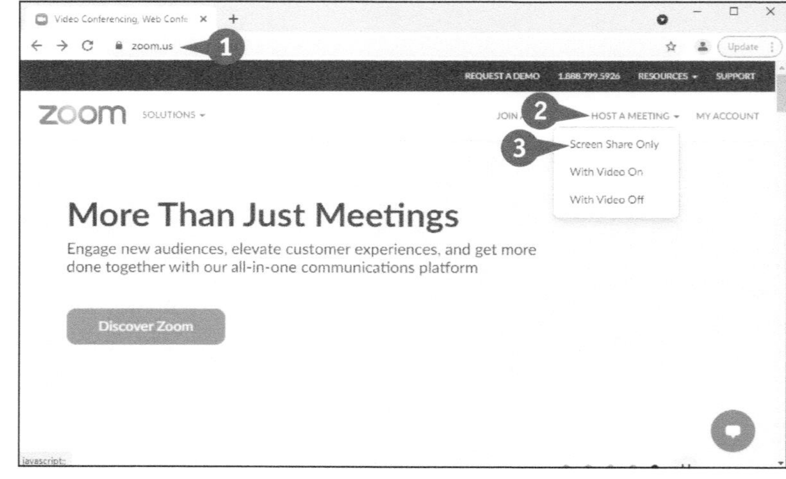

Zoom starts a new meeting and displays the sharing options.

4. Select the sharing option you want to use.
5. Click **Share**.

Zoom shares your content to the meeting.

Note: To stop sharing the content and to end the meeting, click **Stop Share** in the sharing controls.

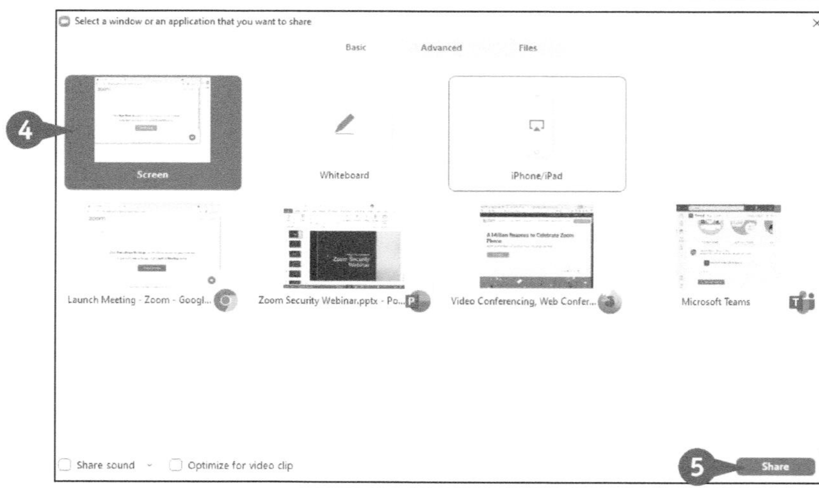

View a Shared Screen in Side-by-Side Mode

You can often make it easier to view a shared screen by switching your Zoom meeting layout to side-by-side mode. When another user shares content in a Zoom meeting, you see the shared screen with either Gallery view or Speaker view floating on top of the shared screen. You can move the floating Gallery view or Speaker view if it is obscuring content on the shared screen. However, if you are using the Zoom desktop app, a better solution is to switch to side-by-side mode, which displays the shared screen on the left and Gallery view or Speaker view on the right.

View a Shared Screen in Side-by-Side Mode

1. In the Zoom desktop app, click **View Options**.
2. Click **Side-by-side mode**.

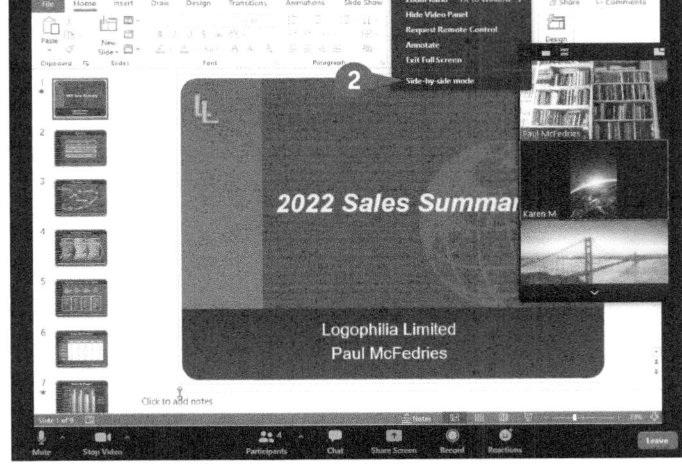

Zoom switches to side-by-side mode.

Ⓐ You can click and drag the separator bar to change the relative sizes of the two screen areas.

Ⓑ You can switch between Speaker view and Gallery view by clicking **View** and then clicking either **Side-by-side: Speaker** or **Side-by-side: Gallery**.

Note: To exit side-by-side mode, repeat steps 1 and 2.

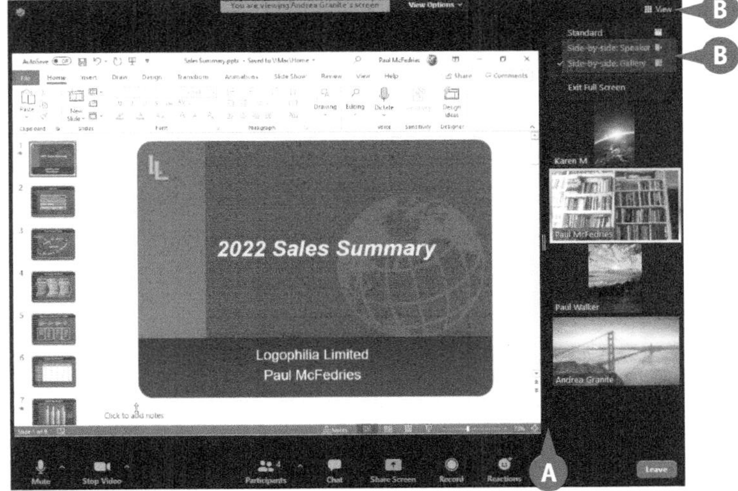

Request Control of a Screen Share

You can ask the user who is sharing a screen for permission to control the share. During a share, you might find that you need help with a particular demonstration or require some troubleshooting to resolve a problem. Rather than asking for verbal instructions on how to proceed, another person can request to control the share remotely. When you approve the request, the remote user can use their local mouse and keyboard to control the screen content just as though they were sitting at your computer. As the content sharer, you can also give control to another meeting user.

Request Control of a Screen Share

Request Remote Control

1. In the Zoom desktop app, click **View Options**.

2. Click **Request Remote Control**.

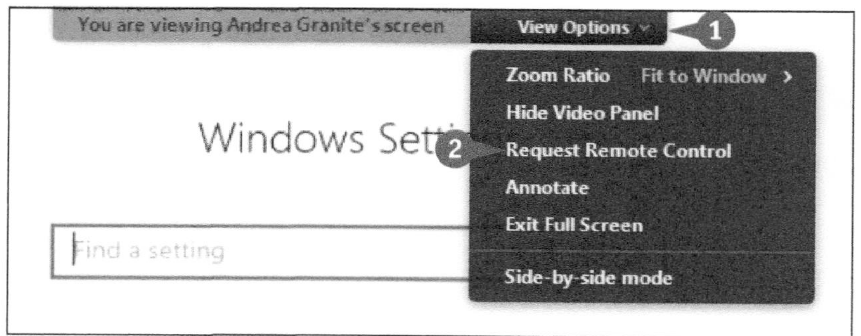

Zoom asks you to confirm that you want to request remote control of the share.

3. Click **Request**.

Zoom sends the request to the person sharing the content.

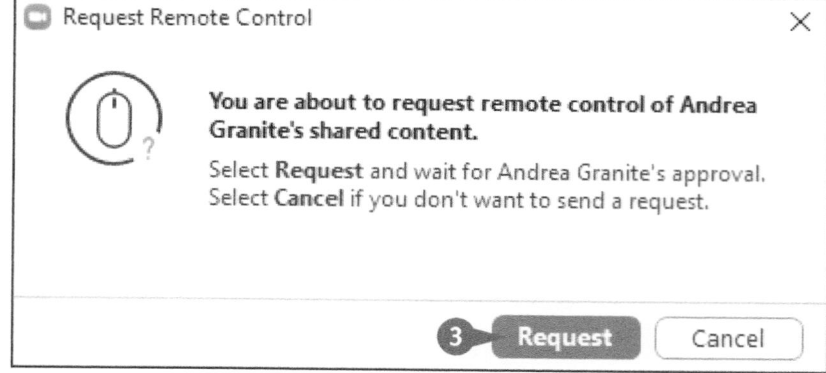

Accept a Remote Control Request

A message appears telling you that a meeting participant is requesting remote control of your screen.

1 Click **Approve**.

Zoom transfers control of the screen to the user who requested remote control.

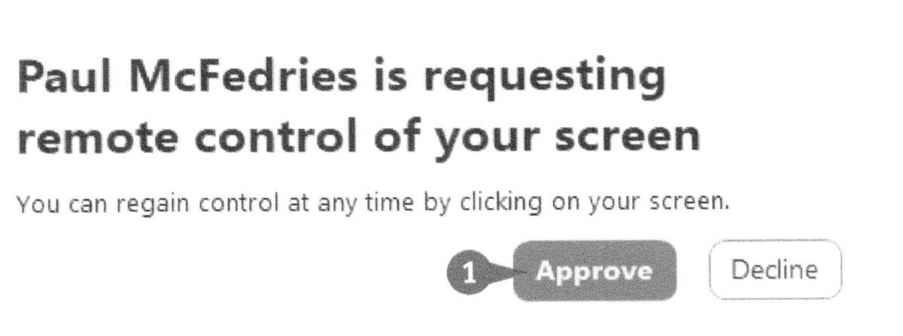

Give a User Remote Control

1 Click **Remote Control**.

2 Click the name of the user.

Zoom transfers control of the screen to the user you selected.

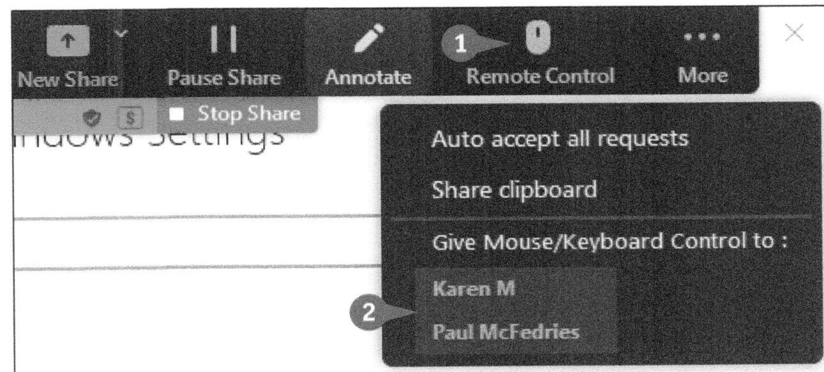

TIPS

Is there an easier way to handle remote control requests?

Yes, you can tell Zoom to accept all remote control requests automatically. Click **Remote Controlled** (A) and then click **Auto accept all requests** (B).

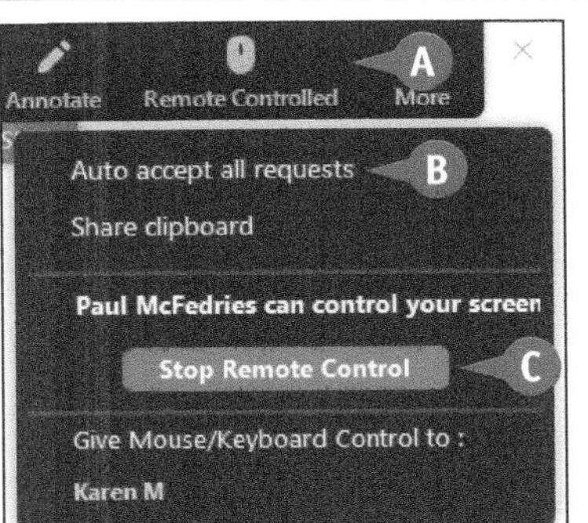

How do I take back control from a user?

In the sharing controls, click **Remote Controlled** (A) and then click **Stop Remote Control** (C).

CHAPTER 7

Recording a Meeting

You can create a recording of a Zoom meeting. Recording a meeting is useful for training purposes or to meet the legal requirements of your business. Having a recording is also handy for users who were unable to attend the meeting. You can save recordings locally on your computer or online in the cloud.

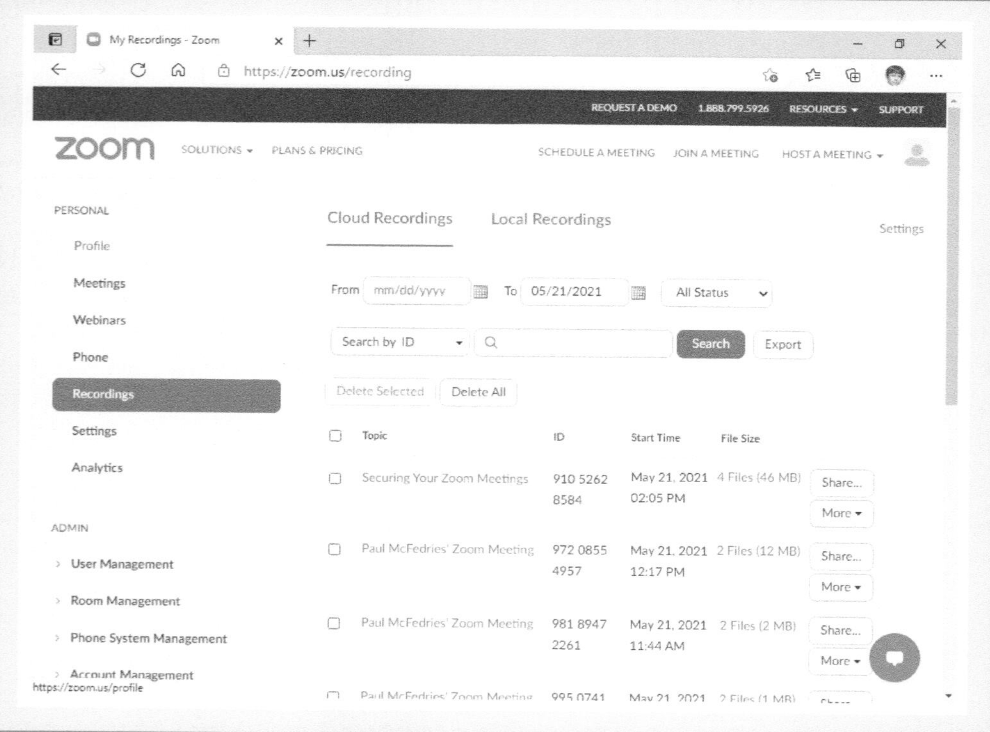

Create a Local Recording

As the meeting host, you can record a Zoom meeting and save the recording to your computer. This is called making a *local* recording of the meeting. See the next two sections if you want to make a cloud recording instead.

After you start the local recording, you can pause if you come to a portion of the meeting that you do not want recorded. Zoom automatically stops the recording when the meeting ends, but you can also stop the recording at any time while the meeting is still on.

Create a Local Recording

Start a Local Recording

1. In the Zoom desktop app, click **Record**.
2. Click **Record on this Computer**.

Note: You can also start a local recording by pressing Alt + R.

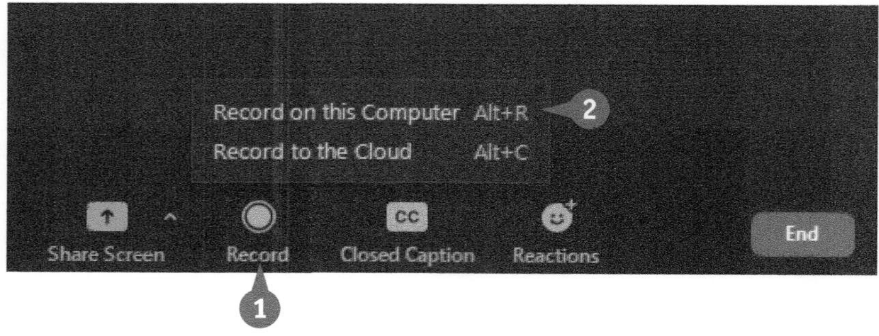

A Zoom displays a **Recording** message in the upper-left corner of the window for each participant.

Note: Zoom mobile app users see a **REC** message with a pulsing red dot.

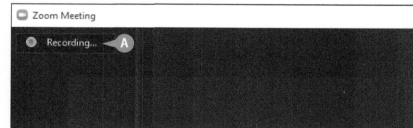

Pause a Local Recording

1. In the Zoom desktop app, click **Pause Recording** (⏸).

Note: You can also pause the recording by pressing Alt+P.

2. To continue the local recording, click **Resume Recording** (▶) (not shown).

Stop a Local Recording

1. In the Zoom desktop app, click **Stop Recording** (□).

Note: You can also pause the recording by pressing Alt+R.

Zoom stops recording and saves the recording to a local file when you end the meeting.

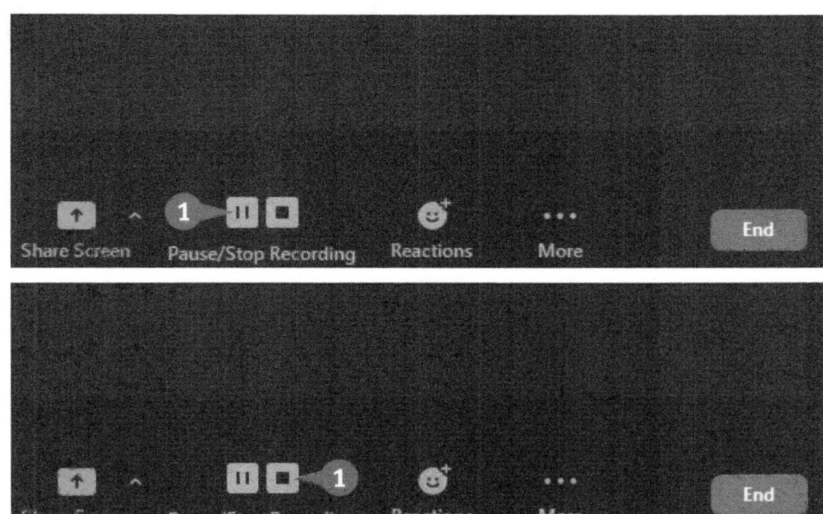

TIPS

Can the host give an attendee permission to record a meeting?
Yes, the host can give attendees permission to make a local recording, as long as the attendee is using the Zoom desktop app. Click the attendee's **More** icon (···) and then click **Allow to Record Local Files**.

What file formats does Zoom use for the recordings?
When the meeting ends, Zoom creates three files on your computer:

- **zoom_0.mp4**. An MPEG-4 file that contains the meeting audio and video
- **audio_only_0.m4a**. An MPEG-4 Audio file that contains the meeting audio
- **chat.txt**. A text file that contains the meeting's chat transcription

Configure Cloud Recording

If you have a paid Zoom account, you have the option of storing your meeting recordings online in the Zoom cloud. Before performing any cloud recordings, however, you should examine the available settings for cloud recordings to make sure this feature is configured the way you want. You also have the option of disabling cloud recordings entirely if you do not want any meeting hosts in your Zoom account to record to the cloud.

Configure Cloud Recording

1. Use a web browser to navigate to https://zoom.us/profile.

   Zoom displays your profile page.

2. Click **Settings**.

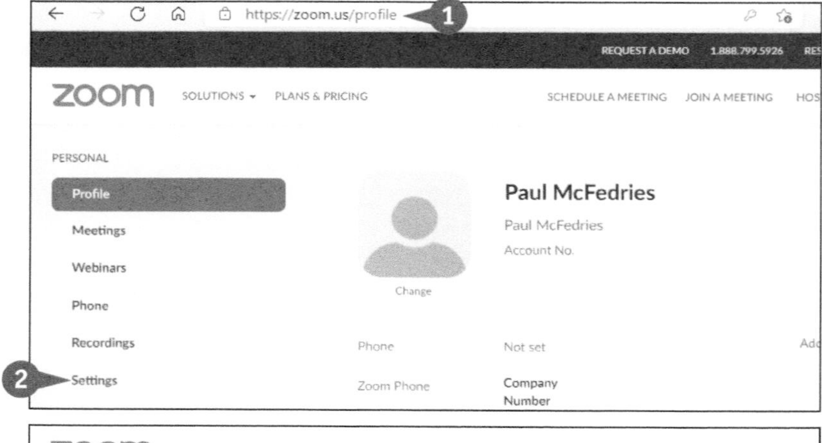

   Zoom displays your account settings.

3. Click **Recording**.

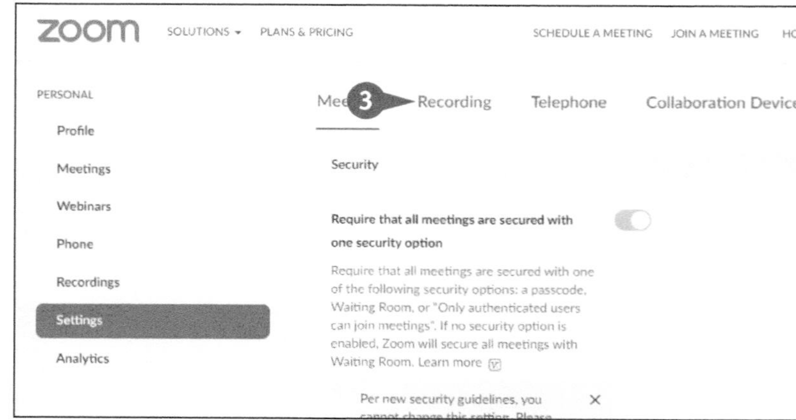

Zoom displays your account's recording settings.

4 Modify the cloud recording settings as needed.

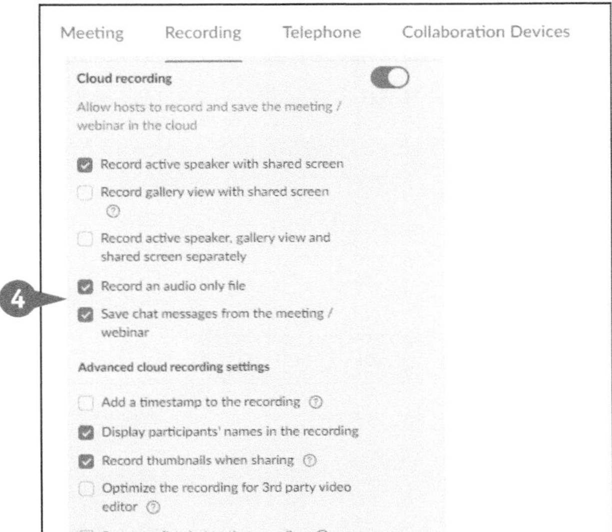

If you disable cloud recording, Zoom asks you to confirm.

5 Click **Disable**.

Zoom saves your changes.

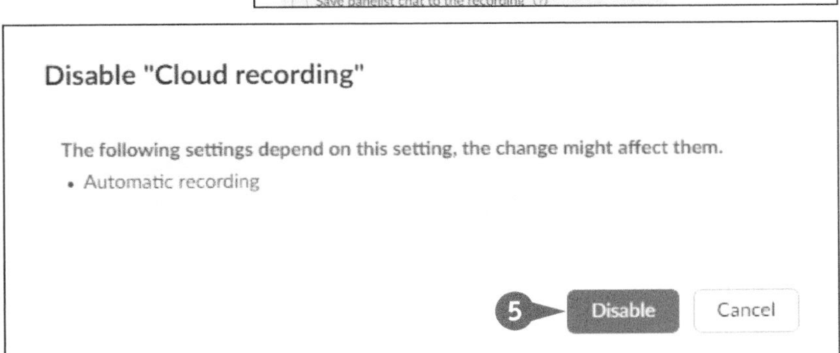

TIPS

If my cloud recordings will be online, is there a way to safeguard the privacy of the meeting participants?

Yes, you can hide participant names when you record to the cloud. Follow steps 1 to 3 to display your account's recording settings. Click **Display participants' names in the recording** (☑ changes to ☐).

Is there a way to make it clear to meeting participants that a recording as started?

Yes, you can display a disclaimer that tells the participant the meeting is being recorded and gives the user to option to leave the meeting. Follow steps 1 to 3 to display your account's recording settings. Click the **Recording disclaimer** switch to **On** (off switch changes to on switch).

Create a Cloud Recording

As the meeting host, you can record a Zoom meeting and save the recording online. This is called making a *cloud* recording of the meeting and it enables others in your Zoom account to view the recording. To create a cloud recording, you must have a paid Zoom account.

After you start the cloud recording, you can pause if you come to a portion of the meeting that you do not want recorded. Zoom automatically stops the recording when the meeting ends, but you can also stop the recording at any time while the meeting is still on.

Create a Cloud Recording

Start a Cloud Recording

1. In the Zoom desktop app, click **Record**.
2. Click **Record to the Cloud**.

Note: You can also start a cloud recording by pressing Alt + C.

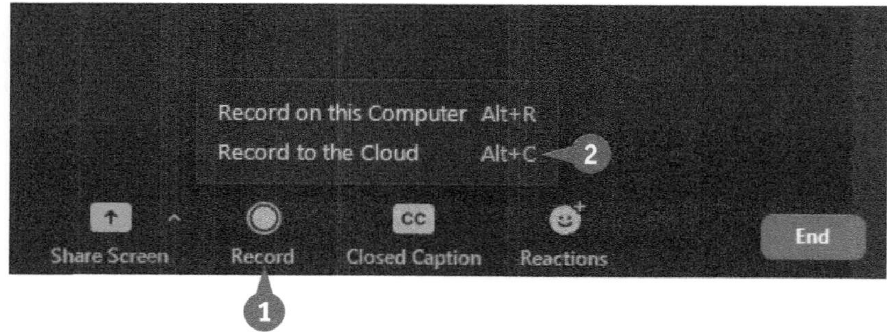

Ⓐ Zoom displays a **Recording** message in the upper-left corner of the window for each participant.

Note: Zoom mobile app users see a **REC** message with a pulsing red dot.

Pause a Cloud Recording

1. In the Zoom desktop app, click **Pause Recording** (⏸).

Note: You can also pause the recording by pressing Alt + P.

2. To continue the local recording, click **Resume Recording** (▶) (not shown).

Stop a Cloud Recording

1. In the Zoom desktop app, click **Stop Recording** (□).

Note: You can also pause the recording by pressing Alt + R.

Zoom stops recording and saves the recording to the cloud when you end the meeting.

TIP

Can I create a cloud recording using the Zoom mobile app?

Yes, cloud recordings are supported in the mobile app. Here are the steps to follow:

1. In the Zoom mobile app, sign in using a paid Zoom account.
2. Tap **More** (···).
3. Tap **Record to the Cloud**.
4. To pause the recording, tap **REC** and then tap **Pause Recording** (⏸).
5. To stop the recording, tap **REC** and then tap **Stop Recording** (□).

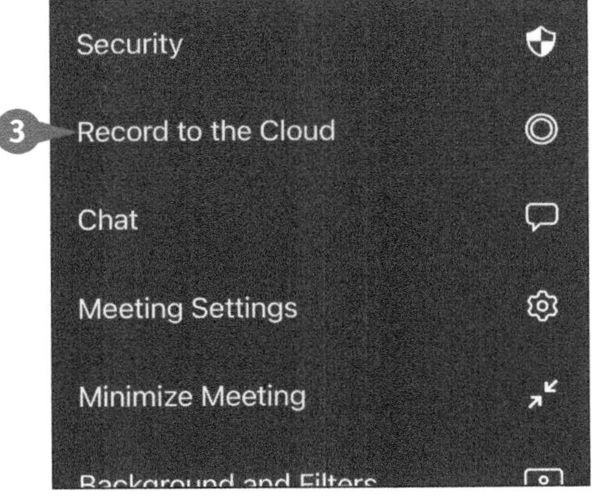

Set Up Automatic Meeting Recording

You can configure your Zoom account to automatically begin recording each meeting as soon as you start the meeting. If you always record your Zoom meetings and you always store your recordings either locally or in the cloud, then you can save several steps each time you start a meeting by configuring Zoom to record your meetings automatically. When you enable this option, Zoom initiates the recording as soon as you join the meeting.

Set Up Automatic Meeting Recording

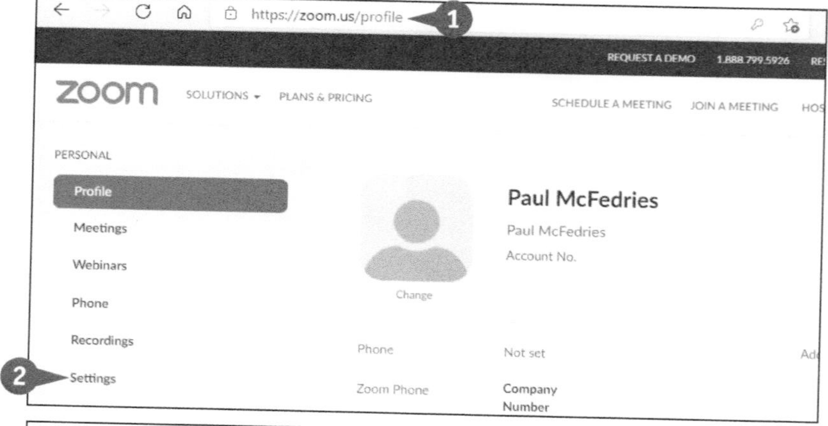

1. Use a web browser to navigate to https://zoom.us/profile.

   Zoom displays your profile page.

2. Click **Settings**.

   Zoom displays your account settings.

3. Click **Recording**.

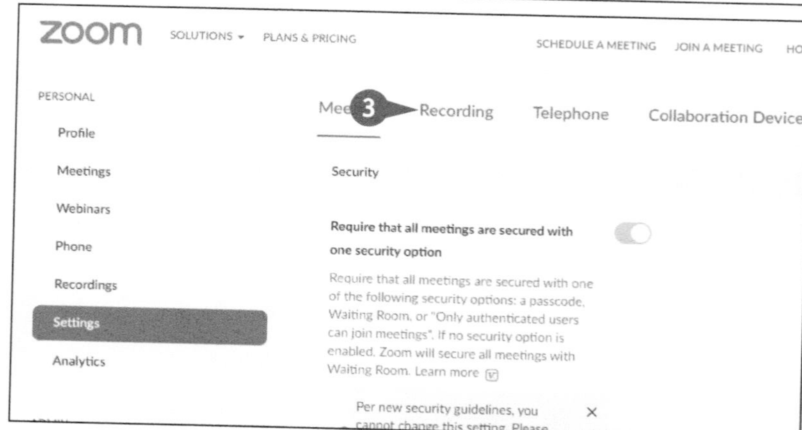

Zoom displays your account's recording settings.

4 Click **Automatic recording** (◯ changes to ◉).

5 Choose whether you want your automatic recording stored locally or in the cloud (○ changes to ◉).

Zoom now starts recording your meetings automatically.

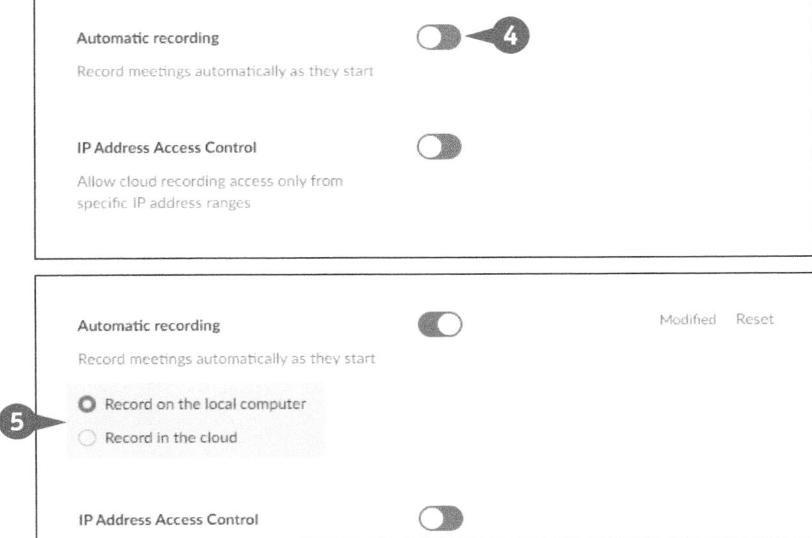

TIPS

Can I set up automatic recording for just a single meeting?

Yes, you can do this for scheduled meetings. In the Schedule Meeting window, click **Advanced Options** (A), click **Automatically record meeting** (☐ changes to ☑) (B), and then choose a location (○ changes to ◉) (C).

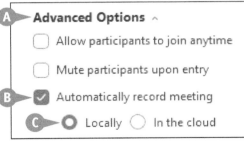

A Advanced Options

☐ Allow participants to join anytime

☐ Mute participants upon entry

B ☑ Automatically record meeting

C ◉ Locally ○ In the cloud

Can I enable automatic recording for everyone in my Zoom account?

Yes. Navigate to your Zoom profile (https://zoom.us/profile), click **Account Management**, click **Account Settings**, and then follow steps 3 to 5 in this section.

View a Recording

After you have recorded a meeting, you can view the recording. If you had to step away from a meeting for a while or if some information was presented during the meeting and you want to review that data, you can watch the recording of the meeting. Whether you recorded the meeting locally or to the cloud, it's easiest to use your Zoom profile interface to access your recordings and start watching them. You can also download cloud recordings to your computer and share cloud recordings with other people.

View a Recording

View a Local Recording

1. Use a web browser to navigate to https://zoom.us/profile (not shown).

   Zoom displays your profile page.

2. Click **Recordings**.
3. Click **Local Recordings**.
4. Click the **Open** button next to the recording you want to view.
5. If your browser asks you to confirm that you want to open the link, click **Open** (not shown).

   Zoom opens the folder containing the local recording files.

6. Double-click the file you want to view.

   Zoom plays or opens the file.

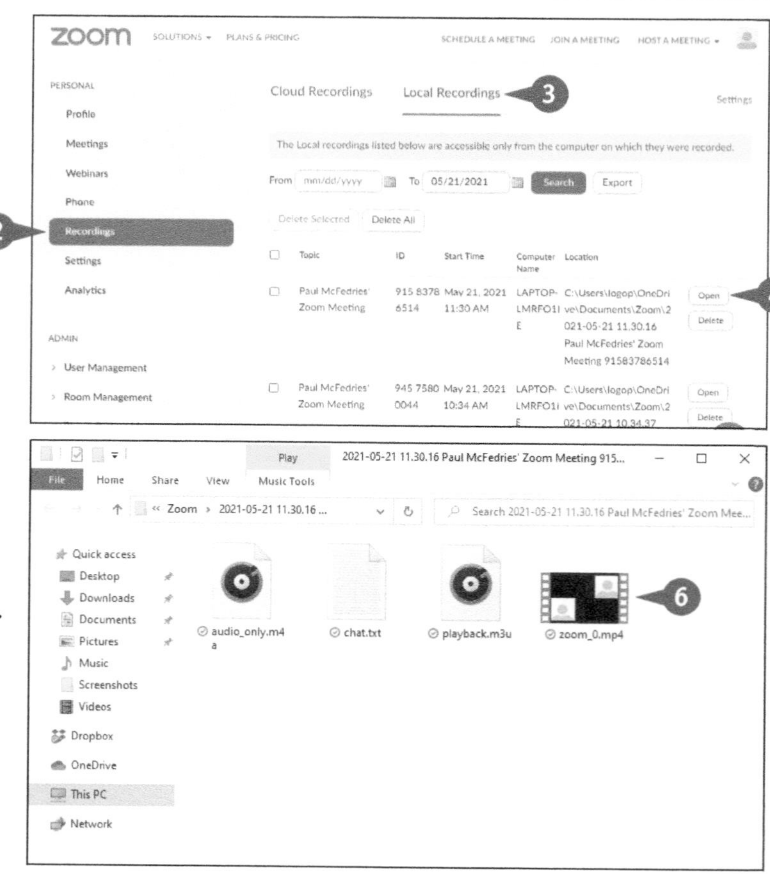

View a Cloud Recording

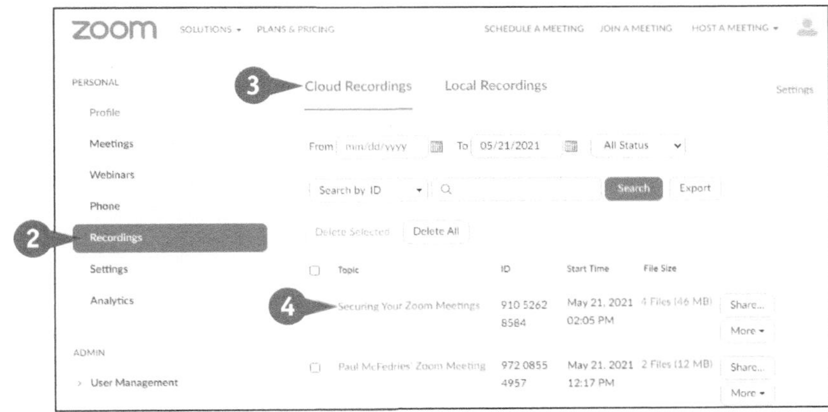

1. Use a web browser to navigate to https://zoom.us/profile (not shown).

   Zoom displays your profile page.

2. Click **Recordings**.
3. Click **Cloud Recordings**.
4. Click the name of the recording you want to view.

   Zoom displays the cloud recording information.

5. Click the recording.

   Zoom plays the recording.

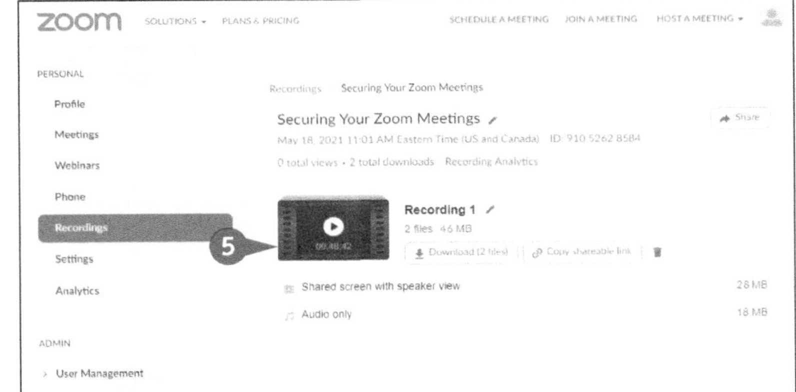

TIPS

How can I download a cloud recording to my computer?

Follow steps 1 to 4 in the "View a Cloud Recording" subsection to open the cloud recording information. Click the **Download** button. If your browser asks for permission to download multiple files, click **Allow**. Zoom downloads the MPEG-4 audio/video file and the MPEG-4 Audio file.

How do I share a cloud recording with others?

Follow steps 1 to 3 in the "View a Cloud Recording" subsection to display your list of cloud recordings. Click the **Share** button next to the recording you want to share. Use the Share This Cloud Recording dialog to set your sharing options, click **Copy Sharing Information**, and then paste the data into a text or email message.

Delete a Recording

If there is a local or cloud recording you no longer need, you can delete it. Meeting recordings are useful, but the more recordings you have, the harder it is to find the one you want. Deleting recordings you no longer need makes it easier to navigate the list of recordings.

Similarly, if you record to the cloud, you have only so much storage space — 1GB for a Pro or Business license — so you can quickly run out of room. To solve storage problems, you can delete those cloud recordings you no longer need.

Delete a Recording

Remove a Local Recording from the List

1. Use a web browser to navigate to https://zoom.us/profile (not shown).

   Zoom displays your profile page.

2. Click **Recordings**.
3. Click **Local Recordings**.
4. Click the **Delete** button next to the recording you want to remove from the list.

   Zoom asks you to confirm.

5. Click **Remove from the List**.

   Zoom removes the recording from the Local Recordings tab.

Note: Zoom does not delete the files associated with the local recording. To delete the files, see the first Tip at the end of this section.

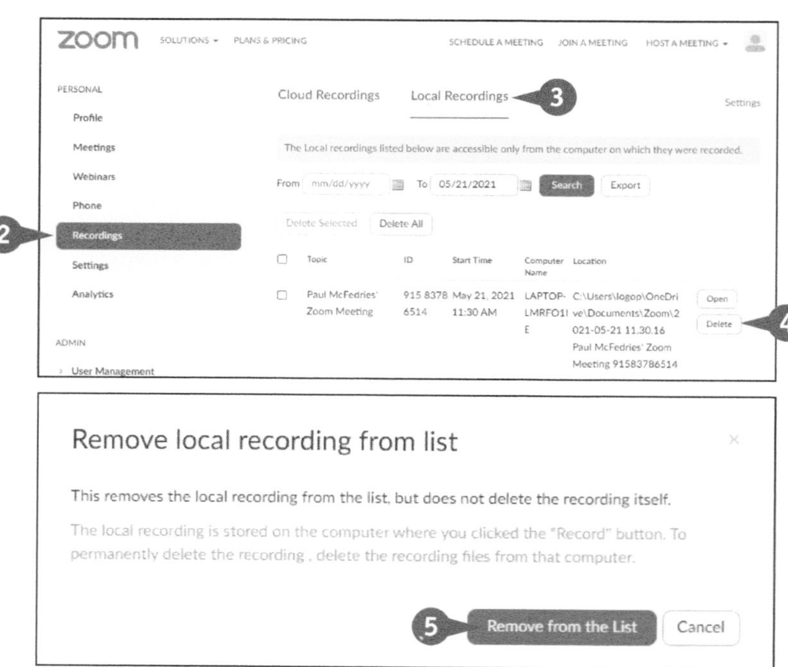

Delete a Cloud Recording

1. Use a web browser to navigate to https://zoom.us/profile (not shown).

   Zoom displays your profile page.

2. Click **Recordings**.
3. Click **Cloud Recordings**.
4. Click **More** beside the recording you want to delete.
5. Click **Delete**.

   Zoom asks you to confirm the deletion.

6. Click **Yes**.

   Zoom deletes the recording.

Note: If you delete a recording accidentally, click **Trash** and then click **Recover** next to the recording you want to recover. When Zoom asks you to confirm, click **Recover**.

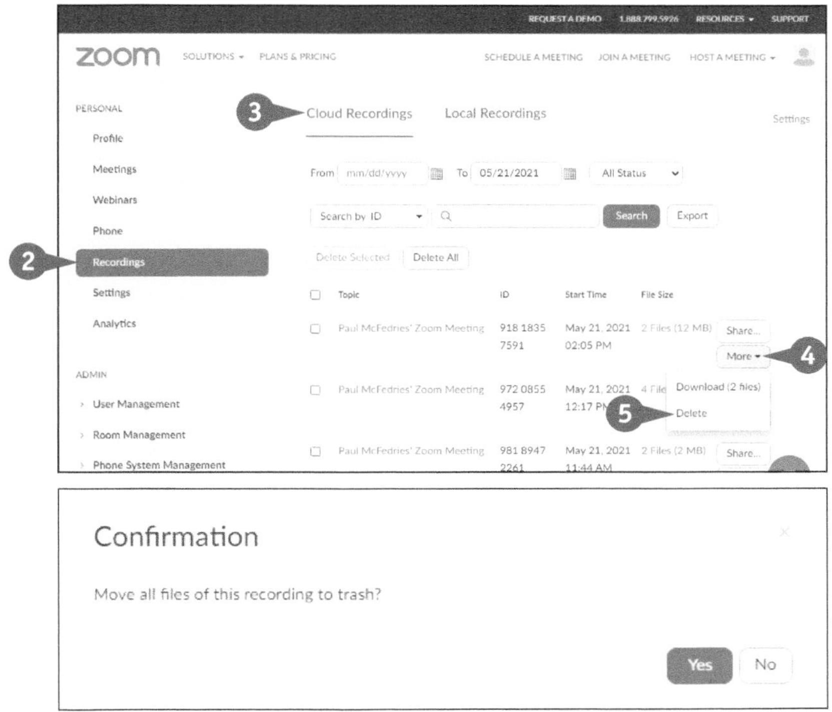

TIPS

How do I delete the files for a local recording?
The easiest way is to follow steps 1 to 3 in the "Remove a Local Recording from the List" subsection. Click **Open** next to the recording to open the folder and then delete the files. If you have already removed the recording from the list, open File Explorer, open your user account's Documents\Zoom folder, and then open the folder for the meeting you removed.

Is there a way to delete recordings automatically?
Yes. Sign in to your Zoom administrator account, click **Settings**, and then click **Recording**. Click **Auto delete cloud recordings after days** (toggle changes to toggle), select the number of days after which recordings are automatically deleted, and then click **Save**.

CHAPTER 8

Configuring Settings

The Zoom mobile app and the Zoom website offer a large number of settings that you can work with to customize Zoom. You can make changes to your Zoom profile, configure meeting defaults, and make Zoom more accessible.

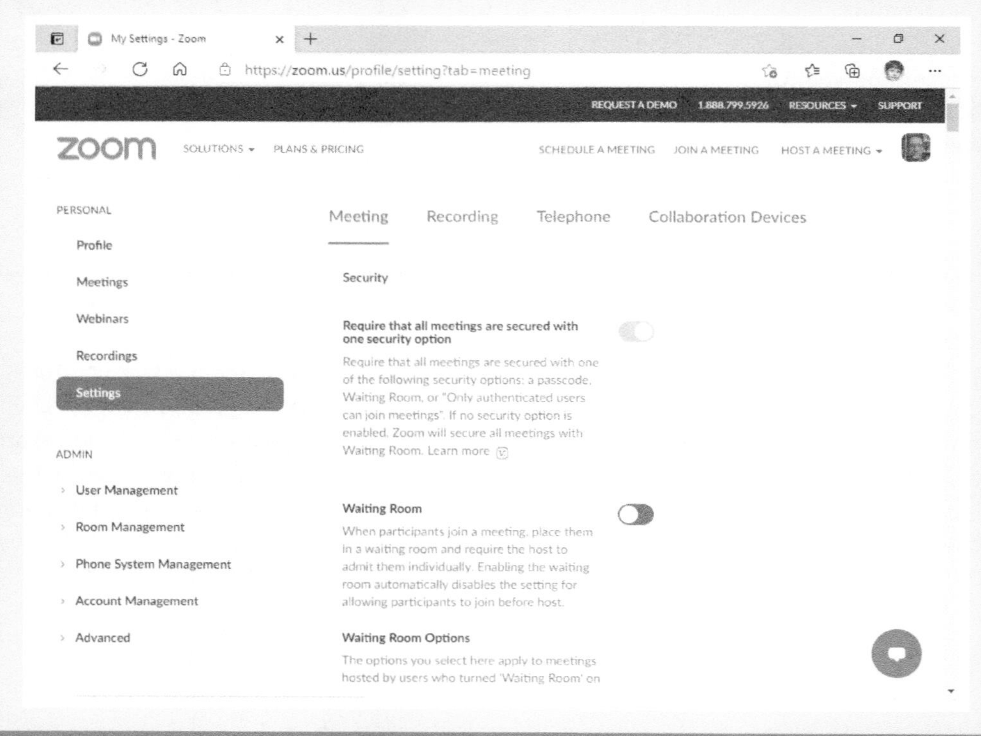

Access Your Zoom Profile

When you sign up for a Zoom account, Zoom automatically creates a profile for you. That profile includes your name, picture, email address, time zone, and date and time format. Zoom supplies default values to these settings, but you can change those defaults to whatever values you prefer.

Before you can make changes to your Zoom profile, you need to know how to access the profile settings. You can access many profile options directly in the Zoom mobile app. For all the profile settings or if you're using the Zoom desktop app, then you need to use the Zoom website.

Access Your Zoom Profile

Using the Zoom Mobile App

1. Tap **Settings**.

   The Settings screen appears.

2. Tap your name.

   The My Profile screen appears.

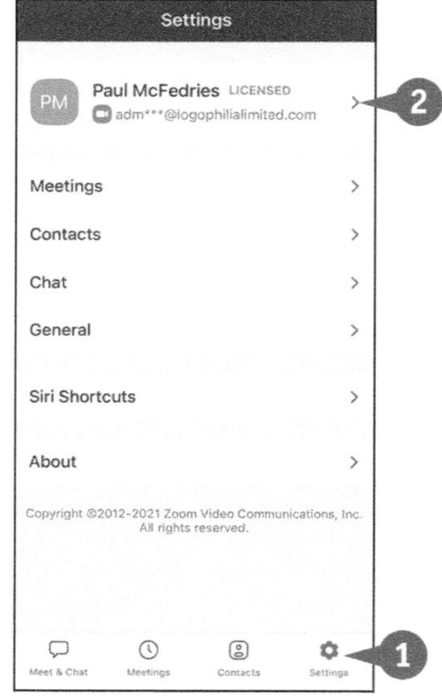

Using the Zoom Desktop App

1. Click your account icon.
2. Click **Settings**.

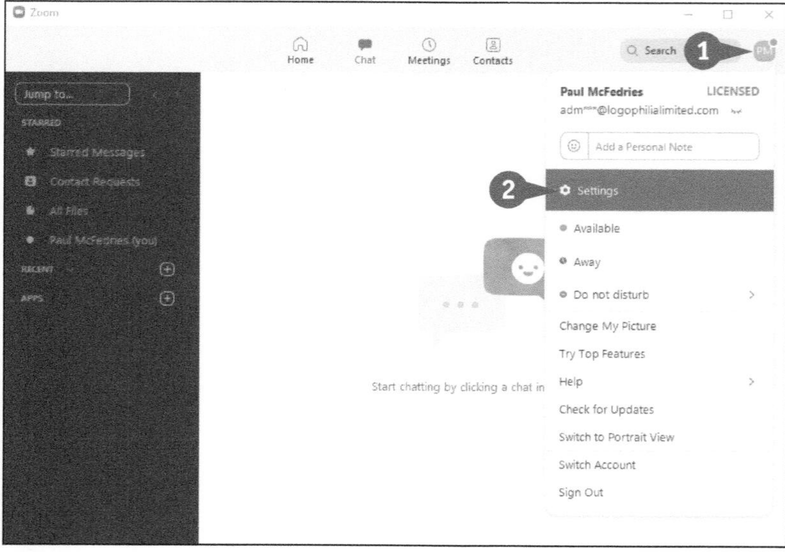

The Settings dialog opens.

3 Click **Profile**.

4 Click **Edit My Profile**.

Your default web browser opens the Zoom website and displays your Profile page.

5 Click **Close** (☒).

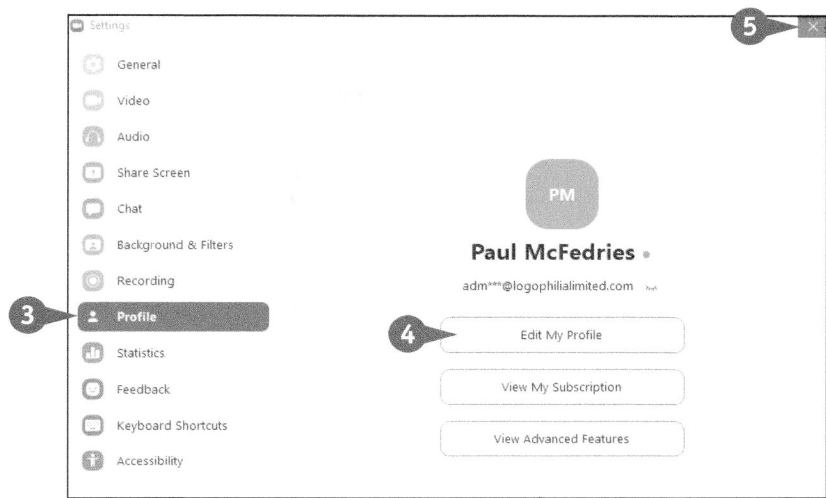

A Your Zoom Profile page appears.

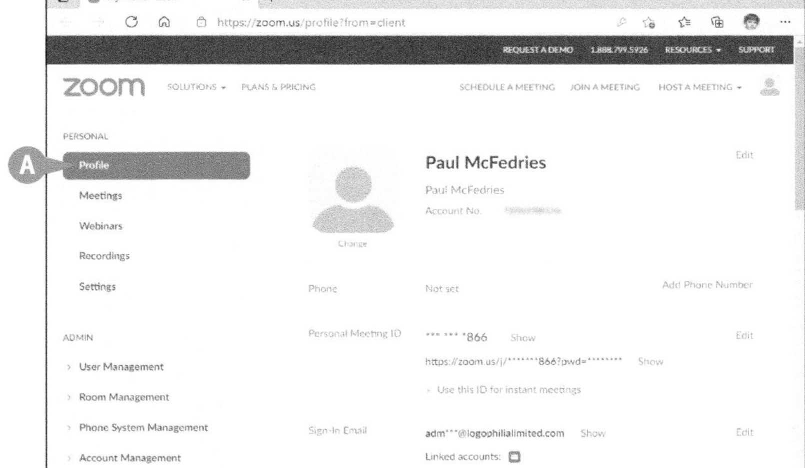

TIP

Is there a more direct way to access my profile?

Yes. If you're already working in your web browser, you can access your profile directly by navigating to https://zoom.us/profile.

If you're already signed in to and working in the https://zoom.us website, you can get to your profile settings by clicking your user account icon, selecting your name, and then selecting the **Profile** tab.

Change Your Profile Picture

You can make your Zoom profile more personable and more business-like by changing your profile picture. Other Zoom users see your profile picture in various places within the Zoom interface. By default, Zoom uses a generic head-and-shoulders icon as the profile picture for all new accounts. That icon makes your Zoom profile look incomplete, so as soon as possible after creating your account you should change the default icon to a picture of yourself that you are comfortable sharing with other Zoom users.

Change Your Profile Picture

1. Open your Profile page on the Zoom website.

Note: See the previous section, "Access Your Zoom Profile," to learn how to open your Profile page.

2. Below the default profile icon, click **Change**.

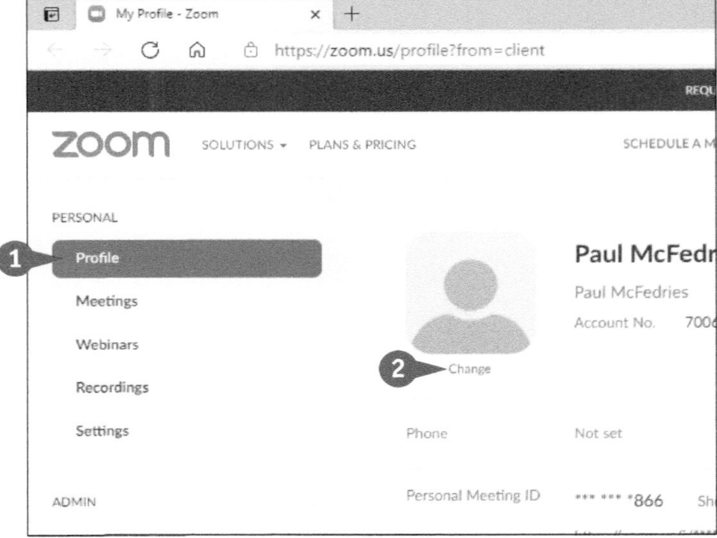

The Change Picture window appears.

3. Click **Upload**.

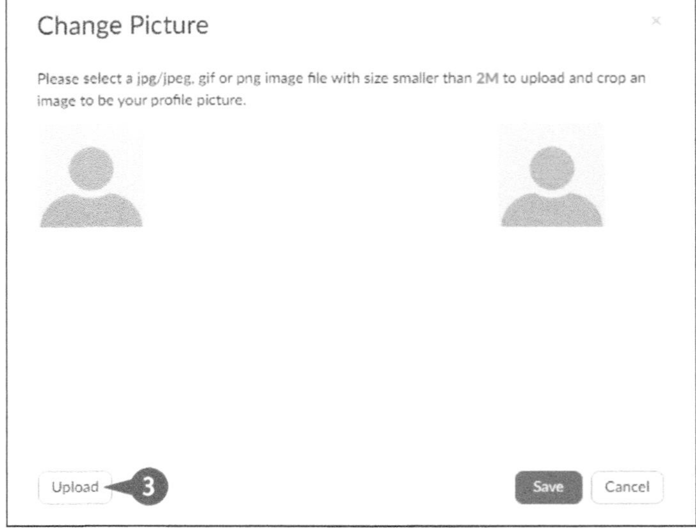

The Open dialog appears.

4 Open the folder that contains the image you want to use.

5 Select the image.

6 Click **Open**.

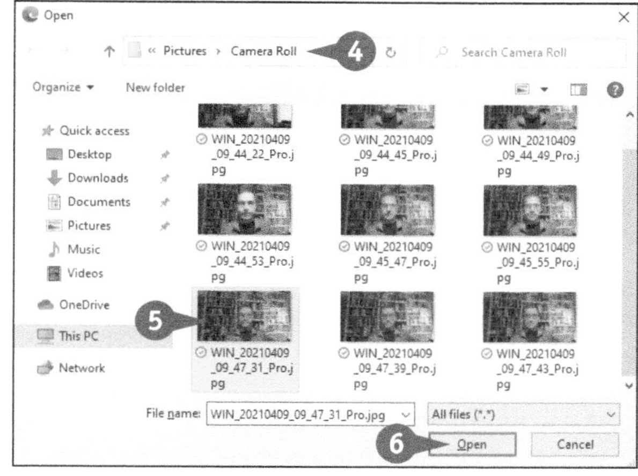

A The image appears in the Change Picture window.

B The area within the dashed line will be used as your profile picture.

C This area shows a preview of the cropped image.

7 Move and/or resize the cropping area as needed.

8 Click **Save**.

Zoom uses the image as your profile picture.

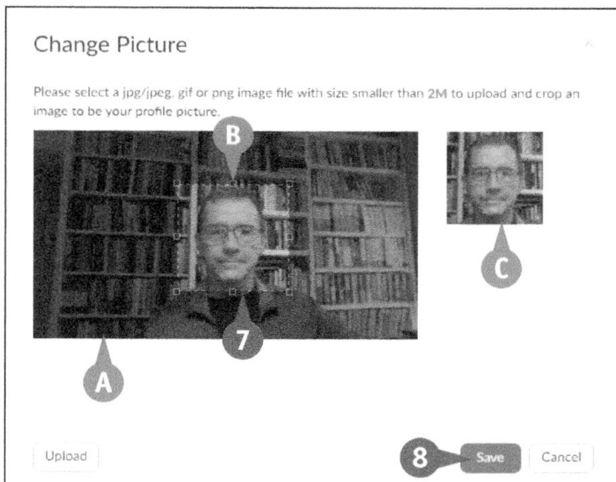

TIP

Can I change my profile using the Zoom mobile app instead of the website?

Yes, by following these steps:

1 Open the My Profile screen in the Zoom mobile app. (See the previous section, "Access Your Zoom Profile," to learn how to open the My Profile screen.)

2 Tap **Profile Photo**.

3 Select how you want to specify your new profile picture:

- **Take Photo** (Android) or **Camera** (iOS): Tap this command and then use your mobile device camera to take your photo.
- **Choose Photo** (Android) or **Select from Photo Album** (iOS): Tap this command and then select an existing photo.

Change Your Email Address

By default, the email address used in your Zoom profile is the same email address that you specified when you first signed up for a Zoom account. However, you are free to update your Zoom profile with a different email address if you prefer.

Note that you must have access to the messages sent to the new email address you want to use. Zoom sends a confirmation email to the new address, and you cannot use the new address until you open that message and confirm the change.

Change Your Email Address

1. Open your Profile page on the Zoom website.

Note: See the section "Access Your Zoom Profile" earlier in this chapter to learn how to open your Profile page.

2. To the right of your current email address, click **Edit**.

3. Type the email address you prefer to use.

4. Type your Zoom account password.

5. Click **I'm not a robot** (☐ changes to ☑).

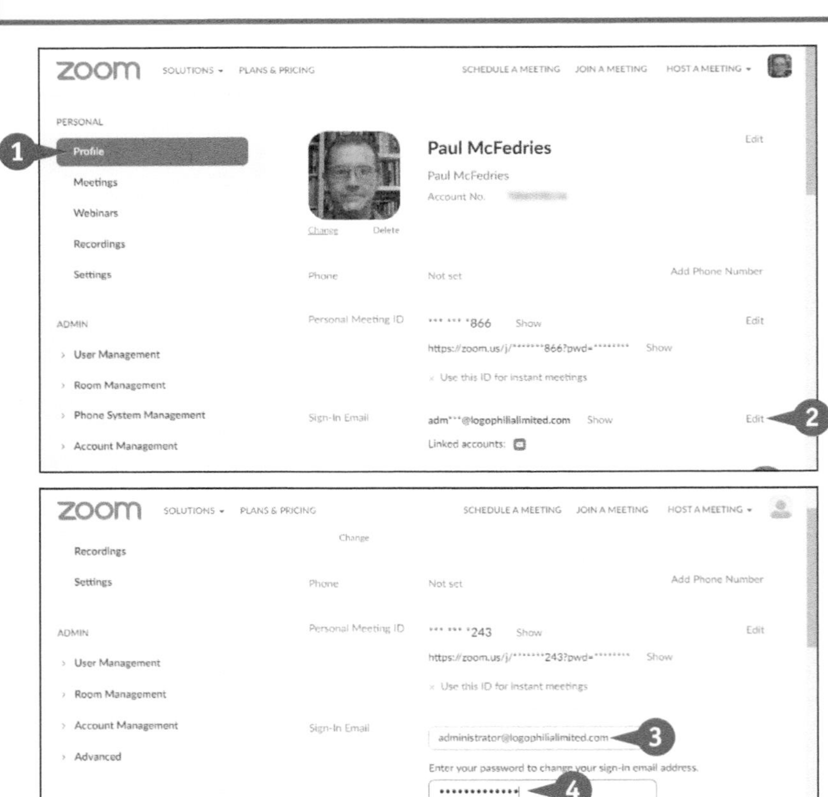

The reCAPTCHA window appears.

6 Click the requested items.

7 Click **Verify**.

Note: You might have to repeat step 6 (and click **Next**) multiple times before you see the Verify button.

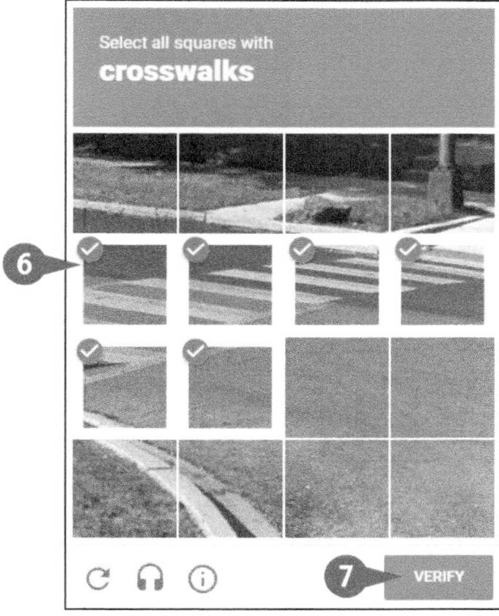

8 Click **Save Changes**.

Zoom sends a confirmation email to the address you specified in step 3.

9 Open the confirmation email and then click **Confirm Change** (not shown).

Zoom updates your profile with your new email address.

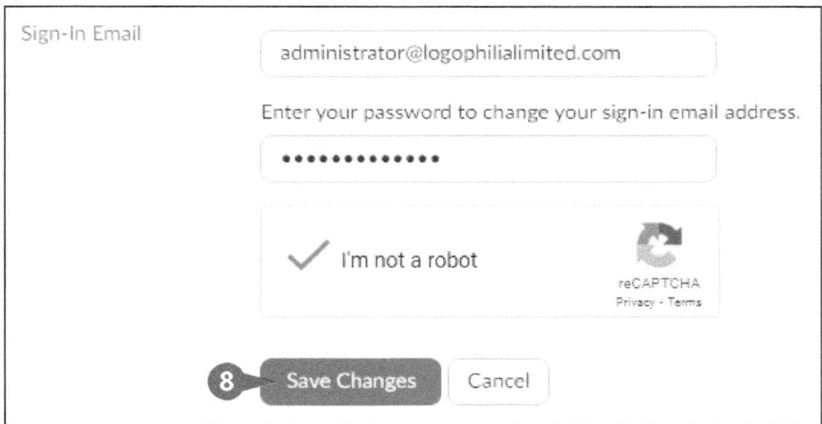

TIPS

I changed my email address, but now I'm having trouble signing in to my Zoom account. Why?

Your email address acts as your Zoom account username. Therefore, after you confirm your new email address, you must use that email address from that point on when you sign in to your Zoom account.

Why do some of the characters in my email address appear as asterisks?

This is a security precaution. Since your profile email address is also your Zoom account username, an unauthorized user who knows that address would only need to guess your password to access your account. By displaying some of the address as asterisks, a malicious user who surreptitiously glances at your profile will not see your full address.

Configure Date and Time Settings

You can modify several Zoom profile settings related to dates and times. Dates and times are important in Zoom because most meetings are scheduled for a particular date and time and some meeting features — such as recordings — rely on the date and time. For these reasons and more, it is vital that your Zoom profile be configured to accurately reflect your date and time preferences. In particular, it is important that your Zoom profile be set to the time zone where you live or work.

Configure Date and Time Settings

1. Open your Profile page on the Zoom website (not shown).

Note: See the section "Access Your Zoom Profile" earlier in this chapter to learn how to open your Profile page.

2. In the Date and Time section, click **Edit**.

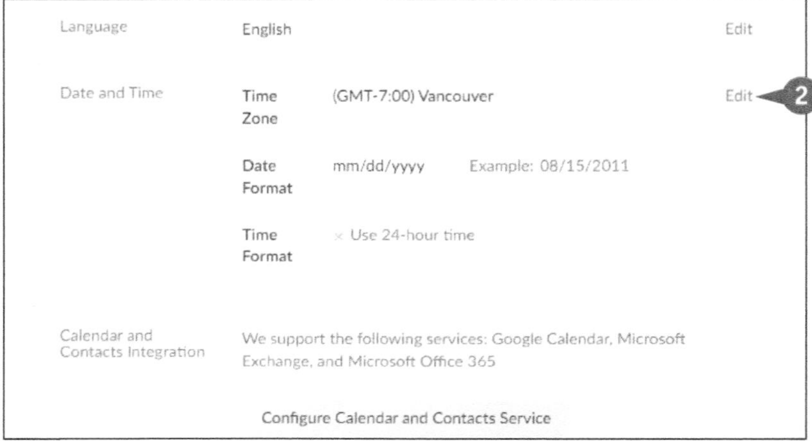

Zoom opens the Date and Time settings for editing.

3. Click the **Time Zone** ⌄.
4. Click the time zone where you live or work.

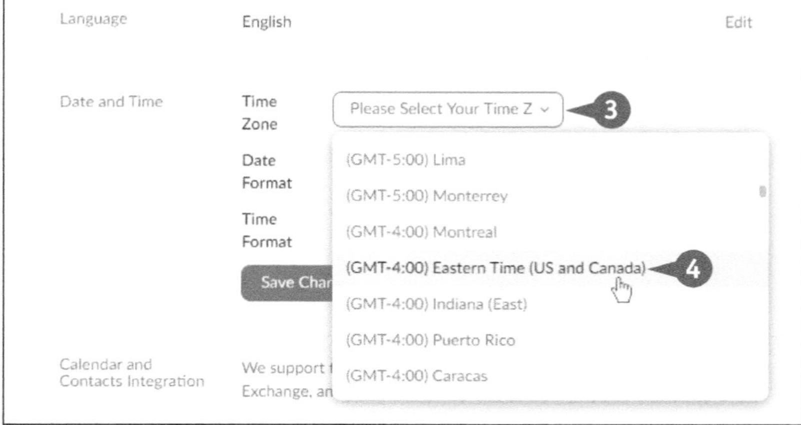

5 Click the **Date Format** ⌄.

6 Click the date format you want to use.

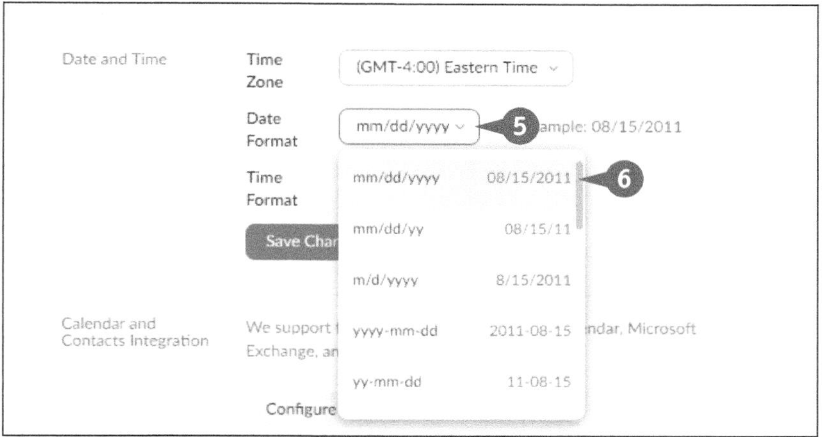

7 If you prefer to use the 24-hour time format, click **Use 24-hour time** (☐ changes to ☑).

Note: If you use 24-hour time, then the time 3:30 PM, for example, is displayed as 15:30 PM.

8 Click **Save Changes**.

Zoom saves your new date and time settings.

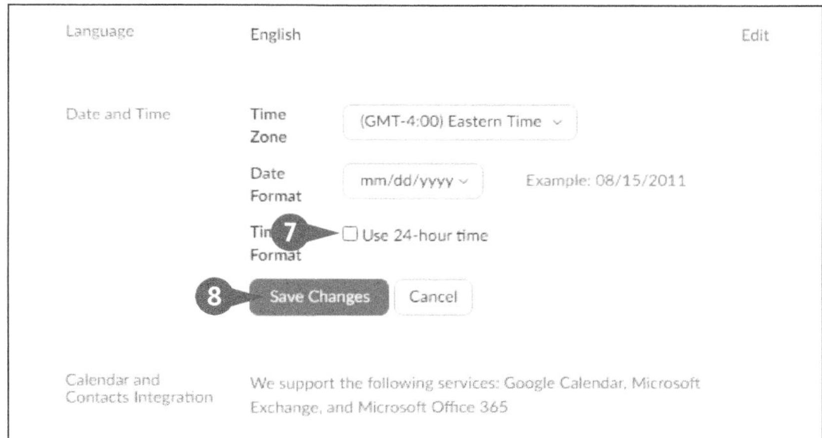

TIP

How do date formats work?

A date format is three sets of letters, separated by a slash (/) or period (.). One set specifies the day of the month using either *d* or *dd* (the latter adds a leading zero to days that are less than 10). A second set specifies the month number using either *m* or *mm* (the latter adds a leading zero to months less than 10). The third set specifies the year using either *yy* (just the last two digits of the year) or *yyyy* (all four digits of the year). For example, if the date is August 3, 2022, then the format *mm/dd/yyyy* displays the date as 08/03/2022, while the format *d.m.yy* displays the date as 3.8.22.

Configure Scheduled Meeting Settings

You can make it easier and faster to schedule Zoom meetings by configuring a few settings related to scheduled meetings. Many meeting hosts find themselves repeating the same steps while creating scheduled meetings. For example, if you always want host and participant video turned on at the start of a meeting, then you need to configure those options each time you schedule a meeting. It is much easier to configure your preferred options in your profile settings and then have Zoom automatically apply those settings each time you schedule a meeting.

Configure Scheduled Meeting Settings

1. Open your Profile page on the Zoom website (not shown).

Note: See the section "Access Your Zoom Profile" earlier in this chapter to learn how to open your Profile page.

2. Click **Settings**.
3. Click **Meeting**.

   Zoom displays the settings related to meetings.

4. Scroll down to the Schedule Meeting section.
5. If you want your host video on automatically when you start a scheduled meeting, click the **Host video** switch to On (◐).
6. If you want participants' video on automatically when you start a scheduled meeting, click the **Participants video** switch to On (◐).

A. Each time you modify a setting, Zoom lets you know your settings have been updated.

B. Zoom also adds the text *Modified* beside each setting you have changed.

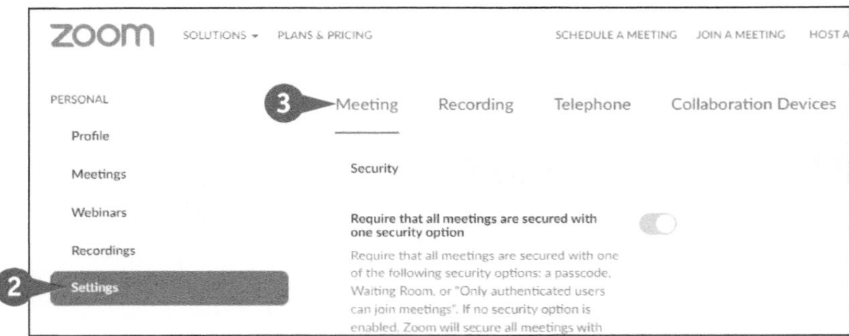

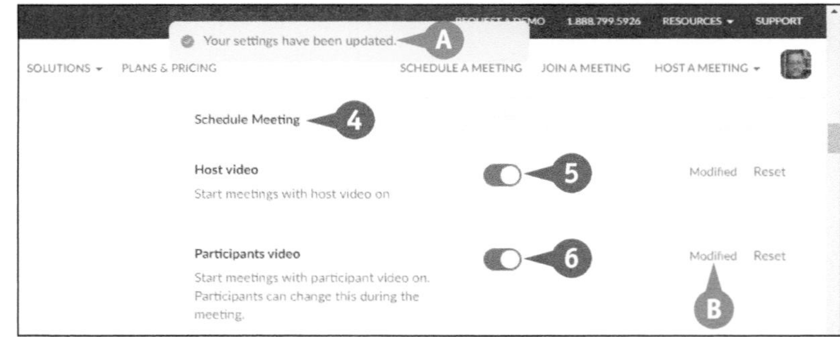

7 For the **Audio Type** setting, click the radio button that represents your preferred audio option for participants (◯ changes to ◉).

8 If you want participants to be able to join the meeting without waiting for the host, click the **Allow participants to join before host** switch to On (◐).

9 To restrict how soon participants can join, click **Participants can join** (☐ changes to ☑) and then click ⌄ to choose a time.

10 Click **Save**.

11 To automatically schedule meetings using your Personal Meeting ID, click the **Use Personal Meeting ID (PMI) when scheduling a meeting** switch to On (◐).

12 To automatically create instant meetings using your Personal Meeting ID, click the **Use Personal Meeting ID (PMI) when starting an instant meeting** switch to On (◐).

13 To automatically mute attendees, click the **Mute all participants when they join a meeting** switch to On (◐).

Your modified settings are now in effect, and Zoom applies them the next time you schedule a meeting.

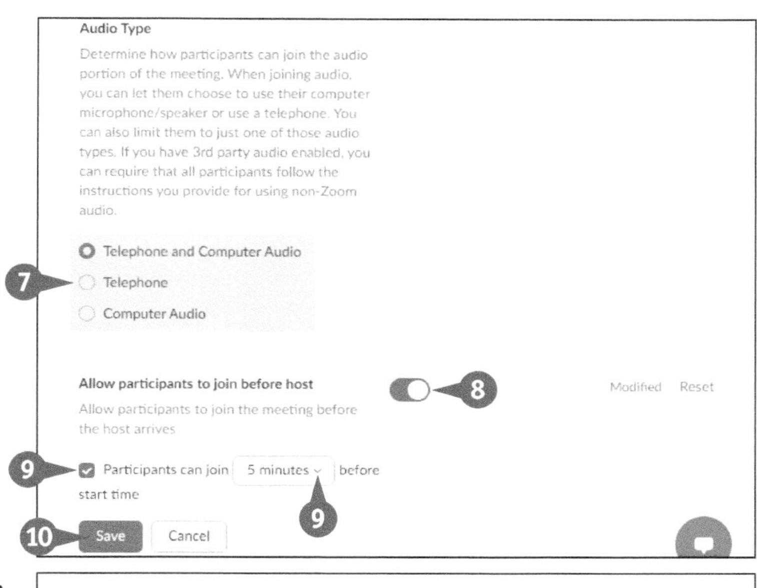

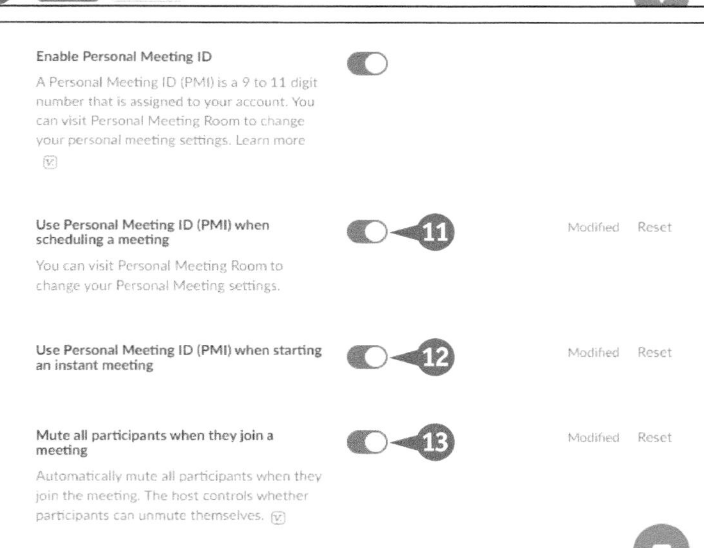

TIPS

Can I turn off the desktop notifications that remind me a scheduled meeting is about to start?

Yes. Follow steps 1 to 4 to display the Schedule Meeting section of the Settings tab. Scroll down to the end of that section and then click the **Upcoming meeting reminder** switch to Off (◑).

I do not use my Personal Meeting ID at all. Can I disable it?

Yes. In the Schedule Meeting section of the Settings tab, click the **Enable Personal Meeting ID** switch to Off (◑). When Zoom asks you to confirm, click **I understand this change will impact PMI meetings immediately** (☐ changes to ☑) and then click **Disable**.

Change Basic Meeting Settings

You can create Zoom meetings more easily and quickly by modifying some basic settings related to both scheduled and instant meetings. For example, if you always turn off chat when creating a meeting, you can configure Zoom to do that for you automatically. There are also settings you can configure related to displaying controls for nonverbal feedback, allowing participants to rename themselves, and hiding participants' profile pictures.

Change Basic Meeting Settings

1. Open your Profile page on the Zoom website (not shown).

Note: See the section "Access Your Zoom Profile" earlier in this chapter to learn how to open your Profile page.

2. Click **Settings**.
3. Click **Meeting**.

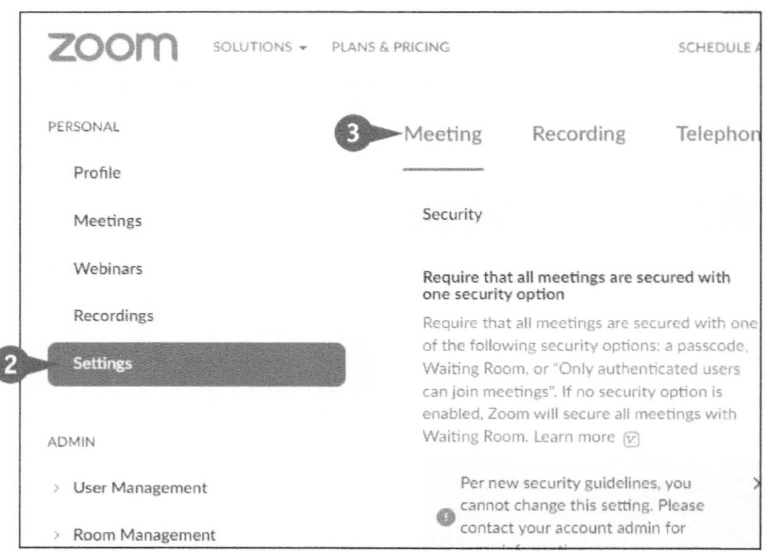

Zoom displays the settings related to meetings.

4. Scroll down to the In Meeting (Basic) section.
5. If you want to prevent meeting participants from chat, click the **Chat** switch to Off (⊂●).

Zoom reminds you that disabling the Chat setting also affects other settings.

6. Click **Disable**.

Zoom disables chat and its related settings.

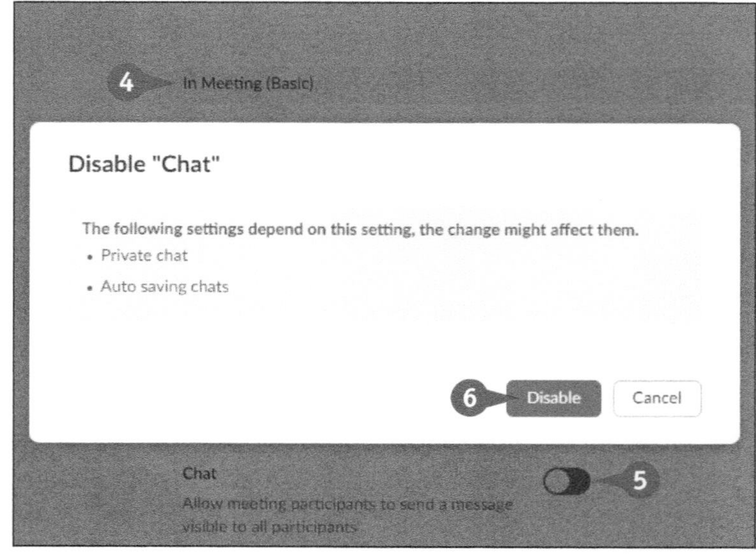

7 To enable attendees to access four extra nonverbal reactions during your meetings, click the **Non-verbal feedback** switch to On.

Note: When the Non-verbal feedback setting is enabled, the meeting Reaction menu displays four new icons: Yes, No, Slow Down, and Speed Up.

Non-verbal feedback
Allow meeting participants to communicate without interrupting by clicking on icons (yes, no, slow down, speed up). These icons are found in the Reactions menu in the toolbar, and when selected, they display on the participant's video and in the participants list until dismissed.
7 Modified Reset

Allow participants to rename themselves
Allow meeting participants and webinar panelists to rename themselves.
8 Modified Reset

Hide participant profile pictures in a meeting
All participant profile pictures will be hidden and only the names of participants will be displayed on the video screen. Participants will not be able to update their profile pictures in the meeting.
9 Modified Reset

8 If you want to prevent meeting participants from changing their display names, click the **Allow participants to rename themselves** switch to Off.

9 If you do not want to see the profile images of nonvideo attendees, click the **Hide participant profile pictures in a meeting** switch to On.

Note: If you hide the profile images of nonvideo participants, you see each person's display name instead.

Your modified settings are now in effect, and Zoom applies them the next time you create a meeting.

TIPS

Is there a way to configure my meetings to automatically disable all nonverbal feedback?
Yes. In the In Meeting (Basic) section, besides leaving the Non-verbal feedback switch Off, you can also click the **Meeting reactions** switch to Off. Modifying this setting completely removes the Reactions menu from the meeting toolbar.

Is there a way to configure my meetings to ask participants for feedback at the end of each meeting?
Yes. In the In Meeting (Basic) section, click the **Display end-of-meeting experience feedback survey** switch to On. By default, Zoom displays the survey at the end of every meeting. If you want the survey to appear only every now and then, click **Display for meetings randomly** (○ changes to ◉).

Change Advanced Meeting Settings

You can gain extra control of your instant and scheduled Zoom meetings by modifying a few advanced meeting settings. Zoom's advanced meeting settings are generally very technical or are needed only in rare situations. However, you might find a few advanced settings useful. For example, you can configure remote support sessions, enabling you to provide one-to-one support by controlling a user's computer. You can also disable participants' video filters and enable attendees to join your meetings using a web browser instead of the Zoom app.

Change Advanced Meeting Settings

1. Open your Profile page on the Zoom website (not shown).

Note: See the section "Access Your Zoom Profile" earlier in this chapter to learn how to open your Profile page.

2. Click **Settings.**
3. Click **Meeting.**

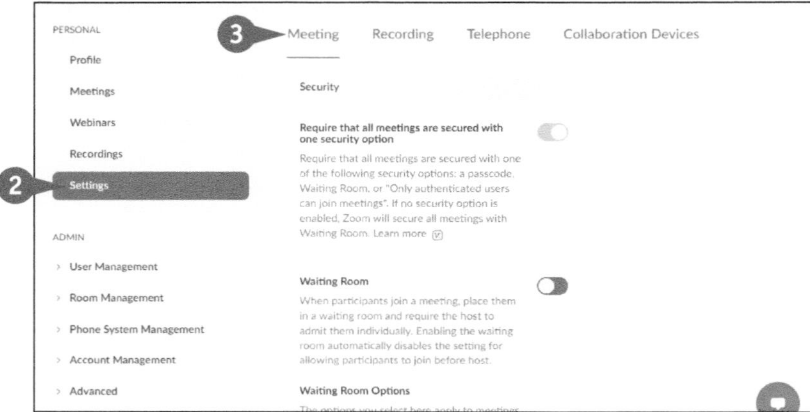

Zoom displays the settings related to meetings.

4. Scroll down to the In Meeting (Advanced) section.
5. If you want to be able to start a remote support session with a meeting participant, click the **Remote support** switch to On (◐).
6. To enable closed captions in your meetings, click the **Closed captioning** switch to On (◐).

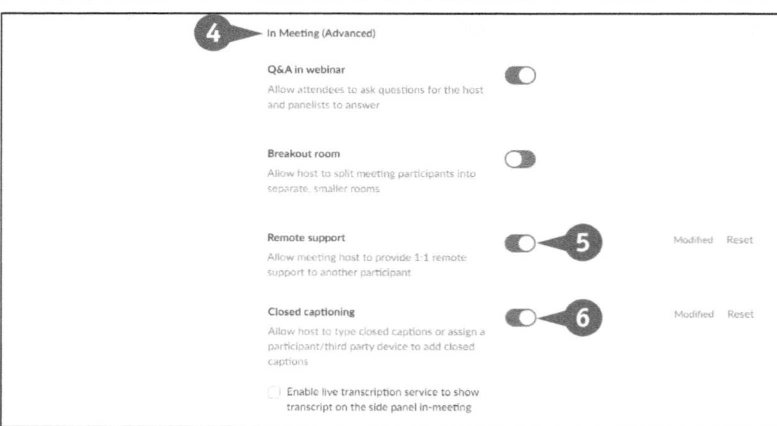

7 If you do not want meeting participants to apply filters to their video feeds, click the **Video filters** switch to Off ().

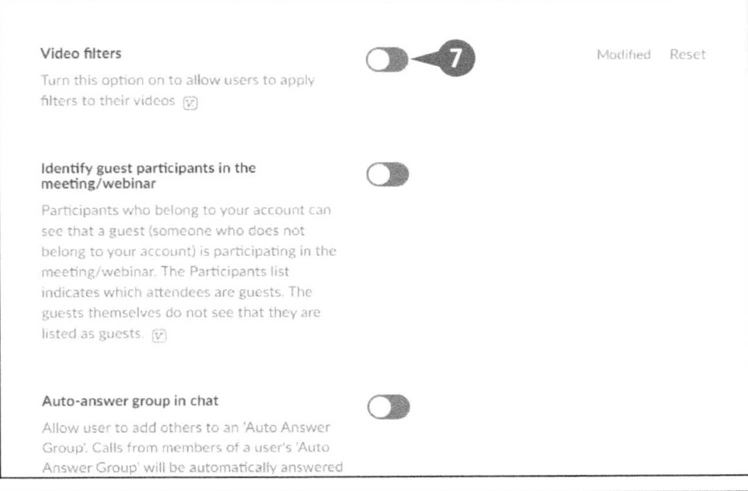

8 To enable participants who do not have the Zoom app to attend the meeting using their web browser, click the **Show a "Join from your browser" link** switch to On ().

9 To enable users who do not have the Zoom app to set the web browser as the default for meetings, click the **Show "Always Join from Browser" option when joining from join.zoom.us** to On ().

Your modified settings are now in effect, and Zoom applies them the next time you create a meeting.

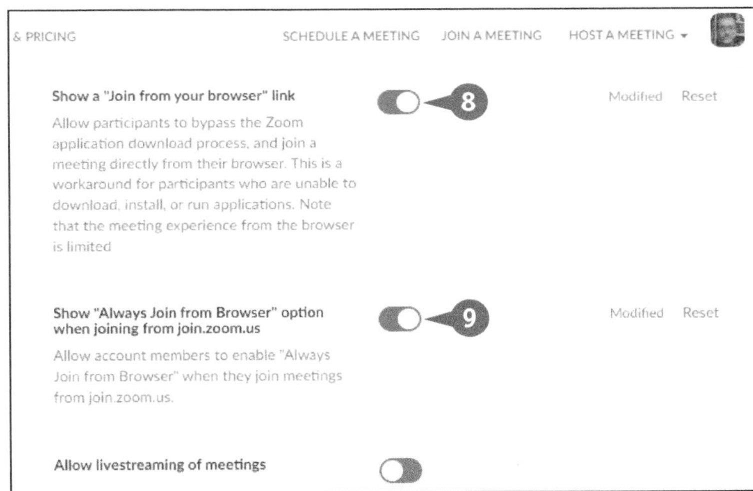

TIPS

What is a remote support session?
Remote support is a feature that enables a meeting host to request control of a meeting participant's computer. When the Remote Support setting is On, the meeting host sees a Support icon in the meeting toolbar. Clicking **Support** displays a menu that enables the host to request permission to control the desktop, control a specific application, or restart the participant's computer.

Is it possible to configure livestreaming for meetings?
Yes. You ordinarily only use livestreaming for webinars, but if you want to livestream a regular meeting, click the **Allow livestreaming of meetings** switch to On (). Then select the check box beside each livestreaming service you want to use (☐ changes to ☑).

Control Email Notifications

You can make Zoom more efficient and your email app less cluttered by configuring Zoom's meeting-related email notifications. By default, Zoom sends you an email notification for many different scenarios. These scenarios include when a cloud recording is available, when attendees join a meeting you are hosting before you do, when a meeting is canceled, and when an alternative host is added or removed during a meeting. You might find some of these notifications useful, but you can disable those notifications that you find unnecessary.

Control Email Notifications

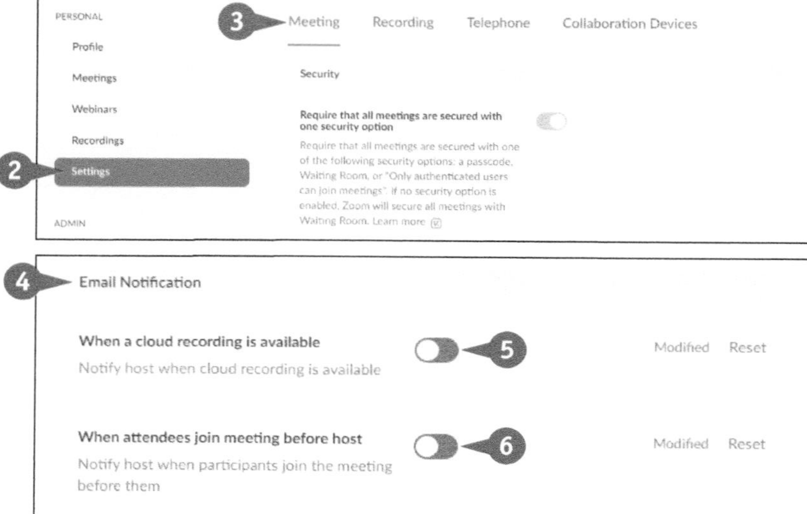

1. Open your Profile page on the Zoom website (not shown).

Note: See the section "Access Your Zoom Profile" earlier in this chapter to learn how to open your Profile page.

2. Click **Settings.**
3. Click **Meeting.**

   Zoom displays the settings related to meetings.

4. Scroll down to the Email Notification section.
5. If you do not want to be notified when a cloud recording of a meeting you hosted is ready, click the **When a cloud recording is available** switch to Off ( ).
6. If you do not want to be notified when participants join a meeting you are hosting before you do, click the **When attendees join meeting before host** switch to Off ( ).

Note: See the section "Configure Scheduled Meeting Settings" earlier in this chapter to learn how to configure scheduled meetings to enable attendees to join before the host.

7 If you do not want to be notified when a meeting is canceled, click the **When a meeting is cancelled** switch to Off (◯).

8 If you do not want a notification sent when someone is added or removed as a meeting's alternative host, click the **When an alternative host is set or removed from a meeting** switch to Off (◯).

9 If you do not want a notification sent when another person schedules a meeting with you as the host, click the **When someone scheduled a meeting for a host** switch to Off (◯).

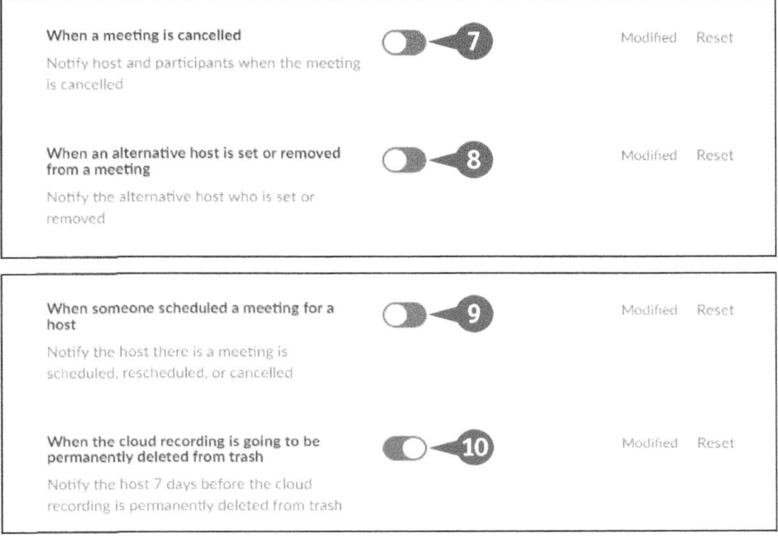

10 If you want to be notified a week before a cloud recording is scheduled to be permanently deleted, click the **When the cloud recording is going to be permanently deleted from trash** switch to On (◯).

Your modified settings are now in effect, and Zoom applies them the next time you create a meeting.

TIP

What does it mean for a cloud recording to be permanently deleted?

As described in the section "Delete a Recording" in Chapter 7, when you delete a cloud recording, Zoom actually moves the recording to the Trash folder. If you discover that you deleted the recording accidentally, you can recover it from the Trash folder.

However, if the recording stays in the Trash folder for 30 days, Zoom permanently deletes the recording by removing it from the Trash folder. This means you can no longer recover the recording.

Make Zoom Accessible

If you have visual or auditory challenges, you can configure several settings that make Zoom easier to use and more accessible. For example, if you have hearing issues, you not only can turn on closed captions (see the section "Change Advanced Meeting Settings" earlier in this chapter) but also can configure the font size of the captions. You can also set the size of the text that Zoom displays in chat windows. If you use Zoom with a screen reader, you can also configure which Zoom alerts the screen reader reads aloud.

Make Zoom Accessible

1. In the Zoom desktop app, click your profile picture.
2. Click **Settings**.

   The Settings window appears.

3. Click **Accessibility**.

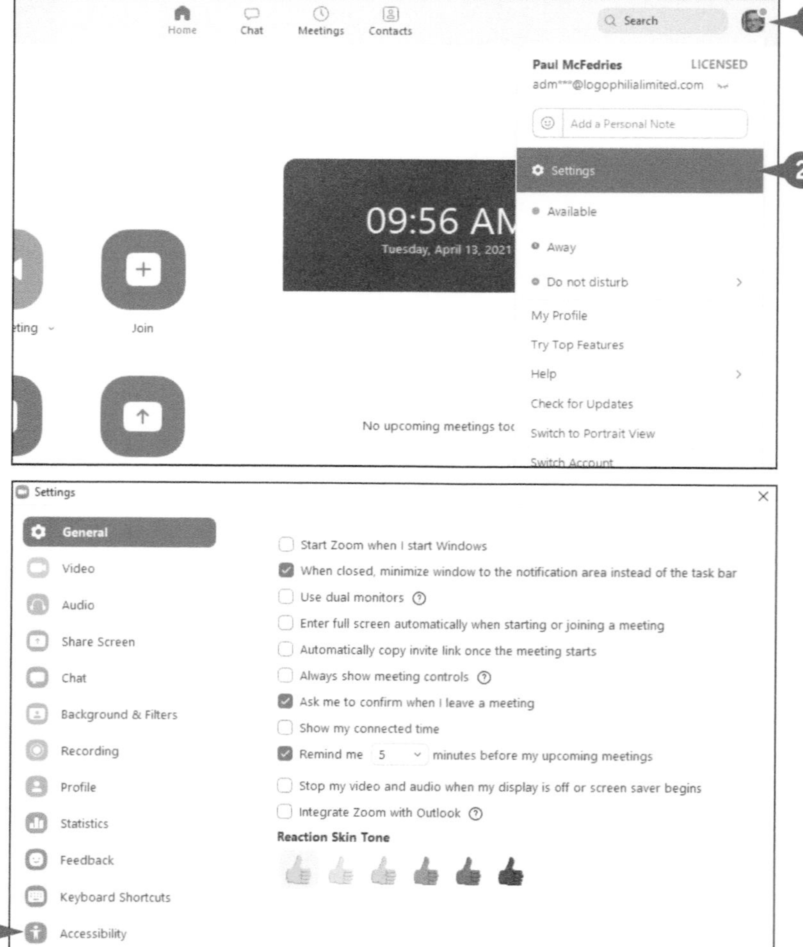

The Accessibility settings appear.

4 In the Closed Caption section, drag the **Font Size** slider (●) to set the size of the caption text.

A This sample text shows a preview of the closed caption font size.

5 Click the **Chat Display Size** ⌄ and then click the percentage increase (greater than 100 percent) or decrease (less than 100 percent) you want to apply to chat text.

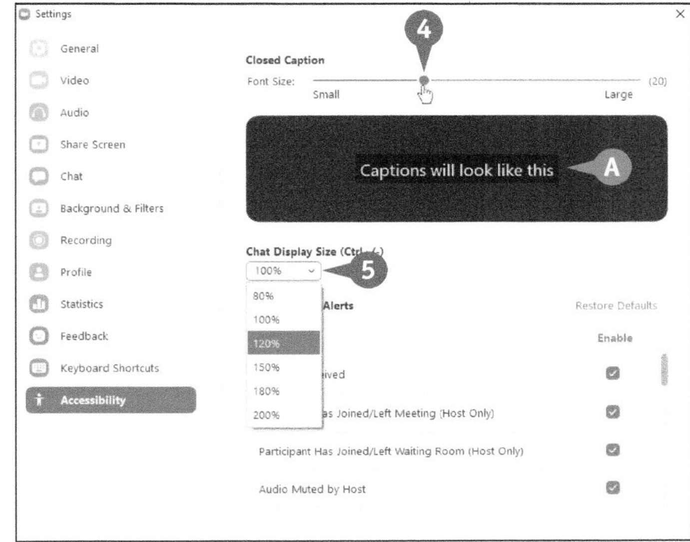

6 If you use a screen reader, use the check boxes in the **Screen Reader Alerts** list to choose which alerts you do not want to hear (☑ changes to ☐).

7 Click **Close** (☒).

Zoom puts your new accessibility settings into effect.

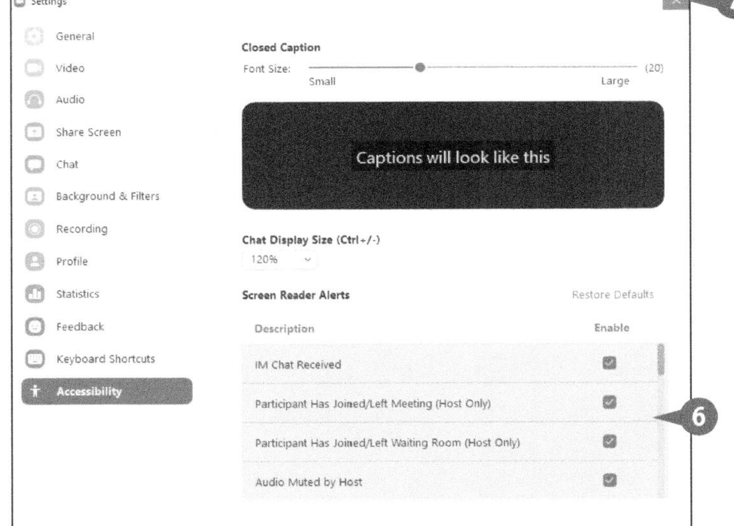

TIP

Can I control the Zoom desktop app from the keyboard?

Yes. The Zoom app supports dozens of keyboard shortcuts, which can be useful if you find it difficult to use a mouse or trackpad. For example, there are keyboard shortcuts for switching the view, starting and stopping video, and muting and unmuting audio. The specific shortcuts depend on whether you are using Windows or a Mac.

To see the shortcuts, start the Zoom app, select your profile picture, select **Settings**, and then select **Keyboard Shortcuts**. To use a different key or key combination, click the existing shortcut key to open it for editing and then press the key or key combination you want to use.

Set Meeting Options at the Account and Group Levels

If you manage users or groups on your account (see Chapter 10), you can more easily apply meeting options across multiple users by working at the account and group levels. The previous sections in this chapter set meeting options at the user level. If you are the only person on your Zoom account, then user-level options are all you require. However, if you administer users on your account, setting meeting options for individual users is time-consuming. It is more efficient to set your preferred meeting options at either the account level for all users or at the group level for just that group's users.

Set Meeting Options at the Account and Group Levels

Set Meeting Options at the Account Level

1. Use a web browser to navigate to https://zoom.us/account/setting.

   A. Zoom displays your Account Settings page.

2. Click the **Meeting** tab.

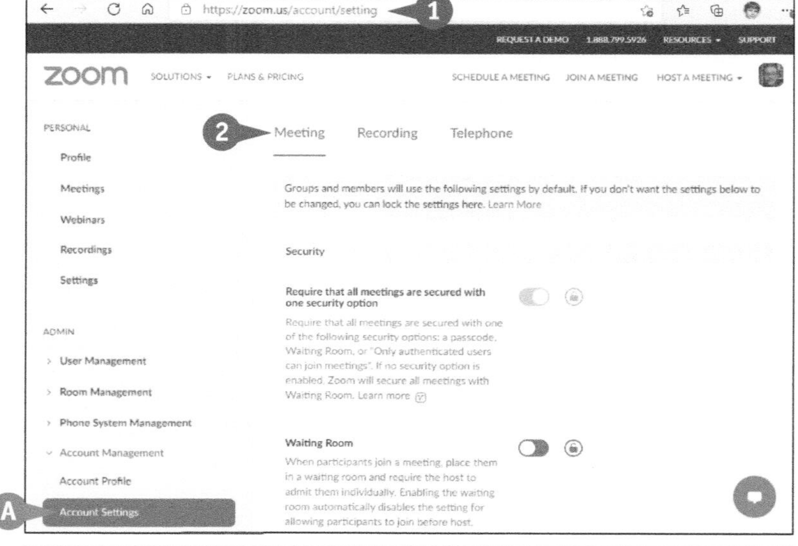

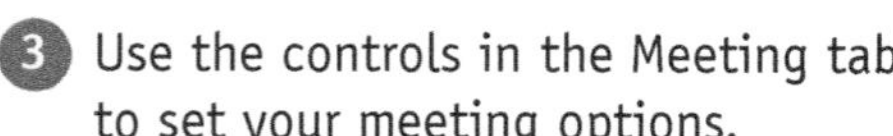

3. Use the controls in the Meeting tab to set your meeting options.

   Zoom applies the settings to all users in your Zoom account.

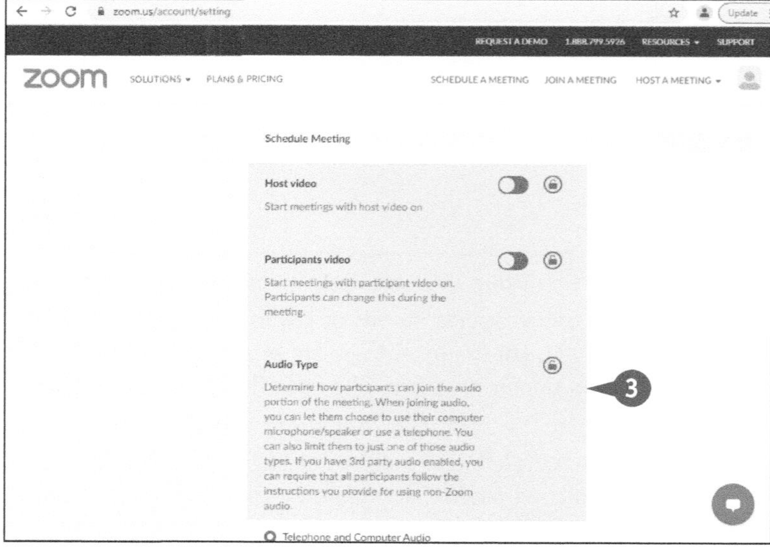

Set Meeting Options at the Group Level

1. Use a web browser to navigate to https://zoom.us/account/ (not shown).

   Zoom displays your account profile page.

Note: Make sure you sign in to Zoom using an administrator account.

2. Click **User Management.**
3. Click **Group Management.**
4. Click the group you want to modify.

   Zoom displays the group's profile page.

5. Click the **Meeting** tab (not shown).
6. Use the controls in the Meeting tab to set your meeting options.

   Zoom applies the settings to all users in the group.

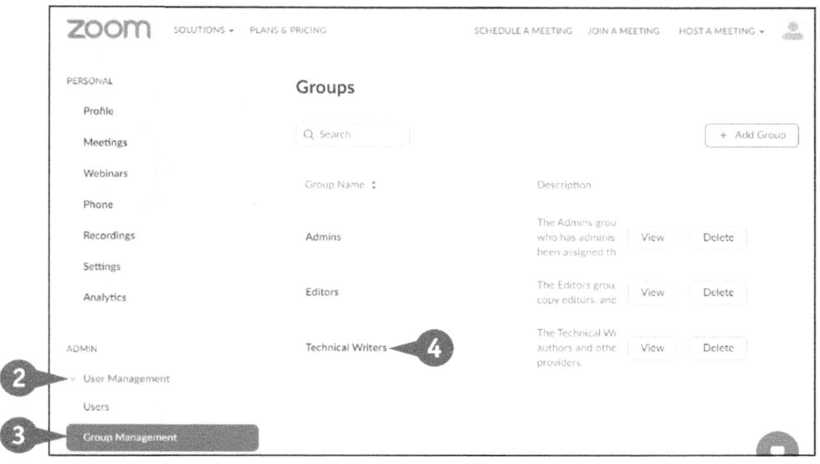

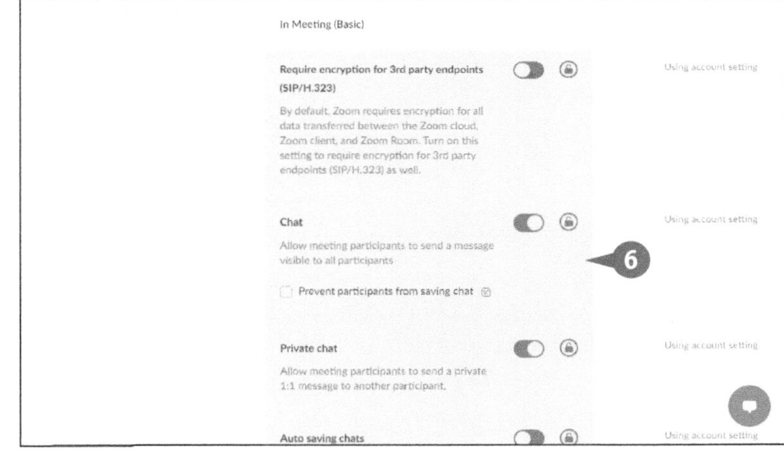

TIPS

What happens if there is a settings conflict for a user who belongs to multiple groups?
Zoom applies the settings based on two rules of precedence. First, a locked setting takes precedence over an unlocked setting (see the next Tip). Second, settings are applied based on the order in which the user was added to the groups, with earlier groups taking precedence over later groups.

Can I prevent account or group settings from being modified at the user level?
Yes, you can lock a setting to prevent changes. Each setting in the Meeting tab of either the Account Settings page or a group's Settings page has a Lock icon (🔒). To lock a setting, click its Lock icon (🔒) and then click **Lock** in the dialog that appears.

Customize Your Host Key

Your Zoom profile comes with a *host key*, which is a six-digit number that you can use to claim host controls in a meeting. You can customize your Zoom profile's host key to make it easier to remember.

The most common scenario when you might need to claim host controls is when you set up a scheduled meeting and allow attendees to join before you, as described in the section "Configure Scheduled Meeting Settings" earlier in this chapter.

Customize Your Host Key

1. Use a web browser to navigate to https://zoom.us/profile.

   Zoom displays your profile page.

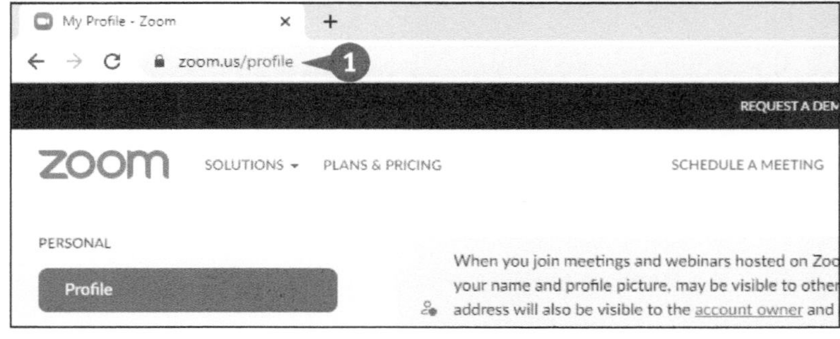

2. Scroll down to the **Host Key** setting.

   A. You can click **Show Host Key** (👁) to view your host key.

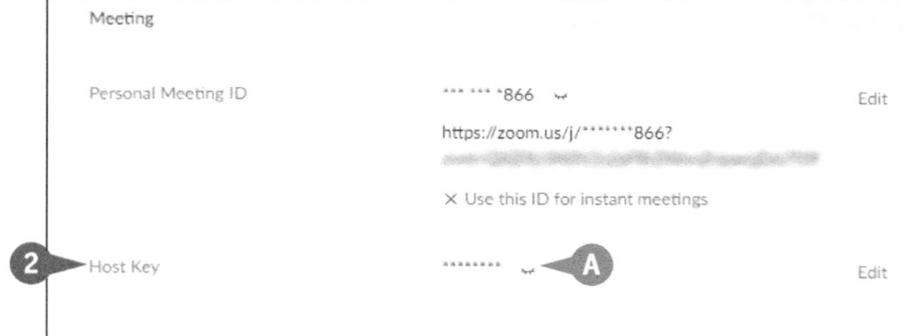

3 Click **Edit**.

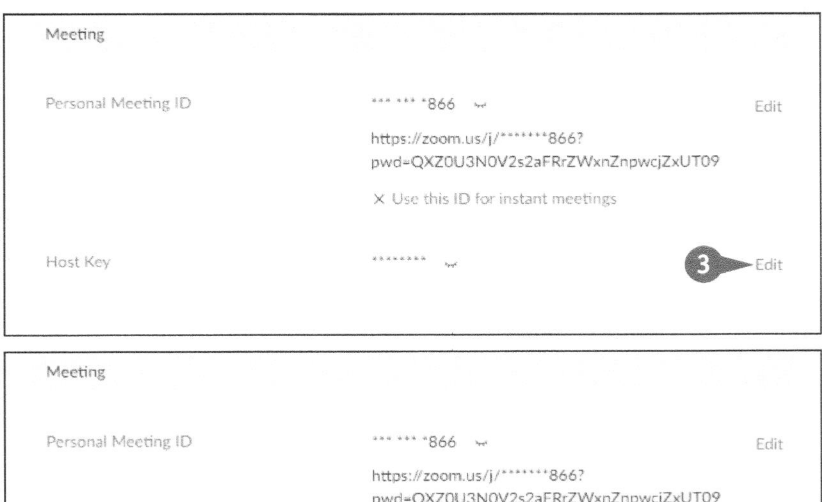

Zoom opens the host key for editing.

4 Type the host key you want to use.

Note: The host key must be a six-digit number. Zoom rejects simple host keys such as 123456 and 111111.

5 Click **Save**.

Zoom saves your new host key.

TIP

How do I use my host key to claim host controls in a meeting?

Follow these steps:

1 In the meeting controls, click **Participants** (not shown).

Zoom opens the Participants pane.

2 Click **Claim Host**.

The Claim Host dialog appears.

3 Type the six-digit host key.

4 Click **Claim Host**.

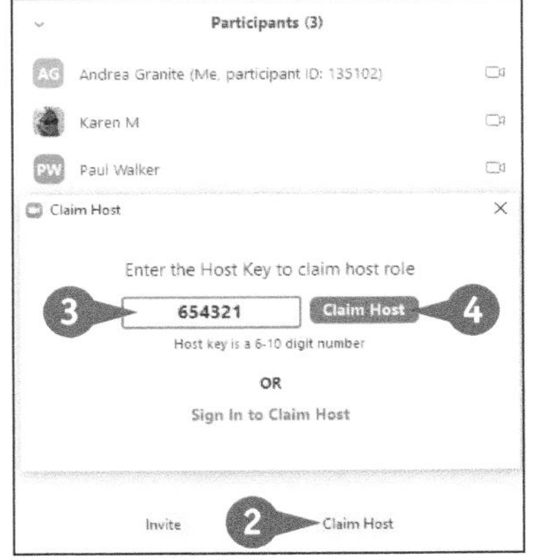

CHAPTER 9

Configuring Security

Whether you are a host or a participant, you can make your Zoom meetings safer and more private by configuring a few security options. These options include strengthening your Zoom password, adding an account authentication method, implementing a meeting waiting room, and setting security options while a meeting is in progress.

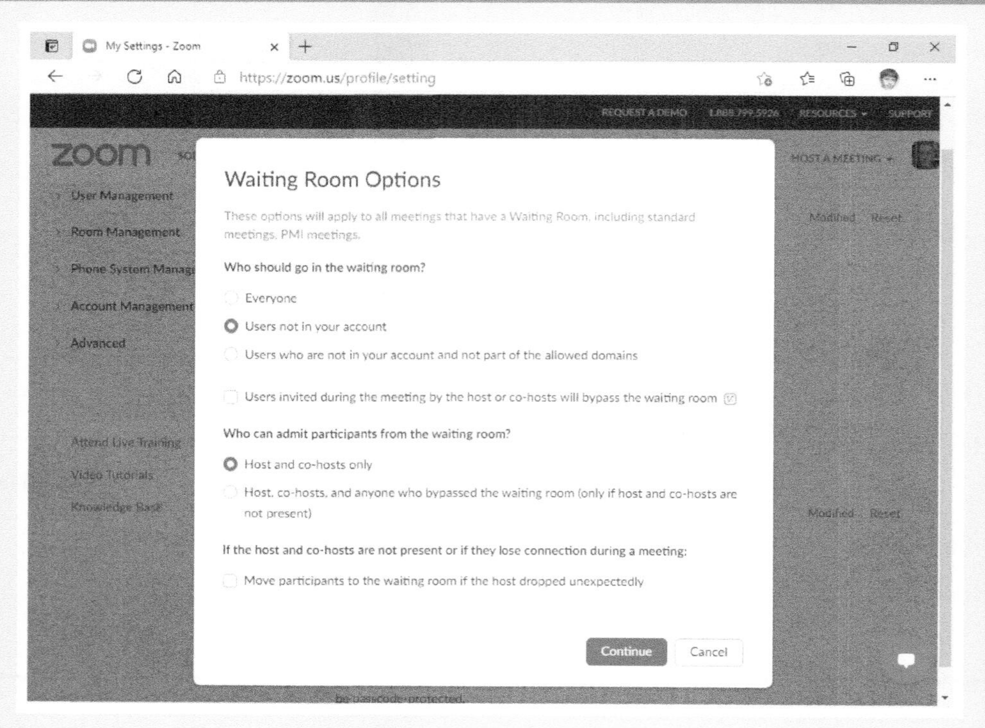

Set a Strong Password

You should assign a strong password to your Zoom account so that a malicious user cannot guess the password and gain access to the system. Your Zoom account's first line of defense is the account password. A *strong password* is one that is at least eight characters long (but is ideally at least twelve characters long) and includes characters from at least three, but ideally from all four, of the following categories: lowercase letters, uppercase letters, numbers, and symbols.

Set a Strong Password

1. Use a web browser to navigate to https://zoom.us.
2. Click **My Account**.

Note: If you are on some other page on the Zoom site, click your profile picture and then click your name.

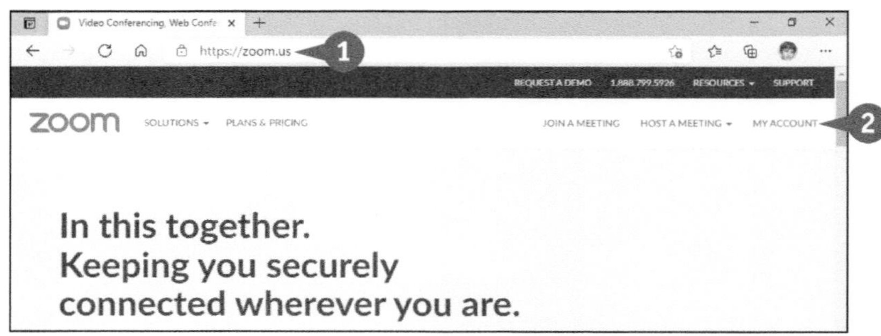

Zoom displays your Profile page.

Note: You can combine steps **1** and **2** by navigating directly to https://zoom.us/profile.

3. Click **Edit** to the right of the Sign-In Password setting.

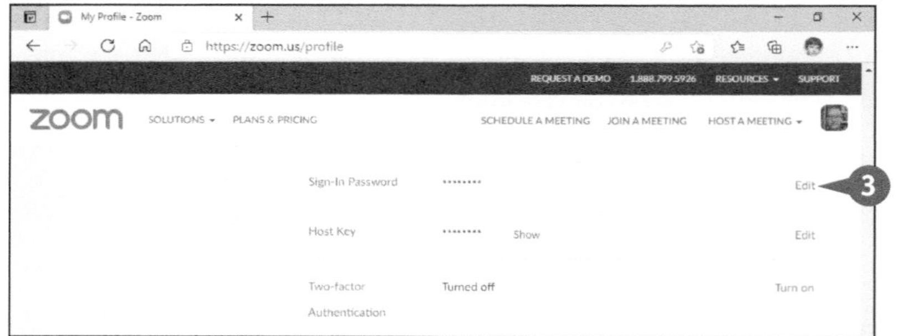

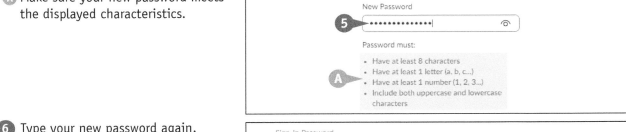

4. Type your existing Zoom password.
5. Type your new password.

A. Make sure your new password meets the displayed characteristics.

6. Type your new password again.
7. Click **Save Changes**.

Zoom updates your account password.

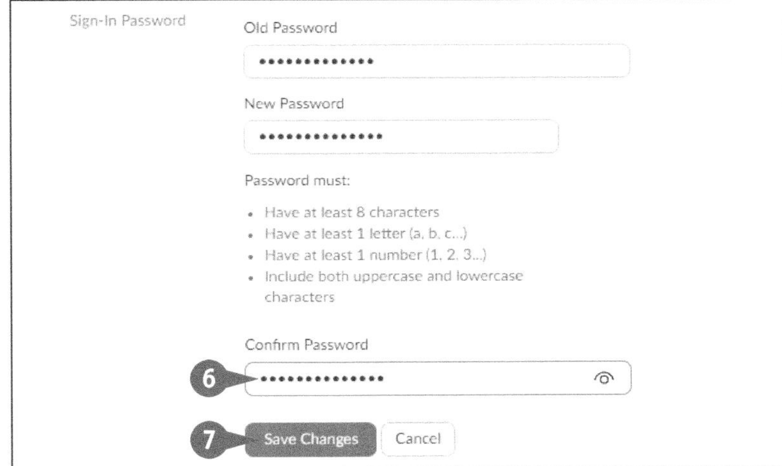

TIP

Can I change my password using the Zoom mobile app?

Yes, by following these steps:

1. Tap **Settings**.
2. Tap your name.

   The Zoom app displays the My Profile screen.
3. Tap **Update Password**.

   The Zoom app displays the Update Password screen.
4. In the Old Password text box, type your existing Zoom password.
5. In the New Password text box, type your new password.
6. In the Confirm text box, type your new password again.
7. Tap **Save**.

Enable Two-Factor Authentication

You can add an extra security layer to your Zoom account by enabling *two-factor authentication*. Also called *two-step verification*, this security feature requires you to provide two ways of verifying your identity before you can access your account. That is, when you sign in to your Zoom account, you enter your credentials as you normally do, but then Zoom also prompts you to enter a code. That code is generated by an app on your mobile device, so only you can see it. So, even if your Zoom credentials are stolen, a malicious user cannot sign in to your account.

Enable Two-Factor Authentication

Turn On Two-Factor Authentication

1. Use a web browser to navigate to https://zoom.us/profile.

   Zoom displays your Profile page.

2. Click **Turn on** to the right of the Two-Factor Authentication setting.

   The Turn On Two-Factor Authentication dialog appears.

3. Type your Zoom account password.

4. Click **Next**.

   Zoom turns on two-factor authentication for your account.

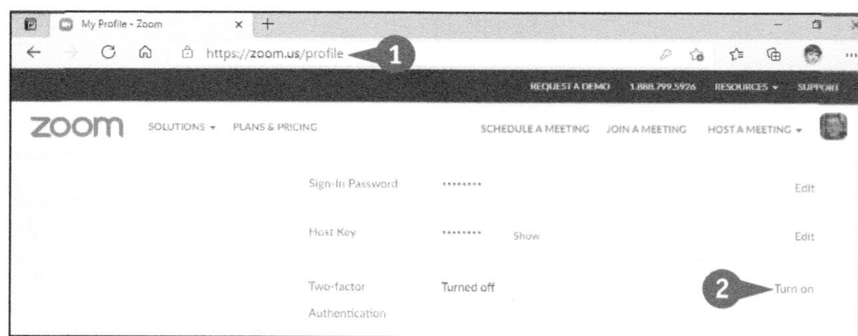

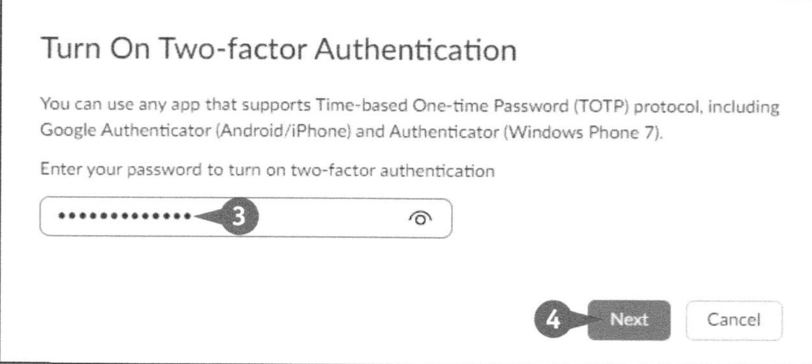

Configure an Authentication App

1 Click the **Set Up** link to the right of the Authentication App setting.

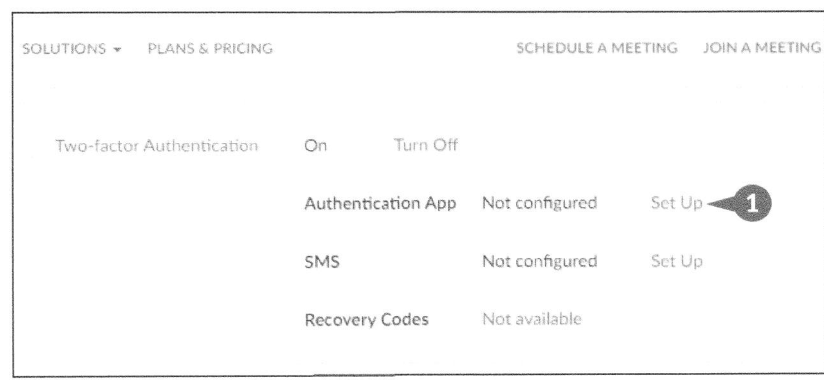

The Set Up Authentication App dialog appears.

2 Type your Zoom account password.

3 Click **Next**.

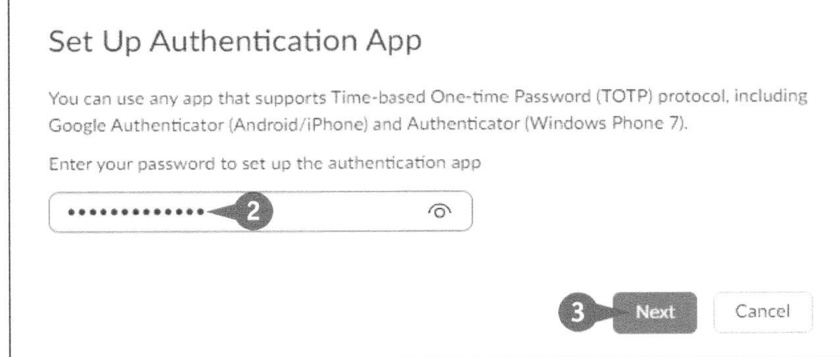

TIP

Can I authenticate my Zoom account via text message instead of an authentication app?
Yes, by following these steps:

1 Click the **Set Up** link to the right of the SMS setting.

2 Enter your Zoom password.

3 Click **Next**.

4 Enter your mobile phone number.

5 Click **Send Code**.

Zoom sends a six-digit code via text message to your phone.

6 Type the six-digit code on the SMS Authentication Setup page.

7 Click **Verify**.

Zoom enables SMS for two-factor authentication.

continued ▶

Although you can configure Zoom's two-factor authentication feature to get authentication codes via text message, almost all security experts recommend using an authentication app instead. An authentication app runs on your mobile device and generates a constantly changing six-digit code for your Zoom account. When prompted by Zoom, you enter the current six-digit code to verify your identity.

Zoom works with many authentication apps, but the free apps recommended by Zoom are Google Authenticator (available for Android and iOS), Microsoft Authenticator (available for Android, iOS, and Windows), and FreeOTP (available for Android and iOS).

Enable Two-Factor Authentication (continued)

The Authentication App Setup page appears.

4 On your mobile device, use an authentication app to scan the QR code.

After your authentication app scans the QR code, the app displays a six-digit code.

5 Click **Next**.

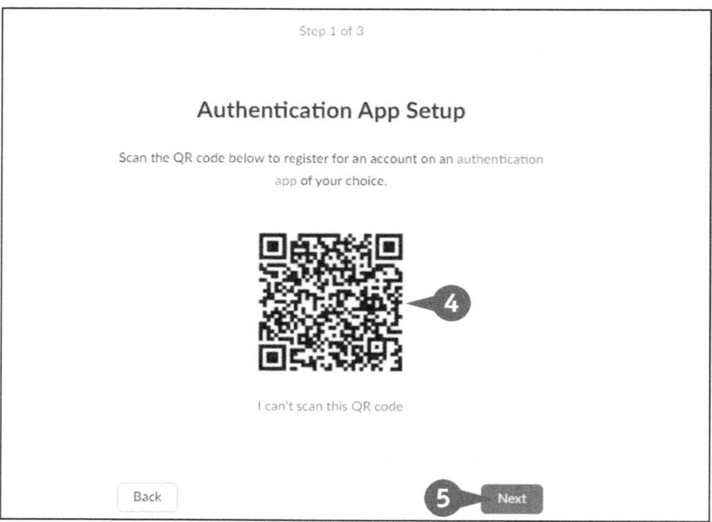

The Authentication App Setup page appears.

6 Type the six-digit code displayed by the authentication app.

Note: The authentication app changes the six-digit code frequently, so be sure you are entering the current code.

7 Click **Verify**.

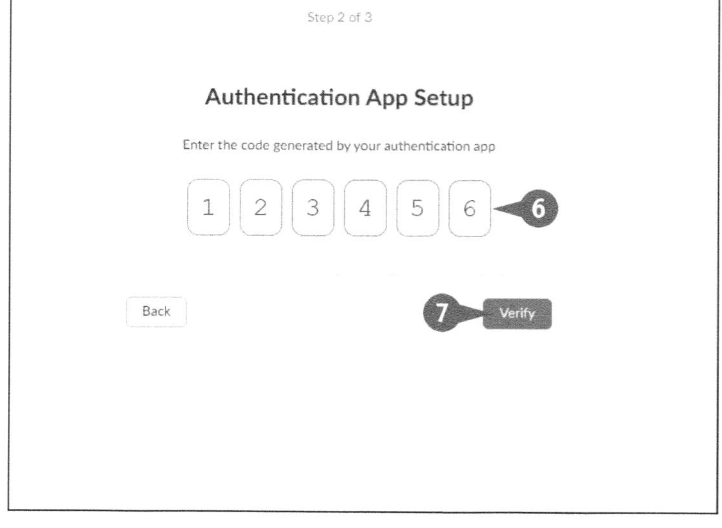

The Two-Factor Authentication Setup Complete page appears.

A Zoom displays your account's single-use recovery codes.

8 Click **Download**.

B Your web browser downloads the Backup-codes.txt file.

Note: Be sure to save this file in a safe and secure location (such as a USB thumb drive or a password-protected online folder).

C If you do not have a secure location in which to store the downloaded file, you can click **Print** to print out a copy of the codes.

9 Click **Done**.

Zoom now protects your account with two-factor authentication.

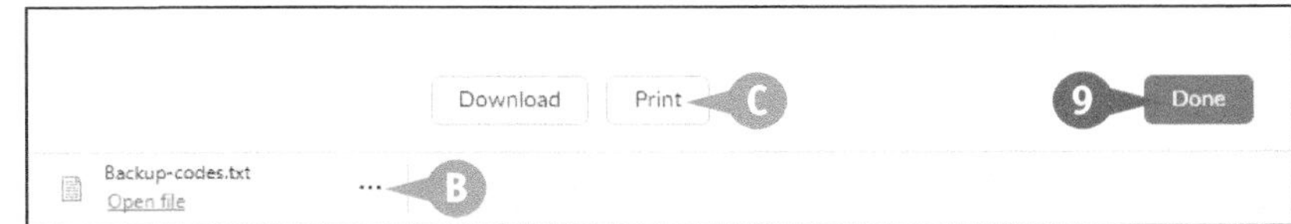

TIPS

What is a single-use recovery code?

A single-use recovery code is a backup method of verifying your identity if you cannot use two-factor authentication. For example, if you lose your mobile device or do not have it with you, you can still sign in to your Zoom account by using one of the recovery codes that you downloaded.

How do I use two-factor authentication?

Sign in to your Zoom account with your email address and password. When you click **Sign In**, you are taken to the Two-Factor Authentication page. On your mobile device, open your authentication app, locate the six-digit code for your Zoom account, enter that code in the Two-Factor Authentication page, and then click **Verify**.

Sign Out of All Devices

You can stop unauthorized use of your Zoom account by forcing all devices that are using your account to sign out. If you suspect that an unauthorized person has gained access to your Zoom account, then you need to change your Zoom password as quickly as possible. Immediately after you have changed your password, tell Zoom to sign your account out from any device that is currently using the account. That way, the unauthorized user will be forced to sign in again but will be unable to access your account because you have changed your password.

Sign Out of All Devices

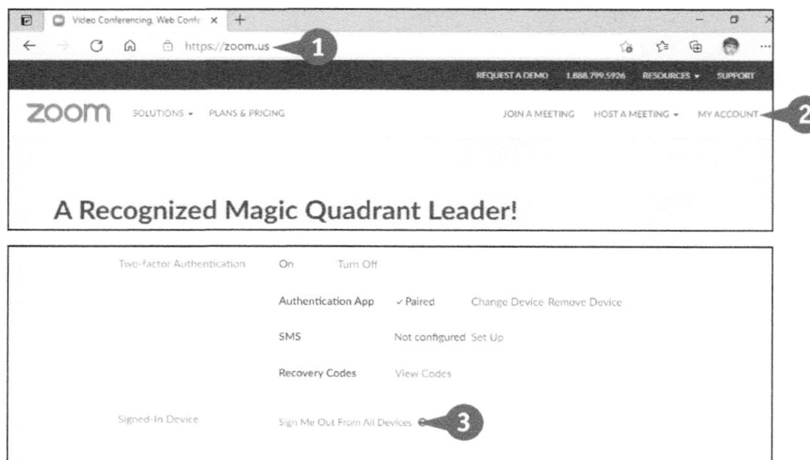

1. Use a web browser to navigate to https://zoom.us.
2. Click **My Account**.

Note: If you are on some other page on the Zoom site, click your profile picture and then click your name.

Zoom displays your Profile page.

Note: You can combine steps 1 and 2 by navigating directly to https://zoom.us/profile.

3. Click **Sign Me Out From All Devices**.

The Sign Me Out From All Devices dialog appears.

4 Click **OK**.

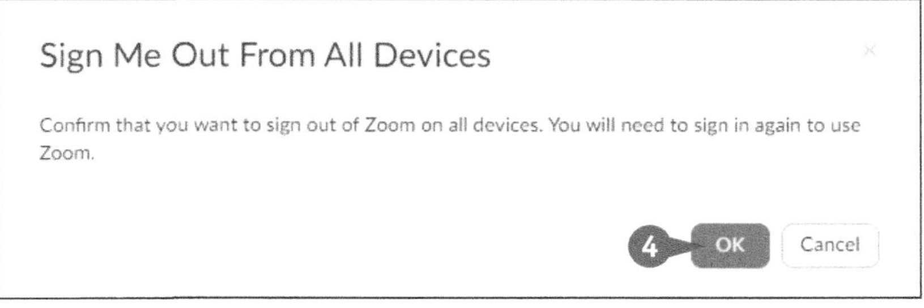

Sign Me Out From All Devices
Confirm that you want to sign out of Zoom on all devices. You will need to sign in again to use Zoom.
4
OK
Cancel

If you have the Zoom app running, it lets you know that your session has ended and you need to sign in again.

5 Click **OK**.

Zoom signs out of all your devices.

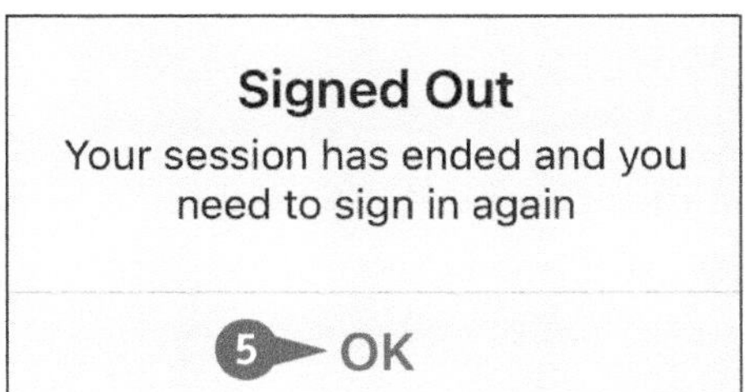

TIP

Should I sign out of the Zoom app when I am not using it?

Yes, it is good practice to sign out from your Zoom account if you will not be using the service for a while. Signing out is particularly important if you will be away from your desk for a time and your computer or mobile device is unlocked. If you have not signed out, an unauthorized user could access your account.

To sign out from the Zoom desktop app, click your profile picture and then click **Sign Out**.

To sign out from the Zoom mobile app, tap **Settings**, tap your name, and then tap **Sign Out**.

Enable the Waiting Room

You can control access to your Zoom meetings by enabling the Waiting Room feature. When the waiting room is enabled for a meeting, participants do not join the meeting directly. Instead, each person is held in a separate area where they see the message *Please wait, the meeting host will let you in soon*. Using the waiting room enables you not only to control when participants can join the meeting but also to prevent unauthorized users from joining.

Zoom gives you several options for controlling which users go into the waiting room and which users bypass the waiting room.

Enable the Waiting Room

Enable the Waiting Room

1. Use a web browser to navigate to https://zoom.us/profile (not shown).

   Zoom displays your Profile page.

2. Click **Settings**.
3. Click **Meeting**.
4. Click the **Waiting Room** switch to On ( ).

   Zoom now enables the waiting room for all your scheduled meetings.

Note: If needed, you can still disable the waiting room for a meeting. When you schedule the meeting, click **Waiting Room** (changes to).

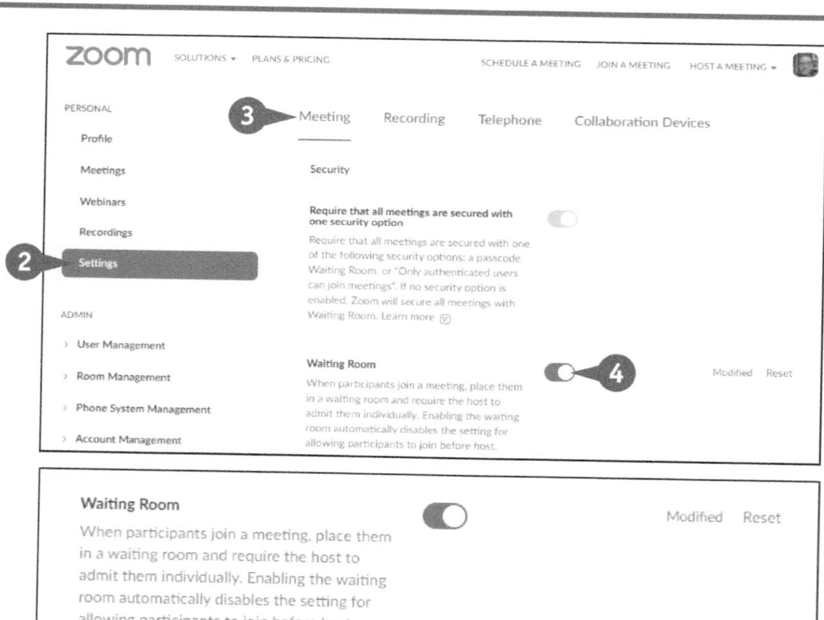

Set Waiting Room Options

1. Click **Edit Options**.

   The Waiting Room Options window appears.

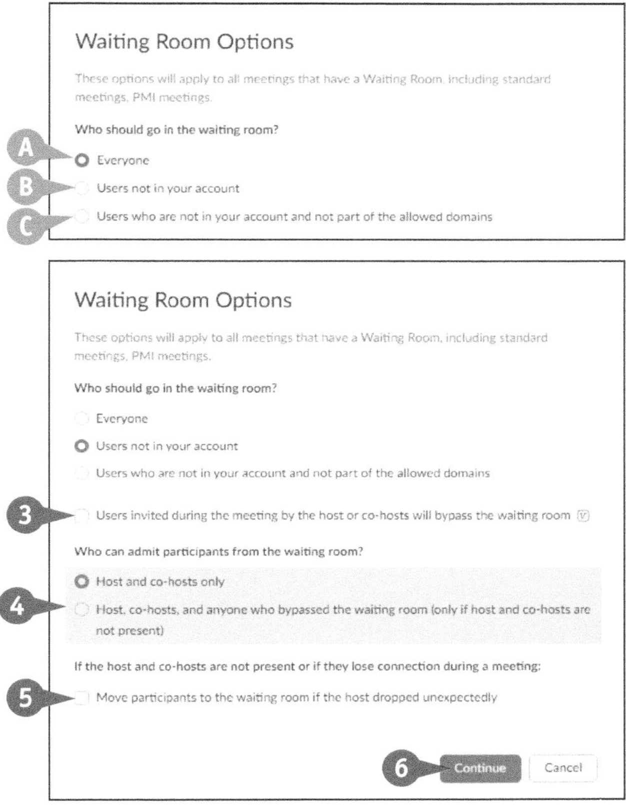

2 Choose which participants you want to go into the waiting room (○ changes to ◉):

A **Everyone:** Puts all participants into the waiting room.

B **Users not in your account:** Puts participants who are not part of your Zoom account into the waiting room.

C **Users who are not in your account and not part of the allowed domains:** Same as previous, but also enables you to specify one or more domain names (not shown). Users who sign in to Zoom using one of these domains will bypass the waiting room.

3 Click this check box if you want people invited during the meeting to bypass the waiting room (☐ changes to ☑).

4 If you selected an option other than Everyone in step 2, select who can admit participants from the waiting room.

5 Click this check box if you want all participants moved to the waiting room if the host loses a connection to the meeting (☐ changes to ☑).

6 Click **Continue**.

Zoom puts your waiting room options into effect.

TIP

Can I customize my waiting room?

Yes, Zoom offers several waiting room customizations. On the **Meeting** tab, under **Waiting Room Options**, click **Customize Waiting Room**. In the Customize Waiting Room window, you can edit the message (A), add a logo (B), and add a description of the meeting room (C). When you are done, click **Close**.

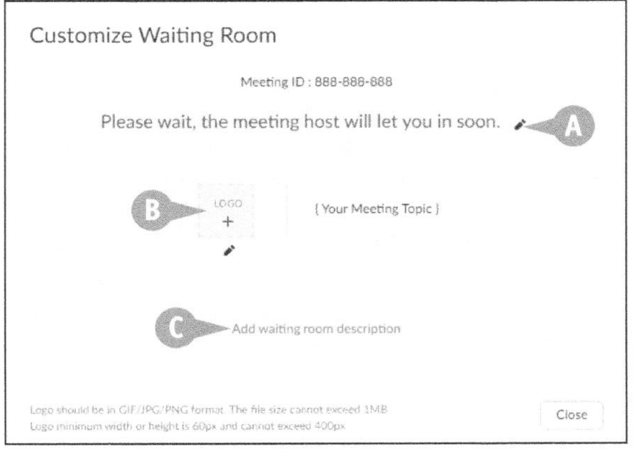

Allow Only Authenticated App Users

You can enhance the security of your Zoom meetings by requiring participants who join using the Zoom app to sign in to their Zoom accounts. By default, anyone who has a link to your meeting or who knows the meeting ID and passcode can join the meeting. If you are concerned that an unauthorized user has access to the meeting information, you can require all attendees to authenticate — that is, sign in to their Zoom accounts.

If you also want participants who join via the Web to authenticate, see the next section, "Allow Only Authenticated Web Users."

Allow Only Authenticated App Users

1. Use a web browser to navigate to https://zoom.us/profile (not shown).

   Zoom displays your Profile page.

2. Click **Settings.**
3. Click **Meeting.**

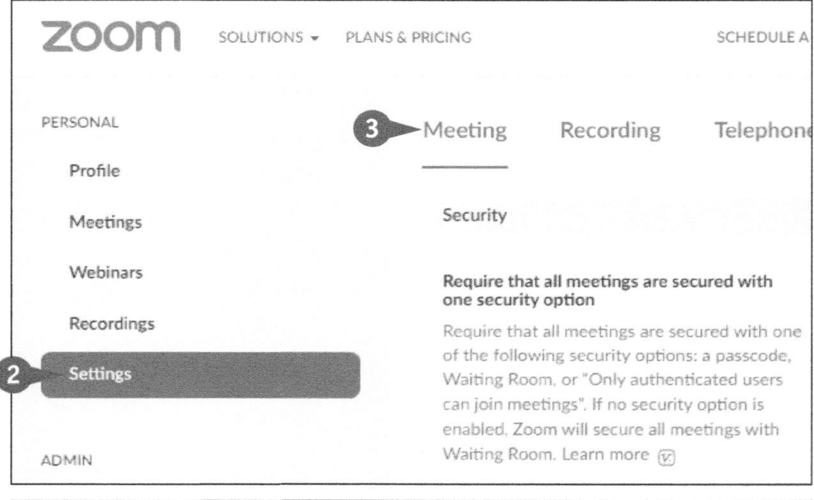

4. Click the **Only authenticated users can join meetings** switch to On (◐).

   Zoom now requires users to sign in to their Zoom accounts before they can join a scheduled meeting.

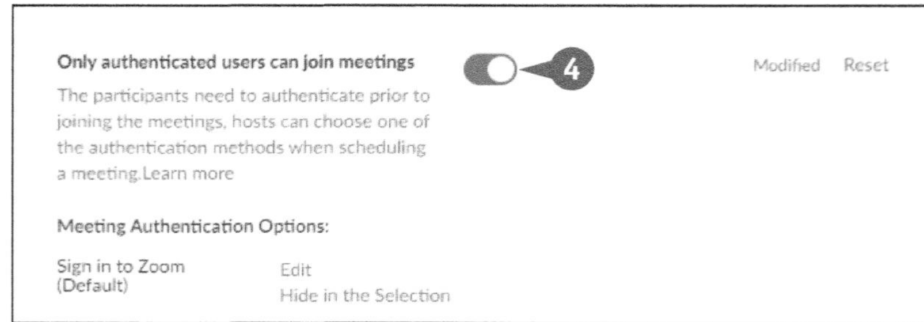

Note: If needed, you can still disable the authentication requirement for a meeting. When you schedule the meeting, click **Require authentication to join** (☑ changes to ☐).

Allow Only Authenticated Web Users

You can help thwart unauthorized users from accessing your Zoom meetings by requiring participants who join using the Zoom website to sign in to their Zoom accounts. By default, web users who have a link to your meeting or know the meeting ID and passcode can join the meeting via the Zoom website. If you are concerned that an unauthorized user has access to the meeting information, you can require all web users to sign in to their Zoom accounts.

If you also want participants who join via the Zoom app to authenticate, see the previous section, "Allow Only Authenticated App Users."

Allow Only Authenticated Web Users

1. Use a web browser to navigate to https://zoom.us/profile (not shown).

   Zoom displays your Profile page.

2. Click **Settings**.
3. Click **Meeting**.

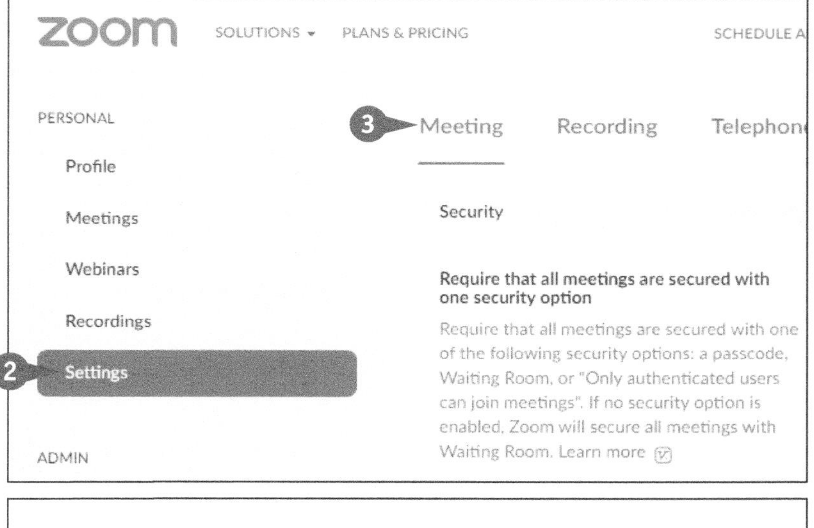

4. Click the **Only authenticated users can join meetings from Web client** switch to On (◉).

   Zoom now requires web users to sign in to their Zoom accounts before they can join a scheduled meeting.

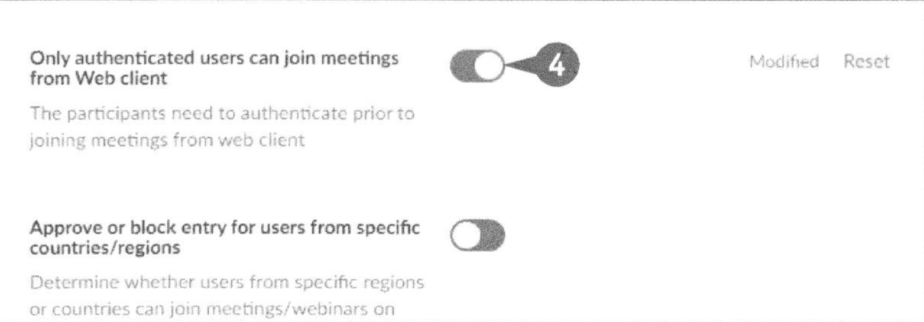

Disable Passcode Embedding

You can help prevent unauthorized or unwanted users from joining a meeting by configuring Zoom to not embed the passcode in the invitation link. By default, the invitation link for a meeting includes encrypted versions of the meeting ID and passcode. Clicking the link enables an invitee to join the meeting automatically without having to specify either the meeting ID or the passcode. This is convenient, but it also means that an unauthorized user who obtains the invitation link can join the meeting automatically. To prevent this, you can configure Zoom to not embed the passcode in the invitation link.

Disable Passcode Embedding

1. Use a web browser to navigate to https://zoom.us/profile (not shown).

   Zoom displays your Profile page.

2. Click **Settings**.
3. Click **Meeting**.
4. Click the **Embed passcode in invite link for one-click join** switch to On (◐).

   Zoom now requires invitees to enter the meeting passcode before joining the meeting.

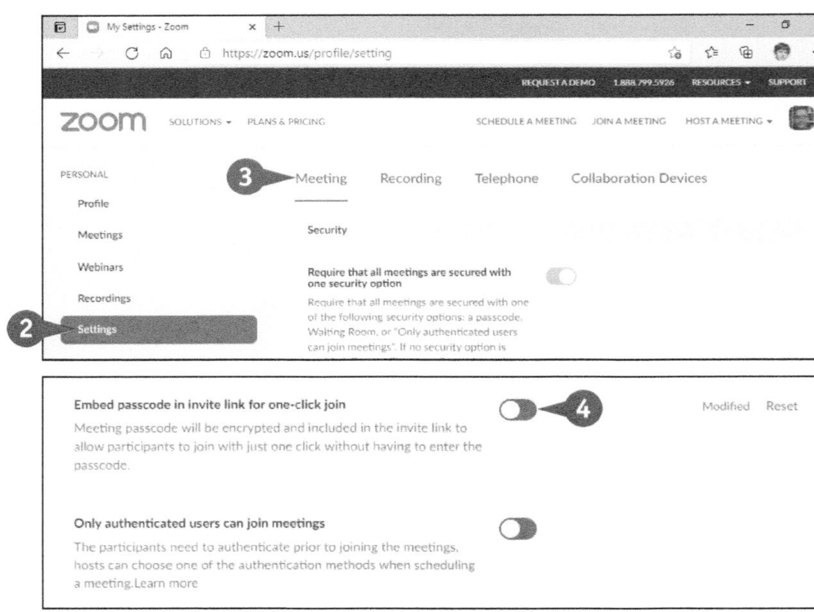

Create a Custom Personal Meeting Passcode

You can make it easier for invitees to join meetings held in your personal meeting room by creating a custom passcode. By default, Zoom assigns a random series of letters and numbers as the passcode for your personal meeting room. This is good practice because it makes it difficult for an unauthorized user to guess the passcode. If you disable passcode embedding as described in the previous section, you might also want to delete the passcode from the meeting invitation email. To make it easier for invitees to enter the passcode manually, create a custom passcode that is memorable.

Create a Custom Personal Meeting Passcode

1. Use a web browser to navigate to https://zoom.us/profile (not shown).

   Zoom displays your Profile page.

2. Click **Settings**.
3. Click **Meeting**.
4. Under the Personal Meeting ID (PMI) Passcode setting, click **Edit**.
5. Type the passcode you want to use.

Note: Make the new passcode memorable, but do not make it easy for an unauthorized user to guess.

6. Click **Save**.

   Zoom now uses your new passcode for all your personal meeting room meetings.

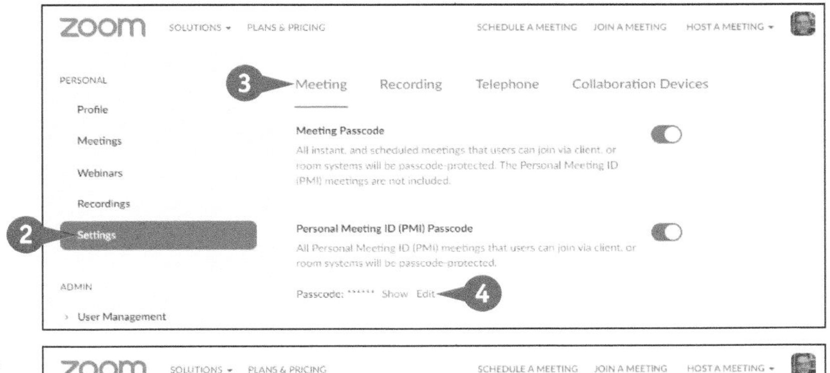

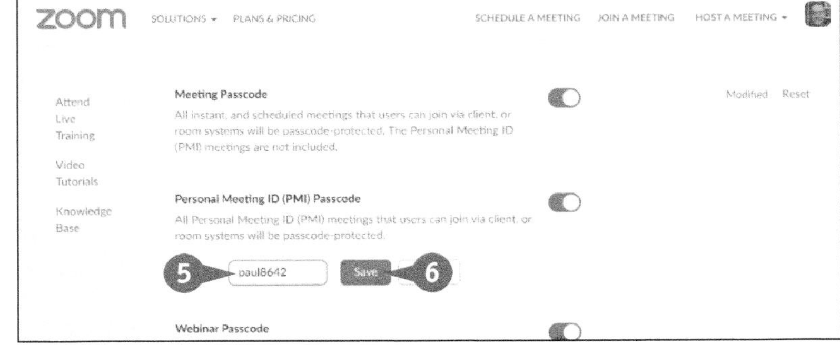

Set Security Options at the Account and Group Levels

If you manage users on your account (see Chapter 10), you can more easily apply security across multiple users by working at the account and group levels. The previous sections in this chapter set security options at the user level. If you are the only person on your Zoom account, then user-level security is all you require. However, if you administer users on your account, setting security for individual users is time-consuming. It is more efficient to set your preferred security options either at the account level for all users or at the group level for just that group's users.

Set Security Options at the Account and Group Levels

Set Security Options at the Account Level

1. Use a web browser to navigate to https://zoom.us/account/.

   Zoom displays your account Profile page.

Note: Make sure you sign in to Zoom using an administrator account.

2. Click **Account Settings**.

Note: You can combine steps 1 and 2 by navigating directly to https://zoom.us/account/setting.

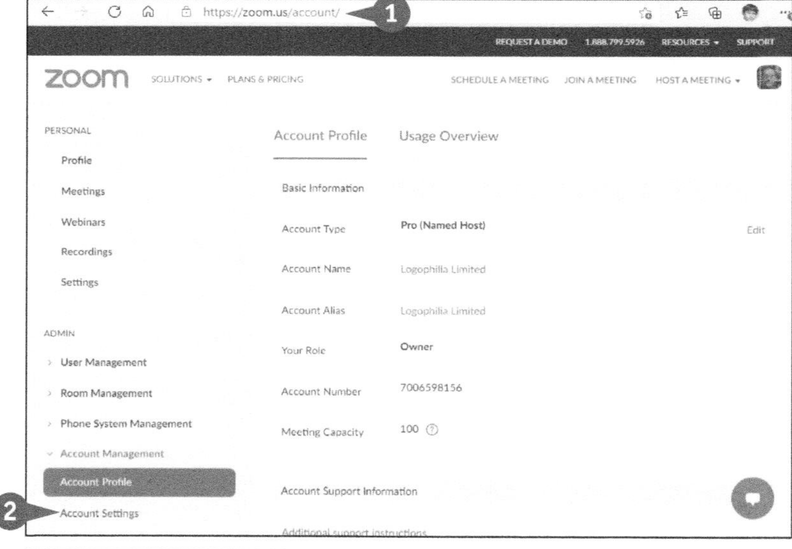

3. Click the **Meeting** tab.
4. Use the controls in the Meeting tab to set your security options.

   Zoom applies the security settings to all users in your Zoom account.

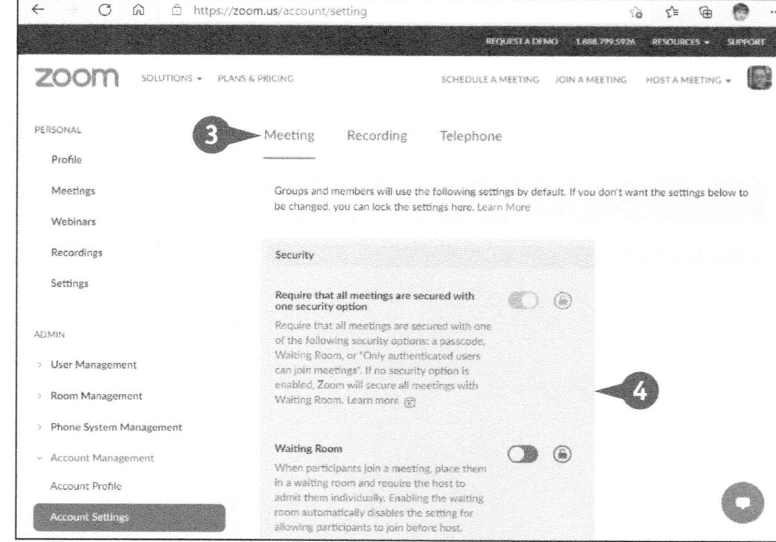

Set Security Options at the Group Level

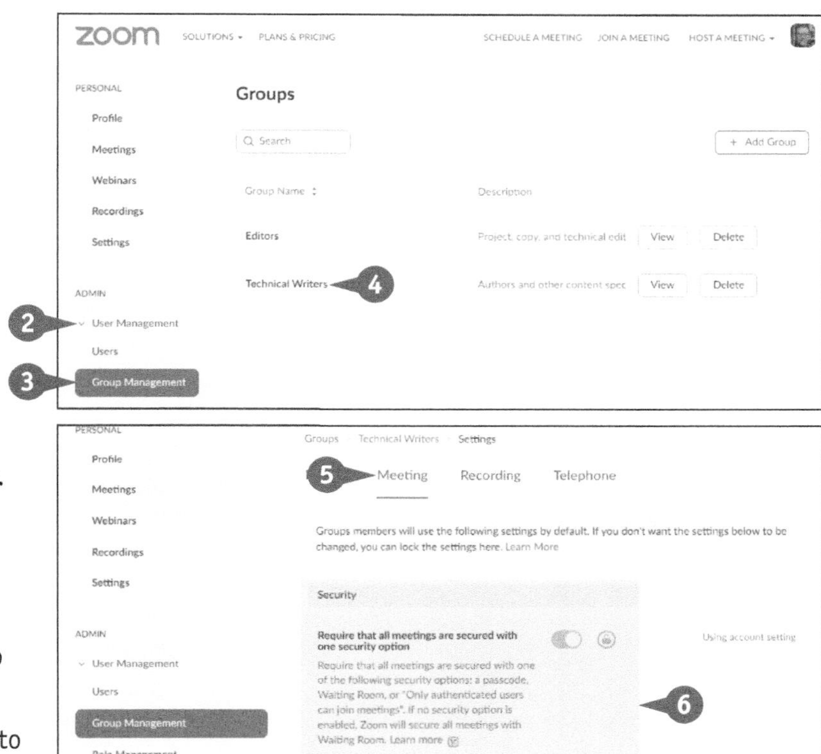

1. Use a web browser to navigate to https://zoom.us/account/ (not shown).

   Zoom displays your account Profile page.

Note: Make sure you sign in to Zoom using an administrator account.

2. Click **User Management.**
3. Click **Group Management.**
4. Click the group you want to modify.

   Zoom displays the group's Profile page.

5. Click the **Meeting** tab.
6. Use the controls in the Meeting tab to set your security options.

   Zoom applies the security settings to all users in the group.

TIP

Can I prevent account or group settings from being modified at the user level?

Yes, you can lock a setting to prevent changes. Each setting in the Meeting tab of either the Account Settings page or a group's Settings page has a Lock icon (🔒). To lock a setting, click its Lock icon (🔒) and then click **Lock** (A) in the dialog that appears.

Lock "Waiting Room"

All group members settings will be enabled and cannot be modified.

Do not remind me again

A Lock Cancel

Set In-Meeting Security Options

If you are a meeting host, you can enhance meeting security by setting security options while the meeting is in progress. For example, if you suspect an unauthorized user is trying to join a meeting, you can lock the meeting to prevent anyone else from joining. You can also activate the meeting waiting room, which enables you to approve anyone else who tries to join the meeting. If a meeting participant is unauthorized or causing problems, you can remove that person from the meeting. Finally, if you are seeing problematic activity in the meeting, you can suspend all participant activity.

Set In-Meeting Security Options

Lock the Meeting

1. Click **Security**.
2. Click **Lock Meeting**.

   Zoom locks the meeting, which prevents anyone else from joining.

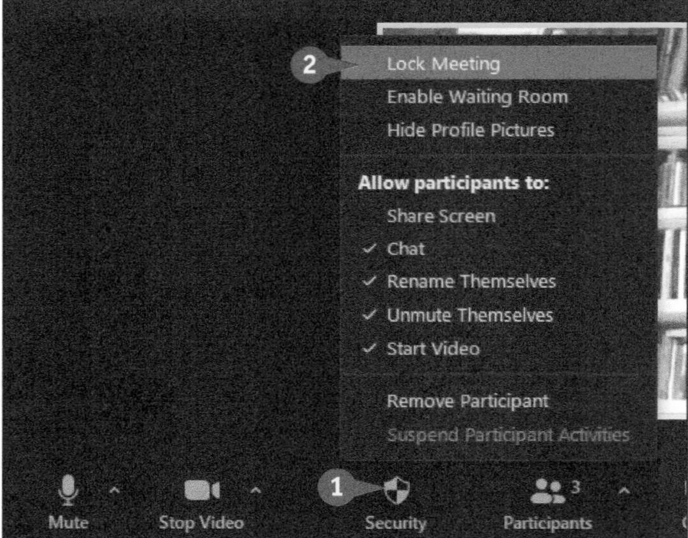

Activate the Waiting Room

1. Click **Security**.
2. Click **Enable Waiting Room**.

   Zoom activates the waiting room for new participants.

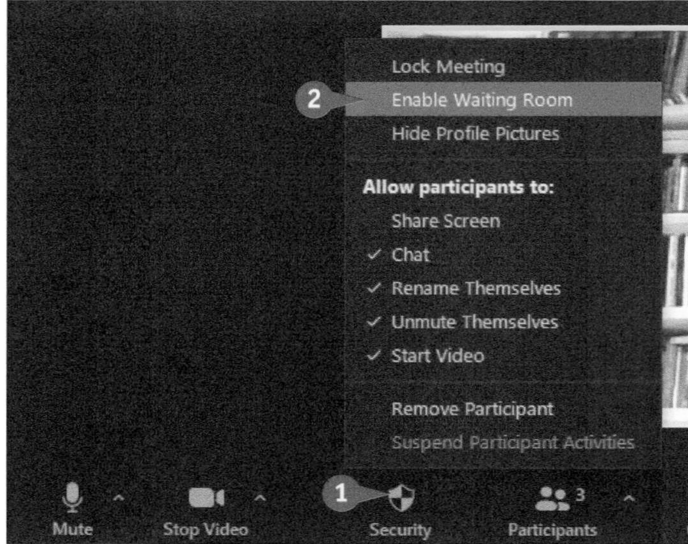

Remove a Participant

1 Click **Security**.

2 Click **Remove Participant**.

The Remove Participant pane appears.

3 Click **Remove** beside the participant you want to remove.

Zoom asks you to confirm.

4 Click **Remove**.

Zoom removes the participant from the meeting.

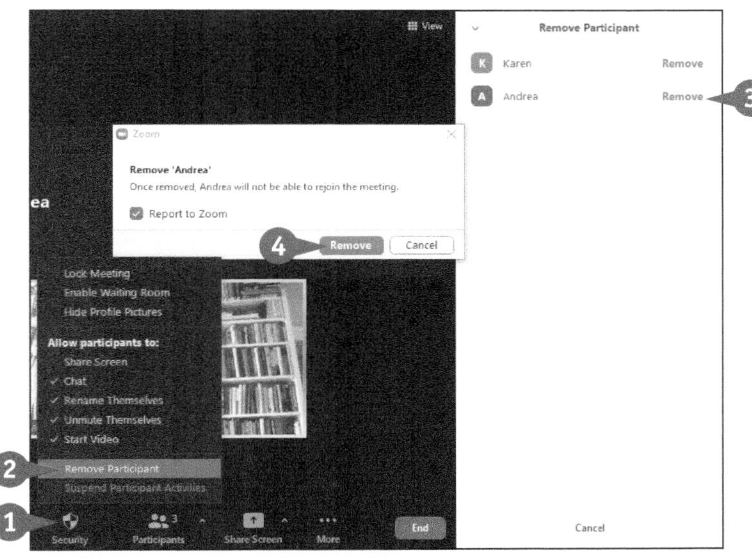

Suspend All Meeting Activity

1 Click **Security**.

2 Click **Suspend Participant Activities**.

Zoom asks you to confirm.

3 Click **Suspend**.

Zoom turns off the audio and video feeds for all participants and locks the meeting.

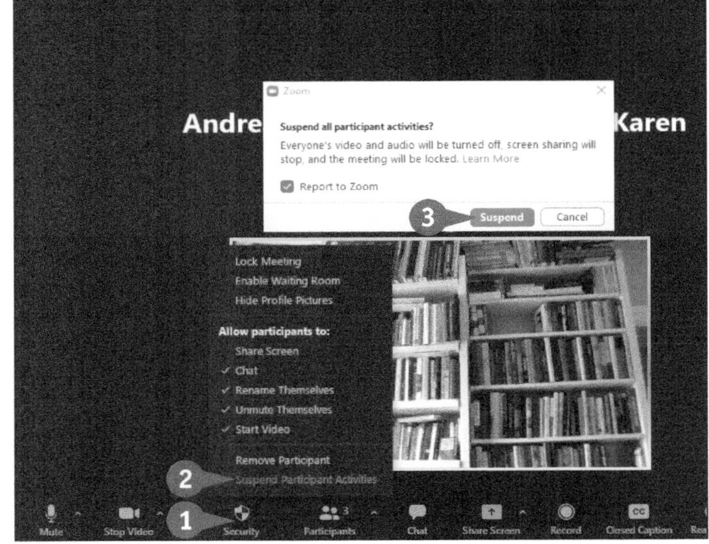

TIPS

Is there a more direct way to remove someone from the meeting?
Yes, you can remove a participant directly by clicking that person's **Menu** icon (...), clicking **Remove**, and then clicking **Remove** again when Zoom asks you to confirm.

Can I move a participant to the waiting room?
Yes. Click the participant's **Menu** icon (...) and then click **Put in Waiting Room**. Zoom moves the person out of the meeting and into the waiting room. To admit the person back into the meeting, click **Participants** in the toolbar and then click the person's **Admit** button. Alternatively, you can click the person's **Remove** button to completely remove that person from the meeting.

CHAPTER 10

Managing Users and Contacts

If you are the owner or administrator of a Zoom account, you can add other Zoom users to your account. This enables you to set meeting options (see Chapter 8) and security options (see Chapter 9) for all users or groups of users. You can also assign roles and add Zoom accounts to your account's contacts.

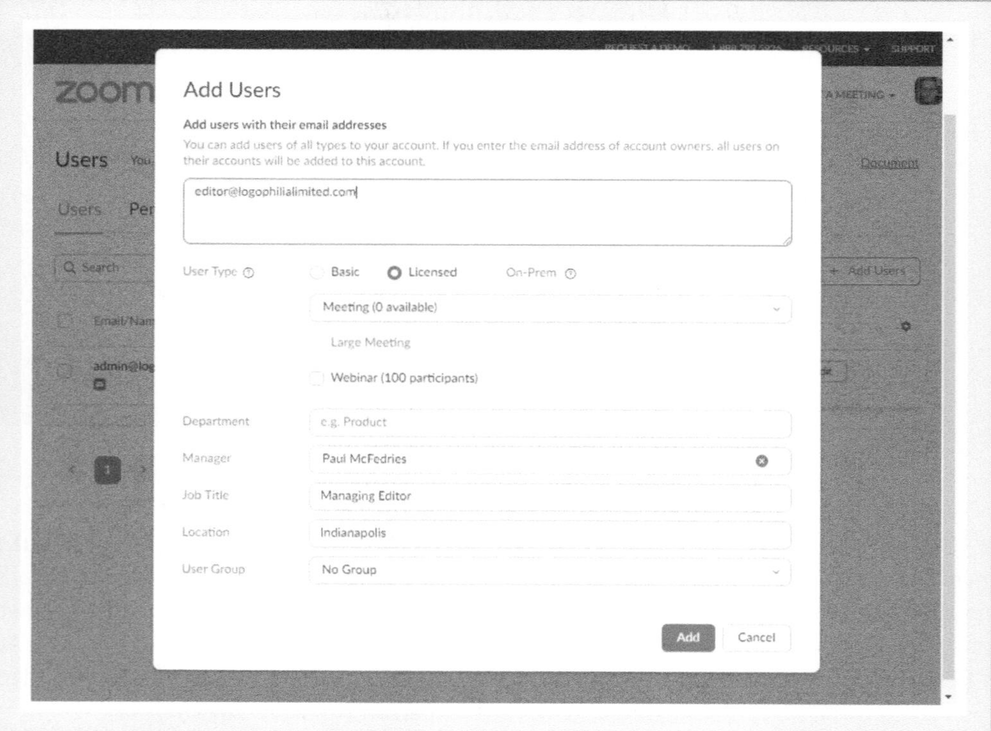

View Users

Your Zoom account has a Users tab where you can view all the Zoom users who belong to your account. At first, just your own account appears on the Users tab. However, you can also use the Users tab to add more users to your account.

Once you have other users added to your account, you can edit users, change user roles, organize users into groups, and more. These tasks all require access to the Users tab, so you need to know how to access that tab on the Zoom website.

View Users

1. Use a web browser to navigate to https://zoom.us.
2. Click **My Account**.

Note: If you are on some other page on the Zoom site, click your profile picture and then click your name.

Zoom displays your Profile page.

Note: You can combine steps 1 and 2 by navigating directly to https://zoom.us/profile.

3. Click **User Management**.

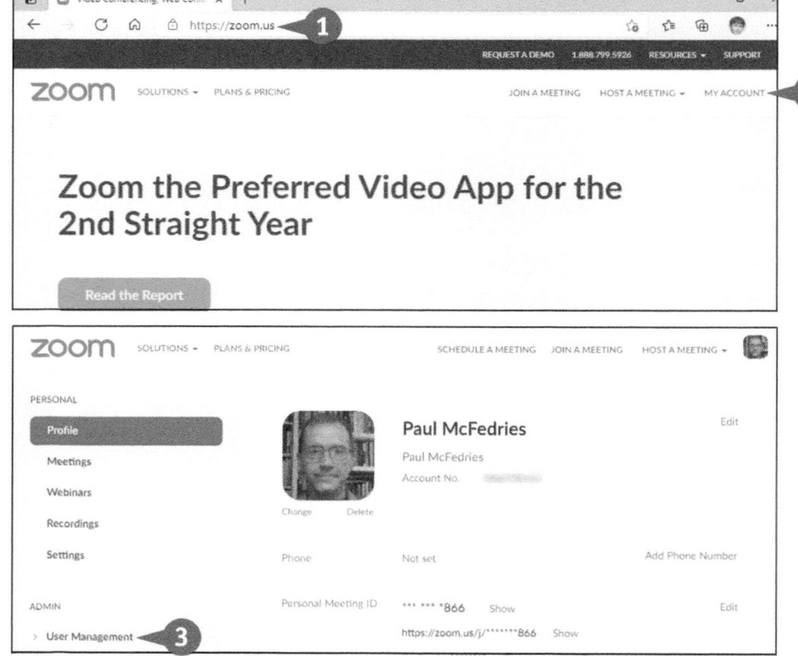

4 Click **Users**.

5 Click the **Users** tab.

Zoom displays the users in your account.

A By default, new accounts contain only your own account as a user.

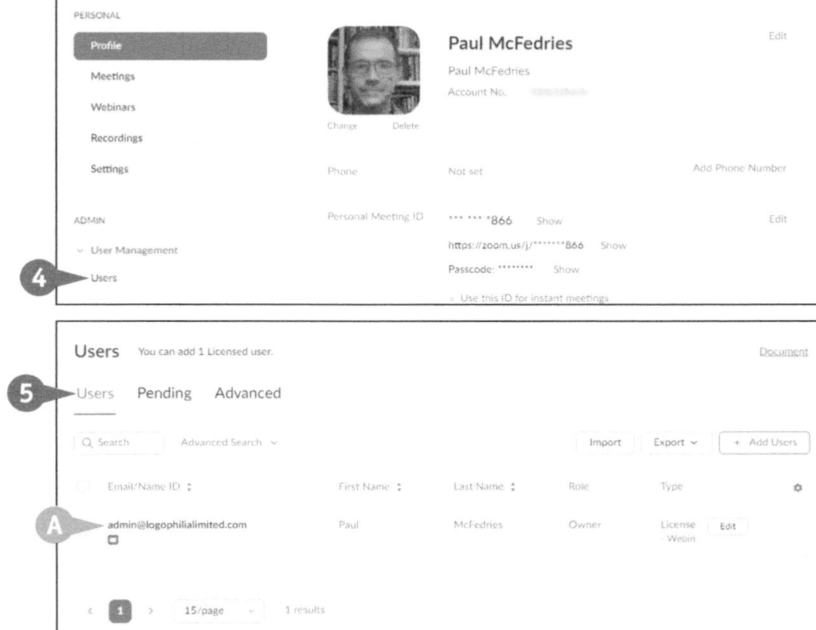

TIP

What types of users does Zoom support?

There are three main types of users on Zoom:

- **Internal user**. A Zoom account holder who belongs to your Zoom account. Note that, by convention, you are an internal user on your Zoom account.
- **External user**. A Zoom account holder who does not belong to your Zoom account.
- **External contact**. An external user who you or some other internal user has added to the contacts directory.

It is important to understand that when you add someone as an internal user on your account, that person relinquishes their own Zoom account and switches to your Zoom account.

Add a User

You can work with, edit, and manage internal users that belong to your Zoom account. By default, your Zoom account includes just you as the only user. Before you can manage users, you must first add those users to your Zoom account. For each potential user, you need to know that person's email address. You can also optionally add information such as the person's department and job title. Each potential user receives an invitation email that includes a link the user must click to accept the request.

You must add Basic Zoom users and Licensed Zoom users separately.

Add a User

Add Basic Zoom Users

1. Display the **Users** tab.

Note: See the previous section, "View Users," to learn how to display the Users tab for your Zoom account.

2. Click **Add Users**.

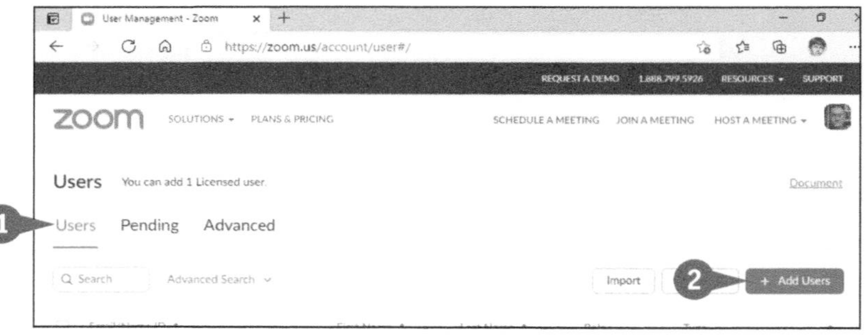

The Add Users dialog appears.

3. Type the user's email address.

Note: You can enter multiple email addresses (separated by commas) if the users all share the same settings.

4. Select **Basic** (○ changes to ◉).
5. Fill in the other fields, as needed.
6. Click **Add**.

Zoom sends an invitation to the email address you entered in step 3.

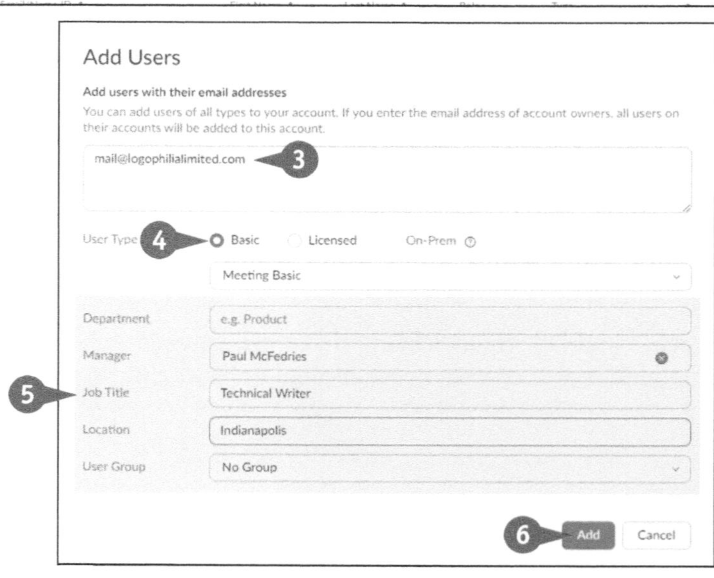

Add Licensed Zoom Users

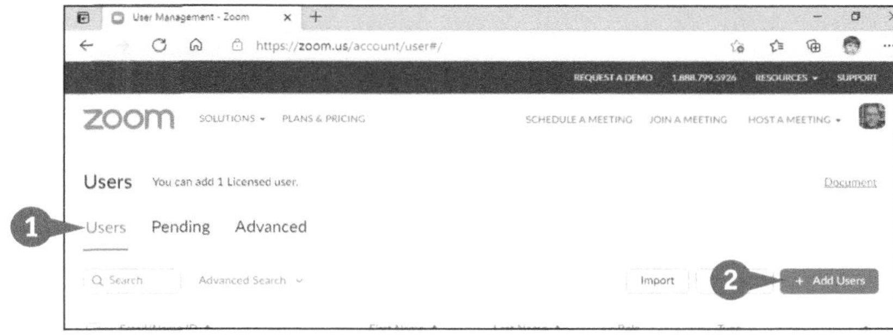

1. Display the **Users** tab.

Note: See the previous section, "View Users," to learn how to display the Users tab for your Zoom account.

2. Click **Add Users**.

The Add Users dialog appears.

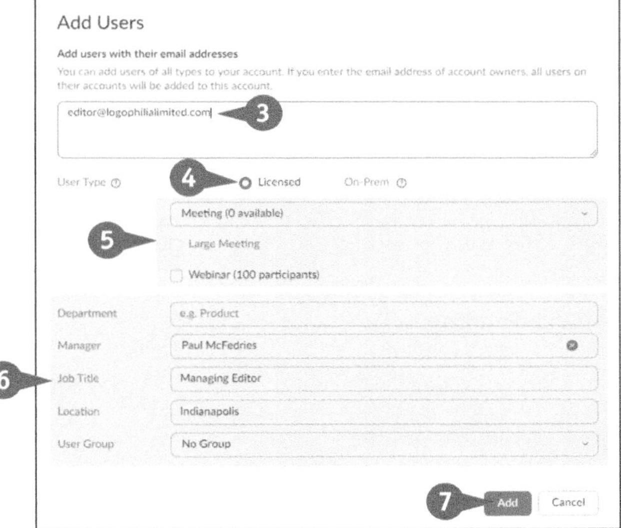

3. Type the user's email address.

Note: You can enter multiple email addresses (separated by commas) if the users all share the same settings.

4. Select **Licensed** (◯ changes to ◉).
5. Select the add-ons you want the user to have.
6. Fill in the other fields, as needed.
7. Click **Add**.

Zoom sends an invitation to the email address you entered in step 3.

TIP

Is there a faster way to add a large number of users?

Yes, you can run a batch import from a file. You must create a comma-separated values (CSV) text file. In this file, each row represents a user, and for each user you insert the person's email address, first name, and last name, separated by commas. You can optionally also include the person's department, manager, user group, IM group, job title, and location, all separated by commas. You need one CSV file for Basic Zoom users and a second CSV file for Licensed Zoom users.

On the Users tab, click **Import**, click **Basic** or **Licensed** (◯ changes to ◉), click **Upload CSV File**, select the appropriate CSV file, and then click **Open**.

Resend a User Invitation

You can resend an invitation for a user to join your Zoom account. When you send someone an invitation to join your account, that person might not receive the invitation message. Similarly, the person might receive the message but delete it accidentally. If you know the person wants to join your account, you can resend the invitation from your account's Pending tab, which lists all the invitations you have sent but that have yet to be accepted.

Note that Zoom gives each user 30 days to accept your invitation. When you resend an invitation, Zoom restarts the 30-day expiration period.

Resend a User Invitation

1 Display the **Users** tab.

Note: See the section "View Users" earlier in this chapter to learn how to display the Users tab for your Zoom account.

2 Click **Pending**.

3 Click the user's **Resend** button.

Zoom sends the invitation again.

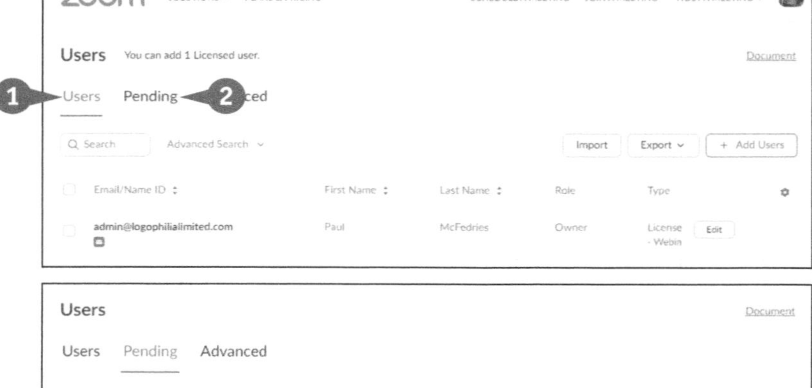

Delete a Pending User

After sending an invitation to a user, you might change your mind and decide you do not want that person to belong to your Zoom account. Similarly, you might find that you sent the invitation to an incorrect email address. Whatever the reason, to cancel an invitation to join your account, you can delete the person from your account's Pending tab.

Note that Zoom automatically deletes a pending user if that person has not accepted your invitation after 30 days.

Delete a Pending User

1. Display the **Users** tab.

Note: See the section "View Users" earlier in this chapter to learn how to display the Users tab for your Zoom account.

2. Click **Pending**.
3. Click the user's **Delete** button.

Zoom asks you to confirm.

4. Click **Delete**.

Zoom deletes the pending user.

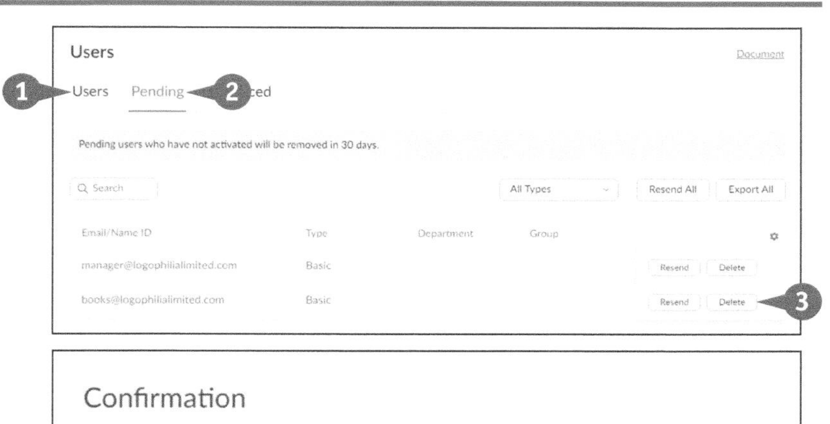

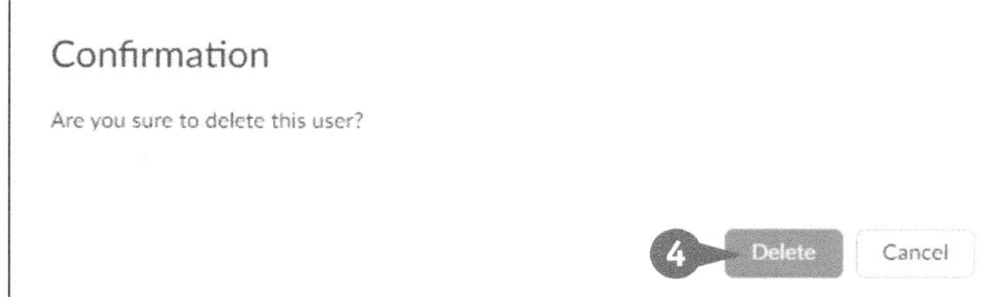

Edit a User

You can edit any user who belongs to your Zoom account. After you add a user to your Zoom account, the user appears on your profile's Users tab. If you need to update a user's existing information or add new information, you can edit the user from the Users tab. You can change the user type and set the user's department, manager, job title, and location.

Edit a User

1. Display the **Users** tab.

Note: See the section "View Users" earlier in this chapter to learn how to display the Users tab for your Zoom account.

2. Click **Edit** for the user you want to edit.

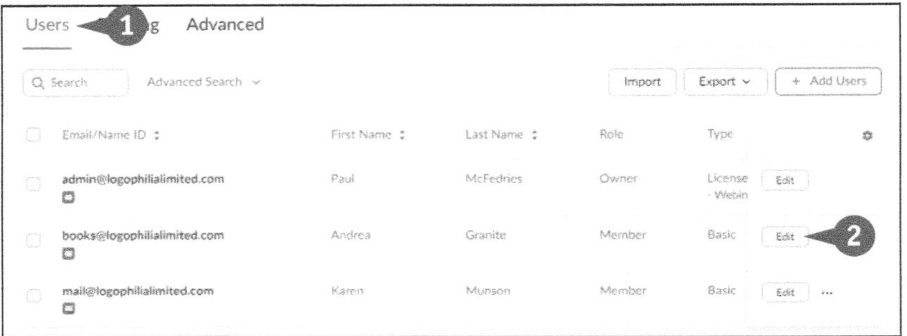

Zoom displays the Edit User dialog.

3. Make your changes to the user's information.

Note: For more information about the user role, see the next section, "Change a User's Role."

4. Click **Save**.

Zoom updates the user's data.

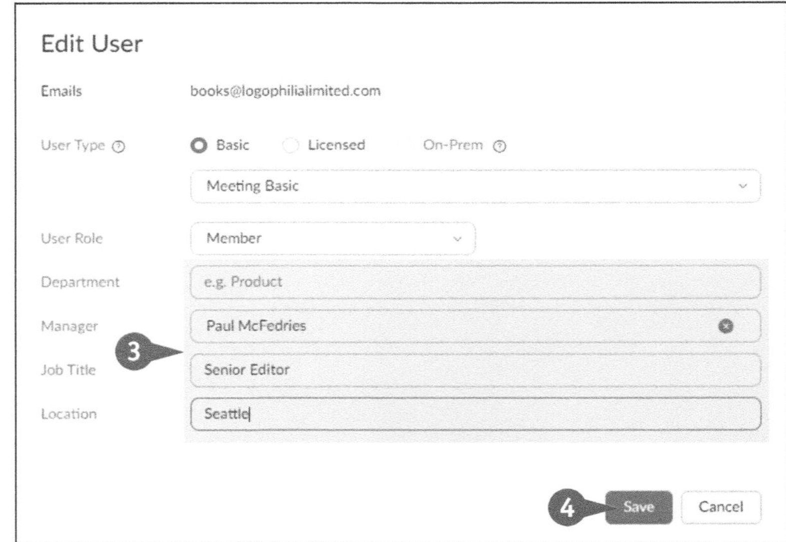

CHAPTER 10

Change a User's Role

After you have added a user to your Zoom account, you can change that user's role within the account. Zoom accounts have three account roles, each of which has certain administrative privileges in the account. The *owner* role, which is assigned to the person who created the Zoom account, can perform all administrative tasks. The *admin* role can add, edit, and remove users, among other tasks (see the section "Customize the Admin Role" later in this chapter). Finally, there is the *member* role, which carries no administrative privileges. If you need help with your account, you can change a member to an admin.

Change a User's Role

1. Display the **Users** tab.

Note: See the section "View Users" earlier in this chapter to learn how to display the Users tab for your Zoom account.

2. Click **Edit** for the user you want to edit.

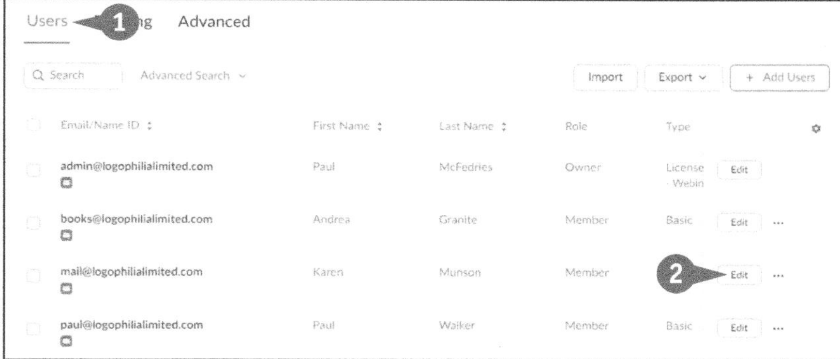

Zoom displays the Edit User dialog.

3. Click the **User Role** ⌄.
4. Click the role you want to assign the user.
5. Click **Save**.

Zoom updates the user's role.

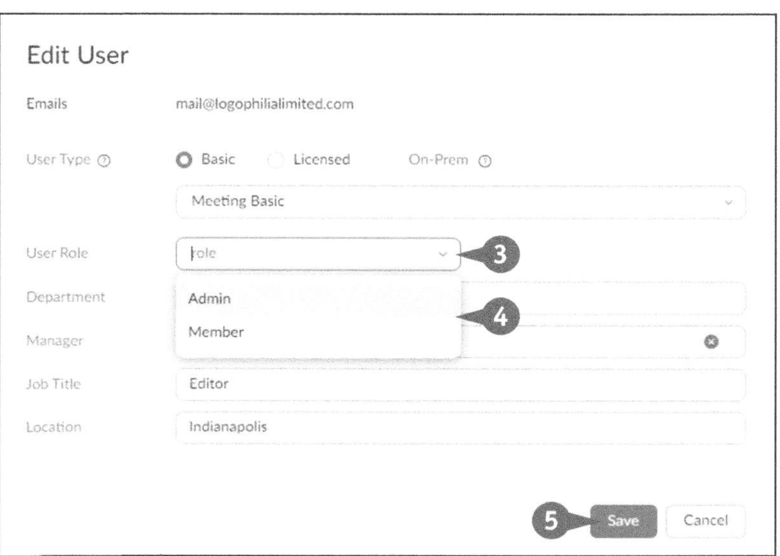

Unlink a User

If you no longer want a user included in your Zoom account, you can remove that user. This is called *unlinking* the user. You might want to unlink a user if that person has moved to a different department or is no longer needed in your Zoom account. The unlinked user retains a Basic Zoom account but is no longer associated with your account.

When you unlink a user, you have the option of transferring that user's data to another user in your account. You can transfer the unlinked user's upcoming meetings, upcoming webinars, and cloud-based recordings.

Unlink a User

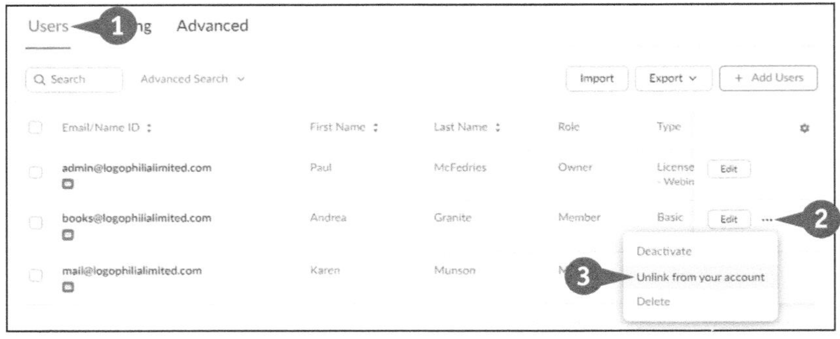

1 Display the **Users** tab.

Note: See the section "View Users" earlier in this chapter to learn how to display the Users tab for your Zoom account.

2 Click **More** (···) for the user you want to edit.

3 Click **Unlink from your account.**

Zoom displays the Unlink User dialog.

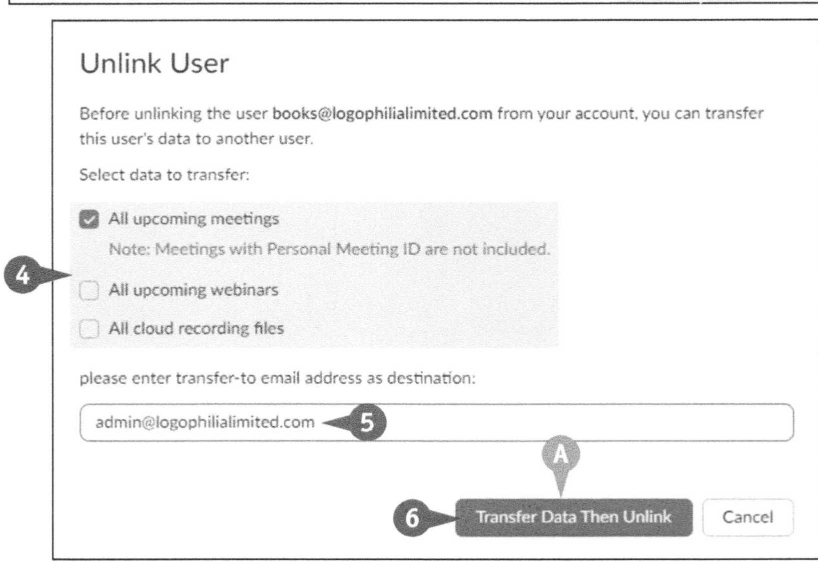

4 Select the check box beside each type of data you want to transfer (☐ changes to ☑).

5 If you are transferring data, type the email address of the user to whom you want the data sent.

6 Click **Transfer Data Then Unlink.**

A If you did not select any check boxes in step 4 — that is, if you are not transferring data — then this button is named **Unlink Now Without Data Transfer.** Click that button instead.

Zoom unlinks the user from your account and transfers the data, if any.

If you want to remove a user from your Zoom account and delete that person's Zoom data and account, you can delete that user. You might want to delete a user if that person no longer works at your company or has exhibited behavior that is abusive, unprofessional, or otherwise problematic. A deleted user is left with no Zoom account.

When you delete someone from your Zoom account, you can transfer that user's Zoom data to another user in your account. For example, you can transfer the deleted user's upcoming meetings, upcoming webinars, and cloud-based recordings.

Delete a User

1 Display the **Users** tab.

Note: See the section "View Users" earlier in this chapter to learn how to display the Users tab for your Zoom account.

2 Click **More** (···) for the user you want to edit.

3 Click **Delete**.

Zoom displays the Delete User dialog.

4 Select the check box beside each type of data you want to transfer (☐ changes to ☑).

5 If you are transferring data, type the email address of the user to whom you want the data sent.

6 Click **Transfer Data Then Delete**.

A If you did not select any check boxes in step 4 — that is, if you are not transferring data — then this button is named **Delete Now Without Data Transfer**. Click that button instead.

Zoom unlinks the user from your account and transfers the data, if any.

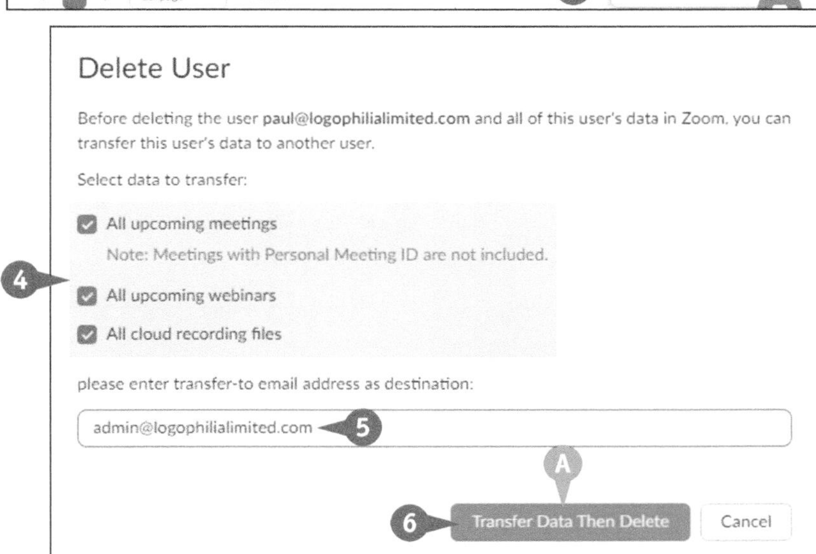

Customize the Admin Role

If your Zoom account contains one or more users in the admin role, you can customize the privileges that Zoom assigns to admins. By default, admins are assigned a long list of privileges in areas such as user management (including adding users and groups), account management (including editing your Zoom account's profile and settings), and billing (including adding subscriptions and editing billing information). As the account owner, you can customize these privileges, either to remove privileges you do not want your admins to have or to add privileges that admins currently lack.

Customize the Admin Role

1. Use a web browser to navigate to https://zoom.us.
2. Click **My Account**.

Note: If you are on some other page on the Zoom site, click your profile picture and then click your name.

Zoom displays your Profile page.

Note: You can combine steps 1 and 2 by navigating directly to https://zoom.us/profile.

3. Click **User Management**.
4. Click **Role Management**.

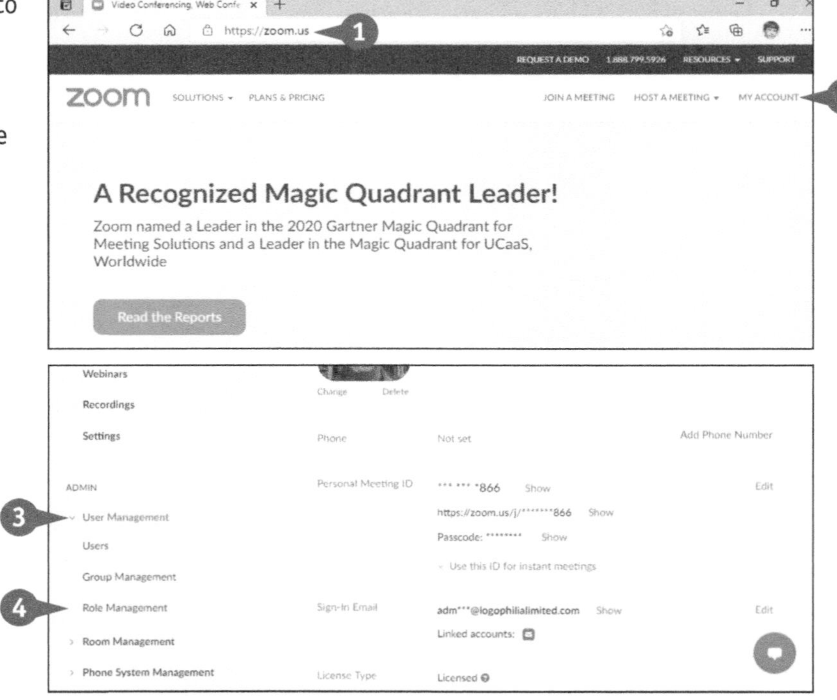

Zoom displays the roles in your account.

Note: See the next section, "Create a New Role," to learn how to add more roles to your account.

5 Click the admin role's **Edit** button.

3 Roles
Each user will belong to one of the roles below, and different roles have their unique privilege.
+ Add Role

Role Name	Description	Number of Members	
Owner	Account owner has full privileges to access and manage a Zoom account.	1	
Admin	Admins have wide range privileges to access and manage a Zoom account.	1	Edit
	Members have access		

6 Click **Role Settings**.

7 To add a privilege, click its **View** or **Edit** check box (☐ changes to ☑).

Note: See the first tip to learn the difference between the View and Edit settings.

8 To remove a privilege, click its **View** or **Edit** check box (☑ changes to ☐).

9 Click **Save Changes**.

Zoom applies your custom privileges to all admin users.

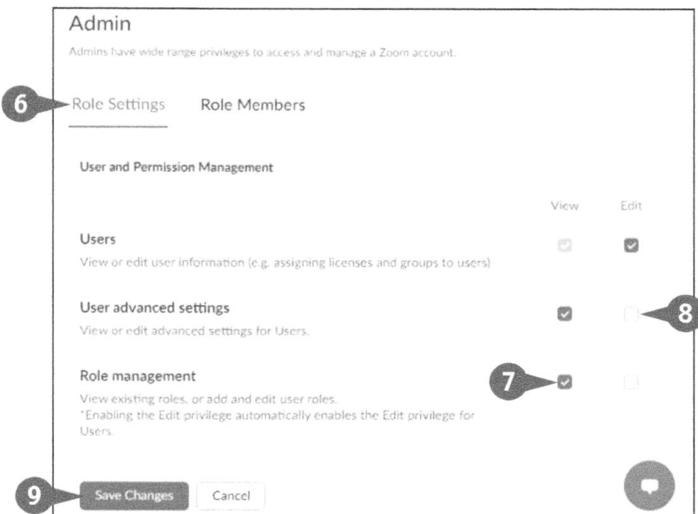

TIPS

What is the difference between the View and Edit settings?
The View setting means admins can examine the information associated with the privilege, but they cannot make changes. The Edit setting means admins can both examine the information associated with the privilege and also make changes to that information.

What is the purpose of the Role Members tab?
You use the Role Members tab to work directly with your admin users. Beside each admin you see two buttons: click **Remove** to remove the user from the admin role; click **Move** to move the user to a different role. You can also click **Add Members** to add other users to the admin role.

Create a New Role

You can create a custom role if Zoom's default roles are not suitable for your users. Zoom's default roles offer either many privileges (the admin role) or none (the member role). However, you might want one or more users to have a special set of privileges. For example, you might want to assign someone to take care of just user-related tasks. This means activating the User Management privileges and deactivating all the other privileges. Rather than modifying an existing role to accomplish this, it is better to create a new role and assign that role the privileges you want.

Create a New Role

1. Use a web browser to navigate to https://zoom.us.
2. Click **User Management.**
3. Click **Role Management.**

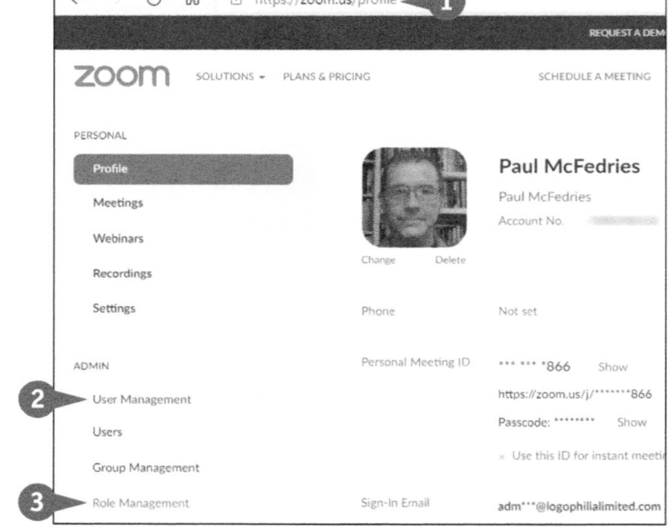

4. Click **Add Role.**

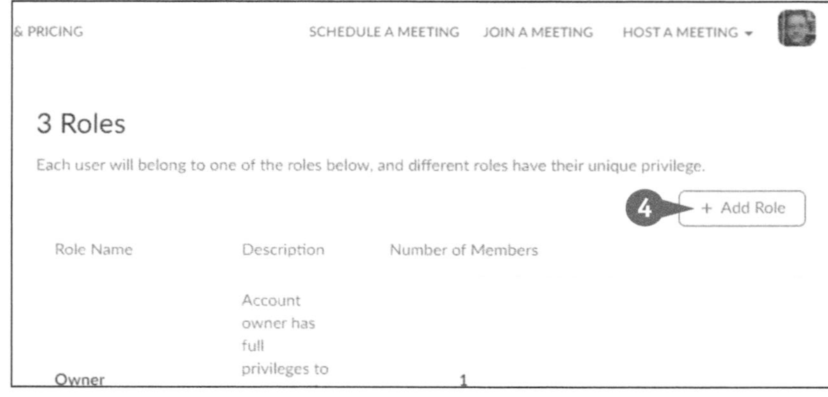

Zoom displays the Add Role dialog.

5 Type a name for the new role.

6 (Optional) Type a description.

7 Click **Add**.

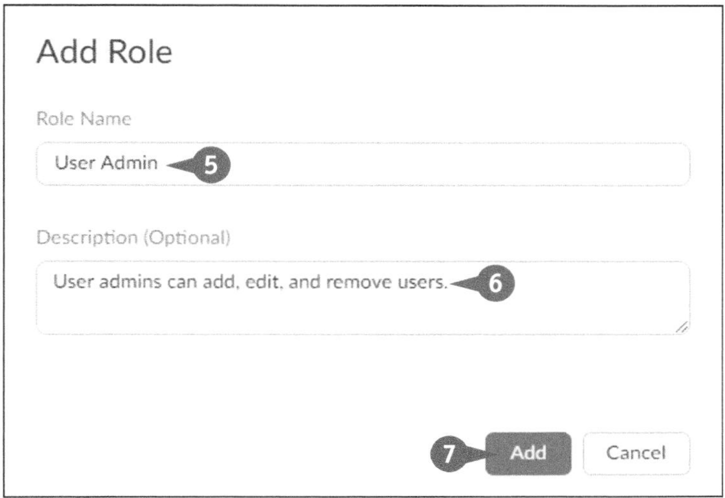

Zoom adds the new role to your account and displays the role's privilege settings.

8 Click the **View** or **Edit** check box (☐ changes to ☑) for each privilege you want to assign to the role.

9 Click **Save Changes**.

Zoom updates the role's privileges.

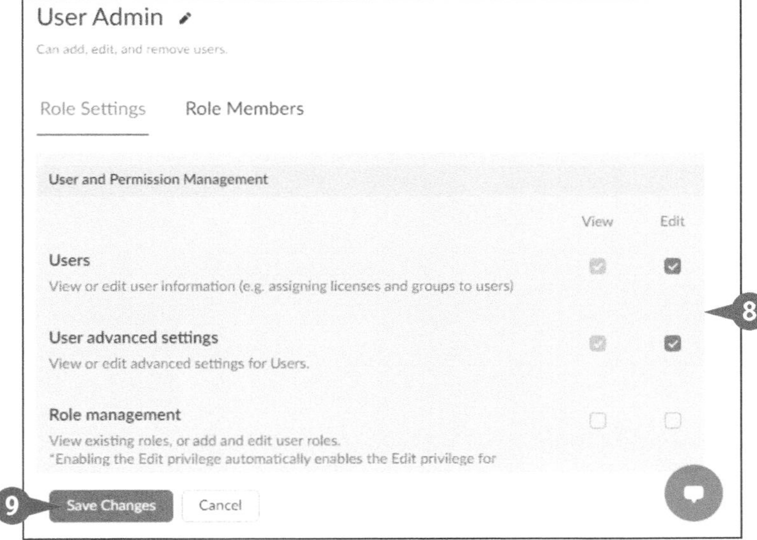

TIPS

Can I make changes to a role that I created?

Yes, you can change the role's privileges and add or remove members. Follow steps 1 to 3 to display your account's roles and then click the **Edit** button beside the role you want to modify.

Can I delete a role that I created?

Yes. If the role currently has one or more members, those users will be assigned to the member role after the deletion. Follow steps 1 to 3 to display your account's roles and then click the **Delete** button beside the role you want to remove. When Zoom asks you to confirm, click **Delete**.

Create a User Group

You can make many user-related tasks easier and more efficient by organizing users into groups. If your Zoom account has only a small number of users, tasks such as setting options for scheduling and securing meetings are not burdensome. However, once your Zoom account has more than a handful of users, such tasks become more time-consuming. It is much quicker and much easier to organize users into a group and then work with the group as a whole. Before you can add users to a group, you must add the group to your Zoom account.

Create a User Group

1. Use a web browser to navigate to https://zoom.us.
2. Click **User Management**.
3. Click **Group Management**.

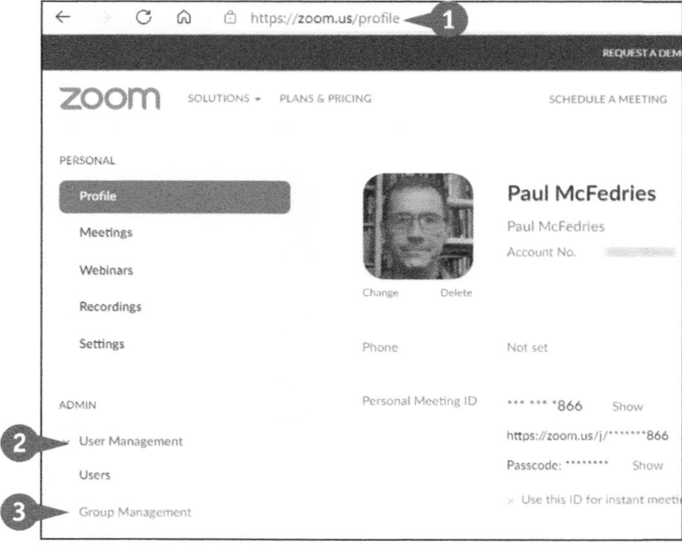

4. Click **Add Group**.

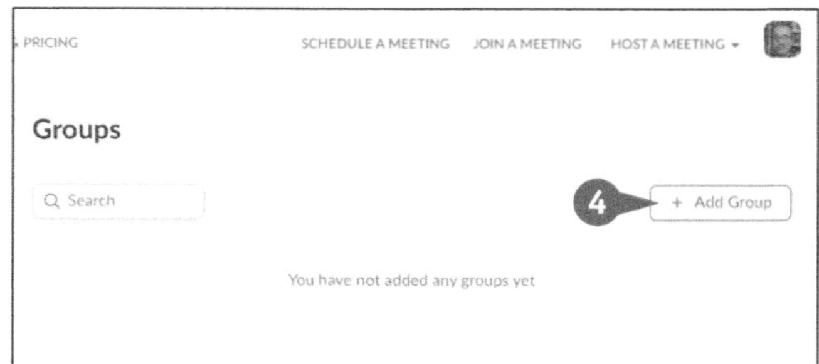

Zoom displays the Add Group dialog.

5 Type a name for the new group.

6 (Optional) Type a description.

7 Click **Add**.

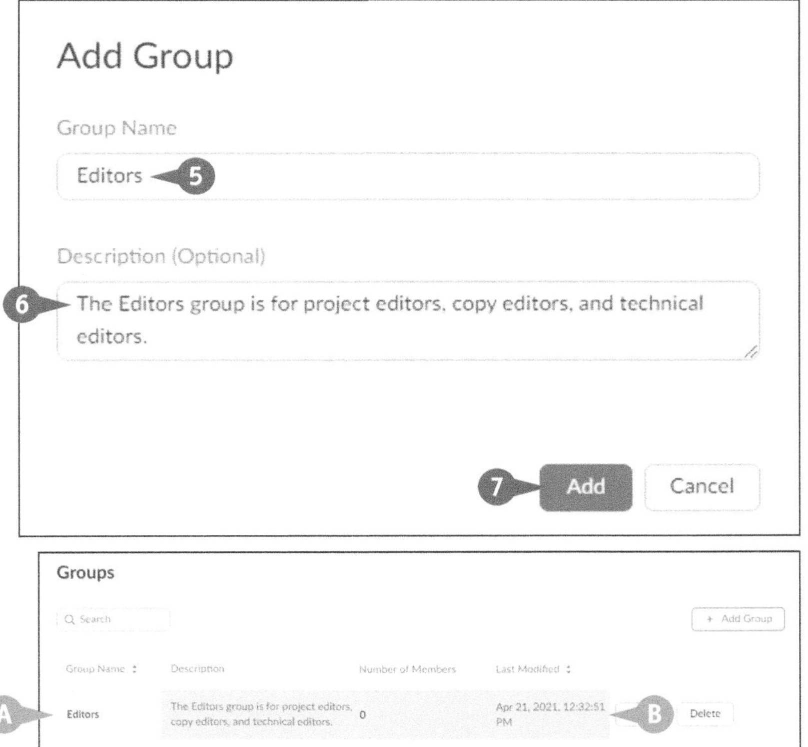

A Zoom adds the group to the Groups page.

B For each group, you see the description, the number of members, and the date and time the group was last changed.

Note: See the next section, "Add Members to a Group," to learn how to add users to your new group.

TIPS

Can I make changes to a group that I created?
Yes, you can change the group's name, description, and other settings. Follow steps 1 to 3 to display your account's groups and then click the **View** button beside the group you want to modify.

Can I delete a group that I created?
Yes. Follow steps 1 to 3 to display your account's group and then click the **Delete** button beside the group you want to remove. When Zoom asks you to confirm, click **Delete**.

Add Members to a Group

After you create a group, your next task is to add the users you want in the group. By default, new groups do not contain any users. As a group administrator, your job is to populate a new group with all the users you want to be in that group. Each user you add to a group is known as a *member* of that group. You can add users one at a time or you can add multiple users. Either way, you need to know the email address of each user you want to add.

Add Members to a Group

1. Use a web browser to navigate to https://zoom.us (not shown).
2. Click **User Management**.
3. Click **Group Management**.
4. Click **View** for the group you want to work with.

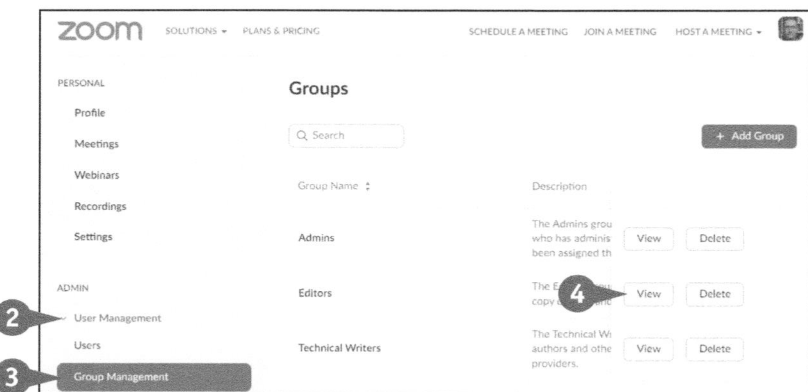

Zoom displays the group's Profile page.

5. Click the number that appears to the right of the **Total Members** label.

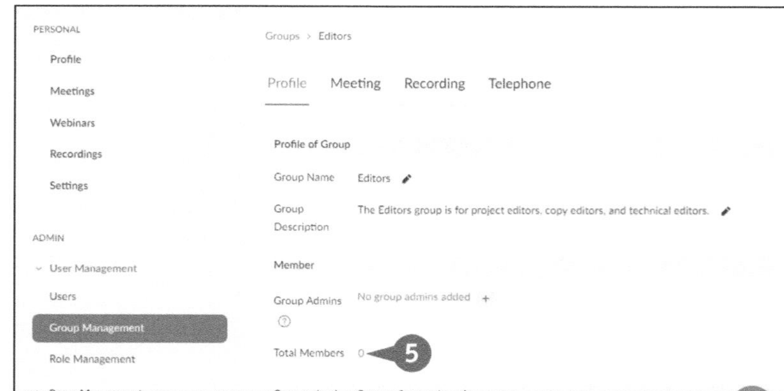

Zoom displays the group's Members page.

6 Click **Add Members**.

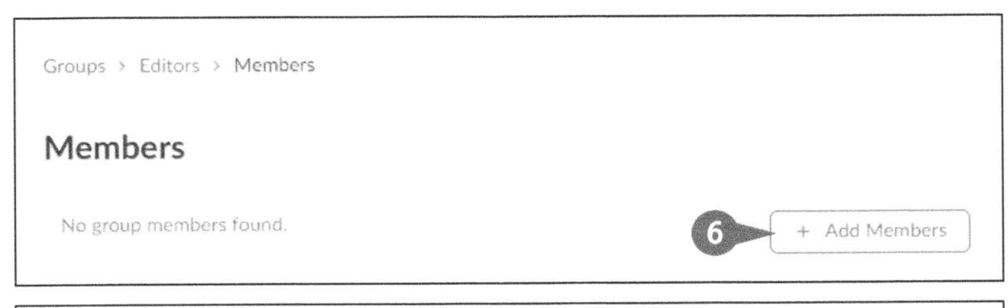

Zoom displays the Add Members dialog.

7 Begin typing the email address of the user you want to add to the group.

A Zoom displays a list of users who match what you have typed.

8 Click the user you want to add.

Note: To add multiple users, repeat steps 7 and 8 as needed.

9 Click **Add**.

Zoom adds the users to the group.

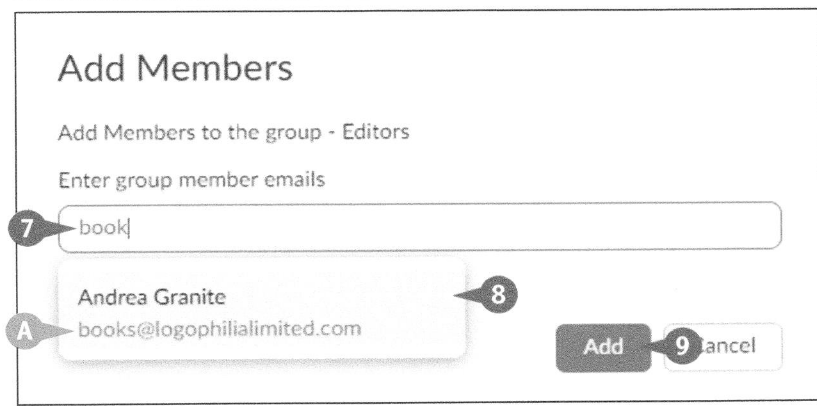

TIPS

How do I apply meeting settings to a group?
Follow steps 1 to 4 to display the group's Profile page. Click the **Meeting** tab and then modify the meeting settings that you want to apply to the group. See Chapters 8 and 9 to learn how to work with these settings.

Can I remove a user from a group?
Yes. Follow steps 1 to 5 to display the group's Members page. Click the **Remove** button for the user you want to remove from the group. When Zoom asks you to confirm, click **Delete**.

Move a User to Another Group

After you add a user to a group, you might later realize that the user would be better suited in a different group. Similarly, you might create a new group and realize that a member of another group might fit better in the new group. For whatever reason, instead of removing the user from the existing group and adding that user to the other group, you can complete everything in one step by moving the user to the other group.

Move a User to Another Group

1. For the group in which the user is currently a member, follow steps 1 to 5 in the previous section, "Add Members to a Group."

   Zoom displays the group's Members page.

2. Click **More** (···).
3. Click **Move To Another Group**.

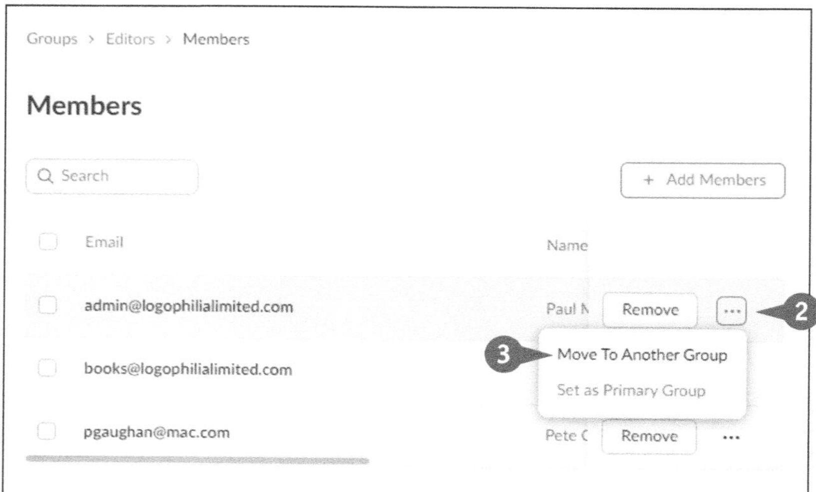

   Zoom displays the Move To Another Group dialog.

4. Click the list ⌄ and then click the group to which you want to move the user.
5. Click **Move**.

   Zoom moves the user to the group you selected.

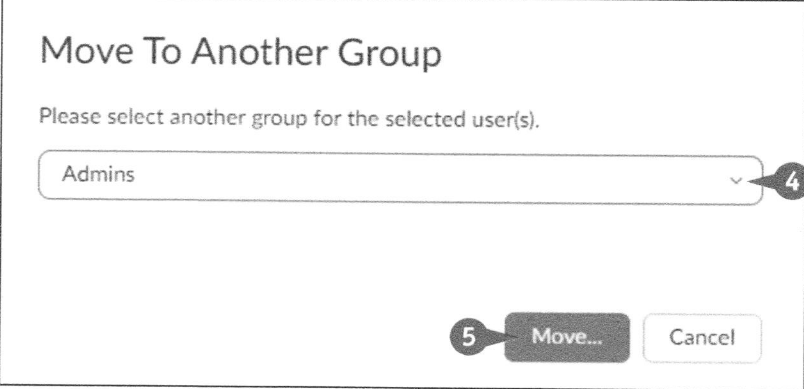

Set a User's Primary Group

If a user is a member of multiple groups, you can change which of those groups defines the user's default settings. One of the advantages of groups is that you can apply settings for meetings and security to the group and those settings automatically apply to each member. If a user is a member of multiple groups, Zoom applies the settings from the user's *primary* group, which is usually the first group to which the user became a member. If you would prefer that another group's settings get applied to a user, you can change that user's primary group.

Set a User's Primary Group

1. For the group in which the user is currently a member, follow steps 1 to 5 in the section "Add Members to a Group," earlier in this chapter.

   Zoom displays the group's Members page.

2. Click **More** (···).
3. Click **Set as Primary Group**.

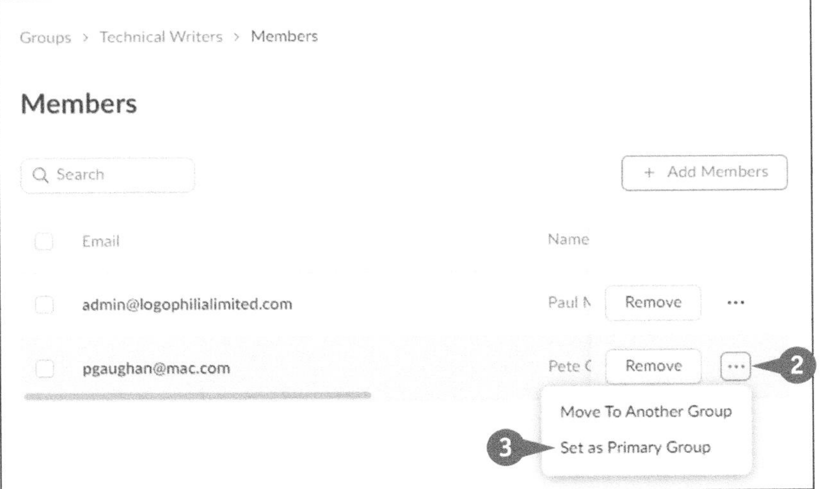

   Zoom displays the Set as Primary Group dialog.

4. Click **Save**.

   Zoom changes the user's primary group.

Add an External Contact

If there are Zoom users with whom you want to communicate, you can add those users as external contacts. Your Zoom account has a Contacts directory that you can use to launch chat sessions with other Zoom users. The Contacts directory also enables you to easily set up meetings with other Zoom users. To add a Zoom user to your Contacts directory, you must invite that user to be a contact, and that user must accept your invitation.

You can invite a Zoom user to be an external contact using either the Zoom desktop app or the Zoom mobile app.

Add an External Contact

Using the Zoom Desktop App

1. Click **Contacts**.
2. Click **Add** (+).
3. Click **Invite a Zoom Contact**.

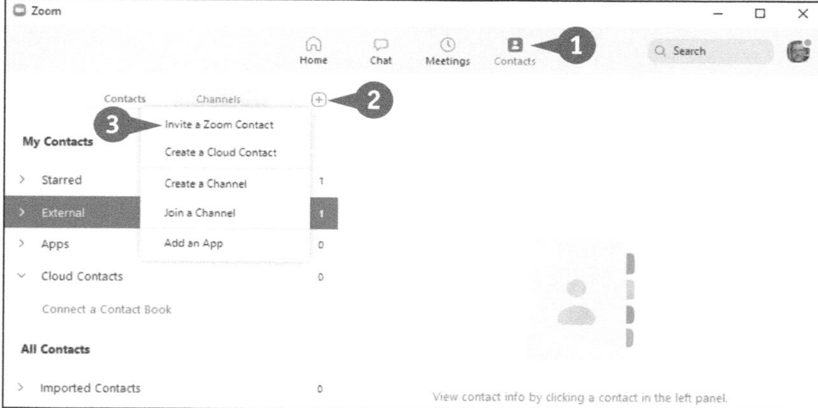

Zoom displays the Invite to Zoom dialog.

4. Type the contact's email address.
5. Click **Invite**.

Zoom lets you know that it has sent the invitation.

6. Click **OK** (not shown).

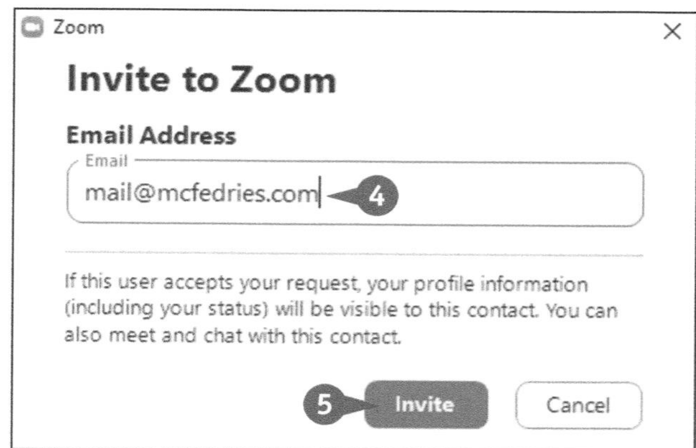

Using the Zoom Mobile App

1. Tap **Contacts**.
2. Tap **Add** (⊕).
3. Tap **Invite a Zoom Contact**.

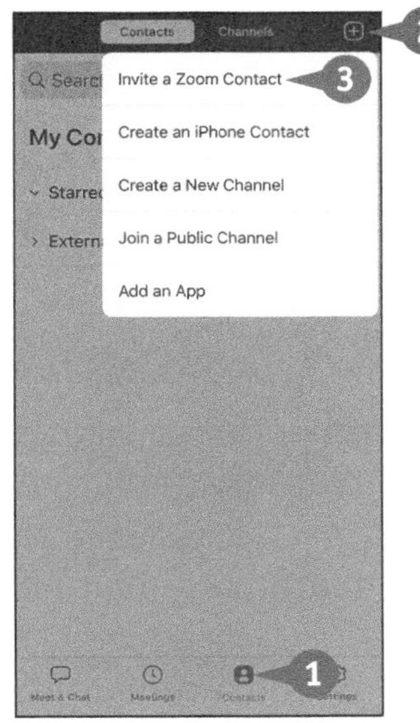

Zoom displays the Invite to Zoom screen.

4. Type the contact's email address.
5. Tap **Add**.

   Zoom lets you know that it has sent the invitation.

6. Tap **OK** (not shown).

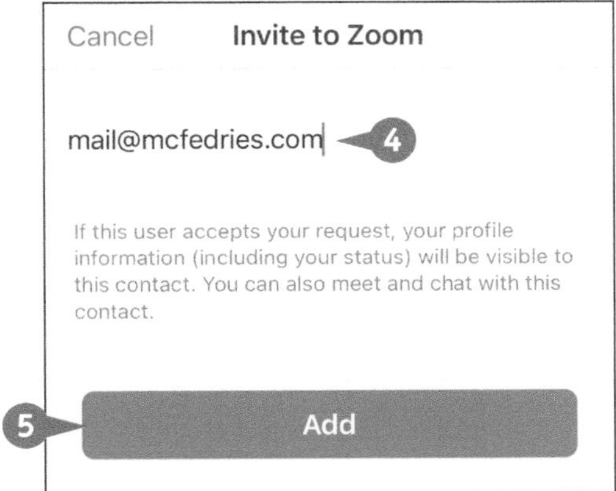

TIPS

How do I block an external contact?
In any Zoom app, select the **Contacts** tab and then select **External** (desktop) or **External Contacts** (mobile) to display your list of external contacts. In the mobile app, tap the external contact you want to remove. Select **More** (···) and then select **Block Contact**. When Zoom asks you to confirm, select **Block**.

How do I delete an external contact?
In any Zoom app, select the **Contacts** tab and then select **External** (desktop) or **External Contacts** (mobile) to display your list of external contacts. In the mobile app, tap the external contact you want to remove. Select **More** (···) and then select **Delete Contact**. When Zoom asks you to confirm, select **Delete**.

Accept a Contact Request

If you receive an invitation to be an external contact for another Zoom user, you need to accept that invitation to complete the request. Just as you can invite other Zoom users to be external contacts in your Zoom account, so too can other Zoom users invite you to be an external contact. Accepting the request enables that person to see your Zoom profile and your current Zoom status.

You can accept a contact request from a Zoom user using either the Zoom desktop app or the Zoom mobile app.

Accept a Contact Request

Using the Zoom Desktop App

1. Click **Chat**.
2. Click **Contact Requests**.
3. Click **Accept**.

A. If you do not want to accept the invitation, click **Decline** instead.

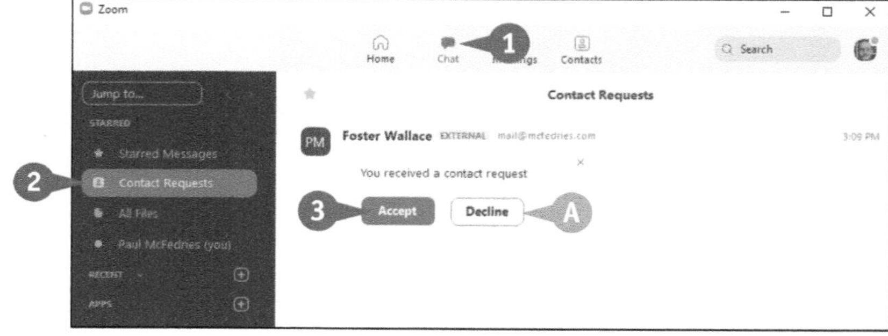

Zoom asks you to confirm.

4. Click **Accept Request**.

Zoom adds you as an external contact for the other user.

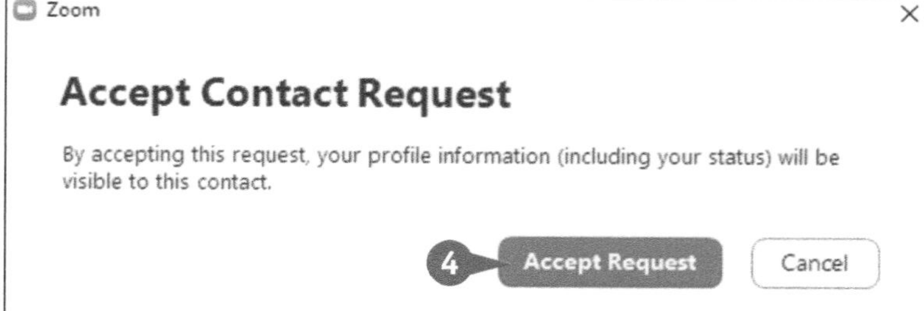

Using the Zoom Mobile App

1 Tap **Meet & Chat**.

2 Tap **Contact Requests**.

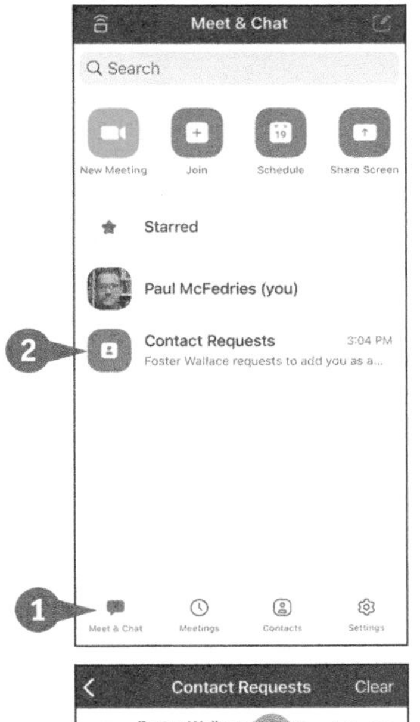

Zoom displays the Contact Requests screen.

3 Tap **Accept** (✓).

B If you do not want to accept the invitation, click **Decline** (✕) instead.

Zoom adds you as an external contact for the other user.

TIP

What does it mean to star an external contact?

Starring an external contact is a way of marking that user as a favorite. This is useful if you frequently chat or meet with someone because a starred contact appears in the Contacts screen's Starred category, which enables you to easily find the contacts you use most often.

To star a contact in the Zoom desktop app, click the **Contacts** tab and then click **External** to display your list of external contacts. Select **More** (···) beside the contact you want to star and then click **Star this Contact**.

In the mobile app, tap **Contacts**, tap **External Contacts**, tap the external contact you want to star, and then tap **Star** (☆ changes to ★).

CHAPTER 11

Chatting with Zoom

Although you will mostly use Zoom for meetings, you can also use Zoom to chat with other people. For example, you can chat with contacts and exchange files and audio messages. You can create a channel for ongoing conversation, add data to your personal chat space, and more.

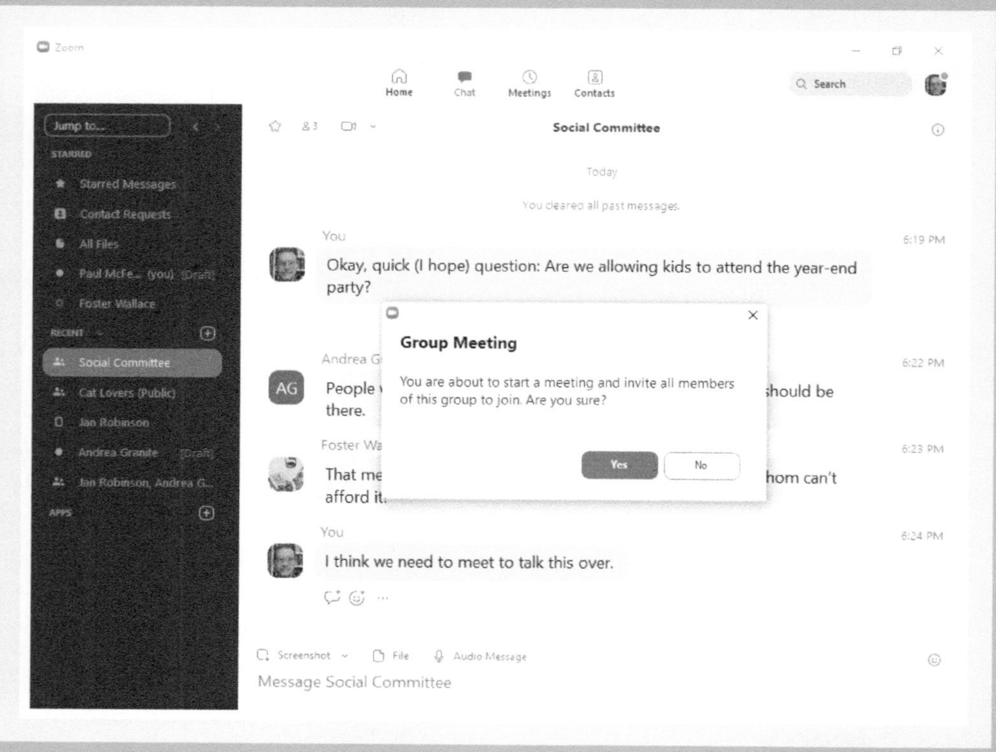

Start a New Chat

You can exchange text messages with any Zoom contact by starting a chat session with that person. Zoom meetings are a great way to exchange information, but they are often overkill if you need to impart only a small amount of information with one person or if you just want to have a short conversation with someone. For these more limited scenarios, a better solution is a chat session where you exchange brief text messages with someone in your Zoom Contacts directory.

Start a New Chat

Using the Zoom Desktop App

1. Click **Chat**.
2. Click the contact with whom you want to chat.

   A The contact's Zoom status (see Chapter 1) appears here.

3. Type your message and then press Enter or Return.

   Zoom sends your message to the contact.

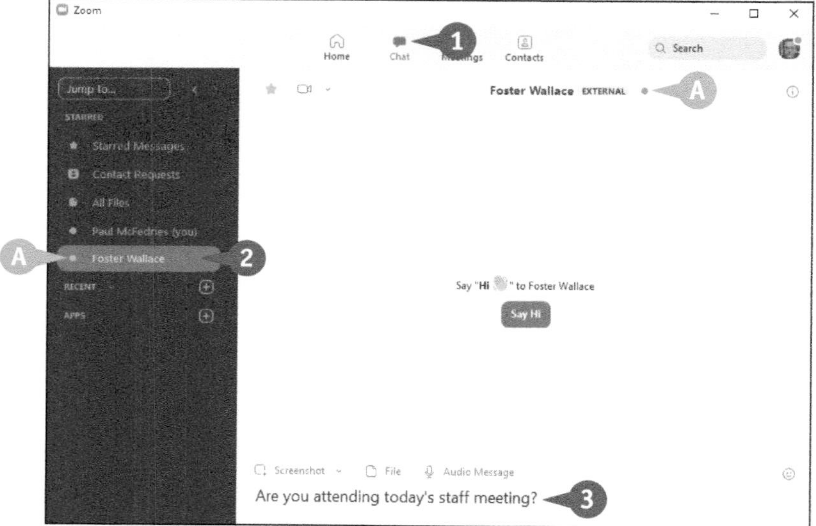

Using the Zoom Mobile App

1. Tap **Contacts**.
2. Click the contact with whom you want to chat.

   B The contact's Zoom status (see Chapter 1) appears here.

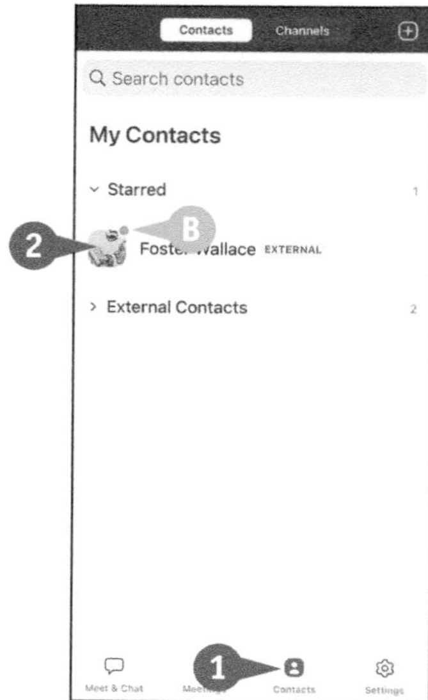

3 Tap **Chat**.

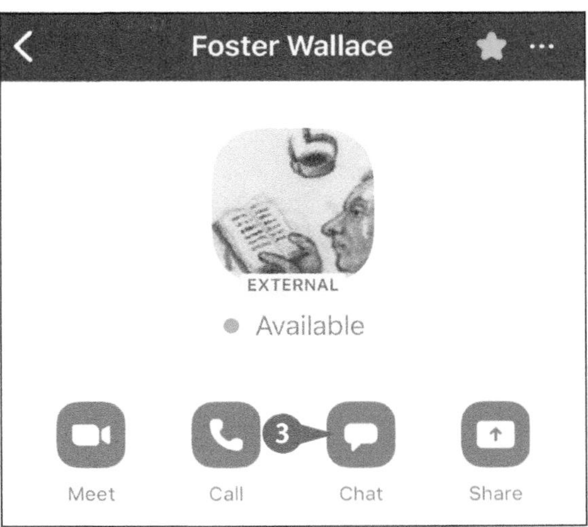

4 Type your message.

5 Tap **Send** (▼) or tap Return.

Zoom sends your message to the contact.

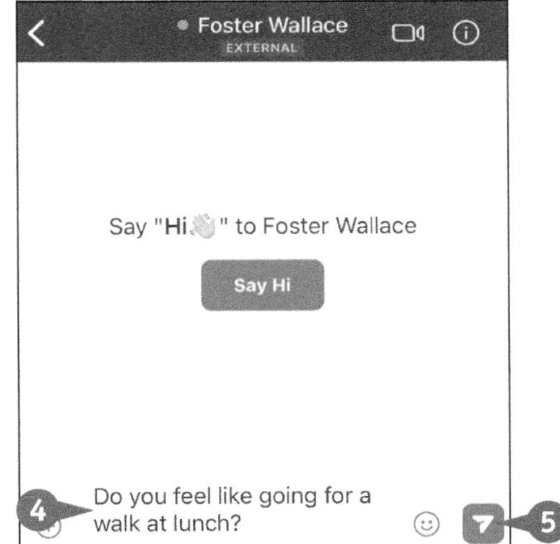

TIP

Is there a way to get notified when a contact becomes available?

Yes, you can configure the chat to display a notification when the contact's status changes to Available.

In the Zoom desktop app, click **Chat**, click the contact, and then click the **More Info** icon (ⓘ) in the upper-right corner of the chat window. In the About This Chat pane that appears, click **More Options** and then click **Notify Me When Available**.

In the Zoom mobile app, tap **Contacts**, tap the contact, tap **Chat**, and then tap the **More Info** icon (ⓘ) in the upper-right corner of the chat screen. In the About Chat screen that appears, tap the **Notify Me When Available** switch to On (◉).

Reply to a Chat Message

If you receive a chat message from a contact, you can reply to that message. Although you will occasionally receive a chat message that requires no response from you, almost all chat messages require some form of reply. The reply could be an answer to a question, information requested by the sender, an acknowledgment that you will perform some task, or a simple thank-you.

How you reply to a chat message varies depending on whether you are using the Zoom desktop app or the Zoom mobile app.

Reply to a Chat Message

Using the Zoom Desktop App

1. Click **Chat**.

   A. The **Unread Messages** icon (1) tells you how many unread chat messages you have.

2. Click the contact to whom you want to reply.

   Zoom displays the latest chat messages the contact has sent to you.

3. Click **Reply** (💬) beside the message to which you want to respond.

4. Type your reply and then press Enter or Return.

   Zoom sends your reply to the contact.

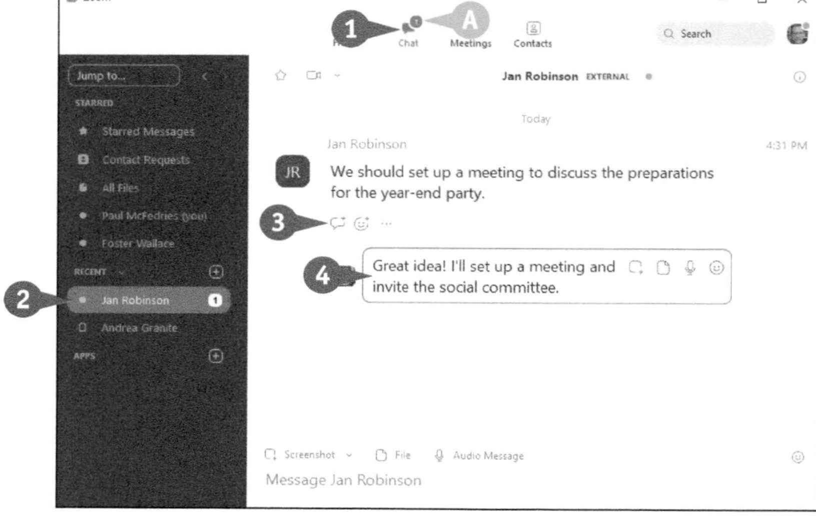

Using the Zoom Mobile App

1. Tap **Meet & Chat**.
2. Tap the contact to whom you want to reply.

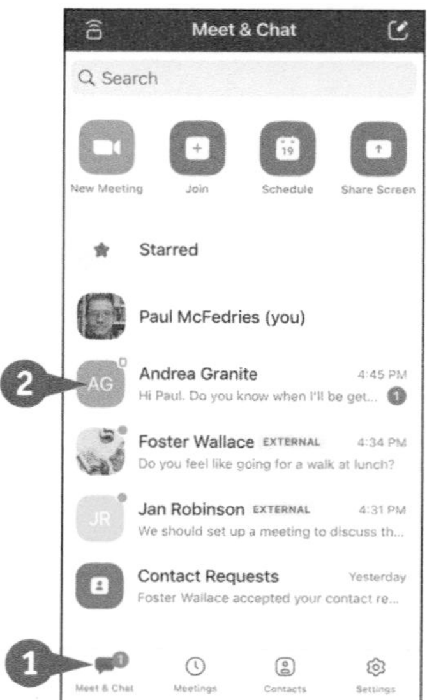

Zoom displays the latest chat messages the contact has sent to you.

3 Tap **Reply** (💬).

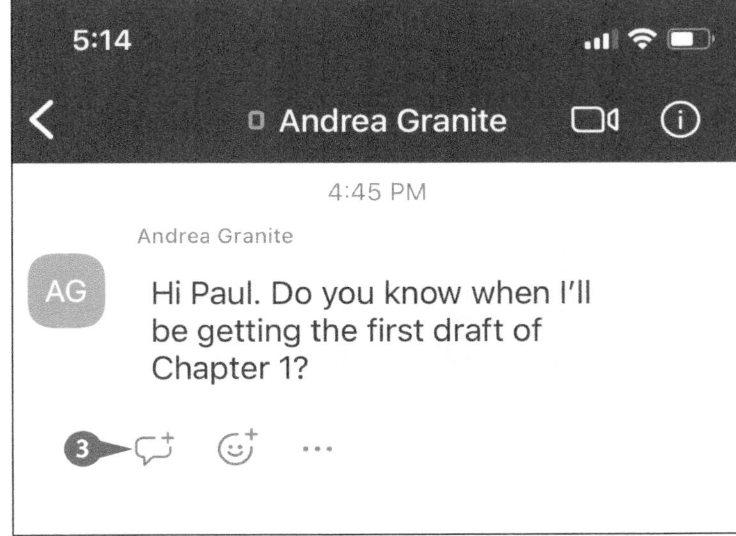

Zoom displays the Replies screen.

4 Type your reply.

5 Tap **Send** (▼) or tap Return.

Zoom sends your reply to the contact.

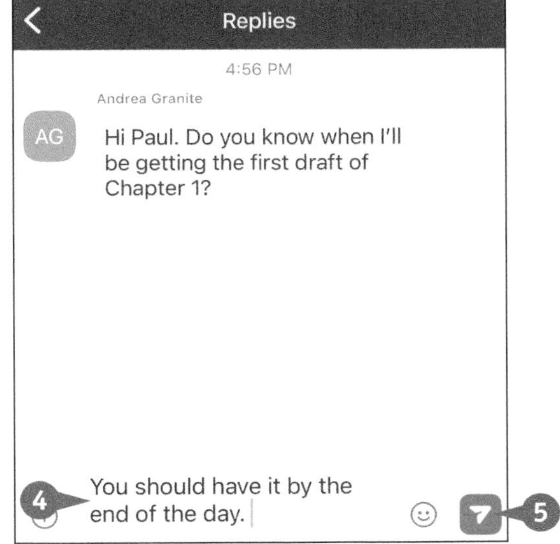

TIPS

Can I reply with an animated GIF?
Yes. In the chat text box, select the **Smiley** icon (☺), select **GIF**, and then select the animated GIF you want to include in your reply.

Can I format my message text?
Yes, the Zoom desktop app offers a limited number of formatting options. In the chat text box, select the text you want to format. In the formatting toolbar that appears over the text, you can click **Bold** (B), **Italic** (/), **Strikethrough** (S), or **Bulleted List** (☰).

Reply with a Screenshot

During a chat conversation, you can send to the other person a reply that includes an image of some or all of your computer screen. If a chat correspondent asks a question or requests information, sometimes the most efficient way to respond is to send an image of your computer screen. The desktop version of the Zoom app includes a Screenshot tool that enables you to capture as much of your computer screen as you need. The Screenshot feature also offers a set of tools to annotate and work with your screenshot.

Reply with a Screenshot

1. Click **Chat**.
2. Click the contact to whom you want to reply.

   Zoom displays the latest chat messages the contact has sent to you.
3. Click **Reply** (💬) beside the message to which you want to respond.

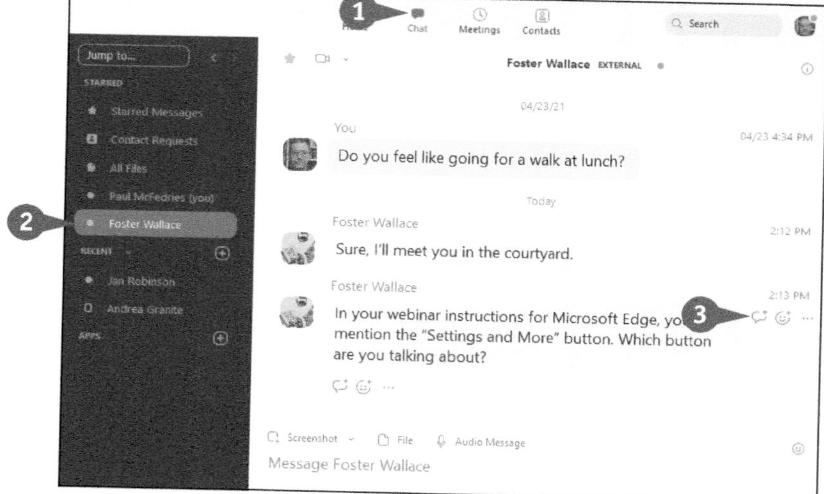

4. Click **Screenshot** (▢).

   The mouse pointer changes from ↖ to +.

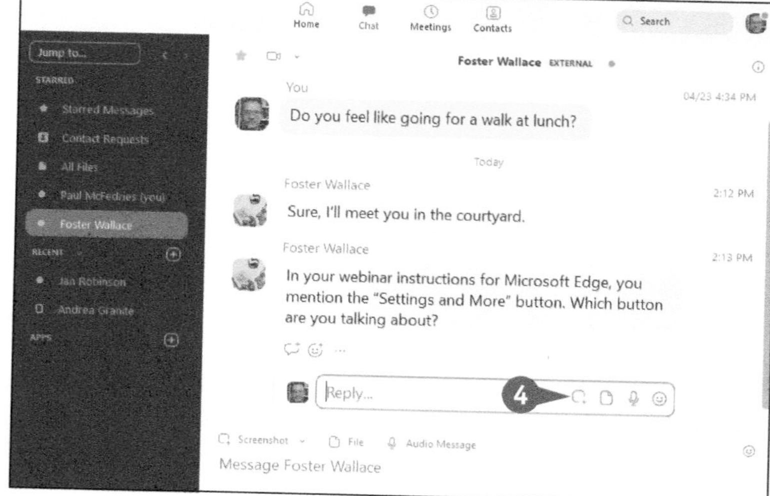

5 Switch to the window or app that has the screen image you want to capture.

6 Drag + over the area of the screen you want to capture.

A When you release the mouse, Zoom displays the screenshot tools.

Note: See the tip at the end of this section to learn more about the screenshot tools.

7 Click **Capture**.

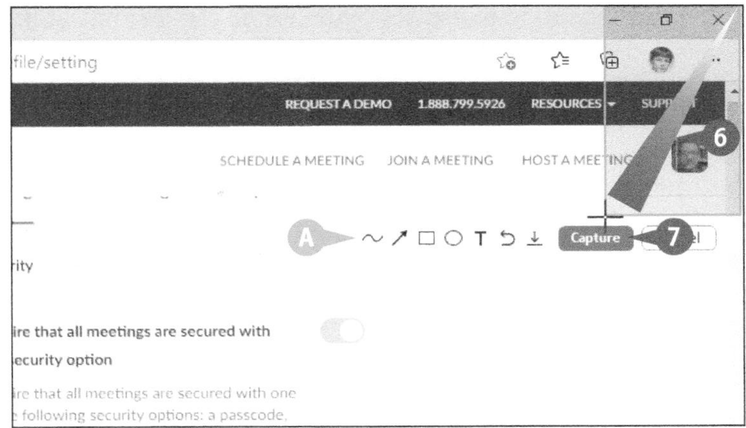

B Zoom adds the screenshot to your reply.

8 Type your reply and then press Enter or Return.

Zoom sends your screenshot and reply to the contact.

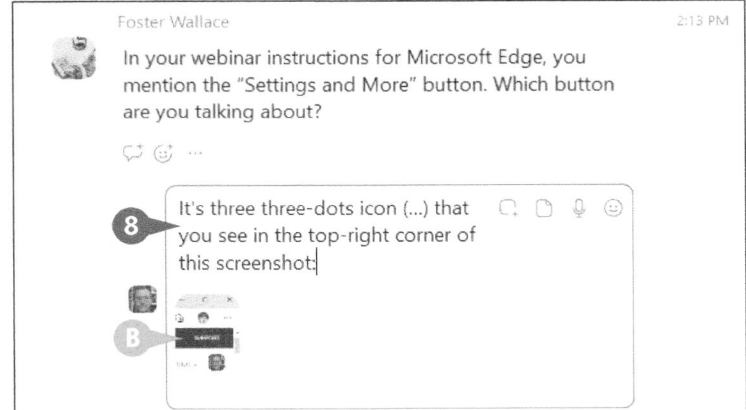

TIP

What do the screenshot tools do?

You use the screenshot tools to annotate or work with your screenshot, as described in the following table.

Tool	Name	Click the Tool to. . .
∼	Freeform	Draw a freeform line inside the screenshot.
↗	Arrow	Draw an arrow inside the screenshot.
□	Rectangle	Add a rectangle or square to the screenshot.
○	Oval	Add an oval or circle to the screenshot.
T	Text	Add text to the screenshot.
↶	Undo	Remove the most recent annotation from the screenshot.
⤓	Download	Save the screenshot as a graphics file.

Send a File

During a chat conversation, you might realize that you need to send the other person a file from your computer. The fastest and easiest way to send the file is to send it directly from the chat window.

If, while chatting with someone, you decide to send that person a file, you might think that the best method is to create an email message and attach the file to that message. However, the Zoom desktop app's Chat feature offers a File tool that you can use to include the file as part of the reply.

Send a File

1. Click **Chat**.
2. Click the contact to whom you want to reply.

   Zoom displays the latest chat messages the contact has sent to you.
3. Click **Reply** (💬) beside the message to which you want to respond.

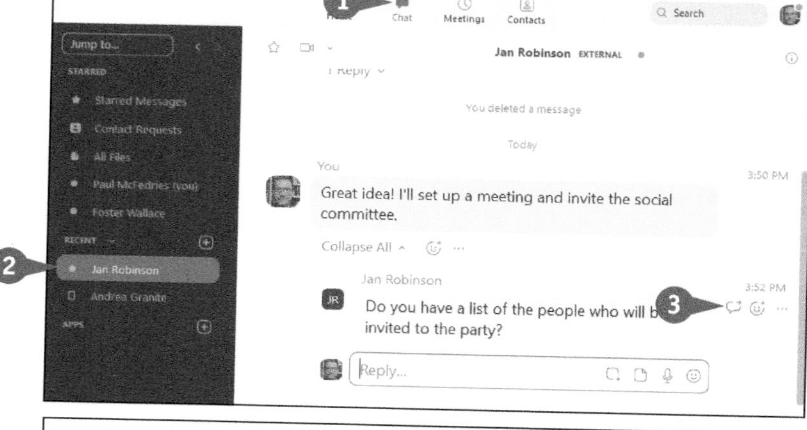

4. Click **File** (🗋).

   Zoom displays a list of locations.
5. Click the location of the file. The steps that follow assume you clicked **Your Computer**.

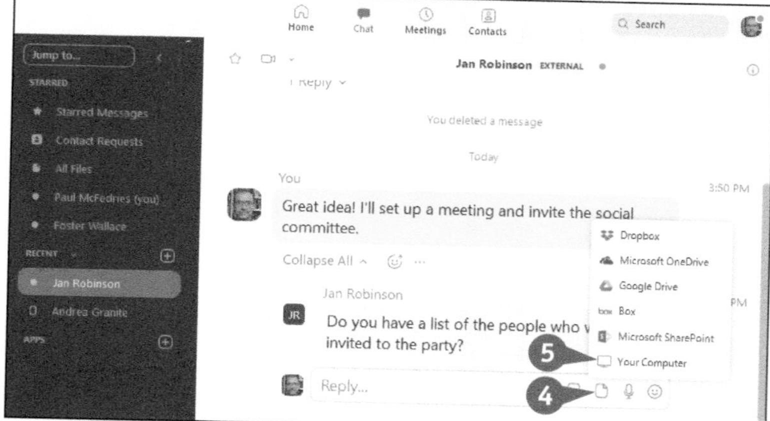

The Upload Files dialog appears.

6 Select the location of the file.

7 Select the file.

8 Click **Open**.

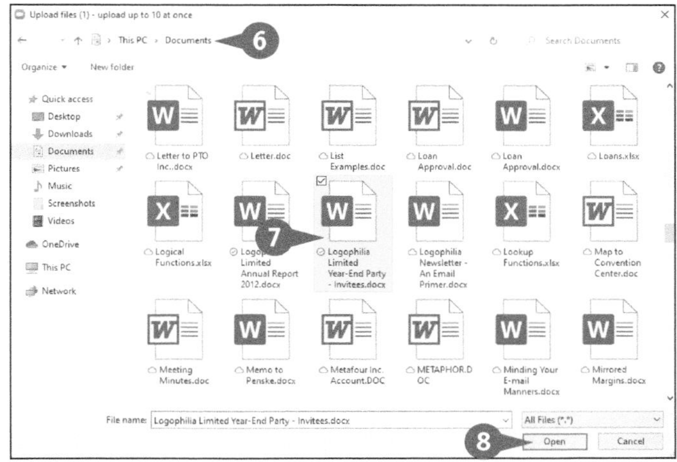

A Zoom adds the file to your reply.

9 Type your reply and then press Enter or Return.

Zoom sends your file and reply to the contact.

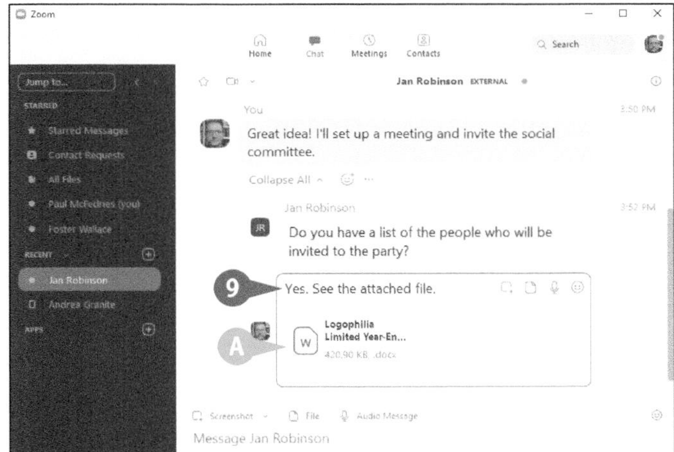

TIP

How do I save a file that I receive during a chat?

When you receive a message that has a file attachment, the message shows the name of the file, with the file's type icon to the left. Follow these steps to save the file to your computer:

1 Click the file's name or icon.

Zoom opens the Save As dialog.

2 Select a folder to store the file.

3 (Optional) Edit the filename.

4 Click **Save**.

Zoom saves the file to the folder you specified.

Reply with an Audio Message

During a chat conversation, you can send to the other person a reply that includes a recorded audio message. Most chat conversations are text-based, but there might be times when it is better to send a voice recording. For example, it might be faster to record something, or you might prefer a voice recording to make sure the other person hears certain vocal nuances.

The desktop and mobile versions of the Zoom app include an Audio Message tool that enables you to record a message using your device microphone. You can record up to 1 minute of audio.

Reply with an Audio Message

Using the Zoom Desktop App

1 Click **Chat**.

2 Click the contact to whom you want to reply.

3 Click **Reply** (💬) beside the message to which you want to respond.

4 Click **Audio Message** (🎙).

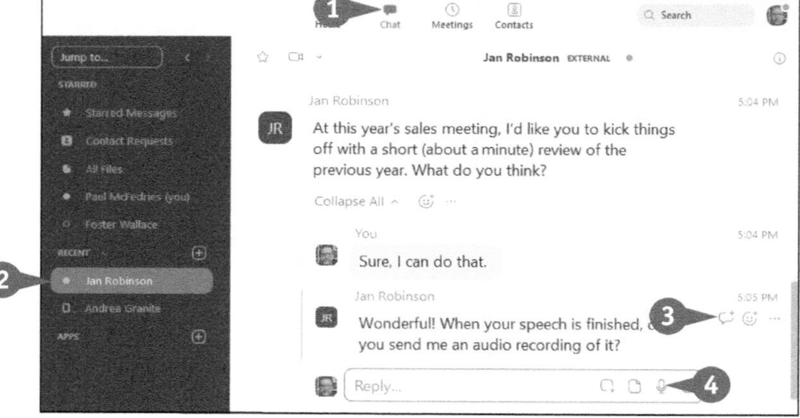

Zoom begins recording your audio.

5 Speak your message into your computer's microphone.

A Zoom displays a waveform for your audio as you speak.

6 When you are done, click **Send** (▶).

Zoom sends the audio message to the contact.

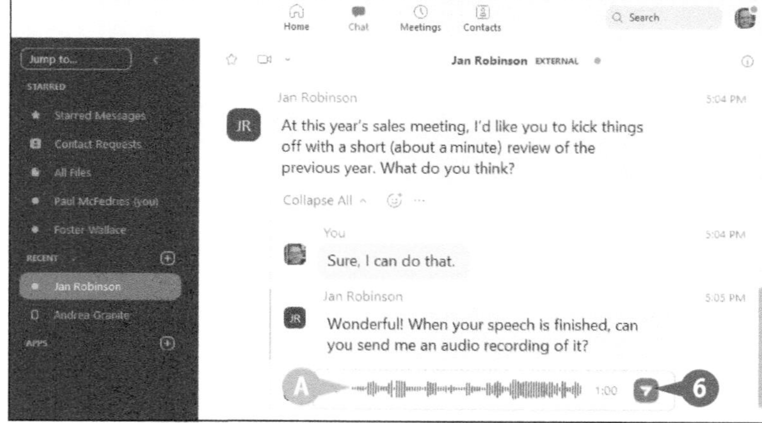

Using the Zoom Mobile App

1 Open the chat conversation.

2 Tap **Audio Message** (🎙).

Note: If your device asks for permission for Zoom to access the microphone, be sure to allow it.

3 Tap and hold the **Hold to record** icon (🎙).

Zoom begins recording your audio.

4 Speak your message into your device's microphone.

5 When you are done, release 🎙.

Zoom sends the audio message to the contact.

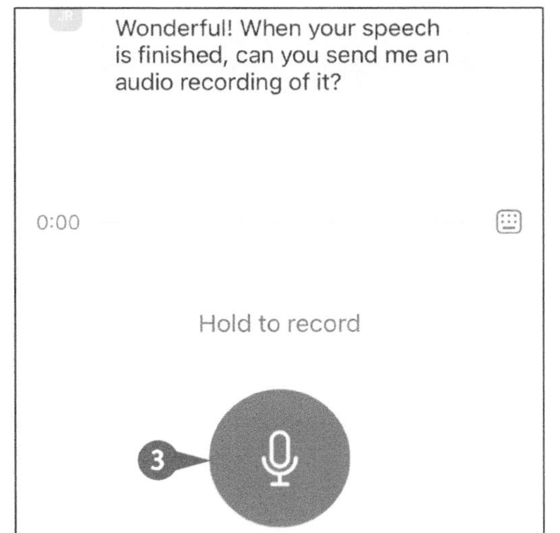

TIPS

How do I listen to an audio message I receive during a chat?
Open the conversation and look for the audio message item. If you are working in the Zoom desktop app, click **Play** (▶) or click the audio message; if you are using the Zoom mobile app, tap the audio message.

Is there a way to send a longer audio message?
Yes. You can use your computer or mobile device to record your message using an app such as Voice Recorder for Windows and Voice Memos for iOS. Save the recorded message as an audio file and then send the other person the audio file using the steps outlined in the previous section, "Send a File."

Manage Important Chat Messages

Zoom gives you several ways to work with chat messages that are important to you. Most chat conversations are used to exchange brief messages or answer quick questions, which means that most chat messages are unimportant. However, you might occasionally have a chat where one or more of the messages are important. In such cases, Zoom gives you three methods for managing those important messages: you can star a message for quick access, you can follow a message to get a notification if someone replies to it, or you can share a message with one or more of your contacts.

Manage Important Chat Messages

Star a Message

1. Locate the message you want to work with.
2. Select **More** (···).
3. Select **Star**.

   Zoom copies the message to the **Starred Messages** section.

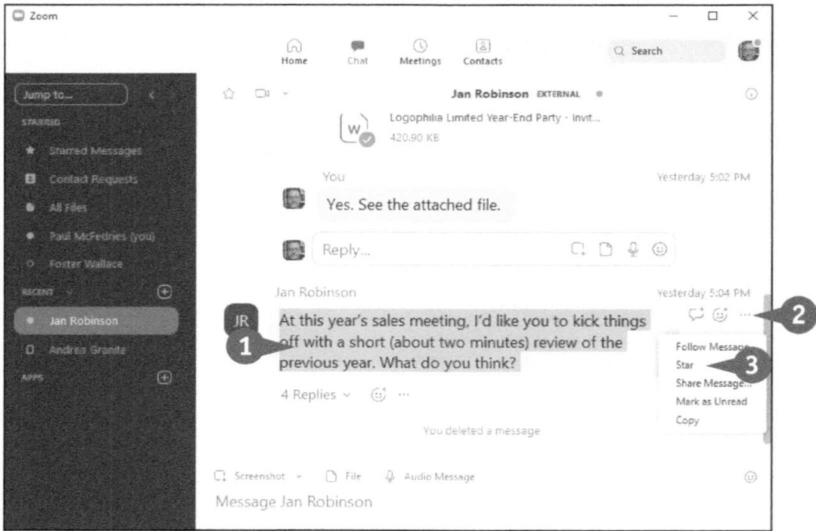

Follow a Message

1. Locate the message you want to work with.
2. Select **More** (···).
3. Select **Follow Message**.

   Zoom will now display a notification if someone replies to the message.

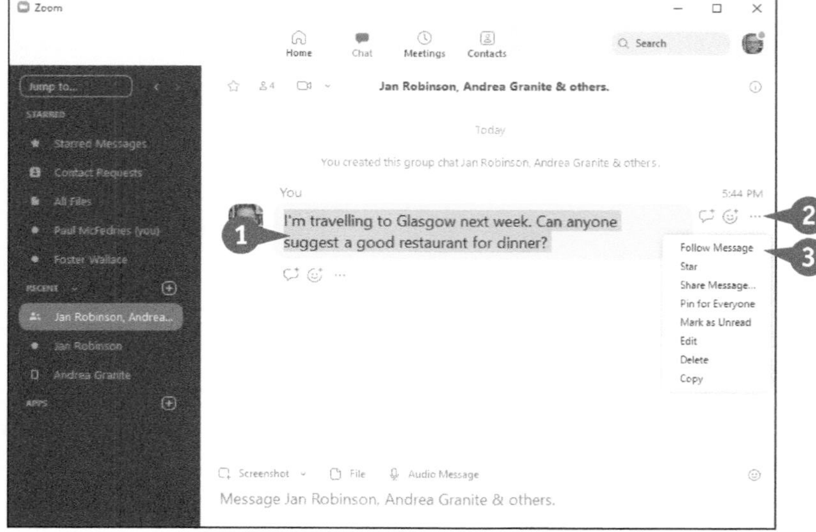

Share a Message

1. Locate the message you want to work with.
2. Select **More** (···).
3. Select **Share Message** (desktop) or **Share** (mobile).

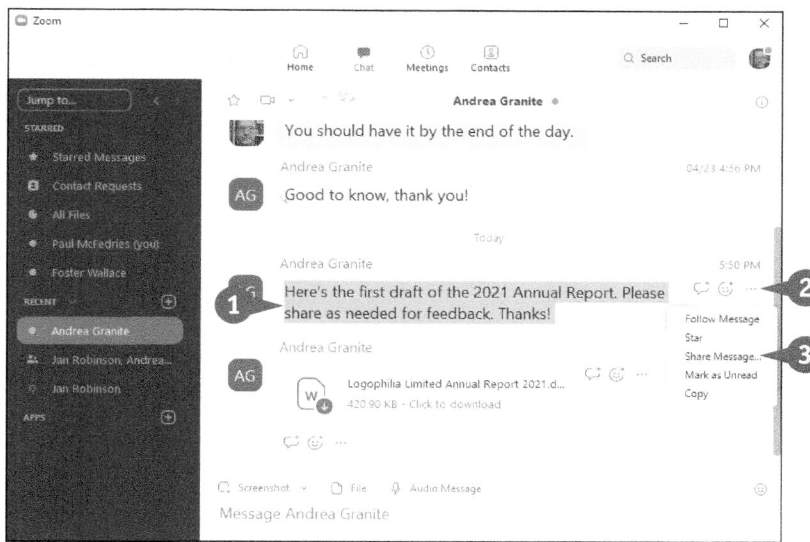

The Share Message window appears.

4. In the Zoom desktop app, select the users and contacts with whom you want to share the message.
5. Click **Share**.

Note: In the Zoom mobile app, tap the user or contact and then tap **OK** to send the message to that person.

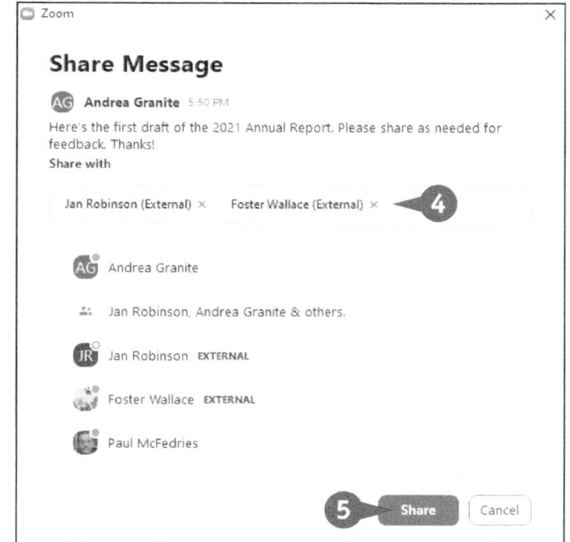

TIPS

How do I unstar a chat message?

There are two methods you can use. First, you can display the original starred message, select **More** (···), and then select **Unstar**. Alternatively, open the Starred Messages screen, select **More** (···) beside the message you want to work with, and then select **Unstar**.

How do I stop following a chat message?

In the chat window, display the message that you are currently following. Select **More** (···) beside the message and then select **Unfollow Message**.

Configure Chat Notifications

You can gain some control over how often the Zoom app displays notifications for chat messages by configuring Zoom's chat notification settings. By default, Zoom displays a push notification for every message you receive. If you find that you are receiving too many push notifications, you can configure Zoom to display notifications only for private (that is, one-on-one) messages and whenever you are mentioned in a chat.

Zoom also offers a collection of settings for configuring various aspects of chat notifications, such as whether Zoom plays a sound with the notification and whether the notification banner stays on-screen.

Configure Chat Notifications

Using the Zoom Desktop App

1. Click your profile picture.
2. Click **Settings**.

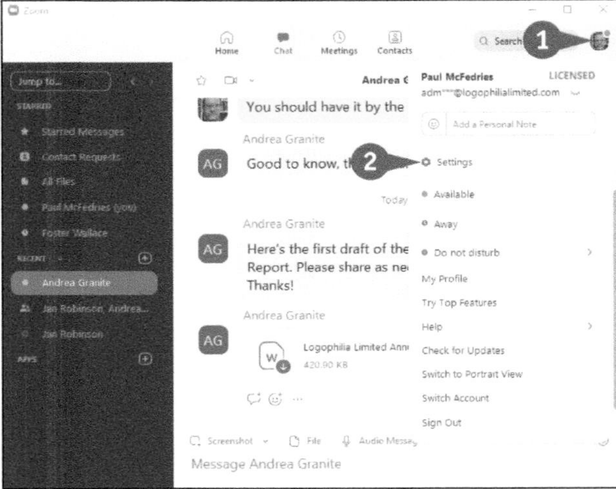

The Settings window appears.

3. Click **Chat**.

Zoom displays the Chat settings.

4. Select the option you prefer for receiving push notifications (○ changes to ◉).
5. Use these settings to configure the notifications displayed by the Zoom app.

Zoom puts your new settings into effect immediately.

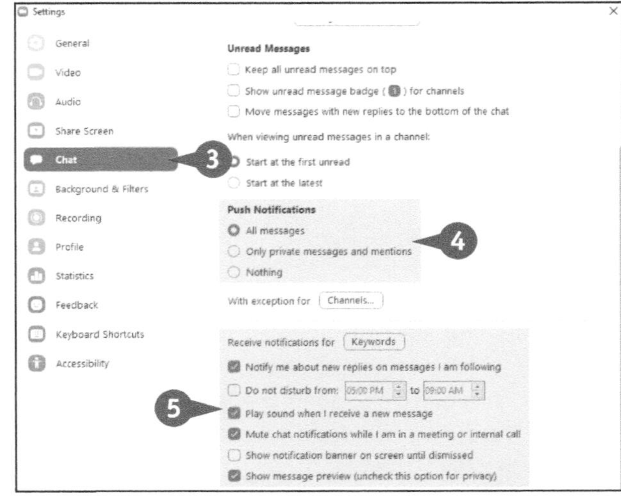

Using the Zoom Mobile App

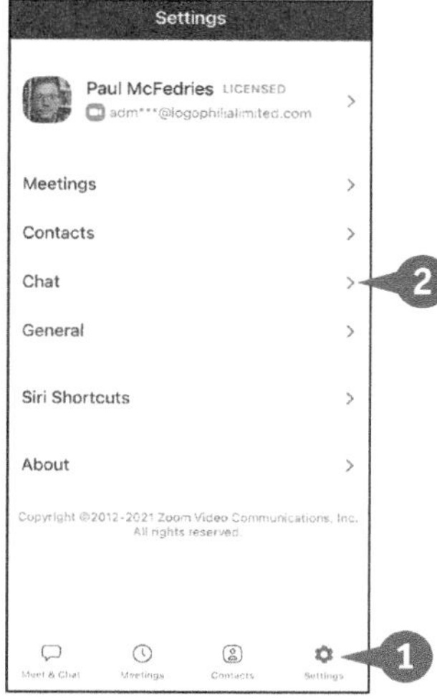

1 Tap **Settings**.

The Settings screen appears.

2 Tap **Chat**.

Zoom displays the Chat settings.

3 Select the option you prefer for receiving push notifications.

4 Use these settings to configure the notifications displayed by the Zoom app.

Zoom puts your new settings into effect immediately.

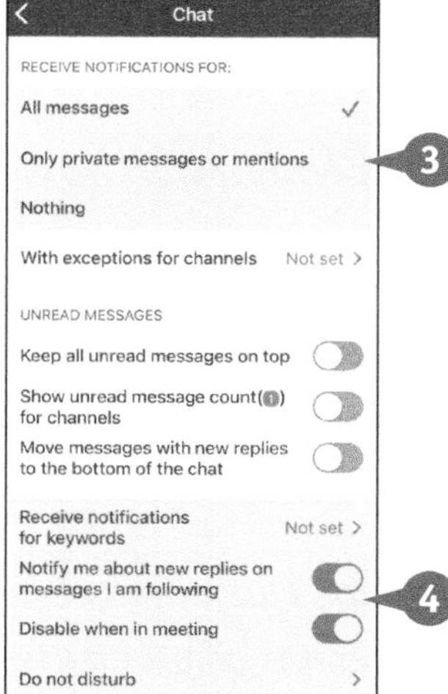

TIPS

What does it mean to receive notifications for keywords?
When you configure this chat notification setting, you specify one or more words (separated by commas) that are of interest to you. Whenever you receive a chat message that includes any of these keywords, you will receive a notification from the Zoom app.

Can I prevent chat notifications from displaying at certain times?
Yes, by enabling the Do Not Disturb feature in Zoom's chat notification settings. When you enable Do Not Disturb, you specify a start time and an end time, and Zoom pauses notifications between those times. When the Do Not Disturb period ends, Zoom displays all the notifications that you missed.

Create a Channel

You can make it easier for groups of people who are either connected in some way or want to discuss a particular topic to chat by creating a channel. A *channel* is a group of people who share chat messages by sending them to the channel rather than to each other. People who join a channel become *members* of that channel. You can create either a public channel that anyone in your organization can join or a private channel where only invited people can join. You can optionally allow people outside your organization to join your channel.

Create a Channel

Using the Zoom Desktop App

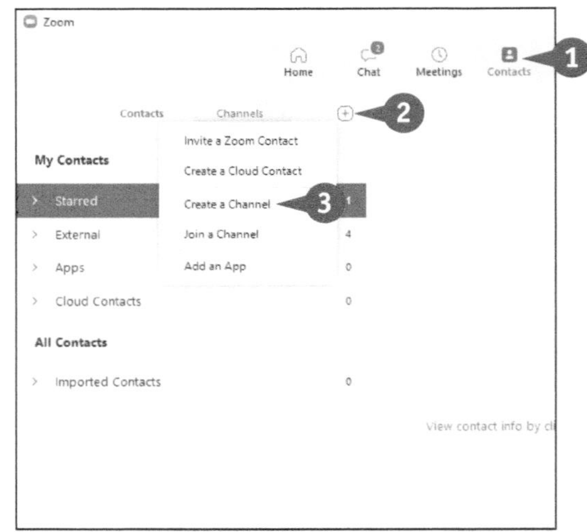

1. Click **Contacts**.
2. Click **Add** (⊕).
3. Click **Create a Channel**.

   The Create a Channel dialog appears.

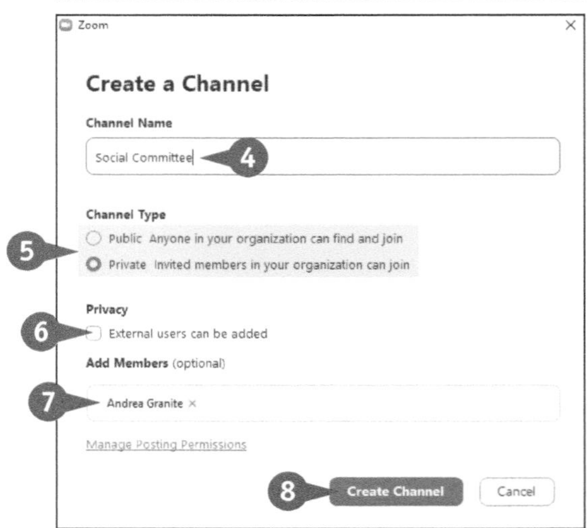

4. Type a name for your channel.
5. Select whether your channel is **Public** or **Private** (○ changes to ◉).
6. If you want to allow people outside of your organization to join the channel, select **External users can be added** (☐ changes to ☑).
7. Enter the names of people you want to add as members.
8. Click **Create Channel**.

   Zoom creates your channel and then adds it to the Channels tab of the Contacts screen.

Using the Zoom Mobile App

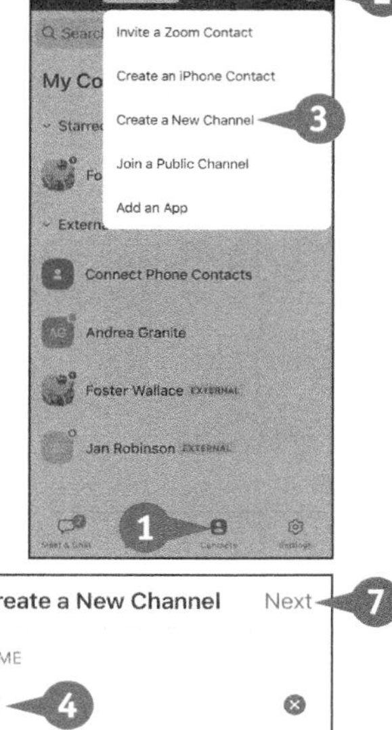

1. Tap **Contacts**.
2. Tap **Add** ().
3. Select **Create a New Channel**.

The Create a New Channel screen appears.

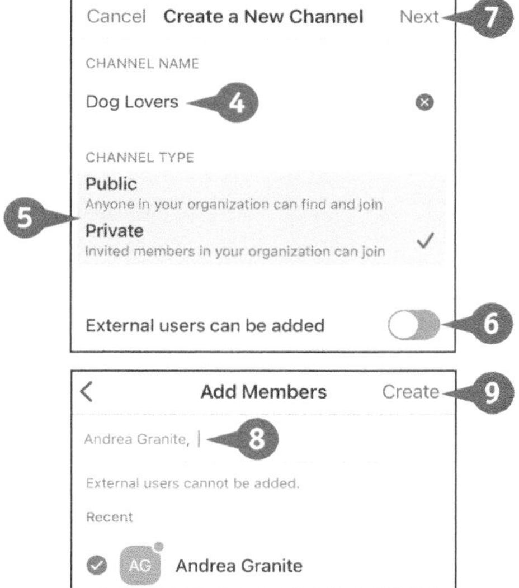

4. Type a name for your channel.
5. Select whether your channel is **Public** or **Private**.
6. If you want to allow people outside of your organization to join the channel, select **External users can be added** (changes to).
7. Tap **Next**.

Zoom displays the Add Members screen.

8. Enter the names of people you want to add as members.
9. Tap **Create**.

Zoom creates your channel and then adds it to the Channels tab of the Contacts screen.

TIPS

Are there any limits on the number of people who can join a channel?
Yes, and the limit depends on the type of Zoom account and on the type of channel. If you have a free Zoom account, private channels can have at most 500 members. If you have a paid Zoom account, private channels can have up to 5,000 members. For all accounts, public channels can have up to 10,000 members.

Can I control who posts to the channel?
Yes. Ordinarily you want to allow every member to post, but in the desktop app you can restrict posting by selecting **Manage Posting Permissions** and then selecting who can post (changes to).

Add Members to a Private Channel

You can populate a private channel by adding one or more members. Although you can add members to a private channel when you create the channel, you might prefer to set up the channel first and then add members. You normally add people who are part of your organization, but you also have the option of adding external users who are not part of your organization.

Add Members to a Private Channel

1. Click **Contacts**.
2. Click **Channels**.
3. Click **More** (···) beside the channel to which you want to add members.
4. Click **Add Members**.

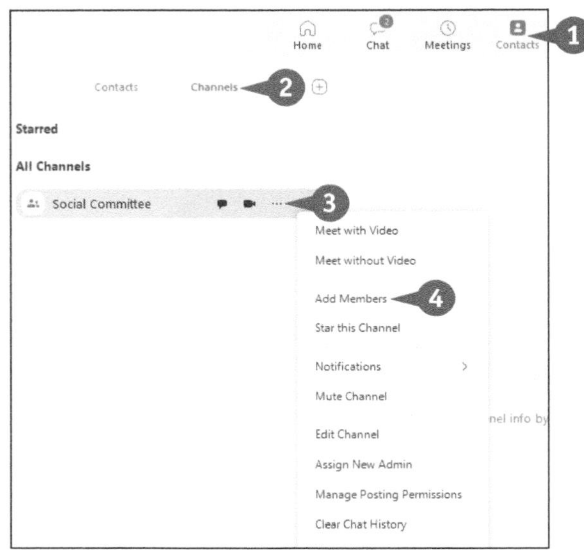

The Add Members dialog appears.

5. To add external users to the channel, select **External users can be added** (☐ changes to ☑).
6. Enter the names of users you want to add as members.
7. Click **Add *X* Members**, where *X* is the number of users you added.

Zoom adds the user as a member of the channel.

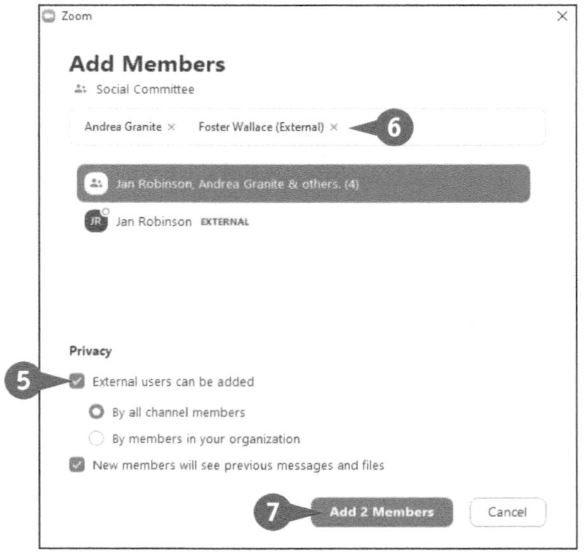

Join a Public Channel

CHAPTER 11

You can participate in group chat within a public channel by joining that channel. If users in your organization have created one or more public channels, you can join one of those channels and become a member so that you can see what other members post and send your own messages to the channel. By definition, anyone in your organization can join a public channel, so there are no restrictions or prerequisites you have to meet.

Join a Public Channel

1. Click **Contacts**.
2. Click **Add** (⊕).
3. Click **Join a Channel**.

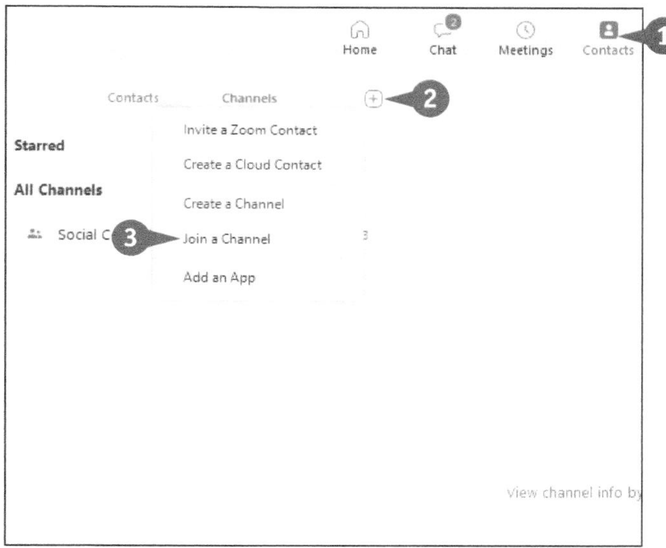

The Join a Channel dialog appears.

4. Type some search text to match the public channel you want to join.
5. Click the channel's **join** button.

Zoom adds you as a member of the public channel.

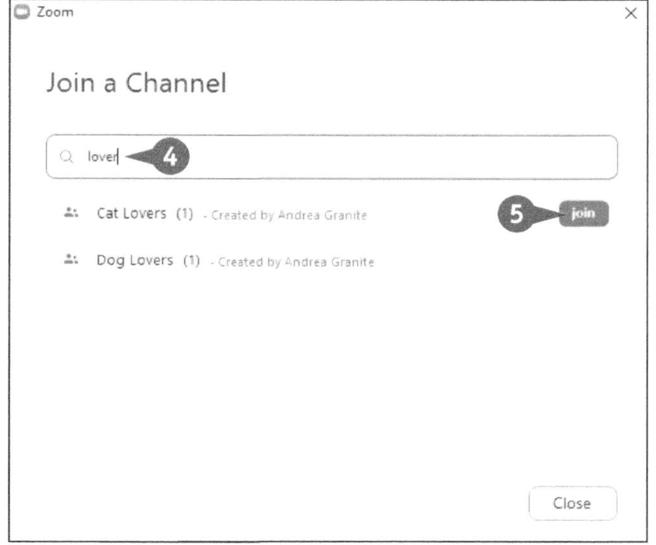

Insert Chat Mentions

You can alert another member of a channel to a channel chat message by inserting a mention of that person's profile name in the message. If you think a chat message you send to a channel is of particular importance to another member of the channel, you might be concerned that the person could miss the message. To increase the chance that the other person sees your message, you can insert a *mention*, which is a special way of invoking the other person's Zoom profile name that sends a notification to that person about your message.

Insert Chat Mentions

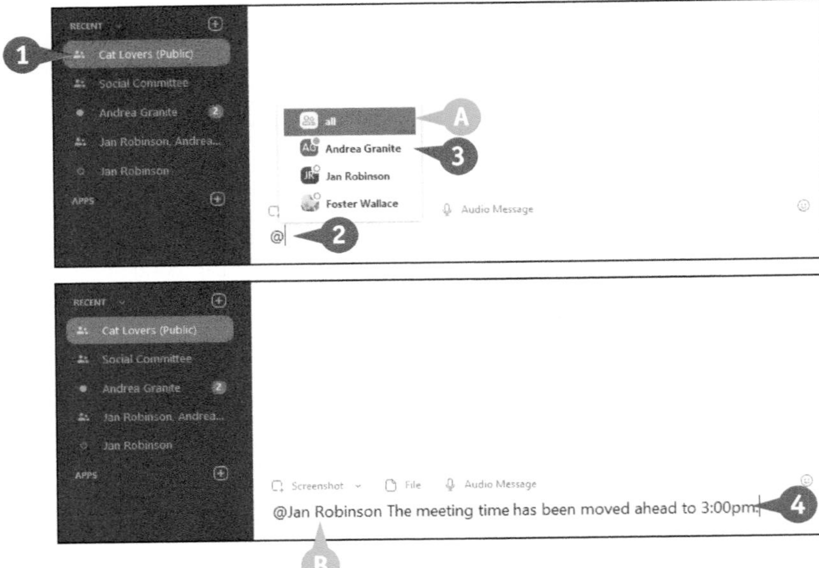

1. Open the chat window of the channel you want to work with.
2. At any point in the message, type **@**.

   Zoom displays a list that includes the channel's members.
3. Click the member you want to mention.

   A. If you want to send a notification to every member, click **all**.

   B. Zoom adds the mention to the message.
4. Complete your message and then press Enter or Return.

   Zoom sends the message to the channel and displays a notification for the user you mentioned.

Start an Instant Meeting from Chat

You can start an instant Zoom meeting from the window of a one-on-one chat or from a channel. Chats are good for exchanging brief messages, but if the discussion becomes more in-depth, you might decide that a meeting with one of the participants is warranted. Rather than creating an instant meeting in the standard way (see Chapter 2), you can start an instant meeting and specify the participant right from the current chat window.

Start an Instant Meeting from Chat

1. Open the chat window of the channel you want to work with.
2. In the chat text box, type **/zoom**, followed by a space.

   Zoom displays a list of users.
3. Click the user with whom you want to meet.

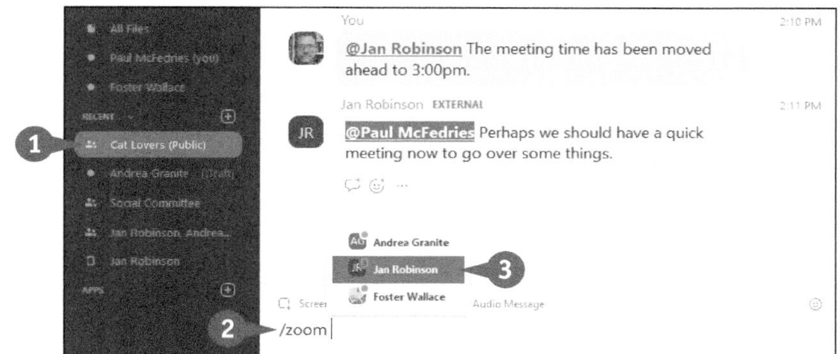

A. Zoom adds the user to the message.

4. Press Enter or Return.

   Zoom creates an instant meeting with the user you specified.

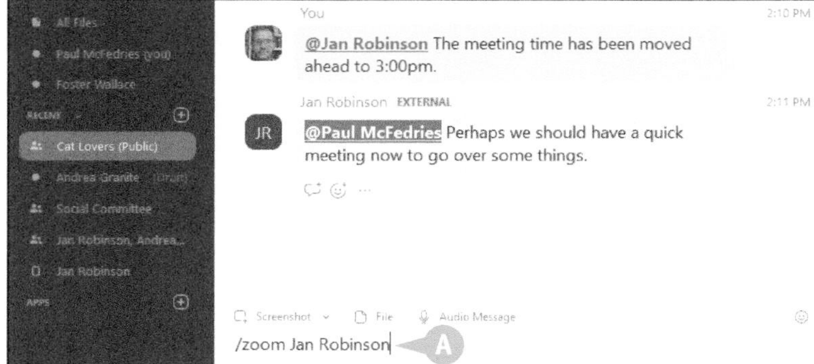

Start a Meeting with a Channel's Members

You can start an instant Zoom meeting with all the members of a channel. Zoom's channels offer an easy way to have text conversations with people who share a common task, project, or interest. You can share screenshots, files, and other data types just as with a regular chat. However, there might be times when the relatively brief and superficial nature of chat is not the right medium for a particular discussion. In that case, you can start an instant meeting with every channel member right from the channel chat window.

Start a Meeting with a Channel's Members

1. Click **Chat**.
2. Open the chat window of the channel you want to work with.
3. Click **Meet with Video** (▭).

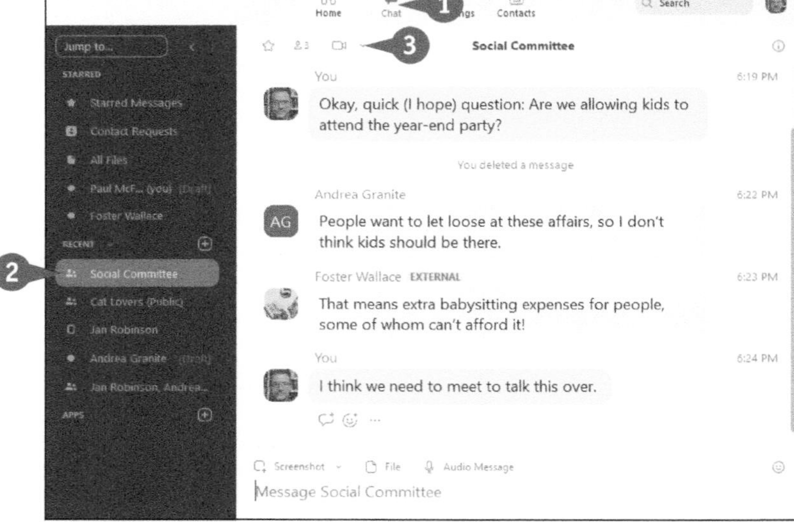

Zoom asks you to confirm that you want to invite all the channel members to a meeting.

4. Click **Yes**.

Zoom starts the meeting and invites all the channel members to attend.

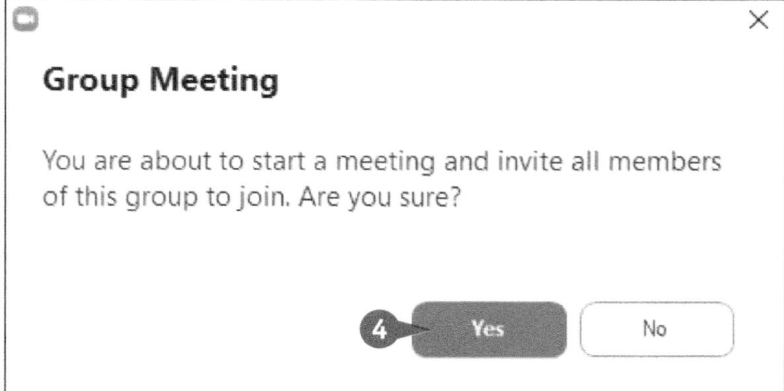

CHAPTER 11

Leave a Channel

If you are a member of a channel, you can leave that channel at any time. Zoom's chat channels are a useful way to have targeted discussions with people who share a common interest or connection. However, you might find that a particular channel is no longer useful to you, either because you no longer share the channel's common interest or because the channel's messages are too numerous or not relevant to you. Whatever the reason, you can leave a channel whenever you feel it is no longer of interest.

Leave a Channel

1. Click **Contacts**.
2. Click **Channels**.
3. Click **More** (···) beside the channel you want to leave.
4. Click **Leave Channel**.

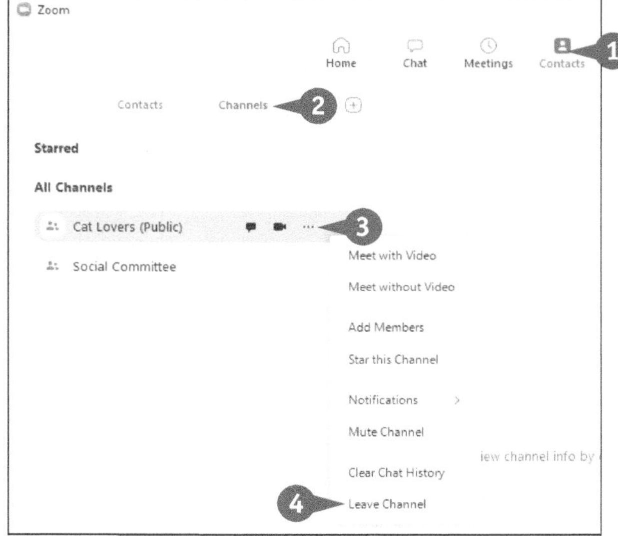

Zoom asks you to confirm.

5. Click **Leave Channel**.

Zoom removes you as a member of the channel.

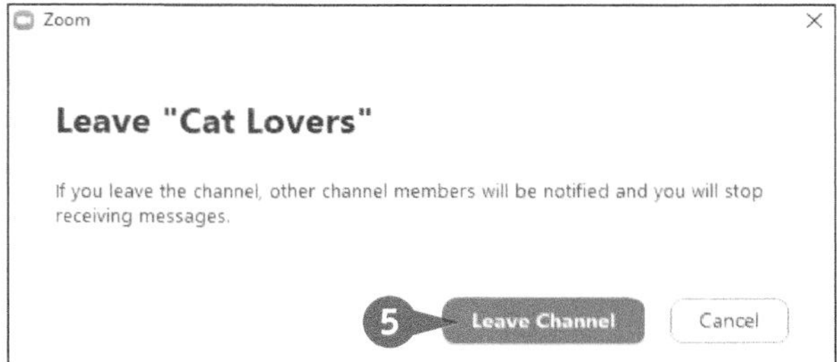

Add Data to Your Personal Chat Space

You can store text, screenshots, images, and other data using the personal chat space that comes with your Zoom account. Earlier sections of this chapter covered how to send text, screenshots, files, and audio messages to other people via Zoom's Chat feature. However, you might have ideas and drafts in the form of messages, images, or files that you want to save just for your own use. To that end, your Zoom account comes with a personal chat space that only you can use and view.

Add Data to Your Personal Chat Space

Using the Zoom Desktop App

1. Click **Chat**.
2. Click your profile name.

   A. Zoom opens your personal chat space.

3. Use the message box to send messages to yourself.
4. Use the **Screenshot**, **File**, and **Audio Message** tools to store these types of data in your personal chat space.

Note: See the sections "Reply with a Screenshot," "Send a File," and "Reply with an Audio Message," earlier in this chapter, to learn how to use these chat tools.

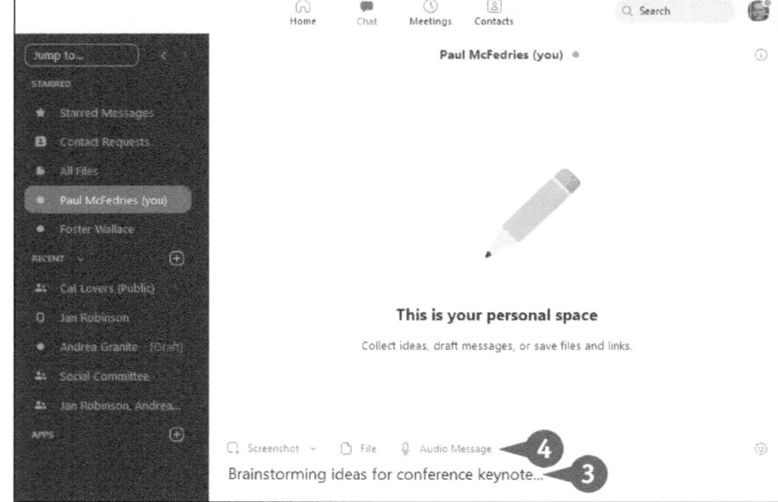

Using the Zoom Mobile App

1. Tap **Meet & Chat.**
2. Tap your profile name.

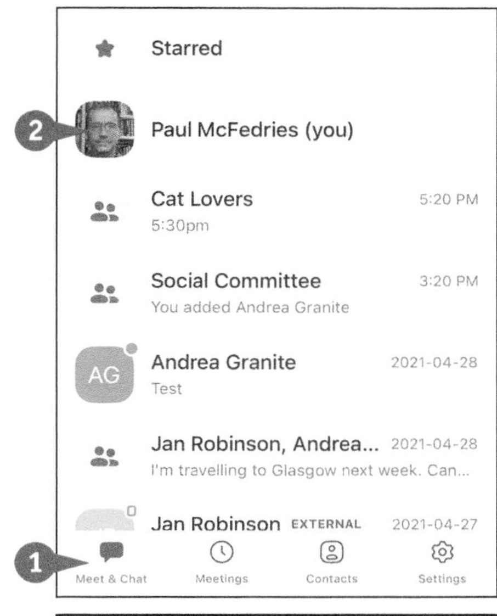

A. Zoom opens your personal chat space.

3. Use the message box to send messages to yourself.
4. Tap **Add** (⊕) to store data such as files or photos in your personal chat space.

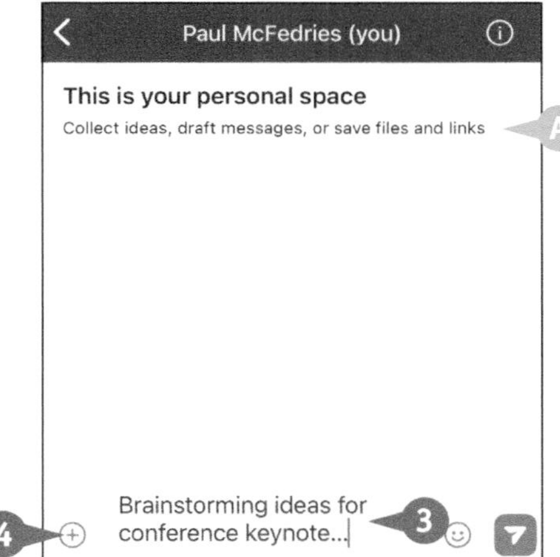

TIPS

Is there an easy way to find particular types of data in my personal chat space?

Yes, Zoom creates separate storage areas for different data types that you create. To see these stores, open your personal chat space, click **More Info** (ⓘ), and then click a data type: **Images**, **Files**, **Whiteboards**, or **Starred Messages**.

Is there a quick way to remove everything from my personal chat space?

Yes, you can clear the chat history in your personal space and start over. Open your personal chat space and then click **More Info** (ⓘ). In the desktop app, click **More Options**. Click **Clear Chat History**, and when Zoom asks you to confirm, click **Clear Chat History**.

CHAPTER 12

Making Calls with Zoom Phone

You can use Zoom Phone to make and receive phone calls from within the Zoom desktop or mobile app. Zoom offers extensive phone features, and you can also launch instant meetings from phone calls. To use Zoom Phone, your company requires a license and a calling plan for each person.

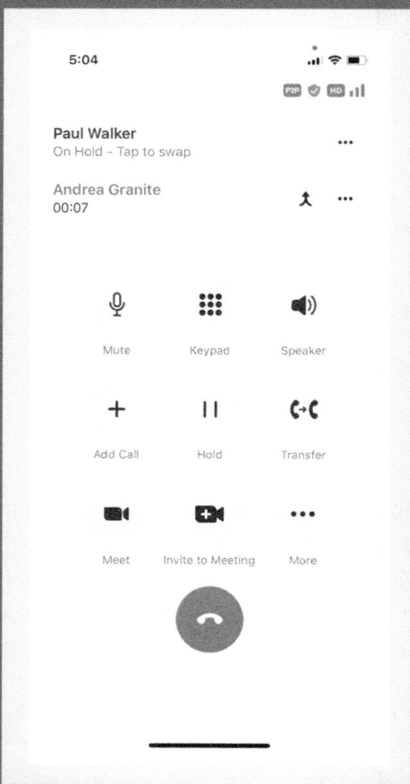

Set Up Zoom Phone

Before you can use Zoom Phone, your Zoom administrator must add a calling plan for you. Once your calling plan is active, the administrator configures the plan with your extension number and a PIN code for accessing your Zoom voicemail. You receive an email message with your extension number and PIN code, and you can then set up your Zoom Phone plan. Once the setup is complete, you can start using Zoom Phone to make and receive calls.

Set Up Zoom Phone

1. Open the Zoom Phone email message.

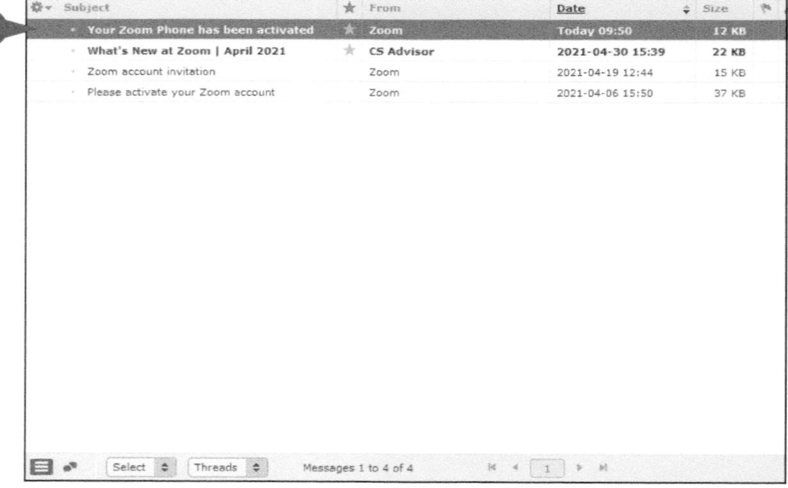

A. Your Zoom Phone extension number appears here.

B. Your Zoom Phone PIN code appears here.

2. Click the link at the bottom of the message.

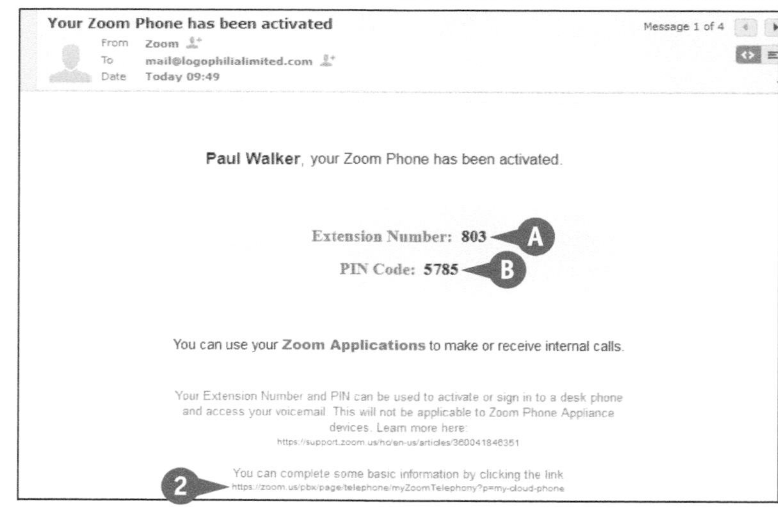

Zoom opens the web page for setting up Zoom Phone.

3 Click the **Select country and area code** ⌄ and then select your country.

4 Click the **Set your time zone** ⌄ and then select your time zone.

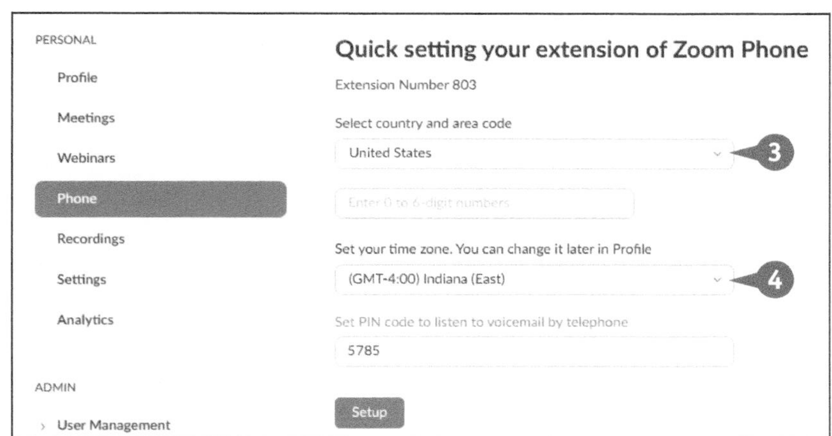

5 (Optional) Edit your PIN code.

6 Click **Setup**.

Zoom completes the setup of your Zoom Phone and displays the Zoom Phone settings.

Note: See the following section, "Configure Zoom Phone Settings," to learn more about the settings that appear.

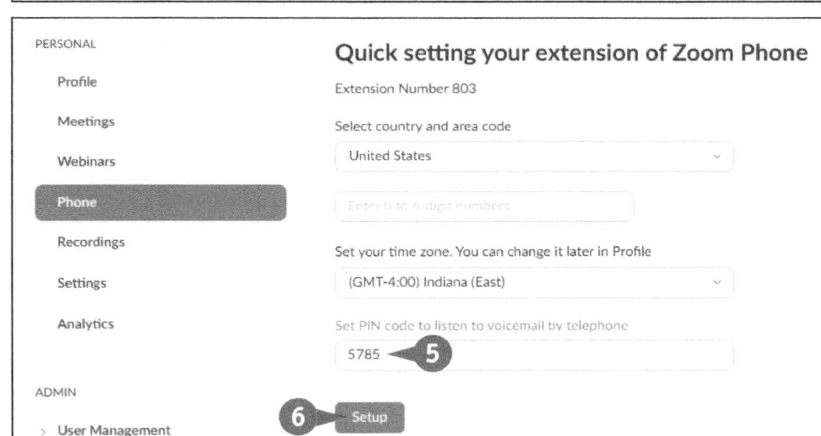

TIP

Is it possible to have a direct line so that I can make and accept external calls?

Yes. If your Zoom administrator assigns you a direct line phone number, you will receive an email message with the subject line "You have been assigned a direct number." Open that message to see the phone number assigned to you (A).

Paul Walker, you have been assigned a direct number

A (647) 555-5925

Configure Zoom Phone Settings

Before you start using Zoom Phone to make and receive calls, you should configure several important settings. In particular, you should configure Zoom Phone with your *business hours*, which are the days of the week you work and the hours on each of those days when you are available to receive Zoom Phone calls. Once you have set your business hours, you can then specify how you want Zoom Phone to handle incoming calls, both during business hours and closed hours.

Configure Zoom Phone Settings

Note: If you have just set up Zoom Phone, as described in the previous section, "Set Up Zoom Phone," and you already have the Settings tab displayed, skip to step 4.

1. Use a web browser to navigate to https://zoom.us/profile.

   Zoom displays your profile page.

2. Click **Phone**.
3. Click **Settings**.
4. To set the hours when you are available to answer your phone, click **Edit** beside **Business Hours**.

   Zoom displays the Business Hours dialog.

5. Click **Custom Hours** (○ changes to ◉).
6. Select the check box for each day you work (☐ changes to ☑).
7. For each day you work, click the **From** ⌄ and **To** ⌄ to set your available hours.
8. Click **OK**.

   Zoom saves your business hours.

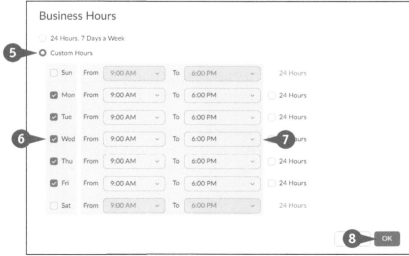

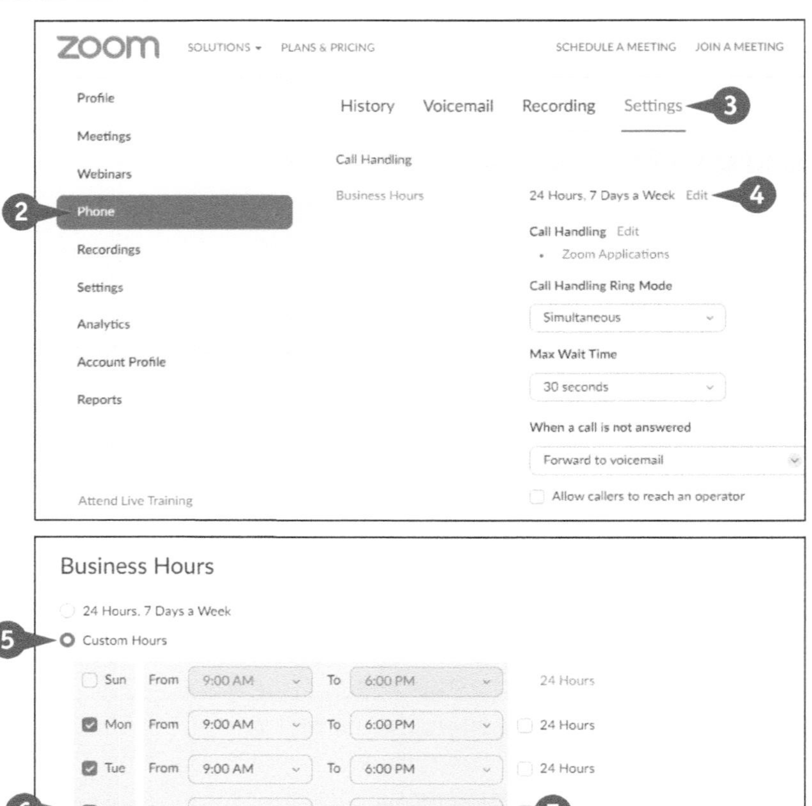

9 Use the settings in the **Business Hours** section to configure how Zoom Phone handles calls during the business hours you specified.

10 For each setting you change, click the **Confirm** button if it appears.

11 Use the settings in the **Closed Hours** section to configure how Zoom Phone handles calls outside of the business hours you specified.

12 For each setting you change, click the **Save** button if it appears.

Zoom Phone puts all your changed settings into effect immediately.

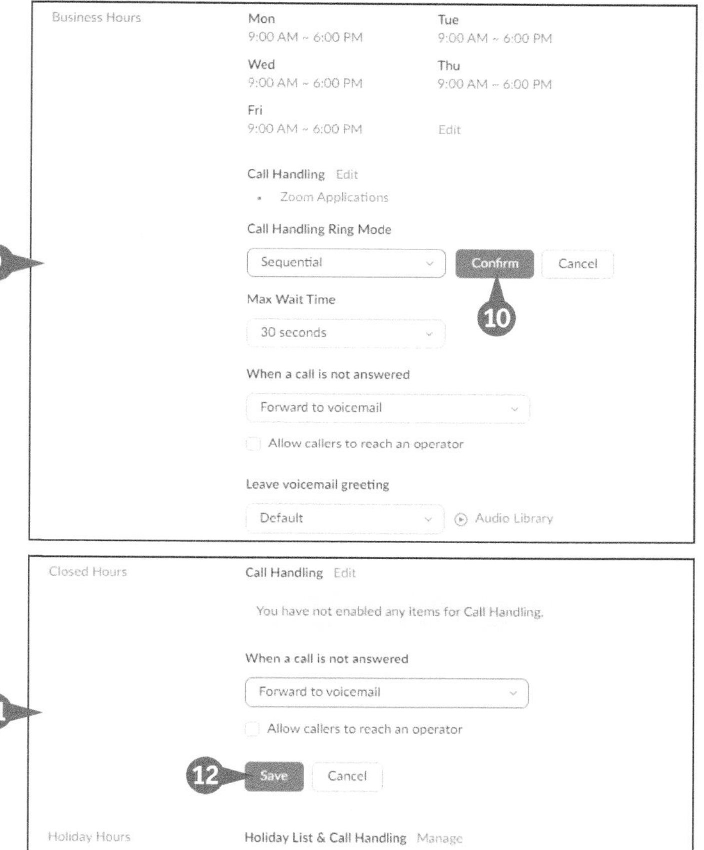

TIPS

What caller ID does Zoom Phone display when I make an external call?

Zoom Phone's caller ID is your Zoom Phone number. You can hide your caller ID when you make calls. On the Zoom Phone Settings tab, click the **Outbound Caller ID** and then click **Hide Caller ID**. If you want to hide your caller ID for only certain calls, see the following section, "Make a Call."

What is the purpose of the Call Handling Ring Mode setting?

This setting determines how incoming calls are handled by your Zoom apps (desktop and mobile) and your phone device. Simultaneous means that all your apps and devices ring at the same time; Sequentially means that your apps and devices ring one after the other for a specified duration.

Make a Call

Once you have been assigned a Zoom Phone calling plan and have configured your Zoom Phone settings, you can start making calls. If you have not been assigned a direct line, you can only call others in your organization. If you have a direct line, you can call either an internal contact or an external contact. You can make internal or external calls using either the desktop app or the mobile app.

Make a Call

Calling a Contact Using the Zoom Desktop App

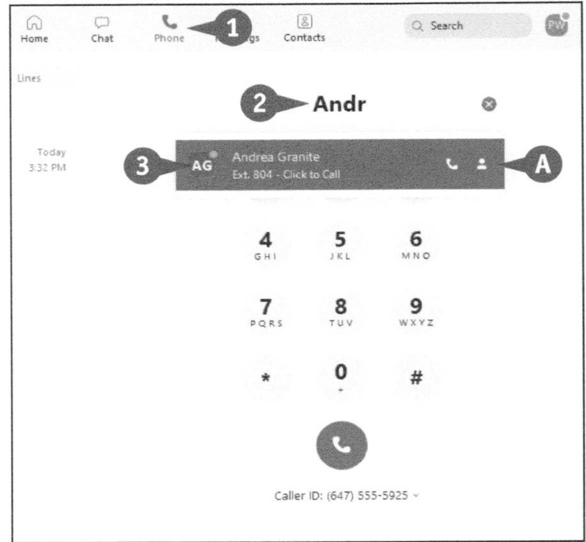

1 Click **Phone**.

2 Start typing the name of the contact you want to call.

A Zoom displays a list of matching contacts.

3 Click the contact you want to call.

Note: You can also click **Contacts**, click the contact you want to call, and then click **Call**.

Zoom Phone calls the contact.

Calling a Number Using the Zoom Desktop App

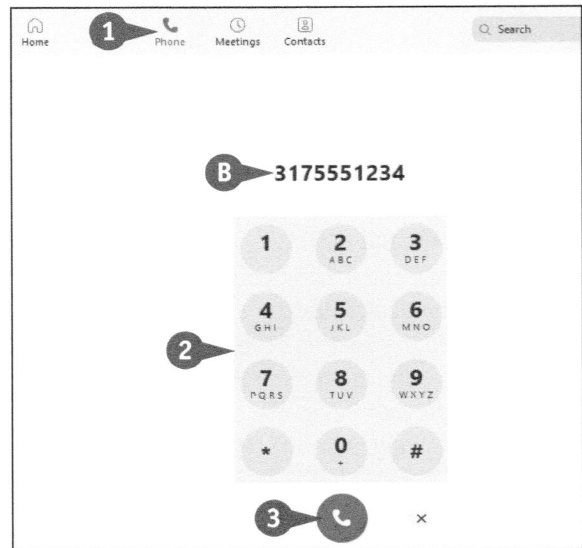

1 Click **Phone**.

2 Use the dial pad to click the phone number you want to call.

Note: You can also use your computer keyboard to type the phone number.

B The numbers appear here.

3 Click **Call** (📞).

Zoom Phone calls the number.

Using the Zoom Mobile App

1. Tap **Phone**.
2. Tap **Dial pad** (⠿).

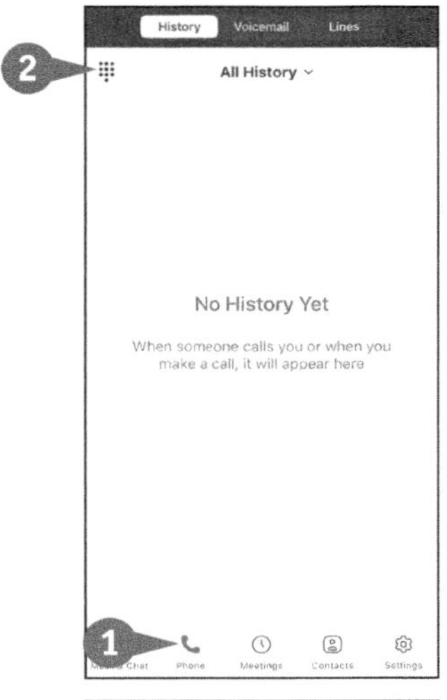

Zoom displays the dial pad.

3. Use the dial pad to tap the phone number you want to call.

   C The number appears here.

   D To call a contact, tap **Contacts** (👤) and then tap the contact you want to call.

4. Tap **Call** (📞).

   Zoom Phone calls the number or contact.

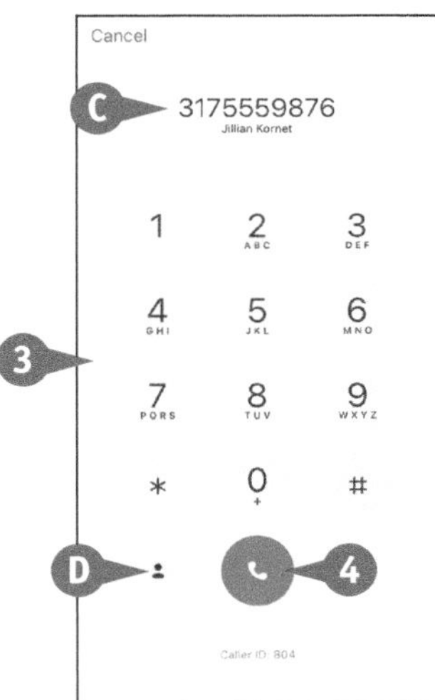

TIP

Can I change or hide my caller ID?

Yes. For external calls in the Zoom desktop app, you can change the caller ID shown by Zoom Phone. Click the **Phone** tab and then click **Caller ID** (A). The options you see depend on how your administrator has set up caller ID, but you usually see the following three:

- **Direct Number (B):** Your caller ID is your Zoom Phone number.
- **Main Company Number (C):** Your caller ID is your organization's main switchboard number.
- **Hide Caller ID (D):** Click this option to hide a caller ID for this call.

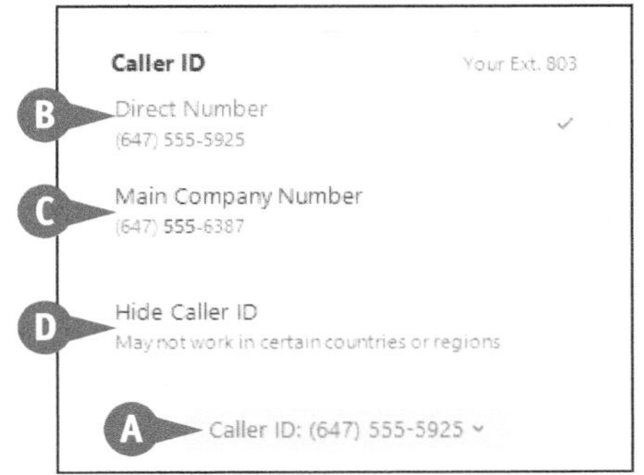

Receive a Call

If someone calls your Zoom Phone number, you can accept the call to talk to that person. By default, Zoom Phone first displays the call notification in the Zoom mobile app; then a few seconds later a similar notification appears in the desktop app. In either app, you can also decline the call if you cannot talk right now.

This section shows you how to accept an incoming call with Zoom Phone. To learn about the features that are available while you are on a call, see the section "Manage a Call" later in this chapter.

Receive a Call

Using the Zoom Desktop App

1. Click **Accept**.

   Zoom accepts the call.

A. If you cannot talk right now, click **Decline** instead.

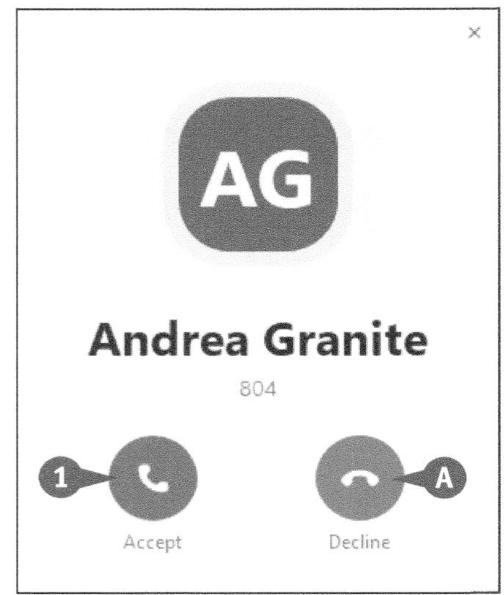

Using the Zoom Mobile App

1. Tap **Accept**.

   Zoom accepts the call.

B. If you cannot talk right now, tap **Decline** instead.

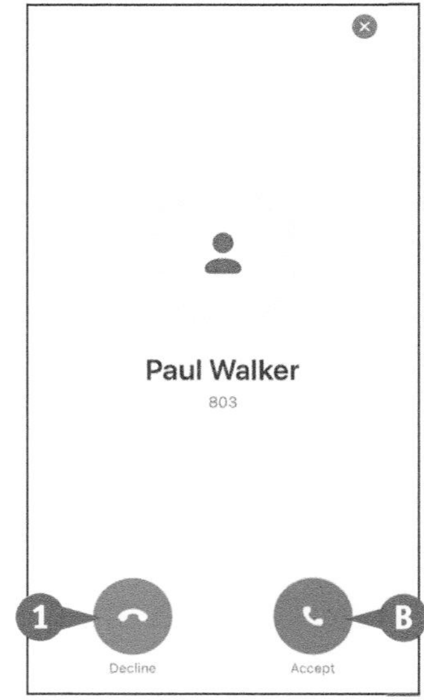

Listen to Voicemail

CHAPTER **12**

If a caller leaves you a message, you can listen to that message by using the voicemail feature in the Zoom desktop or mobile app. When someone calls your Zoom Phone number and you either decline that call or fail to accept the call within about 30 seconds, Zoom Phone automatically sends the caller to your voicemail. By accessing the Voicemail tab in the Zoom app, you can listen to that voicemail message and perform other tasks such as deleting the message.

Listen to Voicemail

1. Select **Phone**.

   A. If you have any new voicemail messages, this badge appears, and the number tells you how many messages you have.

2. Select **Voicemail**.

   Zoom displays a list of your voicemail messages.

3. Select the message you want to hear.

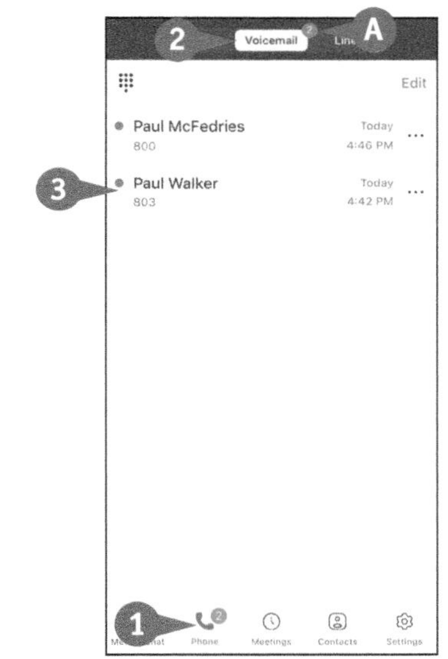

B. Zoom plays the recording.

C. Zoom also displays a transcript of the recording.

D. You can select **Call** ( ) to return the person's call.

E. You can select **Delete** ( ) to delete the recording.

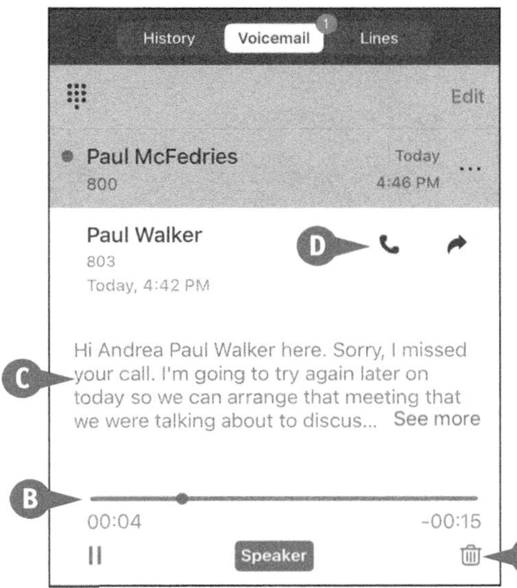

Manage a Call

You can use Zoom Phone's in-call controls to manage the call and perform various tasks. When you answer an incoming call or another person accepts your call, Zoom Phone displays its in-call controls. These controls are a collection of buttons that enable you to perform tasks such as putting the caller on hold, adding a third person to the call, and transferring the caller to another person. When you are ready to end the call, you can also use an in-call control button to hang up the call.

Manage a Call

Put the Caller on Hold

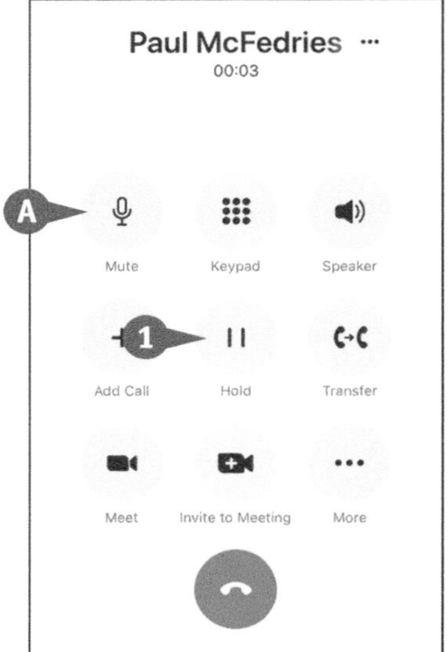

1. Select the **Hold** button (**Hold** changes to **Unhold**).

   Zoom Phone puts the caller on hold and plays the on-hold audio. (See the next tip to change the audio.)

   A. If you prefer to mute the caller, select the **Mute** button instead.

2. To resume the call, select **Unhold** (not shown).

Add Another Person to the Call

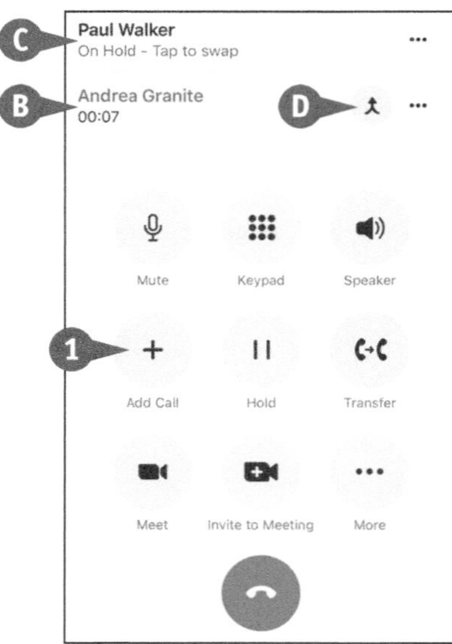

1. Select **Add Call**.

   Zoom Phone displays the dial pad.

2. Select a contact or enter a phone number and then select **Call** (📞) (not shown).

   B. If the person answers, Zoom Phone adds the person to the call and puts the original person on hold.

   C. Select the original person to switch to that caller.

   D. Select **Merge** (⅄) to create a three-way call.

Transfer the Caller to Someone Else

1. Select **Transfer**.

   Zoom Phone displays the dial pad.

2. Select a contact or enter a phone number and then select **Call** (📞) (not shown).

   If the person answers, Zoom Phone transfers the caller to that person.

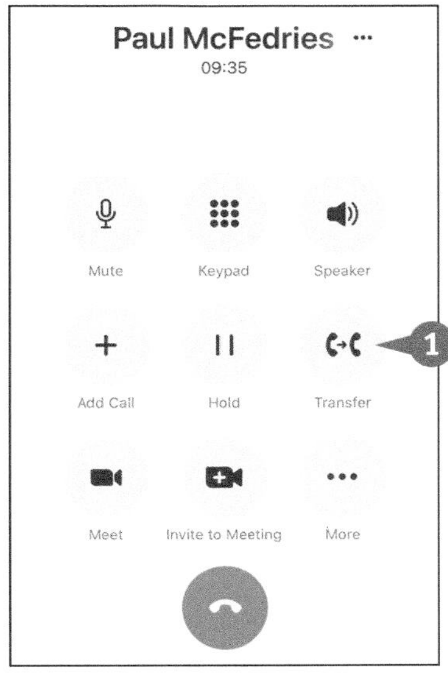

Hang Up the Call

1. Select **End Call** (📞).

   Zoom Phone hangs up the call.

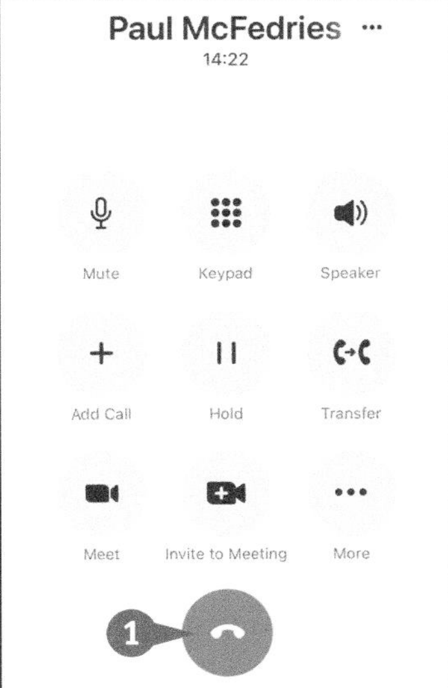

TIPS

Can I change the audio that plays while my caller is on hold?

Yes. Follow the steps in the earlier "Configure Zoom Phone Settings" section to access the Zoom Phone settings. For the Hold Music setting, select **Audio Library** and then use the Audio Library dialog to add the audio you want to use.

Is there a way to access the Zoom app while I am on a call?

Yes, you can minimize the phone call. In the desktop or mobile app, select **More** and then select **Minimize**. Zoom Phone shrinks the in-call controls to a thumbnail and exposes the app so you can work with it. To return to the in-call controls, select the thumbnail.

Exchange SMS Messages

Zoom Phone includes a Short Message Service (SMS) feature that enables you to send or receive text messages. You can send text messages to or receive text messages from Zoom users, external contacts, or any smartphone. You can also use SMS to exchange images with your recipients.

You can exchange text messages using either the Zoom desktop app or the Zoom mobile app.

Exchange SMS Messages

Using the Zoom Desktop App

1. Click **Phone**.
2. Click the **SMS** tab.
3. Click **New SMS** (✍).

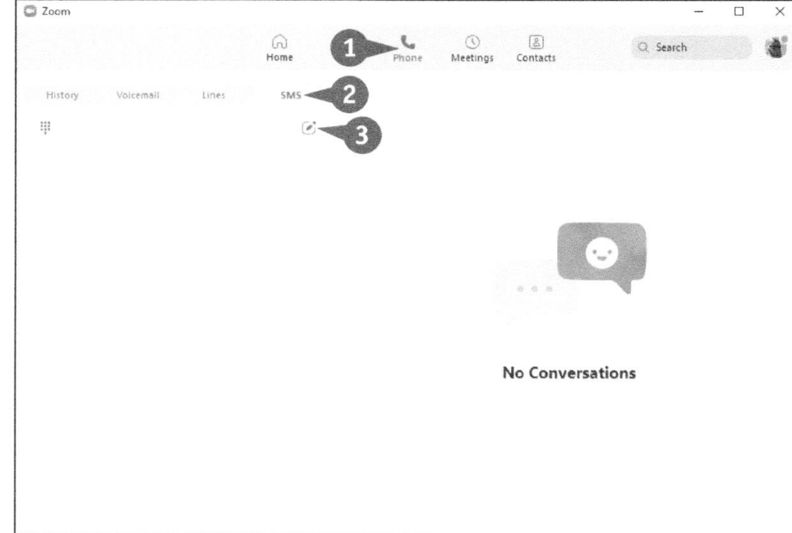

Zoom begins a new SMS message.

4. Start typing the name of the person you want to message.

   A. Zoom displays a list of matching contacts.

5. Click the contact you want to message.
6. Type your message.

   B. If you want to include an image file in your message, click **File**.

7. Click Enter or Return.

Zoom Phone sends the message.

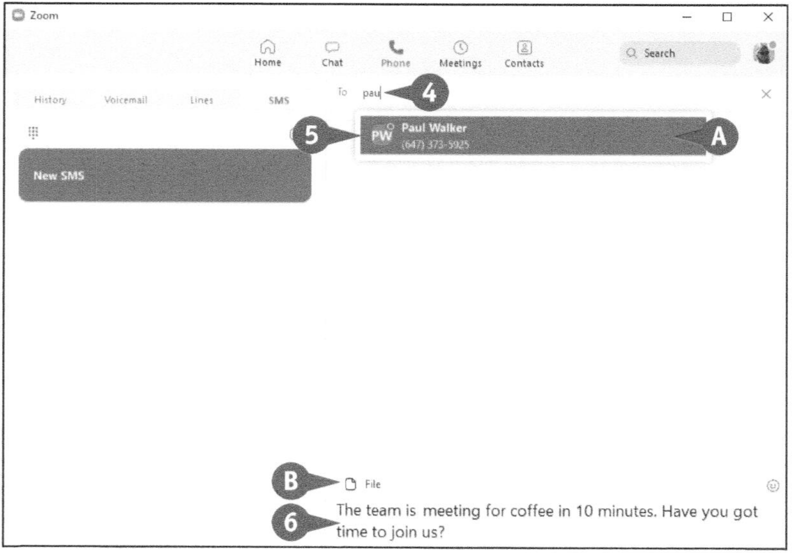

Using the Zoom Mobile App

1. Tap **Phone**.
2. Tap the **SMS** tab.
3. Tap **New SMS** ().

The New SMS screen appears.

4. Start typing the name of the person you want to message.

C Zoom displays a list of matching contacts.

5. Tap the contact you want to message.
6. Type your message.

D If you want to include an image in your message, Tap **Add** ().

7. Tap **Send** ().

Zoom Phone sends the message.

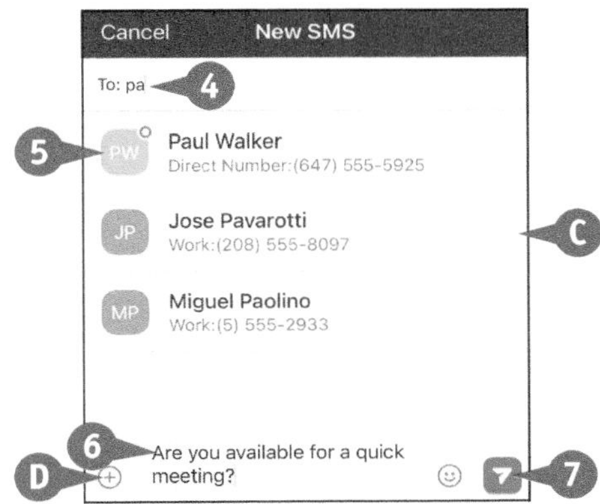

TIP

Why do I not see the SMS tab?

SMS is disabled by default in Zoom Phone, so you do not see the SMS tab if your Zoom administrator has not enabled this feature.

If you are a Zoom administrator, here are the steps to follow to enable SMS in Zoom Phone:

1. Use a web browser to navigate to https://zoom.us/profile and sign in using your Zoom administrator credentials.
2. Click **Phone System Management**.
3. Click **Company Info**.
4. Click **Account Settings**.
5. Click **Policy**.
6. Click the **SMS** switch (A) to On (changes to).

Invite a Caller to a Meeting

You can invite someone to a Zoom meeting from a Zoom Phone call. If you are talking to someone on Zoom Phone, you might you want to meet with that person. If you want to meet right away, you can invite that person to an instant meeting. If the meeting is in progress, you can send that person the URL of the meeting. Finally, if the meeting is in the future, you can invite the person to the scheduled meeting. In each case, the other person must accept the invitation to be added as a meeting participant.

Invite a Caller to a Meeting

Start an Instant Meeting

1. Select **Meet**.

   Zoom Phone starts an instant meeting and sends a meeting invitation to the other person on the call.

Invite a Caller to an Existing Meeting

1. Select **More**.
2. Select **Invite to Meeting**.

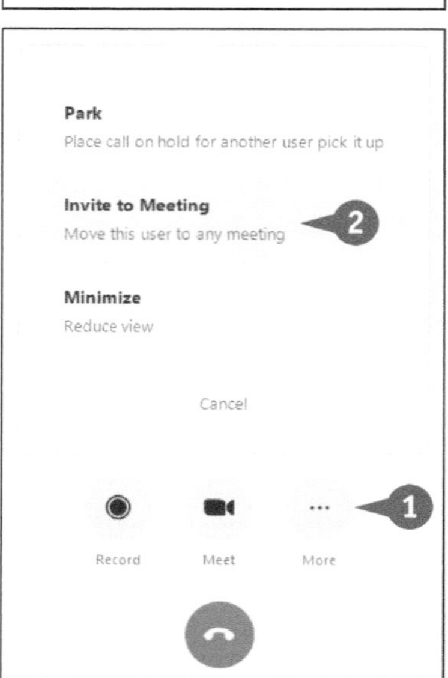

The Choose Meeting dialog appears.

3 Click the scheduled meeting to which you want to invite the caller.

A Alternatively, if the meeting is in progress, paste the meeting URL here.

4 Select **Invite**.

Zoom Phone sends a meeting invitation to the other person on the call.

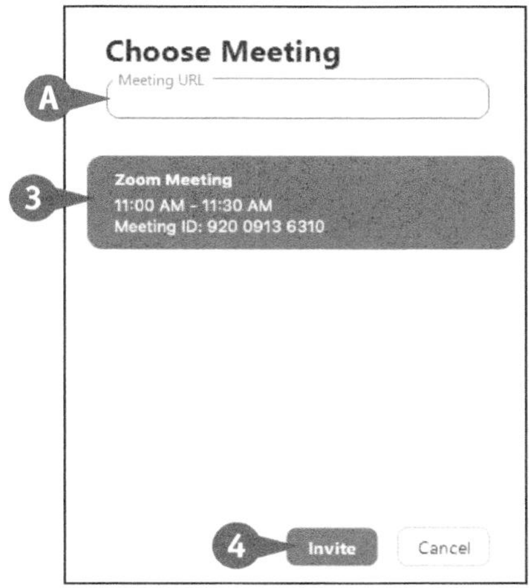

Accept a Meeting Invitation

1 Select **Accept**.

B If you cannot meet right now, select **Decline** instead.

Zoom adds you to the meeting.

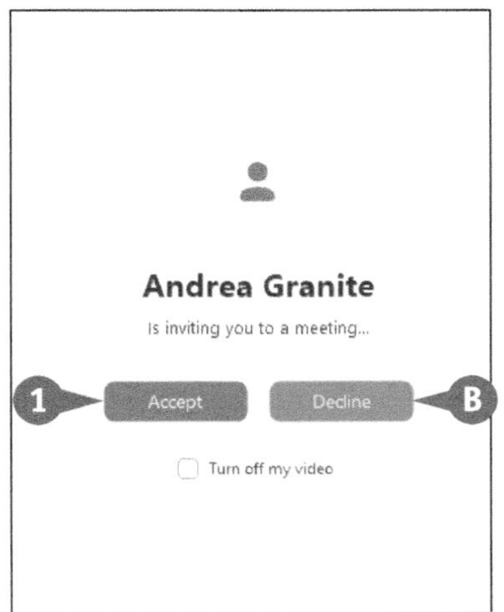

TIPS

If I have multiple people on a call, can I invite them all to a meeting?
Yes. However, if you do not merge the call, then when you select Meet or Invite to Meeting, Zoom Phone sends the invitation only to the active caller. If you want to send the invitation to both callers, you must first merge the call, as described in the earlier "Manage a Call" section.

What happens if I am in a Zoom meeting and I receive a Zoom Phone call?
You have three choices:

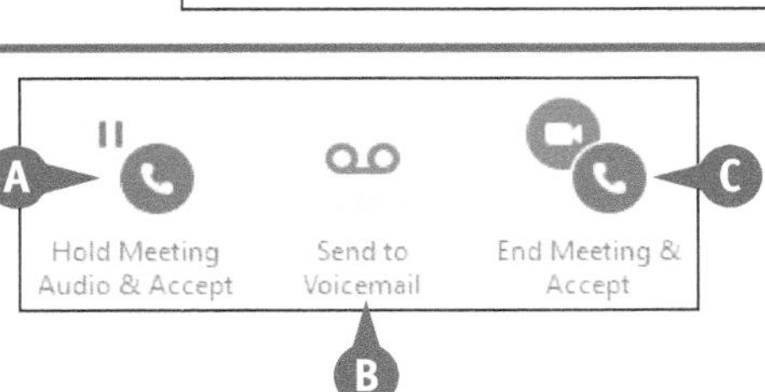

- **Hold Meeting Audio & Accept (A):** Select this option to put the meeting audio on hold and take the call.
- **Send to Voicemail (B):** Select this option to decline the call and send it directly to voicemail.
- **End Meeting & Accept (C):** Select this option to stop the meeting and take the call.

Manage Call History

Zoom Phone keeps track of both the calls you receive and the calls you make by storing these calls in the History list. For the calls you receive, Zoom Phone shows both the calls you accepted and the calls you declined or missed. To manage your call history, you can access the History tab. From there, you can filter the list to show just the calls you missed and the calls that you recorded. You can also delete items from the list and clear the entire list.

Manage Call History

View Call History

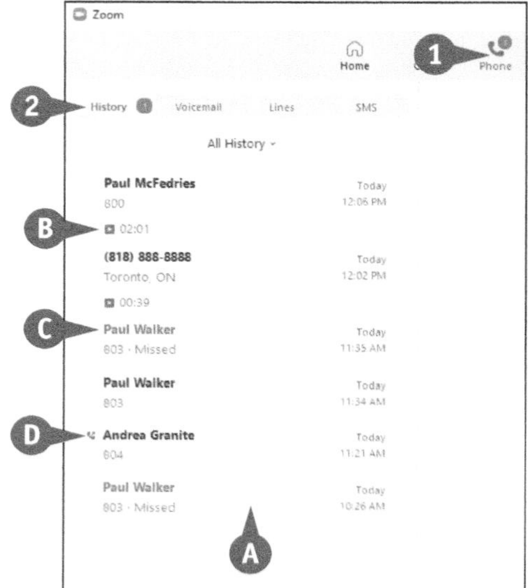

1 Select **Phone**.

2 Select the **History** tab.

A Zoom displays your Zoom Phone call history.

B The Recording icon (■) indicates that some or all of the call was recorded.

C A red caller name indicates a missed call.

D The Outgoing Call icon (☏) indicates that you initiated the call.

Filter Call History

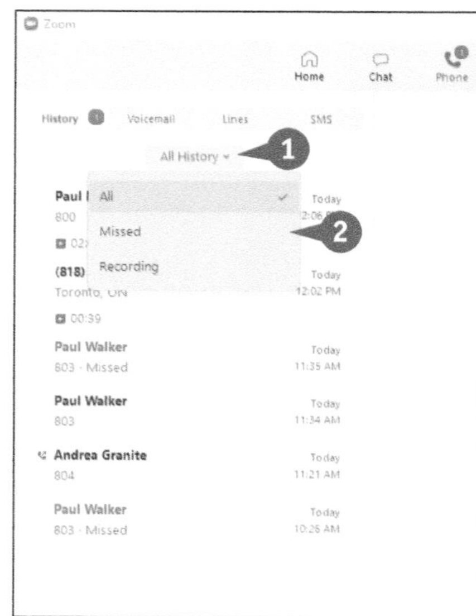

1 Select **All History**.

2 Select the calls you want to see:

- **All.** Displays the entire call history.
- **Missed.** Displays only the phone calls that you did not accept.
- **Recording.** Displays only the phone calls that you recorded.

Delete a Call from Call History

1. Next to the call you want to delete, select **More** (···).
2. Select **Delete**.

   Zoom deletes the call.

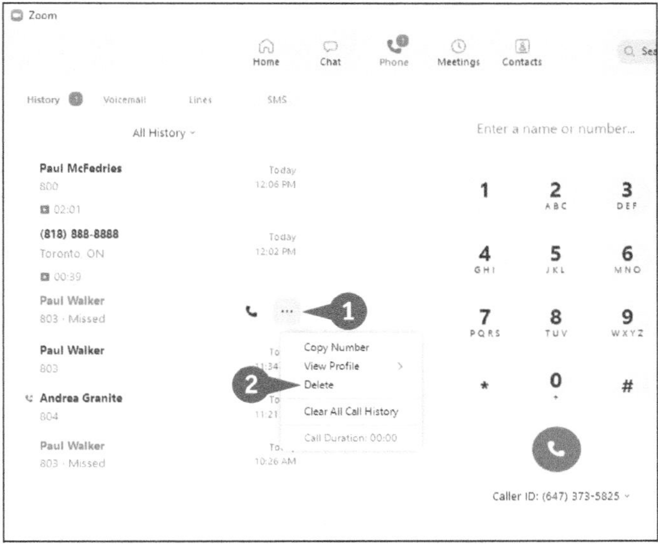

Clear Call History

1. Next to any call, select **More** (···).
2. Select **Clear All Call History**.

   Zoom asks you to confirm that you want to clear everything from your call history.
3. Select **Clear All**.

   Zoom deletes every call from the History tab.

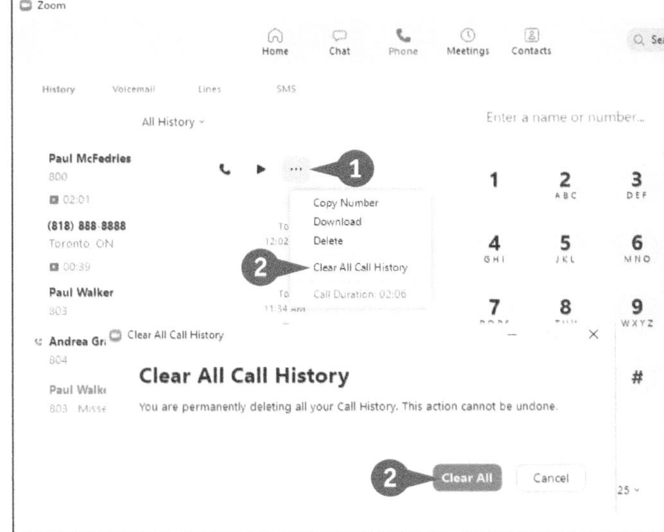

TIPS

How do I listen to a recorded call from call history?

Display your call history and then display the call controls by hovering the mouse over the call that has the recording you want to hear. Click **Play** (▶) to listen to the recording.

Why do I not see the Record button or any recorded calls in the Zoom mobile app?

Call recording is not available in the Zoom mobile app. To record calls and to listen to those recordings, you must use the Zoom desktop app.

CHAPTER 13

Setting Up Webinars

You can use Zoom to host a webinar that can have anywhere from 100 to 10,000 attendees. Webinar hosts can create polls and surveys for attendees to fill in, can share a screen, and can record the webinar. Hosts can also answer questions asked by the attendees.

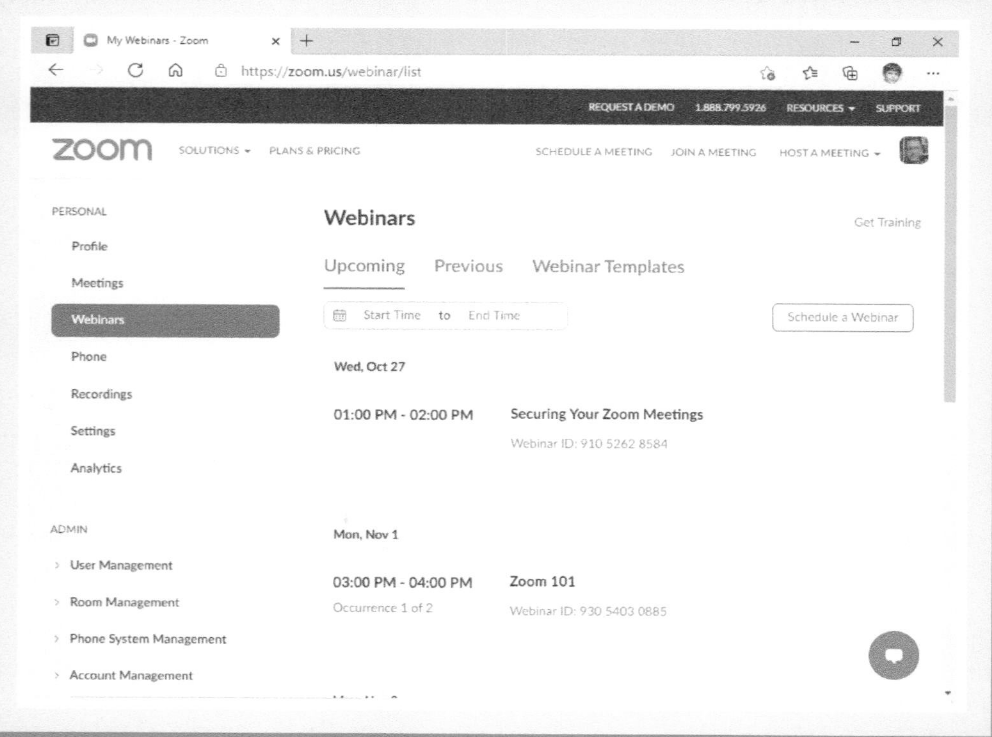

Create a Webinar

Zoom's Video Webinar product enables you to create a *webinar* — from the phrase *web seminar* — which is a special kind of Zoom meeting. A webinar has a host and optionally one or more panelists, who broadcast audio and video to up to 10,000 view-only attendees (the maximum number depends on your license). To create a webinar, you require a webinar license from Zoom, and that license determines the maximum number of people who can attend your webinar. This section and the rest of the host tasks in this chapter assume you have already purchased a webinar license from Zoom.

Create a Webinar

1. Use a web browser to navigate to https://zoom.us.
2. Click **My Account**.

Note: If you are on some other page on the Zoom site, click your profile picture and then click your name.

Zoom displays your profile page.

Note: You can combine steps 1 and 2 by navigating directly to https://zoom.us/profile.

3. Click **Webinars**.
4. Click **Schedule a Webinar**.

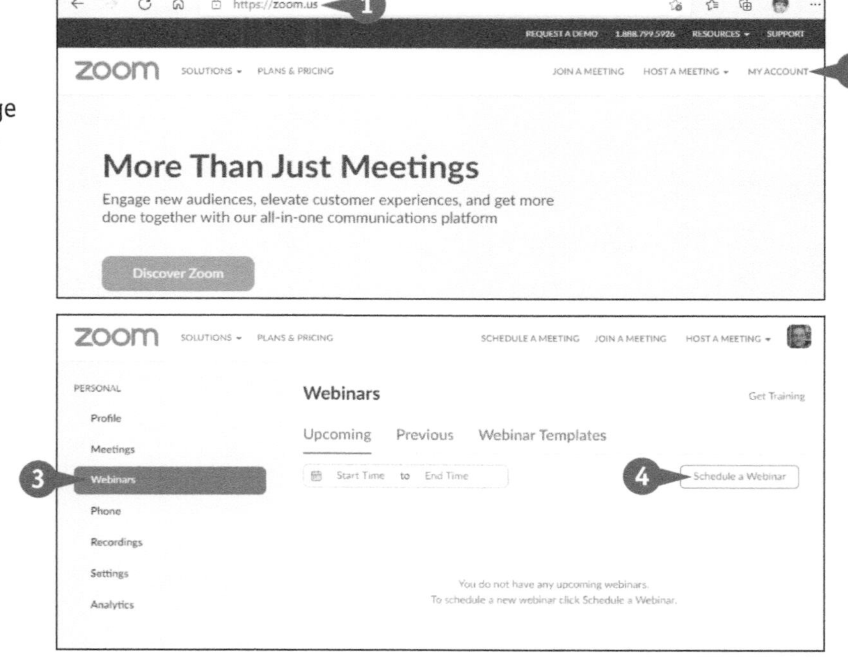

The Schedule a Webinar page appears.

5 Type a name for your webinar.

6 (Optional) Type a description for your webinar.

7 Select the webinar date.

8 Select the webinar time.

9 Select the webinar duration.

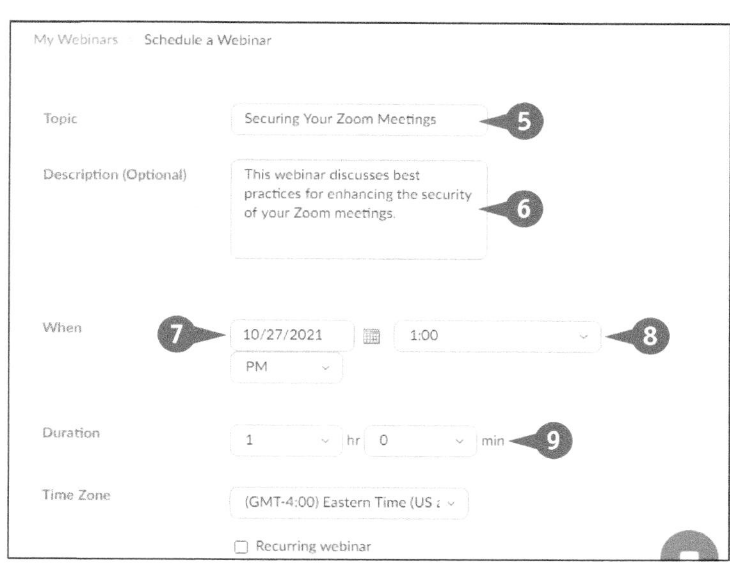

10 Select the other meeting options, as required (not shown).

A If you want to allow attendees to ask questions for the host and/or panelists to answer, select the **Q&A** check box (☐ changes to ☑).

B If you want to invite one or more people to co-host the webinar, enter their usernames or email addresses here.

11 Click **Schedule**.

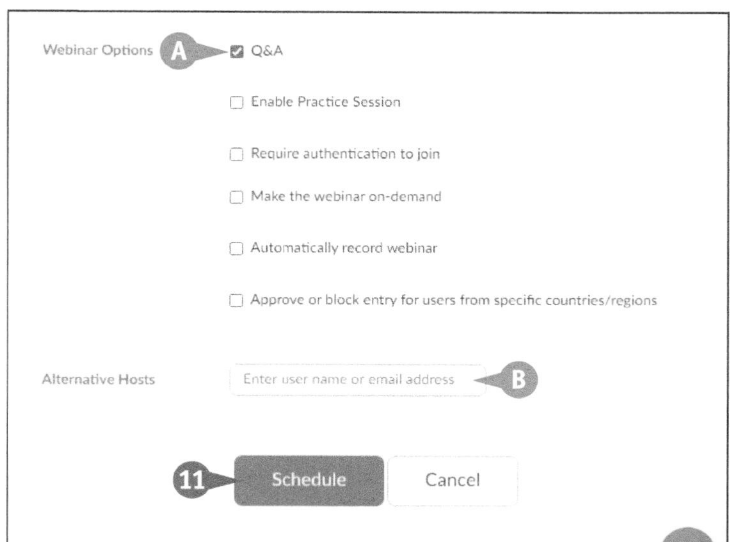

TIPS

How do I create a recurring webinar?

On the Schedule a Webinar page, click the **Recurring webinar** check box (☐ changes to ☑). Select a recurrence interval (such as Weekly or Monthly), how often you want the webinar to repeat, and when you want the recurrence to end.

How do I create a webinar that requires registration?

In the Schedule a Webinar page's **Registration** section, click the **Required** check box (☐ changes to ☑). If this is a recurring webinar, you then click an option that specifies how often attendees must register (○ changes to ◉). See the second tip in the following section, "Invite People to Your Webinar," to learn how to change the registration settings.

Invite People to Your Webinar

You can invite panelists and attendees to a webinar. Most webinars are hosted by a single person, but it is also common to have one or more panelists, each of whom can be seen and heard by the attendees and can share their screens. To add panelists to a webinar, you must first invite each person.

Most webinars generate attendees through online promotions, such as social media posts. However, if there are people you want to notify about the webinar, you can invite those people directly. You can invite up to the number of attendees supported by your webinar license.

Invite People to Your Webinar

Display the Webinar Details

1. Use a web browser to navigate to https://zoom.us/webinar/list.

   Zoom displays your upcoming webinars.

2. Click the webinar you want to work with.

   Zoom displays the webinar details.

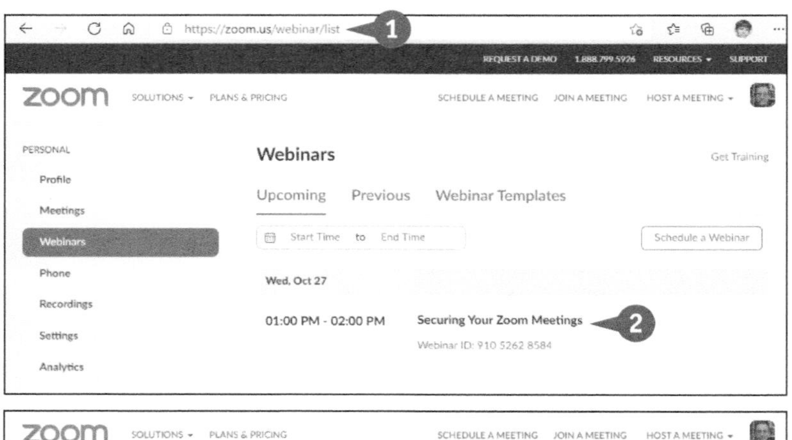

Invite Panelists

1. Open the webinar information, as described in the "Display the Webinar Details" subsection.

A. This value tells you the maximum number of webinar attendees based on your webinar license.

2. Scroll down and click the **Invitations** tab.
3. In the **Invite Panelists** section, click **Edit**.

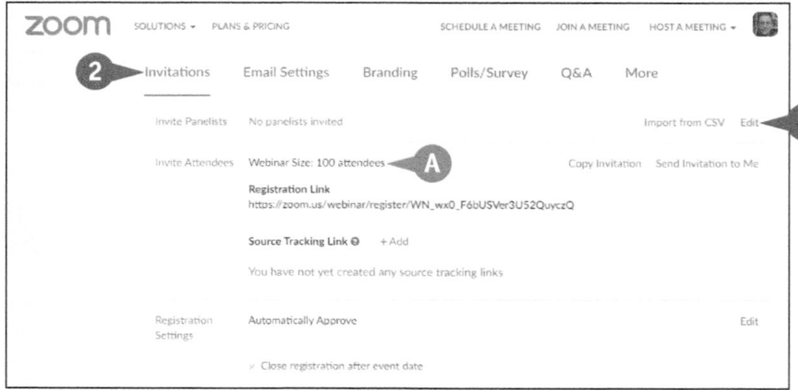

The Panelists dialog appears.

4 Type the name and email address of each panelist you want to invite.

5 Click **Save**.

Zoom sends an invitation to each panelist.

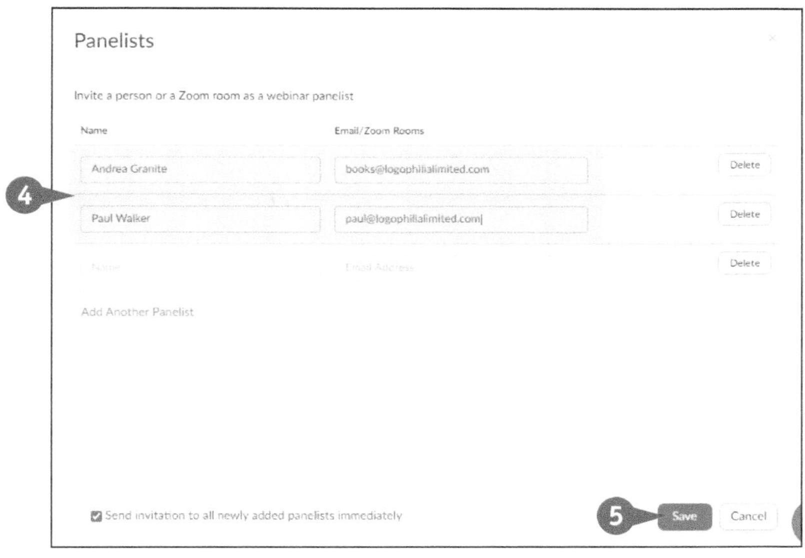

Invite Attendees

1 Open the webinar information, as described in the "Display the Webinar Details" subsection.

2 Scroll down and click the **Invitations** tab.

3 In the **Invite Attendees** section, click **Copy Invitation**.

4 Use your email app to send the copied invitation to each person you want to invite to the webinar (not shown).

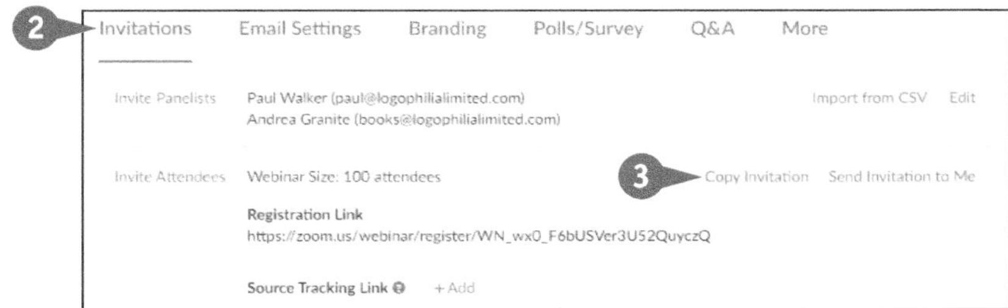

TIPS

I have quite a few panelists I want to invite. Is there an easier method I can use?

Yes, you can import the panelist data from a comma-separated values (CSV) file, where each panelist is on a separate line and each panelist's email address and name is separated by a comma. Open the webinar details and, in the **Invite Panelists** section, click **Import from CSV**.

How do I configure a webinar's registration settings?

Open the webinar details and then click **Edit** in the **Registration Settings** section. In the Registration dialog that appears, use the **Registration** tab to set your webinar's registration options. Use the **Questions** tab to specify which fields users must fill in to register.

Create a Poll

You can get feedback from your webinar attendees by creating a poll to display during the meeting. A poll consists of one or more questions, each of which can be either single-choice or multiple-choice. With a single-choice question, attendees must choose one answer from those that you provide; with a multiple-choice question, attendees can choose one or more answers from those that you provide. You can add up to 10 questions per poll and you can create up to 25 polls per webinar.

Create a Poll

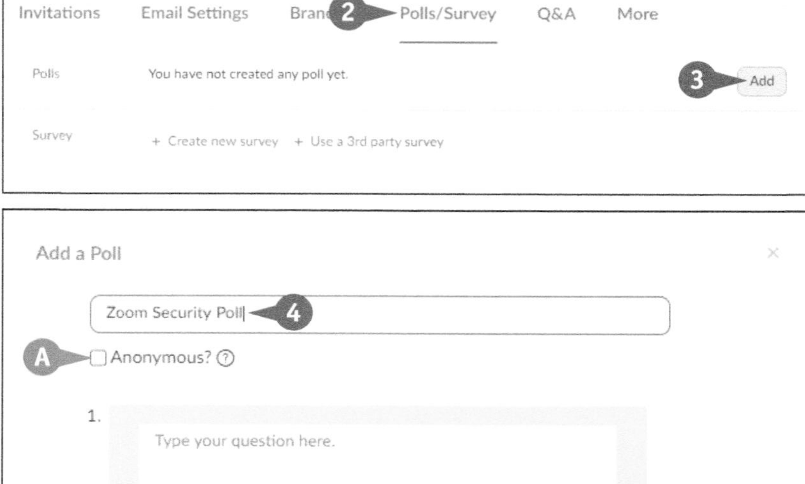

1. Open the webinar information as described in the earlier "Invite People to Your Webinar" section.
2. Scroll down and click the **Polls/Survey** tab.
3. In the **Polls** section, click **Add**.

   Zoom displays the Add a Poll dialog.
4. Type a title for the poll.

A. If you want each participant's polling answers to be anonymous, you can select the **Anonymous** check box (☐ changes to ☑).

5 Type your poll question.

6 Select the type of question (◯ changes to ◉).

7 Type your possible answers.

Note: Your question and your possible answers can each be a maximum of 255 characters.

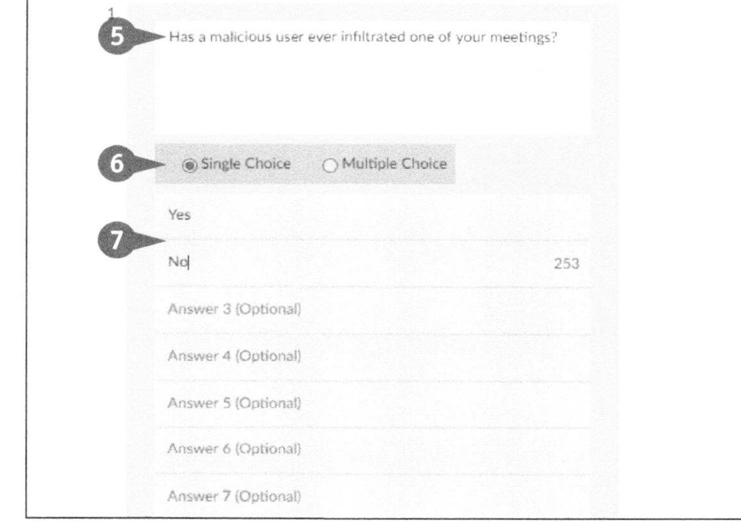

8 To include another question in the poll, click **Add a Question** and then repeat steps 5 to 7.

9 Click **Save**.

Zoom adds your poll to the webinar configuration.

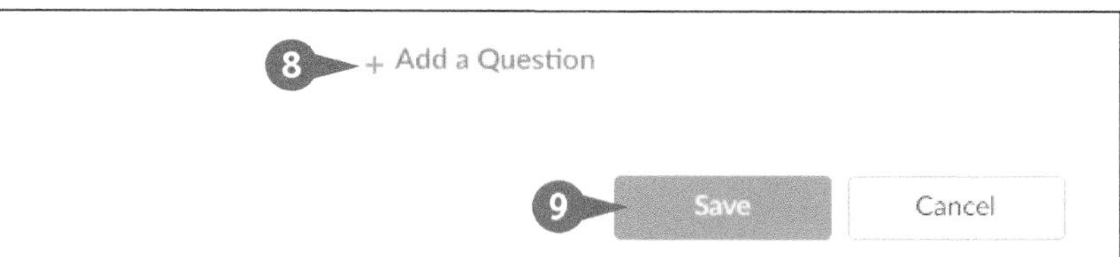

TIP

How do I present a poll during my webinar?

During your webinar, when the time comes to run your poll, follow these steps:

1 Click **Polls** in your host controls.

The Polls dialog appears.

2 If you want to make some last-minute changes, click **Edit**.

3 If you want your webinar panelists to be included in the poll, click **Allow Panelists to vote** (☐ changes to ☑).

4 Click **Launch Polling**.

Zoom shows you the progress of the poll.

5 When the polling is complete, click **End Poll**.

6 If you would like to show attendees the poll results, click **Share Results**.

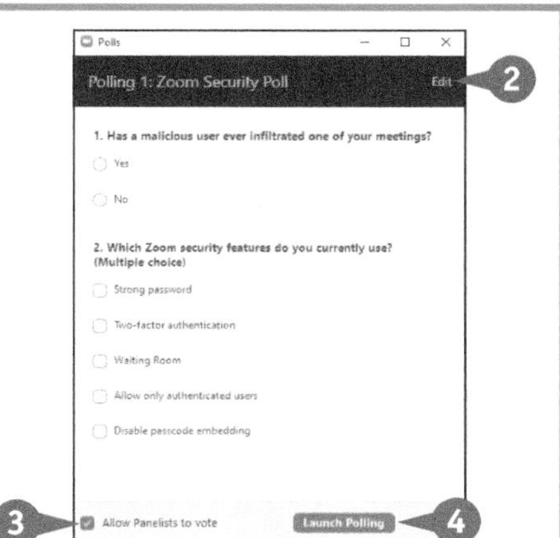

Create a Survey

You can get participant feedback about a webinar by creating a survey that you distribute to the attendees after your webinar is over. A survey consists of one or more questions, each of which can be one of the following: single-choice, where attendees must choose one answer from those that you provide; multiple-choice, where attendees can choose one or more answers from those that you provide; rating scale, where the answer is a value within a range that you specify; and short text, where attendees provide a written response.

Create a Survey

Start the Survey

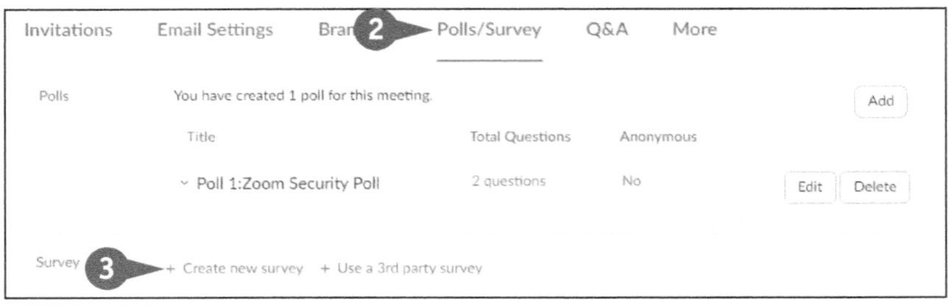

1. Open the webinar information, as described in the earlier "Invite People to Your Webinar" section.
2. Scroll down and click the **Polls/Survey** tab.
3. In the **Survey** section, click **Create new survey**.

   Zoom displays the Create New Survey dialog.

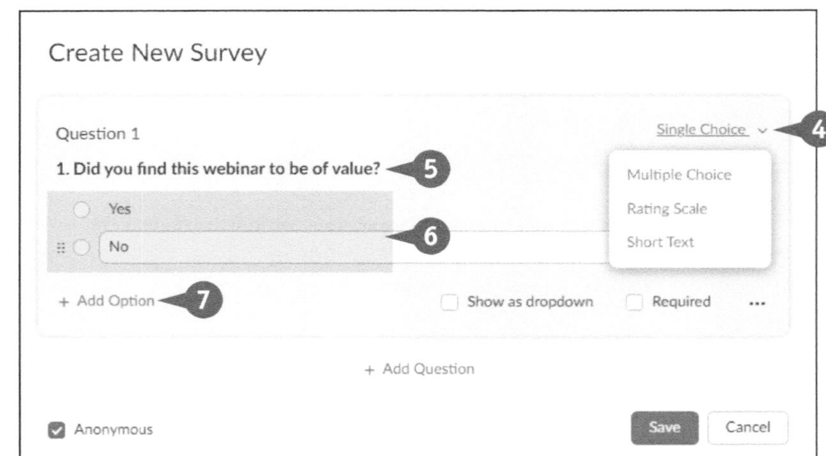

Add a Single- or Multiple-Choice Question

4. Click ⌄ and then click either **Single Choice** or **Multiple Choice**.
5. Type your question.
6. Type the answer choices you want to present.
7. To add more choices, click **Add Option** and enter the answer text, as needed.

Add a Rating Scale Question

8 Click **Add Question**.

9 Click ⌄ and then click **Rating Scale**.

10 Type your question.

11 Use the **From** and **To** text boxes to specify the range of values from which the user can choose.

12 Type labels that describe the low end and high end of the scale.

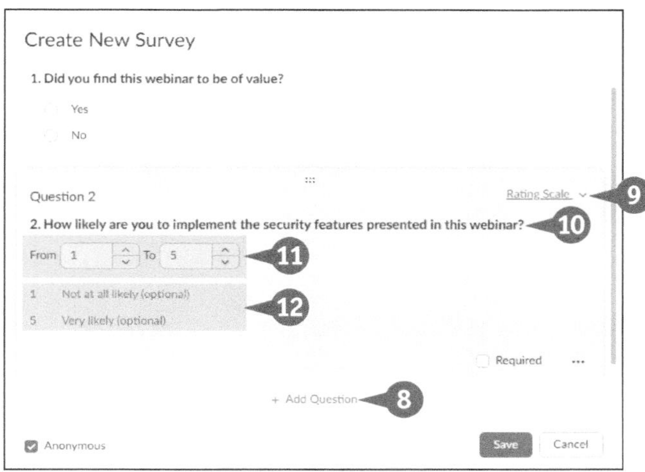

Add a Short Text Question

13 Click **Add Question**.

14 Click ⌄ and then click **Short Text**.

15 Type your question.

16 To include more questions in the survey, click **Add Question** and then repeat the corresponding steps based on the type of question you add.

17 Click **Save**.

Zoom adds your survey to the webinar configuration.

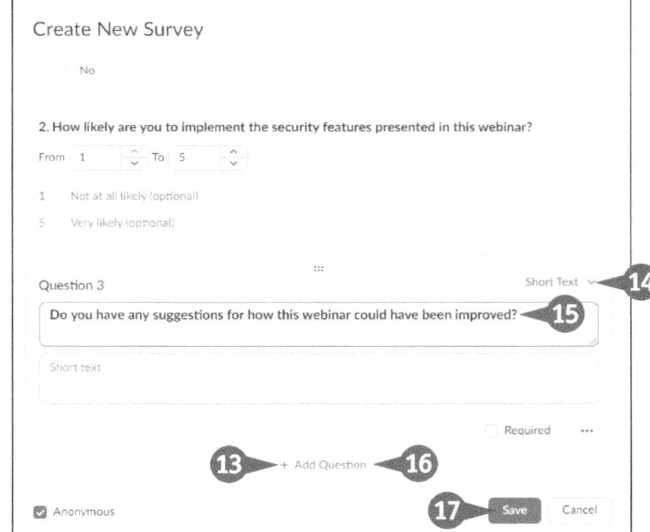

TIPS

How do I show the survey to the attendees?

By default, Zoom shows the survey in the web browser as soon as you end the webinar. You can also add a link to the survey page to your webinar follow-up email. Open the webinar details, click **Edit Setting** in the **Survey** section, click **Show the link in the follow-up email** (☐ changes to ☑), and then click **Save**.

Can I try the survey before my webinar?

Yes. Open the webinar details and then click **Preview** in the **Survey** section. Zoom opens the survey page for you to view the survey. If you need to make changes, return to the webinar details and click **Edit Survey**.

Configure Q&A Settings

You can customize your webinar's Q&A feature by configuring a few settings. If you enabled the Q&A option when creating your webinar, attendees can submit questions for the webinar host and/or panelists to answer. By default, participants do not need to provide a name when posting a question, but you can configure your webinar to not allow anonymous questions. You can also configure your webinar to allow attendees to see all questions (even unanswered ones) and to upvote and post comments about questions.

Configure Q&A Settings

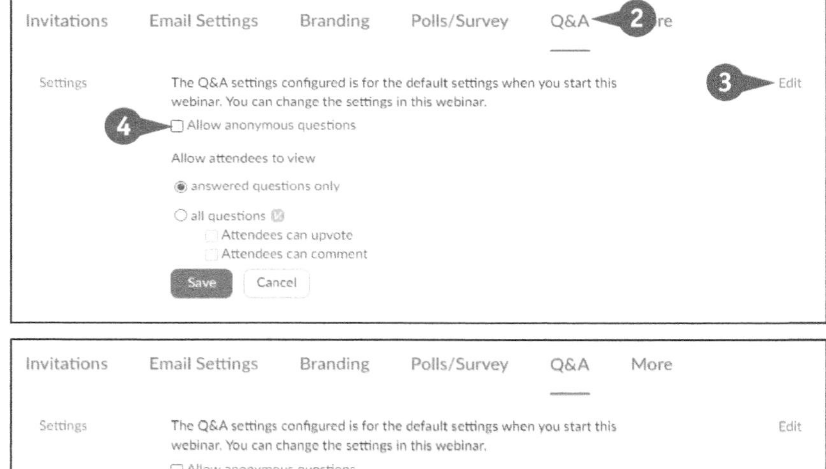

1. Open the webinar information, as described in the earlier "Invite People to Your Webinar" section.
2. Scroll down and click the **Q&A** tab.
3. Click **Edit**.

   Zoom opens the Q&A settings for editing.
4. If you do want attendees to provide a name when posting a question, click **Allow anonymous questions** (☑ changes to ☐).
5. If you want attendees to see both answered and unanswered questions, click **all questions** (○ changes to ◉).
6. If participants can view all questions, click **Attendees can upvote** (☐ changes to ☑) to enable them to cast a vote in favor of any question they think is useful.
7. If participants can view all questions, click **Attendees can comment** (☐ changes to ☑) to enable them to post comments about any question.
8. Click **Save.**

   Zoom updates your webinar's Q&A settings.

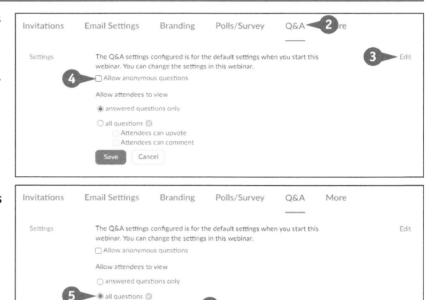

Start Your Webinar

CHAPTER 13

When your webinar's scheduled date and time arrives, you can start the webinar. This launches a new Zoom meeting that is configured to broadcast the video and audio of only the webinar audio and, optionally, the webinar panelists. Webinar attendees cannot participate directly in the webinar, but they can ask questions, respond to any polls you have configured, and take the survey that appears after you end the webinar.

You can start your webinar either from the Zoom website or from the Zoom desktop or mobile app.

Start Your Webinar

From the Zoom Website

1. Open the webinar information, as described in the earlier "Invite People to Your Webinar" section.
2. Click **Start this Webinar**.

   Zoom launches your webinar.

From the Zoom App

1. Select **Meetings**.
2. Select the webinar.
3. Select **Start**.

   Zoom launches your webinar.

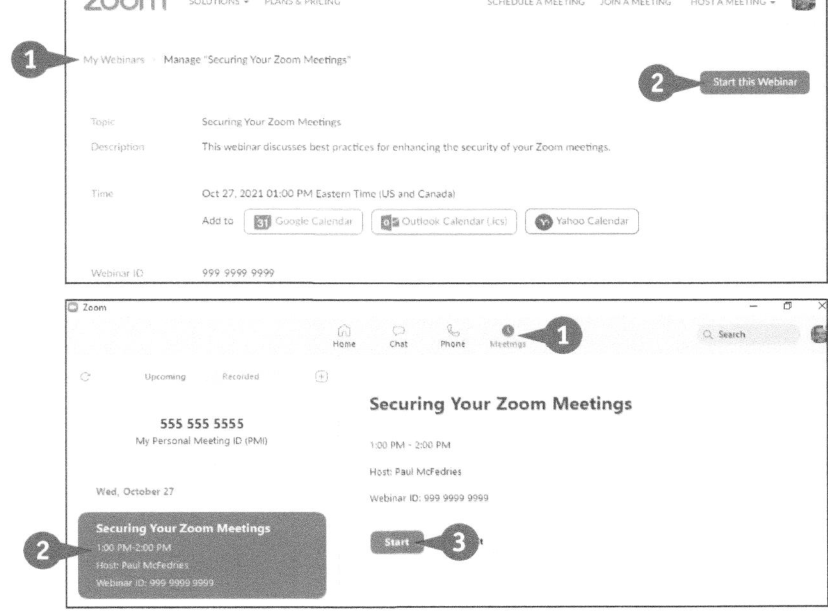

Share Your Screen

You can share content from your computer with your webinar participants. Just like in a regular Zoom meeting, the host of a webinar can share content with the attendees. The host can share the full computer screen, an open application window, part of the screen, a whiteboard, a mobile screen, an audio or video clip, or the contents of a file. If configured in the webinar settings, panelists can also share screen content from their computers.

The webinar sharing options are the same as the ones available for regular Zoom meetings. For details on sharing, see Chapter 6.

Share Your Screen

1. In the webinar host controls, click **Share Screen**.

   The sharing options appear.

2. Select what you want to share.

3. Click **Share**.

   Zoom shares your content with the webinar attendees.

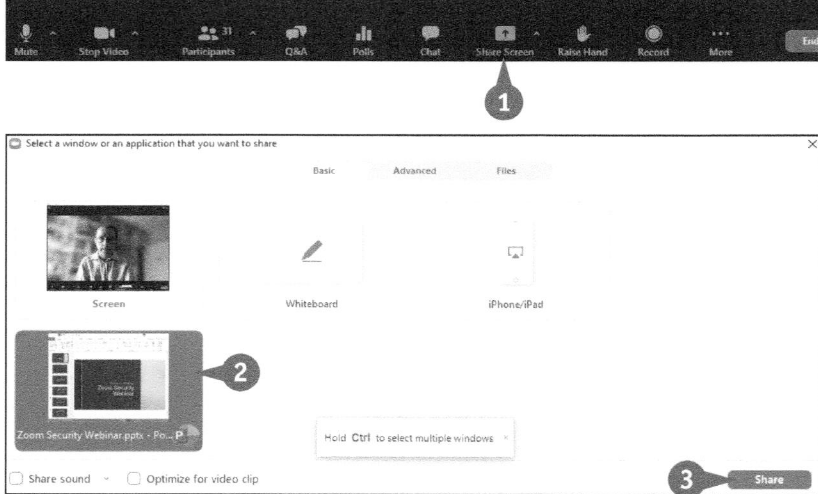

Record the Webinar

CHAPTER 13

You can save your webinar for you or others to watch later by recording the meeting. Recording a webinar has many uses. For example, you can watch the recording to critique your presentation. Similarly, if some attendees could not attend the webinar, you can make the recording available to those users. Finally, if you have a webinar license that only allows for a relatively small number of attendees, you can use the recording to make your webinar available to a larger audience.

Webinar recordings are identical to recordings of regular Zoom meetings. For details on recording meetings, see Chapter 7.

Record the Webinar

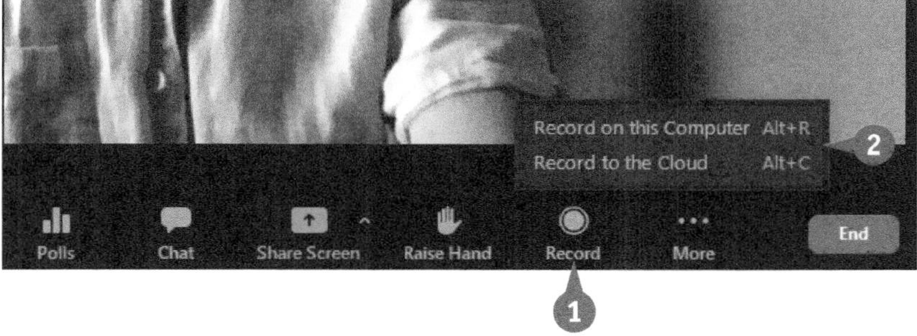

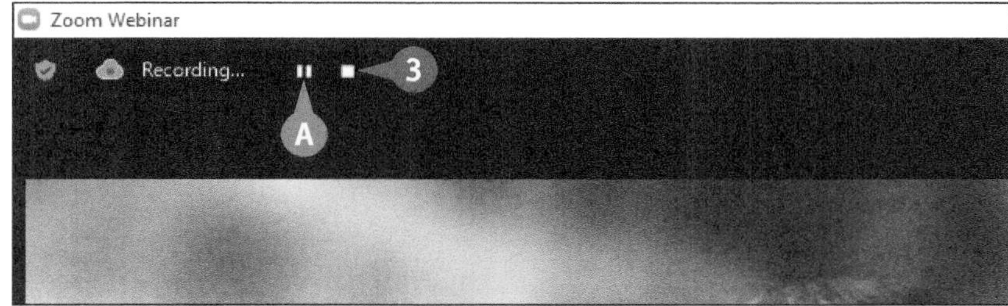

1. In the webinar host controls, click **Record**.
2. Click the recording option you want to use:
   - **Record on this Computer**. Click this option to save the webinar recording on your computer's hard drive.
   - **Record to the Cloud**. Click this option to save the webinar recording online.

   Zoom begins recording the webinar.

   A. You can click **Pause Recording** (⏸) at any time to temporarily stop the recording.
3. When you are done, click **Stop Recording** (□).

Handle Q&A

You can use the webinar's Q&A feature to view, answer, and manage attendee questions. If you enabled the Q&A feature in your webinar, attendees see a Q&A button in their webinar controls, and they can use that button to post questions to the host and/or panelists. As the webinar host, you can monitor the open questions by displaying them. You can then decide to answer a question with either a voiced or typed reply. You can also manage off-topic or unsuitable questions by dismissing or deleting them.

Handle Q&A

Display the Open Questions

1. In the host controls, select **Q&A**.

   The Q&A screen appears.

2. Click the **Open** tab.

Ⓐ Zoom displays a list of the unanswered questions.

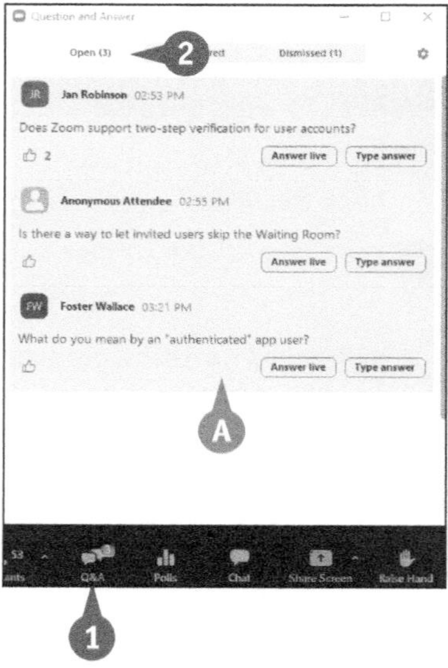

Answer a Question

1. Click **Type answer**.

Ⓑ Alternatively, you can answer the question with a voiced reply by clicking **Answer live**.

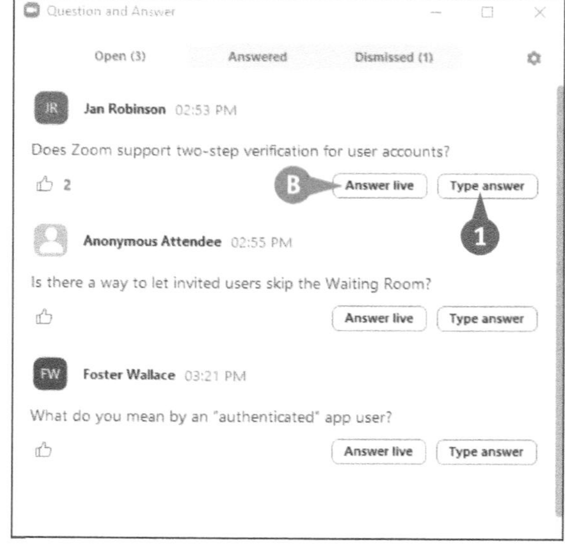

2 Type your answer.

C If you want only the attendee who asked the question to see your reply, click **Send privately** (☐ changes to ☑).

3 Click **Send**.

Zoom posts your answer. If you did not choose to answer privately, your reply appears on the **Answered** tab.

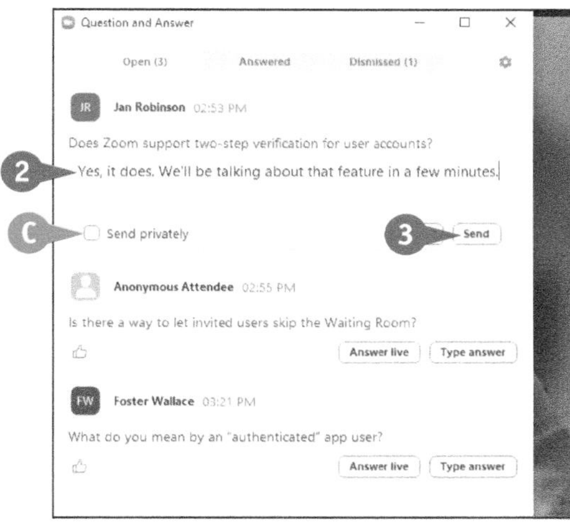

Dismiss or Delete a Question

1 Click **More** (···) to the right of the question.

2 Click **Dismiss**.

Zoom moves the question to the Dismissed tab.

Note: To reinstate a dismissed question, click the **Dismissed** tab and then click the **Reopen** button that appears to the right of the question.

D Alternatively, you can remove the question entirely from the Q&A by clicking **Delete**.

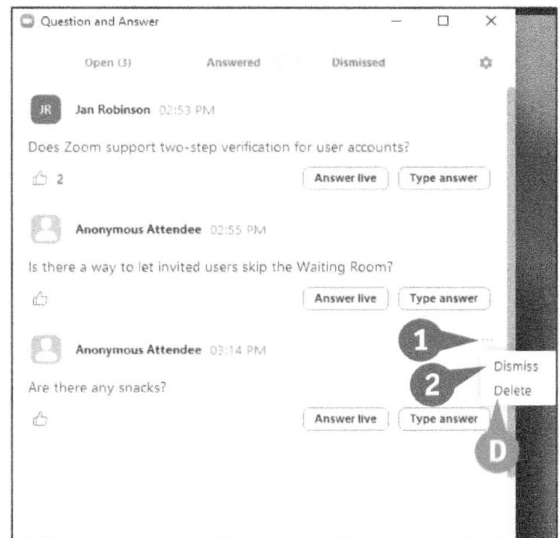

TIPS

How do I ask a question as a webinar attendee?

In the attendee controls, select **Q&A** to open the Q&A screen. Select **Ask a Question** and then type your question in the text box that appears. If the webinar supports anonymous questions, you can select **Send anonymously** (☐ changes to ☑) to send your question without giving your name.

How do I upvote or comment on a question?

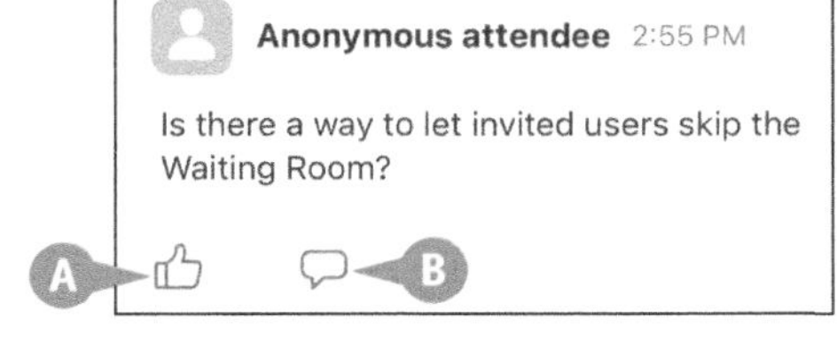

In the attendee controls, select **Q&A** to open the Q&A screen. To upvote a question, select the question's **Upvote** icon (👍) (A). To comment on a question, select the question's **Comment** icon (💬) (B), type your comment, and then select **Send** (▼).

Live-Stream the Webinar

If your webinar reaches capacity, you can redirect more users to a live stream of the webinar. If you have set up your webinar without requiring users to register in advance, you might find that attendance is greater than expected and reaches the maximum number of attendees as dictated by your Zoom webinar license. Rather than leaving would-be attendees disappointed, you can live-stream your webinar on YouTube, Facebook, or Workplace by Facebook. That way, when your webinar reaches capacity, new users see a Watch Live Stream button they can click to watch the webinar on a live-streaming service.

Live-Stream the Webinar

Enable the Live-Streaming Link

1. Open the webinar information, as described in the earlier "Invite People to Your Webinar" section.
2. Scroll down and click the **More** tab.
3. Click **Edit.**
4. Click **Remind users to watch the live stream** (☐ changes to ☑).
5. Click **Save Changes.**

When your webinar reaches capacity, subsequent users will now see a Watch Live Stream button they can click to watch the webinar on the live-streaming service you select.

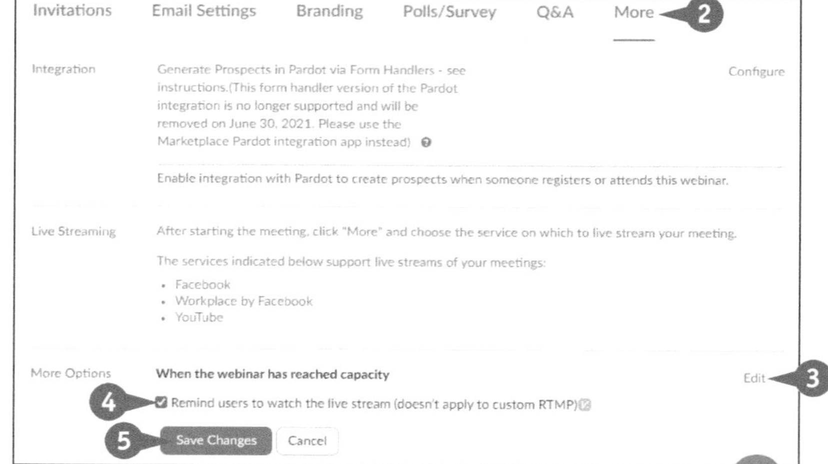

Select a Live-Streaming Service

1. In the webinar host controls, click **More.**
2. Click the streaming service you want to use.

When your webinar reaches capacity, Zoom redirects new attendees to the live-streaming service you selected.

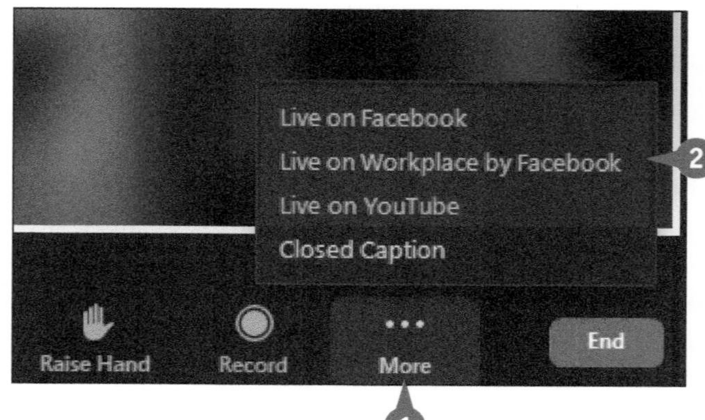

CHAPTER 13

End the Webinar

When your webinar is complete, you can end the session for all users. If you created a survey for your webinar, attendees see the survey web page immediately after you end the webinar. (See the earlier "Create a Survey" section for details.)

Note that webinar panelists and co-hosts cannot end the meeting. Only the webinar host can end the meeting.

End the Webinar

1 In the webinar host controls, click **End**.

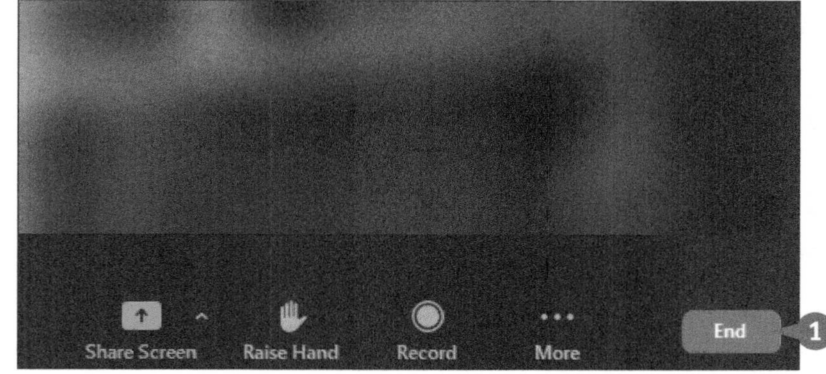

2 Click **End Meeting for All**.

Zoom ends the webinar.

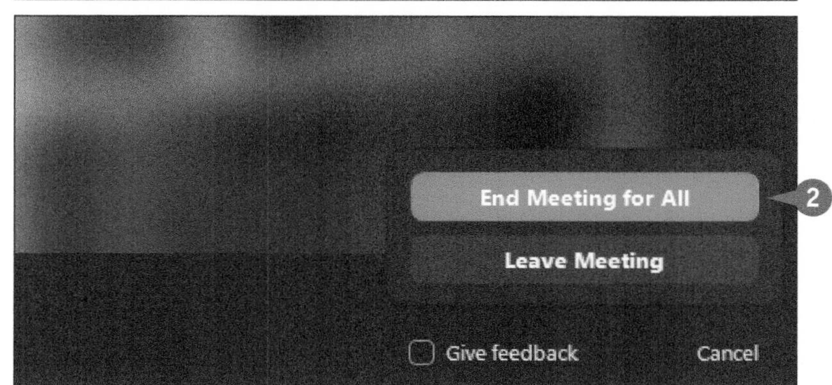

CHAPTER 14

Integrating with Other Apps

You can help get the most out of Zoom by setting up integrations with other apps. Integrations enable you to access and share content from other apps, including Dropbox; Google's Gmail, Calendar, and Contacts; and Microsoft 365's Calendar and Contacts. There is also a large collection of Zoom-compatible apps that you can install.

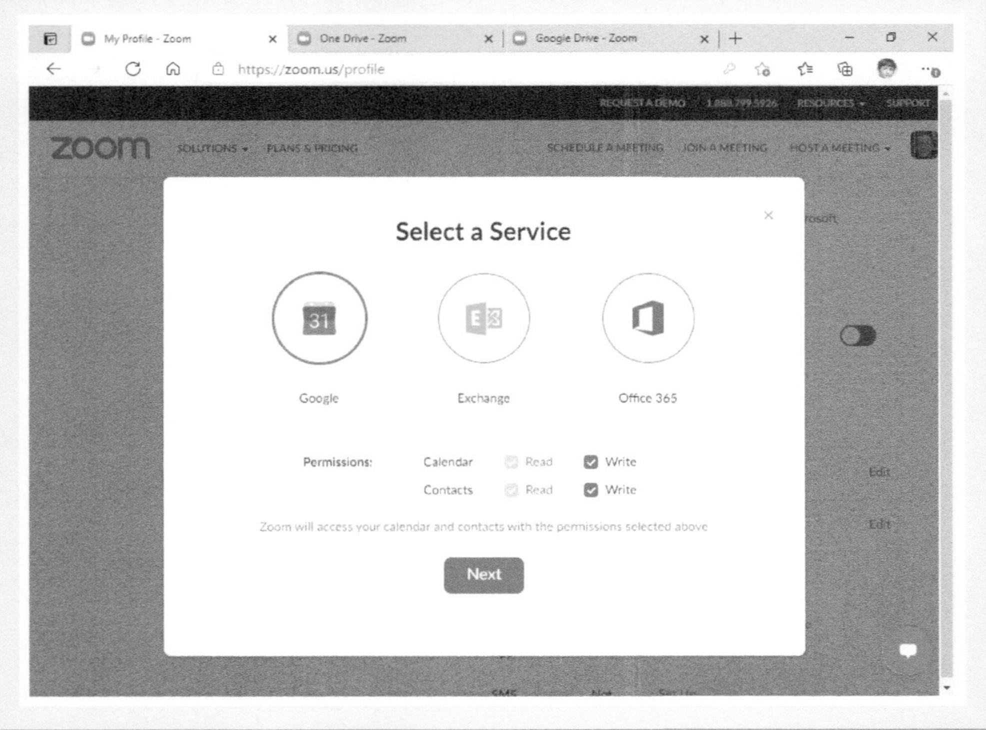

Set Up File-Sharing Integration

You can make your Zoom file sharing even more powerful by setting up one or more integrations with file-sharing apps. Zoom offers many file-sharing integrations, but the most popular are with Box, Dropbox, Google Drive, Microsoft OneDrive, and Microsoft SharePoint. When you enable any of these integrations, you can share files from the enabled services in a meeting or a chat. You can also present content from any enabled service in a meeting.

Set Up File-Sharing Integration

Enable File-Sharing Integrations

1. Use a web browser to navigate to https://zoom.us/profile.

   Zoom displays your profile page.

2. Click **Advanced**.
3. Click **Integration**.
4. Click the switch to On (changes to) for each file sharing integration you want to use.

   Zoom configures your profile with the enabled file-sharing integrations.

Using File-Sharing Integrations in Chat

1. In the desktop app, in a Zoom chat window, click **File**.

Note: In the mobile app, tap **Add** (+) and then tap **Send a File**.

2. Select the file-sharing service you want to use.

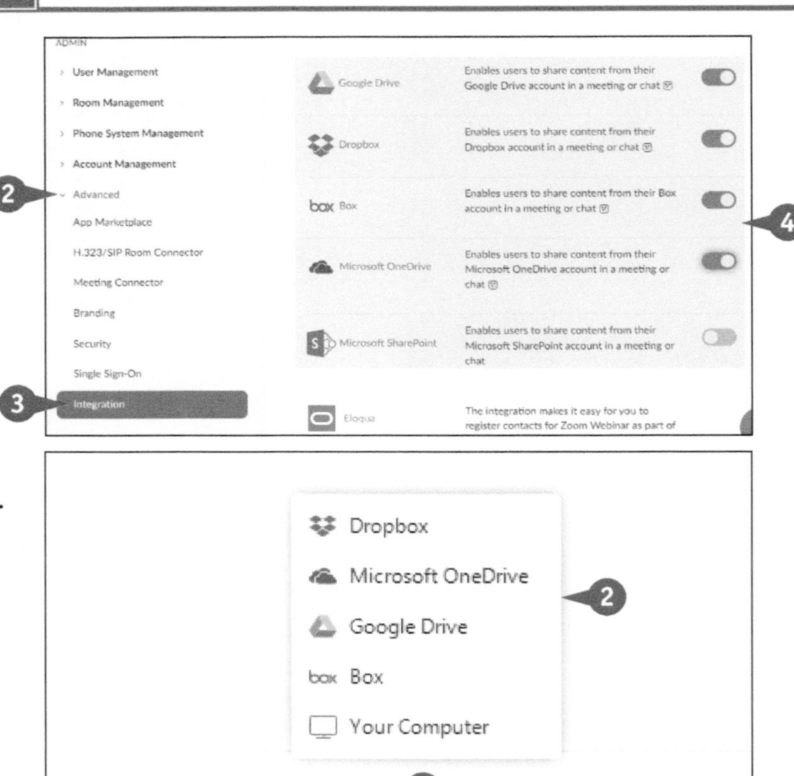

Zoom displays the Connect to *Service* page, where *Service* is the file-sharing service you clicked in step 2.

3 Select **Connect**.

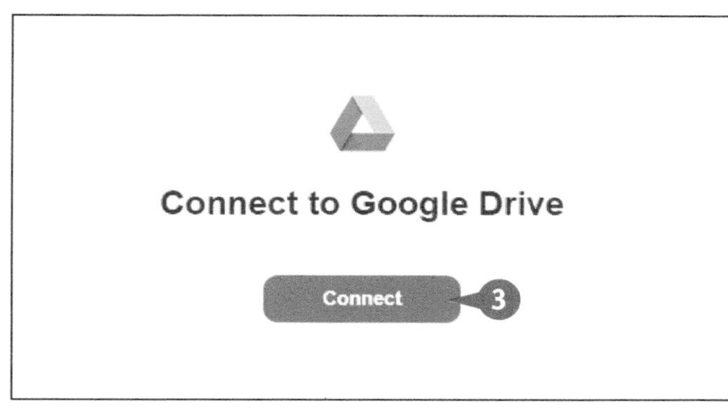

The file-sharing service asks you to authorize the connection to Zoom.

4 Select **Authorize**.

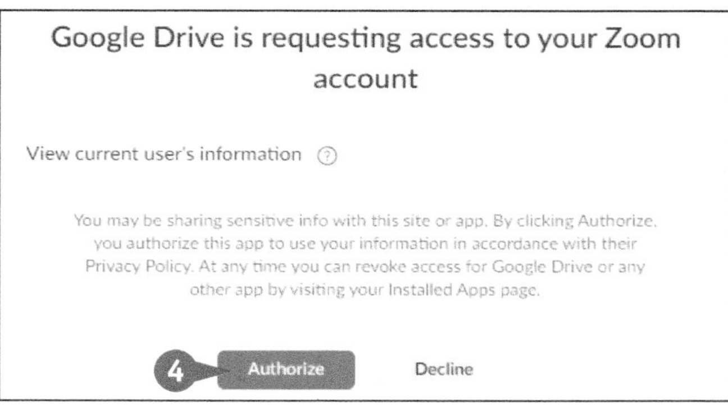

5 If requested, sign in to your account on the service (not shown).

The service asks you to provide permission for Zoom to access your data.

6 Select **Allow**.

You can now share files on the service.

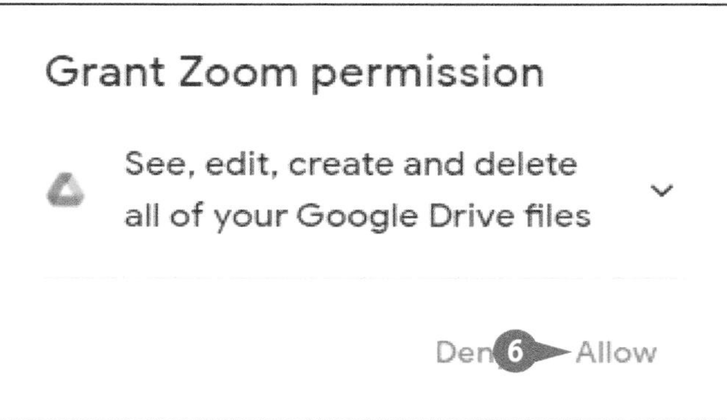

Note: To present a file from a file-sharing service in a meeting, select **Share Screen**, select **Files**, and then select the file-sharing service you want to use.

TIP

Why do I not see either the Integration tab or the service I want to use?

As this book went to press, Zoom announced that future versions of the Zoom web portal will move the Integrations content to Zoom's App Marketplace. If you do not see the Integration tab or the service you want to use, you can still set up the integration you want by installing the corresponding app. See the section "Install Zoom Apps" later in this chapter.

Integrate Calendar and Contacts

You can make Zoom more efficient and easier to use by integrating your existing online calendar and contacts into your Zoom profile. Zoom supports three services for calendar and contact integration: Google, Microsoft 365, and Microsoft Exchange. This enables you to see your scheduled Zoom meeting in the service's calendar. After you integrate contacts from your preferred service, they appear in the Zoom app's Contacts tab in the Cloud Contacts section.

Note that calendar and contacts integration can be used only with institutional (that is, work or school) accounts, not with personal accounts.

Integrate Calendar and Contacts

1. Use a web browser to navigate to https://zoom.us/profile.

   Zoom displays your profile page.

2. Click **Configure Calendar and Contacts Service**.

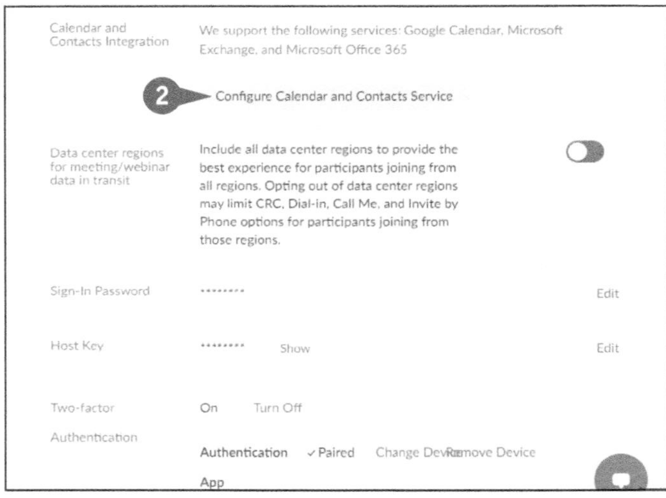

   The Select a Service dialog appears.

3. Click the service you want to use for calendar and contacts integration.

4. Click **Next**.

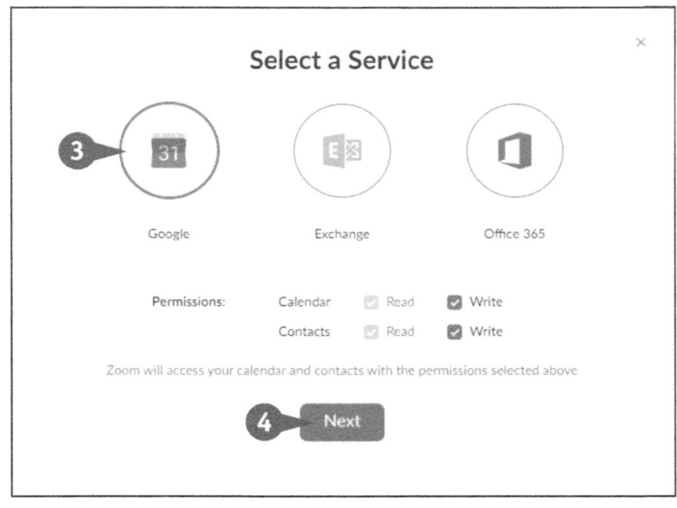

The service asks you to confirm that you want to grant Zoom permission to access your data.

Note: The exact steps required to grant this permission depend on which service you choose. The steps that follow show the steps for Google.

5 Click **Allow**.

6 Depending on the service, you might have to grant multiple permissions, so be sure to click **Allow** each time.

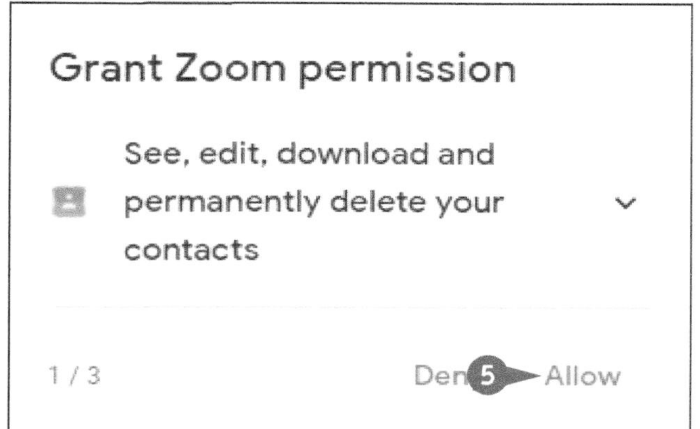

The service asks you to confirm.

A Disabled permissions cannot be changed.

B Enabled permissions are optional, but it is best to leave all the permissions selected.

7 Click **Allow**.

Zoom integrates the service's calendar and contacts.

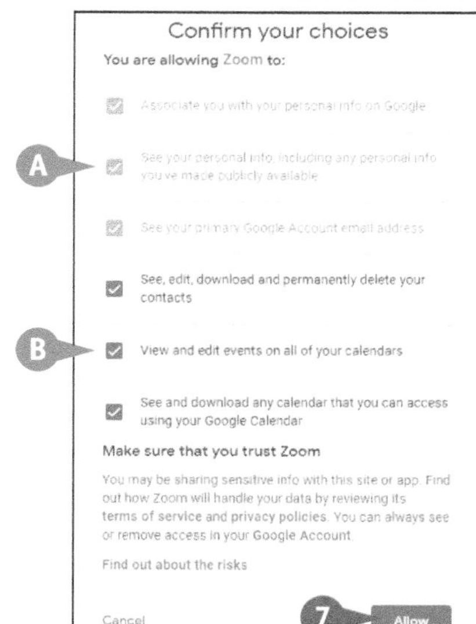

TIP

Can I change which service I use for calendar and contacts integration?

Yes, you can switch to a different service at any time. Here are the steps:

1 Use a web browser to navigate to https://zoom.us/profile.

Zoom displays your profile page.

2 For the Calendar and Contacts Integration setting, click **Configure**.

3 Click the service you want to use.

4 Click **Next**.

5 Follow the on-screen instructions for granting Zoom permission to use the services calendar and contacts.

Integrate Dropbox

Dropbox integration enables you to perform several Zoom-related tasks from within the Dropbox app. Although you can integrate Dropbox file sharing in Zoom (see the earlier "Set Up File-Sharing Integration" section), you can also modify the Dropbox app to perform Zoom tasks. These tasks include presenting a file in Zoom from Dropbox, messaging Zoom contacts from Dropbox, and joining a Zoom meeting from Dropbox.

This task requires that you first connect either your Google calendar or your Microsoft 365 calendar to Dropbox.

Integrate Dropbox

1. Use a web browser to navigate to https://www.dropbox.com/apps.
2. In the **Search App Center** text box, type **zoom**.
3. Click **Zoom**.

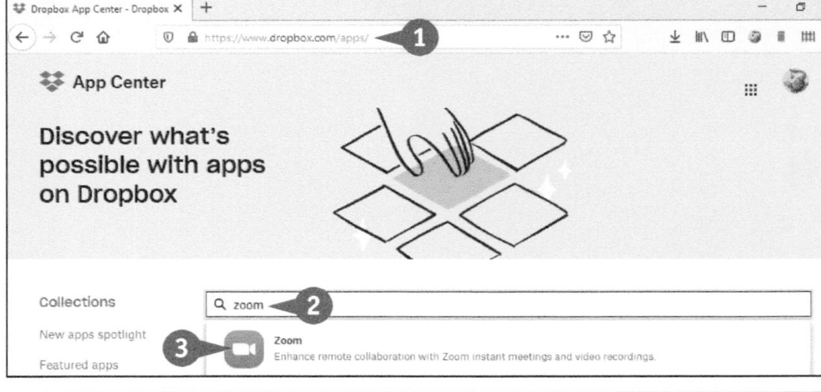

The Dropbox Zoom app appears.

4. Click **Connect**.

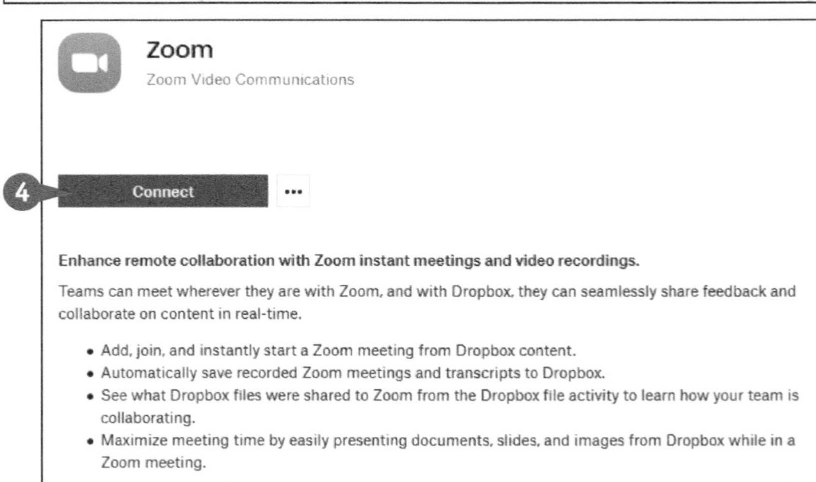

Dropbox lets you know that some people might see how to contact you on Zoom.

5 Click **Got it**.

6 If Zoom asks you to sign in to your account, complete the sign-in process (not shown).

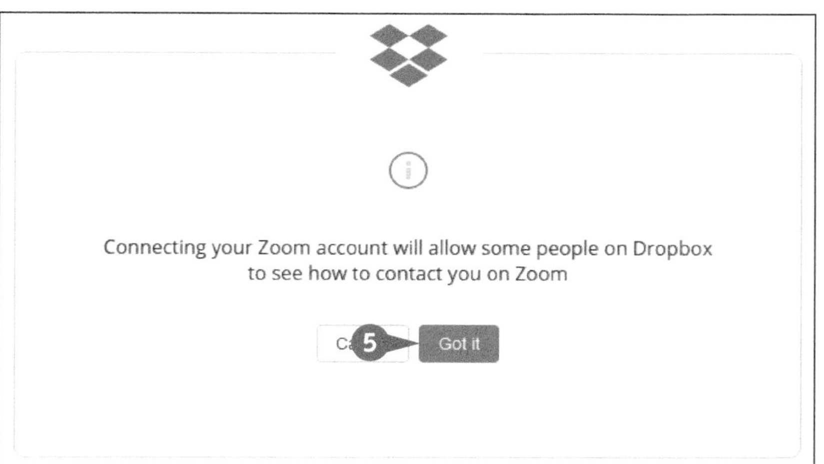

Zoom asks you to authorize Dropbox to access your account.

7 Click **Authorize**.

8 If Zoom asks whether you want to copy your cloud recordings to Dropbox, click **Enable** (not shown).

9 Click **Done** (not shown).

Your Zoom account is now integrated with Dropbox.

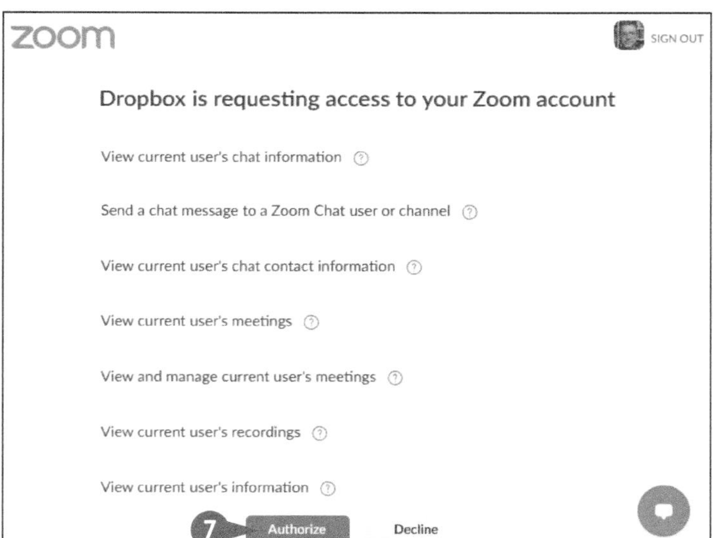

TIP

What Zoom-related tasks can I perform in the Dropbox app?

There are three main tasks you can perform in the Dropbox desktop app:

- **Present files in a Zoom meeting.** In Dropbox, hover the mouse over the file you want to present and then click **Present in Zoom**.
- **Message a Zoom contact.** In Dropbox, open a file, click the profile of a contact you are sharing the file with, and then click **Message on Zoom**.
- **Join a Zoom meeting.** In Dropbox, open a file, click the profile of a contact you are sharing the file with, and then click **Join Zoom Meeting**.

Navigate App Marketplace

Zoom offers a feature called App Marketplace that enables you to install apps that work with Zoom products such as Meetings, Webinars, Phone, and Chat. Most apps enable you to connect third-party services such as Gmail, Slack, and Zapier. There are hundreds of available apps, so you need to know how to navigate the App Marketplace interface by searching for an app and browsing app categories. You can also filter the app marketplace to show only pre-approved apps, apps that only account administrators can install, and apps that only account members can install.

Navigate App Marketplace

Open App Marketplace

1. Use a web browser to navigate to https://marketplace.zoom.us/.

Note: From your Zoom profile page (https://zoom.us/profile), you can also click **Advanced** and then click **App Marketplace**.

The App Marketplace page appears.

2. Click **Sign in**.
3. Enter your Zoom account credentials (not shown).

Search for an App

1. Use the **Search** text box to type some or all of the app name.

A. App Marketplace displays a list of the apps with names that match your search text.

2. Click the app you want to view.

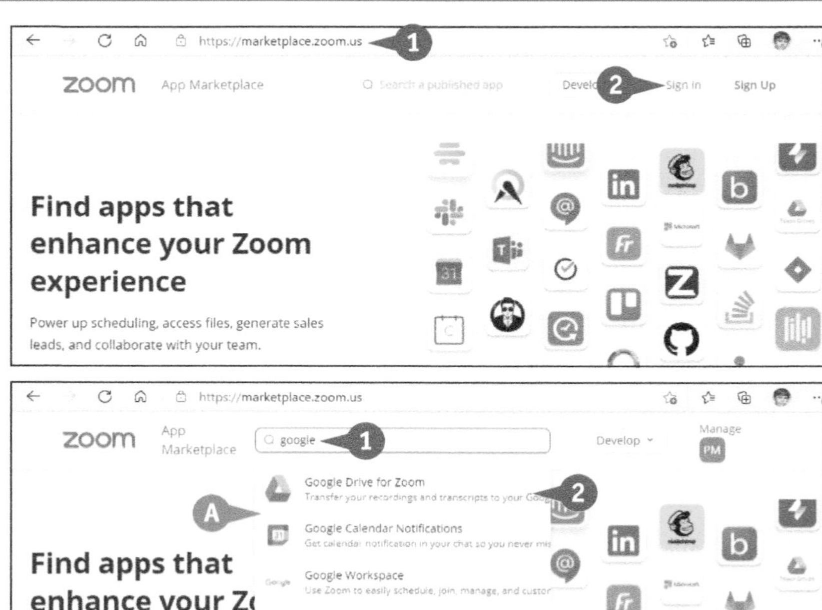

Browse by Category

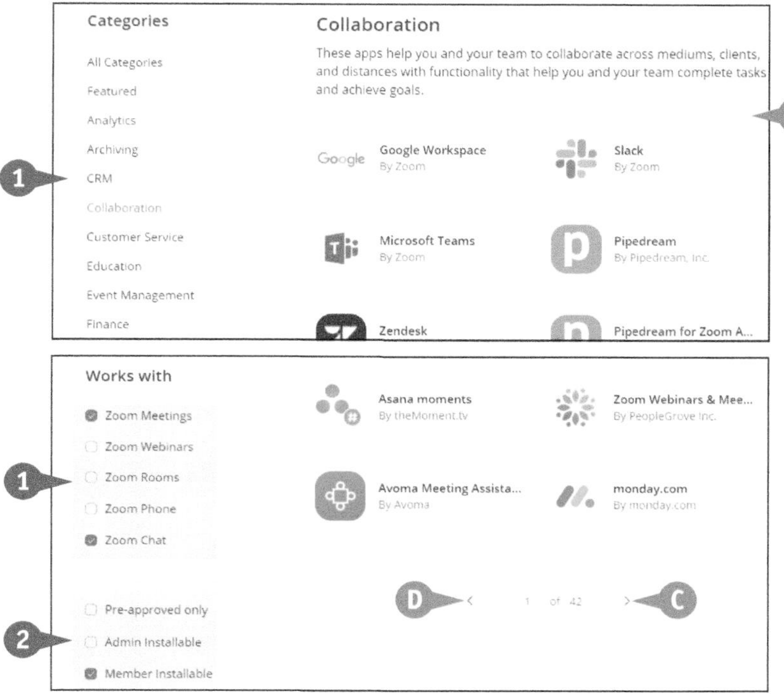

1. In the **Categories** list, click the category that contains the app you want to view.

B. App Marketplace opens a page that lists all the available apps in the category.

1. To show only apps that work with a particular Zoom product, click that product's check box (☐ changes to ☑).

2. Click any of these check boxes (☐ changes to ☑) to show only apps of that type.

C. In the app list, click **Next** (>) to see the next screenful of apps.

D. In the app list, click **Previous** (<) to return to the previous screenful of apps.

TIP

What is a pre-approved app?

A *pre-approved* app is an app that your Zoom account owner or administrator has configured in advance to allow account member installations.

If you are an account owner or administrator, you pre-approve an app by displaying the app's page in App Marketplace and then clicking the **Pre-approve** switch (A) to On (changes to).

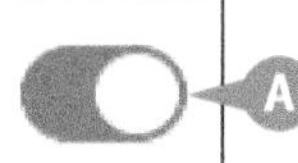

By default, all account members can install a pre-approved app. To control who can install the app, click the **Allow all users on the account with the required permissions to install this app** switch to Off (changes to) and then add the users or groups who can install the app.

Install Zoom Apps

You can make your work and personal lives easier and more efficient by installing a Zoom app. Zoom's App Marketplace offers hundreds of apps in categories such as Collaboration, Education, Games, Lifestyle, and Productivity. In most cases, an app connects your Zoom account to an account you have with a third-party service. Once your accounts are connected, you can use the third-party service to perform Zoom tasks such as scheduling meetings.

See the earlier "Navigate App Marketplace" section to learn how to navigate and search for apps in App Marketplace.

Install Zoom Apps

Request App Pre-Approval

1. In App Marketplace, open the page of the app you want to install.
2. Click **Request pre-approve**.

   Zoom sends the request to your Zoom account's owner and/or administrator for approval.

Install an App

1. In App Marketplace, open the page of the app you want to install.

Note: If you requested pre-approval for the app, you might need to refresh the page.

2. Click **Install**.

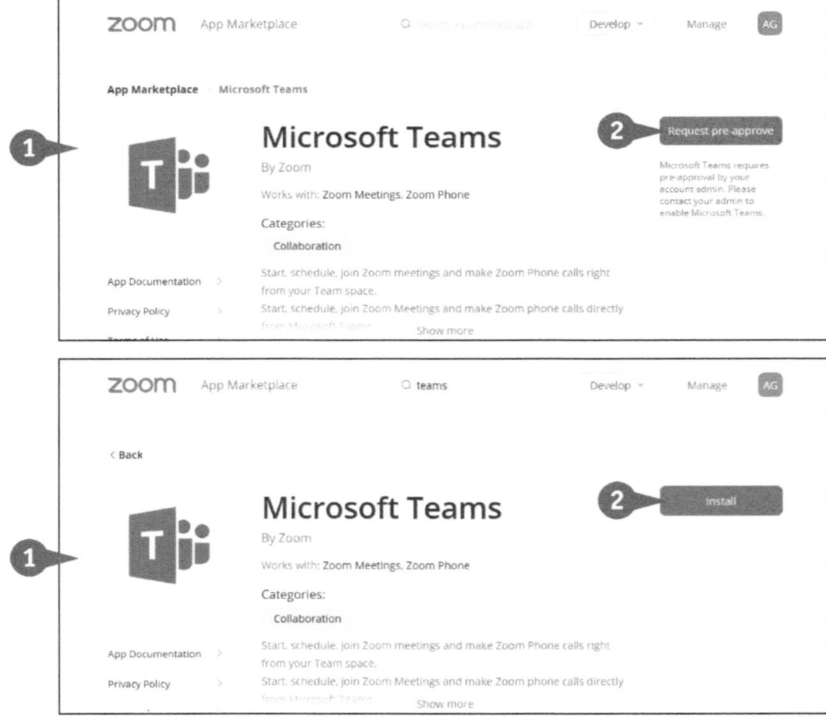

App Marketplace displays the permissions that the app is requesting for your Zoom account.

3 Click **Authorize**.

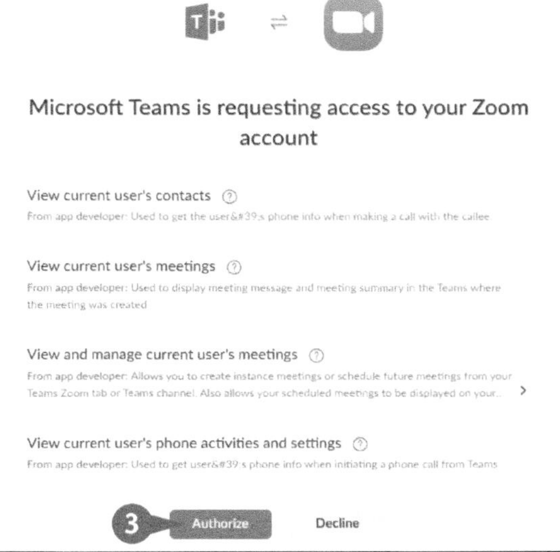

App Marketplace loads the third-party app or website.

4 Sign in to (or, if necessary, create) your account with the service (not shown).

5 Follow the on-screen instructions to complete the installation process.

You can now use the third-party service in conjunction with your Zoom account.

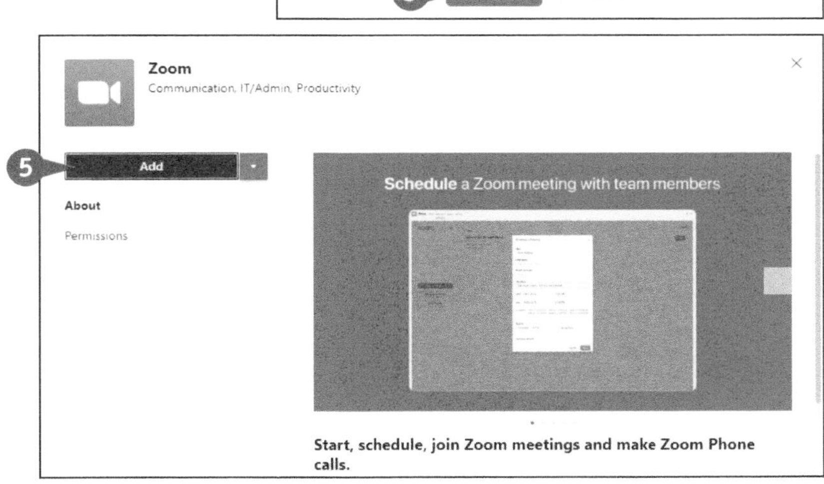

TIPS

As the Zoom account owner/administrator, how do I pre-approve app installation requests?
Sign in to App Marketplace with your Zoom owner or administrator credentials, click **Manage**, and then click **App Requests**. On the **Pre-approval Requests** tab, click **Pre-approve** beside each request you want to pre-approve. To disallow a pre-approval request, click **Reject** instead.

An app's Install button is disabled. Why?
If an app's Install button is disabled, it means you cannot install the app. There are two main reasons why you cannot install the app:

- Your Zoom account owner or administrator has pre-approved the app but has not included you in the list of users or groups that can install the app.
- Your Zoom account does not have sufficient permissions to install the app.

Index

D

H

I

J

K

L

M

W

Z